VIZ GRAPHIC NOVEL

ONE-POUND GOSPEL™ Vol. 3

KNUCKLE SANDWICH

STORY AND ART BY
RUMIKO TAKAHASHI

CONTENTS

This volume contains ONE-POUND GOSPEL ROUND TWO #1 through #8 in their entirety.

**STORY AND ART BY
RUMIKO TAKAHASHI**

English Adaptation/Gerard Jones & Mari Morimoto
Touch-Up Art & Lettering/Mary Kelleher
Cover Design/Hidemi Sahara
Editor/Annette Roman

Managing Editor/Hyoe Narita
Editor-in-Chief/Satoru Fujii
Publisher/Seiji Horibuchi

Printed in Canada

Published by Viz Communications, Inc.
P.O. Box 77010 • San Francisco, CA 94107

10 9 8 7 6 5 4 3 2 1
First printing, February 1998

Vizit us at our World Wide Web site at **www.viz.com** and
our new Internet magazine, **j-pop.com**, at **www.j-pop.com**!

ONE-POUND GOSPEL GRAPHIC NOVELS TO DATE
ONE-POUND GOSPEL
HUNGRY FOR VICTORY
KNUCKLE SANDWICH

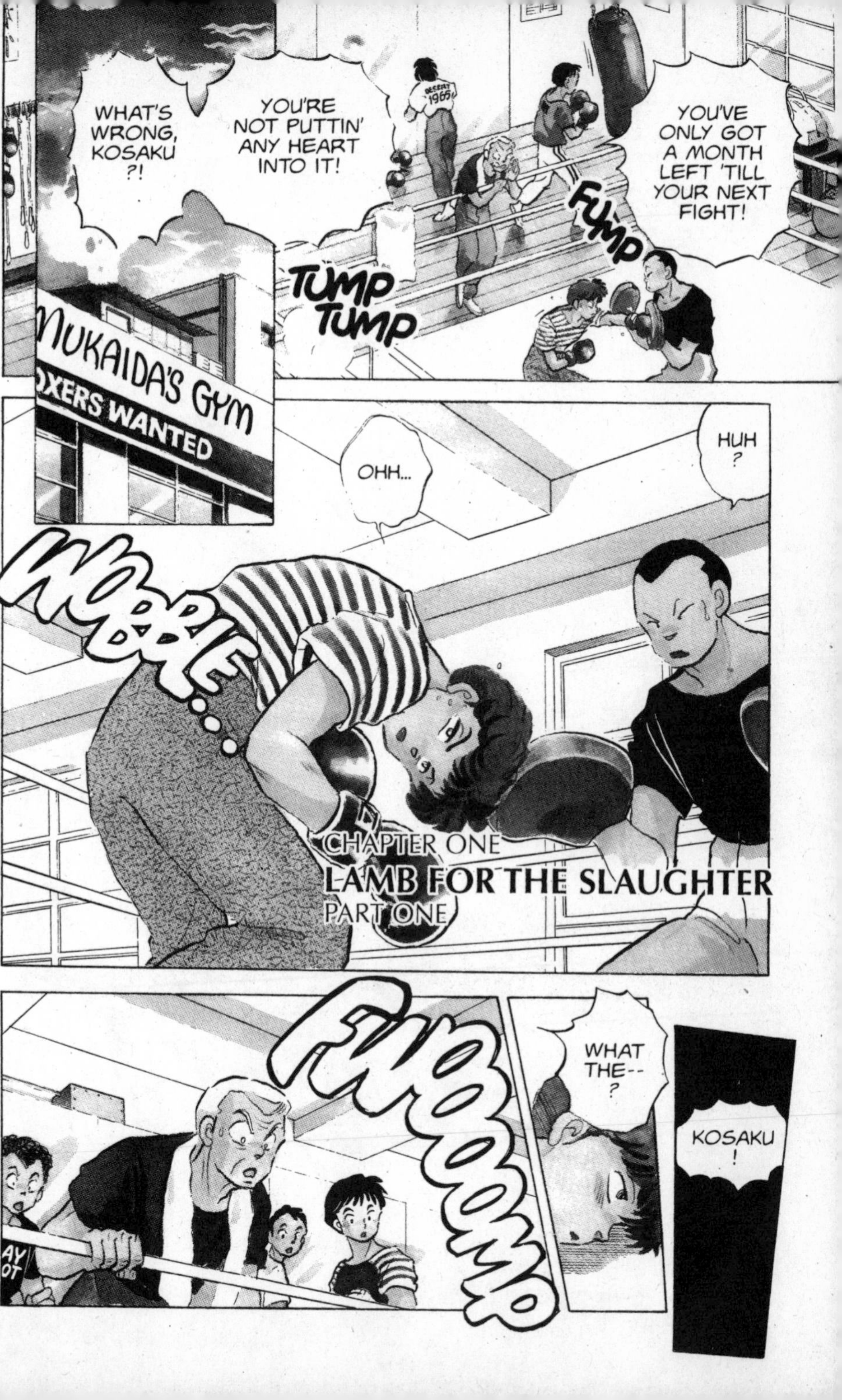
WHAT'S WRONG, KOSAKU ?!
YOU'RE NOT PUTTIN' ANY HEART INTO IT!
YOU'VE ONLY GOT A MONTH LEFT 'TILL YOUR NEXT FIGHT!
FUMP
TUMP TUMP
MUKAIDA'S GYM
OXERS WANTED
OHH...
HUH ?
WOBBLE...
CHAPTER ONE
LAMB FOR THE SLAUGHTER
PART ONE
FWOOOOMP
WHAT THE-- ?
KOSAKU !

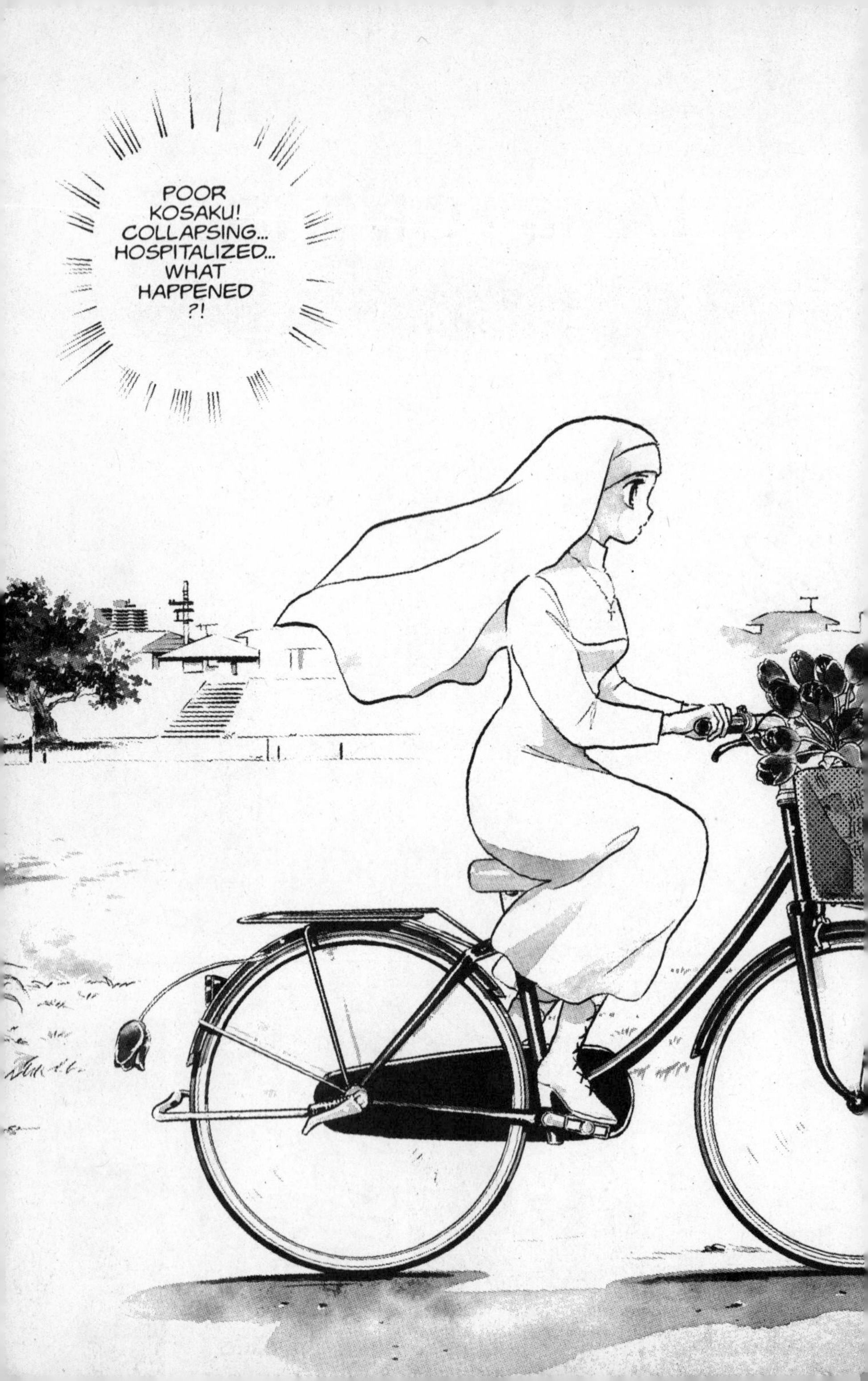
POOR KOSAKU! COLLAPSING... HOSPITALIZED... WHAT HAPPENED ?!

CHAPTER ONE

LAMB FOR THE SLAUGHTER

PART ONE

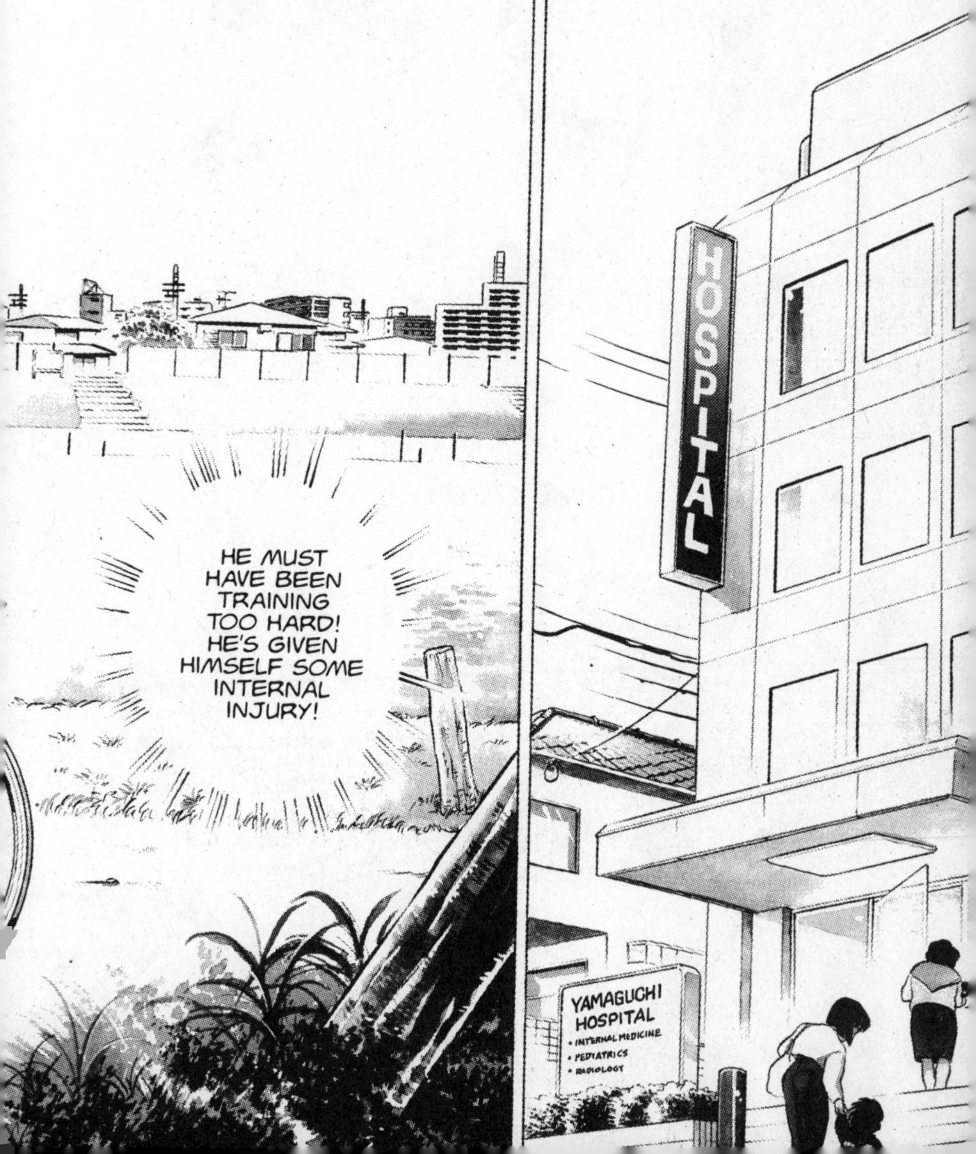
HE MUST HAVE BEEN TRAINING TOO HARD! HE'S GIVEN HIMSELF SOME INTERNAL INJURY!
HOSPITAL
YAMAGUCHI HOSPITAL
• INTERNAL MEDICINE
• PEDIATRICS
• RADIOLOGY

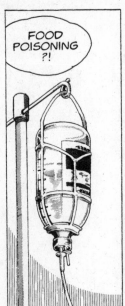

FOOD POISONING?!

HEH HEH HEH HEH HEH HEH.

BONK

IT'S NOT *FUNNY*!

PLEASE, COACH!

DON'T CHASTISE HIM FOR GETTING FOOD POISONED.

IT'S NOT AS IF HE OVER ATE OR SOMETHING.

HE ATE *THREE* SPOILED BOX LUNCHES-- DURING WEIGHT TRAINING!

. . . . .

THAT'S A LIE, COACH!

YOU DON'T KNOW THAT *ALL THREE* WERE BAD.

ACCEPT MY APOLOGY!

BONK

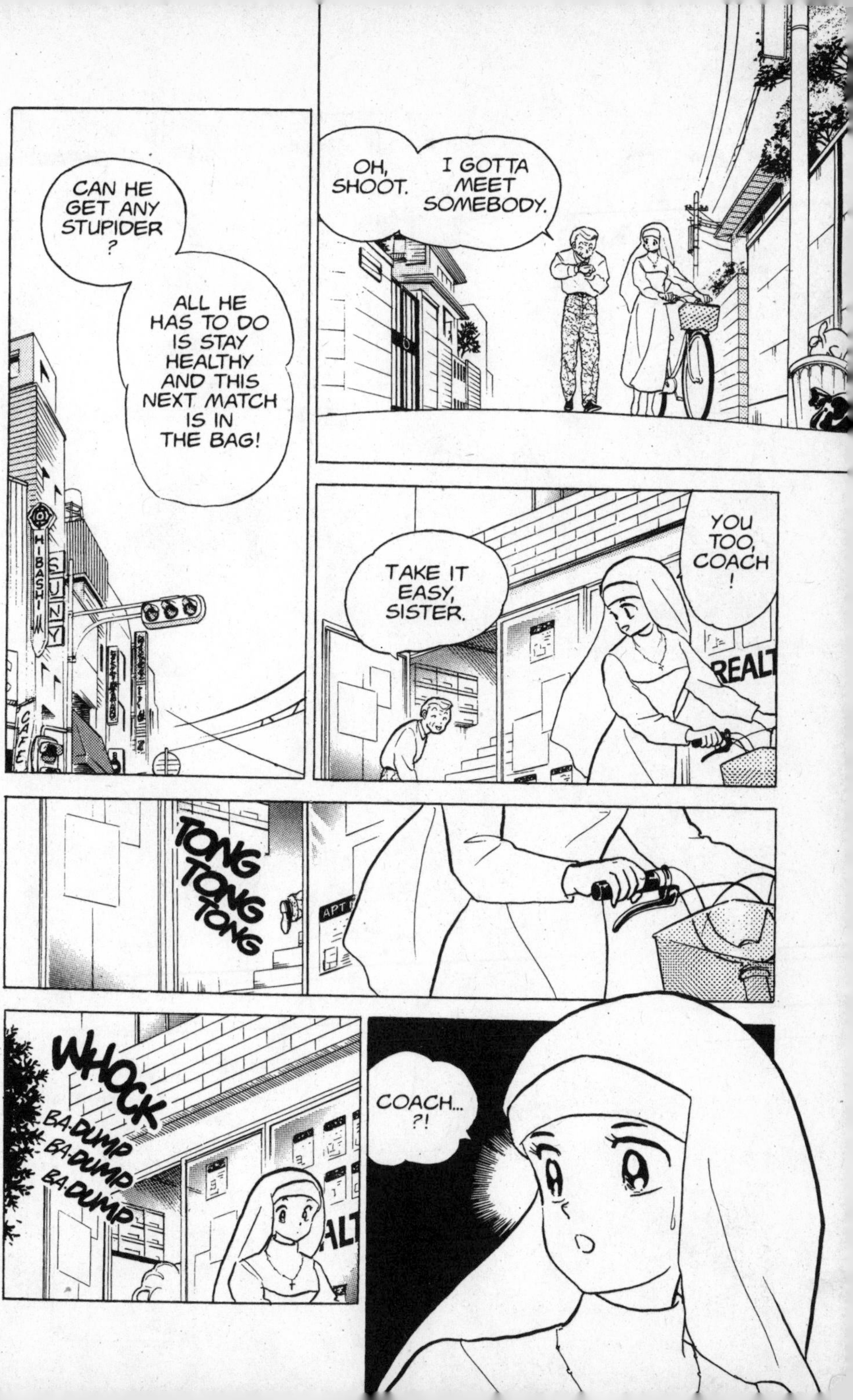
CAN HE GET ANY STUPIDER?
ALL HE HAS TO DO IS STAY HEALTHY AND THIS NEXT MATCH IS IN THE BAG!
HIBASHI
SUNNY
CAFE
OH, SHOOT.
I GOTTA MEET SOMEBODY.
TAKE IT EASY, SISTER.
YOU TOO, COACH!
REALT
TONG TONG TONG
APT
WHOCK
BA-DUMP BA-DUMP BA-DUMP
ALT
COACH... ?!

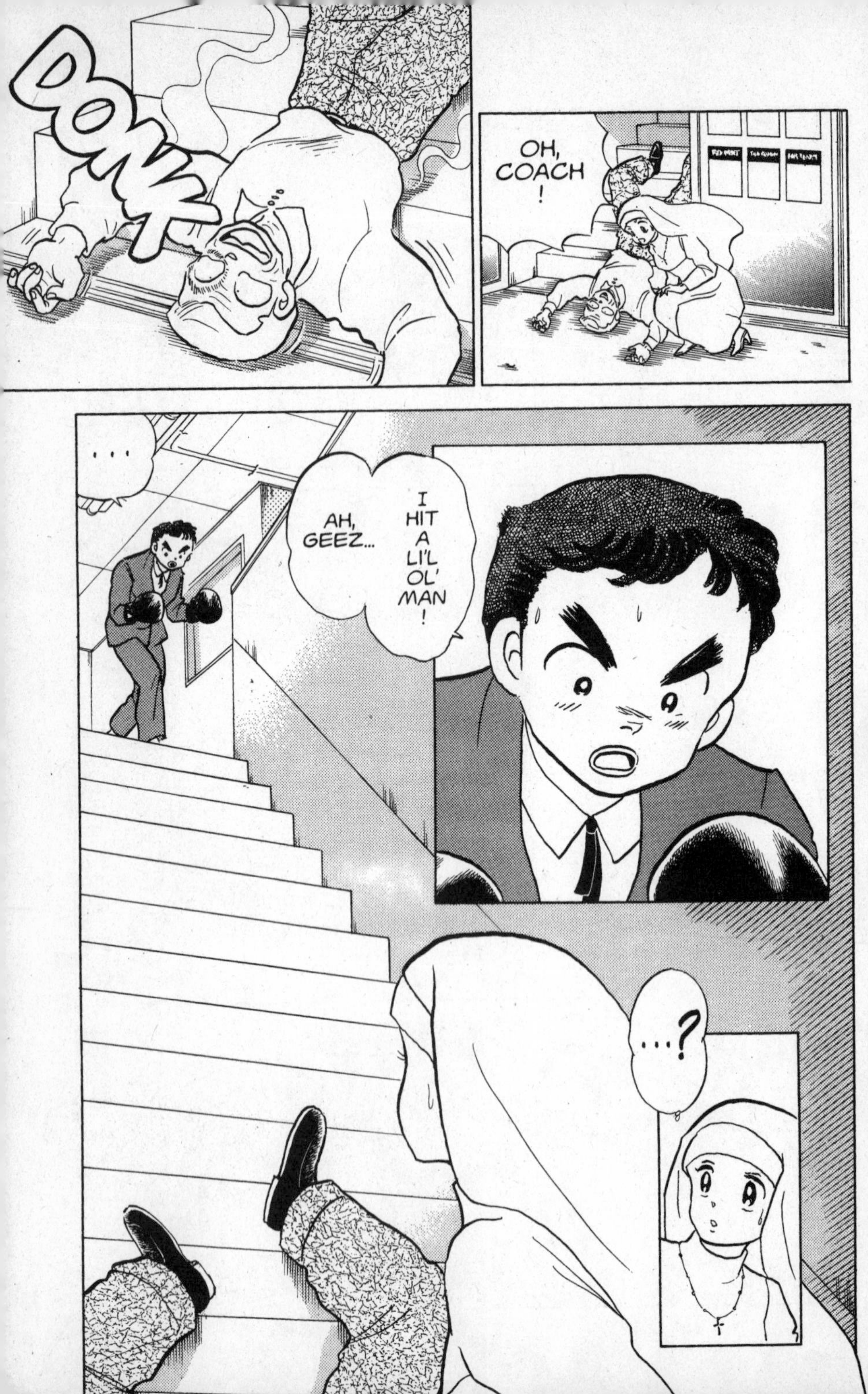
DONK
OH, COACH!
...
AH, GEEZ...
I HIT A LI'L OL' MAN!
...?

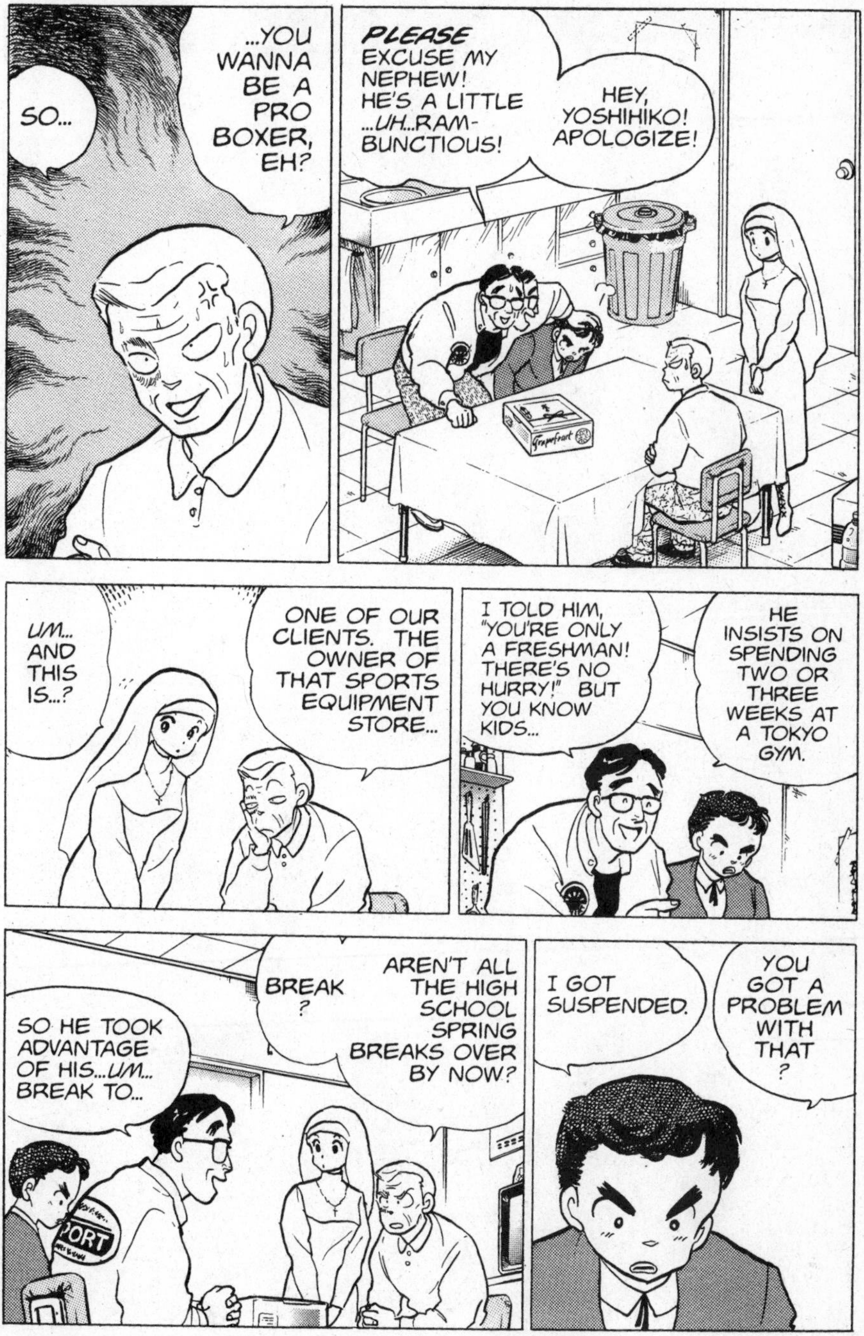
SO...
...YOU WANNA BE A PRO BOXER, EH?
PLEASE EXCUSE MY NEPHEW! HE'S A LITTLE ...UH...RAM-BUNCTIOUS!
HEY, YOSHIHIKO! APOLOGIZE!
Grapefruit
UM... AND THIS IS...?
ONE OF OUR CLIENTS. THE OWNER OF THAT SPORTS EQUIPMENT STORE...
I TOLD HIM, "YOU'RE ONLY A FRESHMAN! THERE'S NO HURRY!" BUT YOU KNOW KIDS...
HE INSISTS ON SPENDING TWO OR THREE WEEKS AT A TOKYO GYM.
SO HE TOOK ADVANTAGE OF HIS...UM... BREAK TO...
BREAK?
AREN'T ALL THE HIGH SCHOOL SPRING BREAKS OVER BY NOW?
PORT
I GOT SUSPENDED.
YOU GOT A PROBLEM WITH THAT?

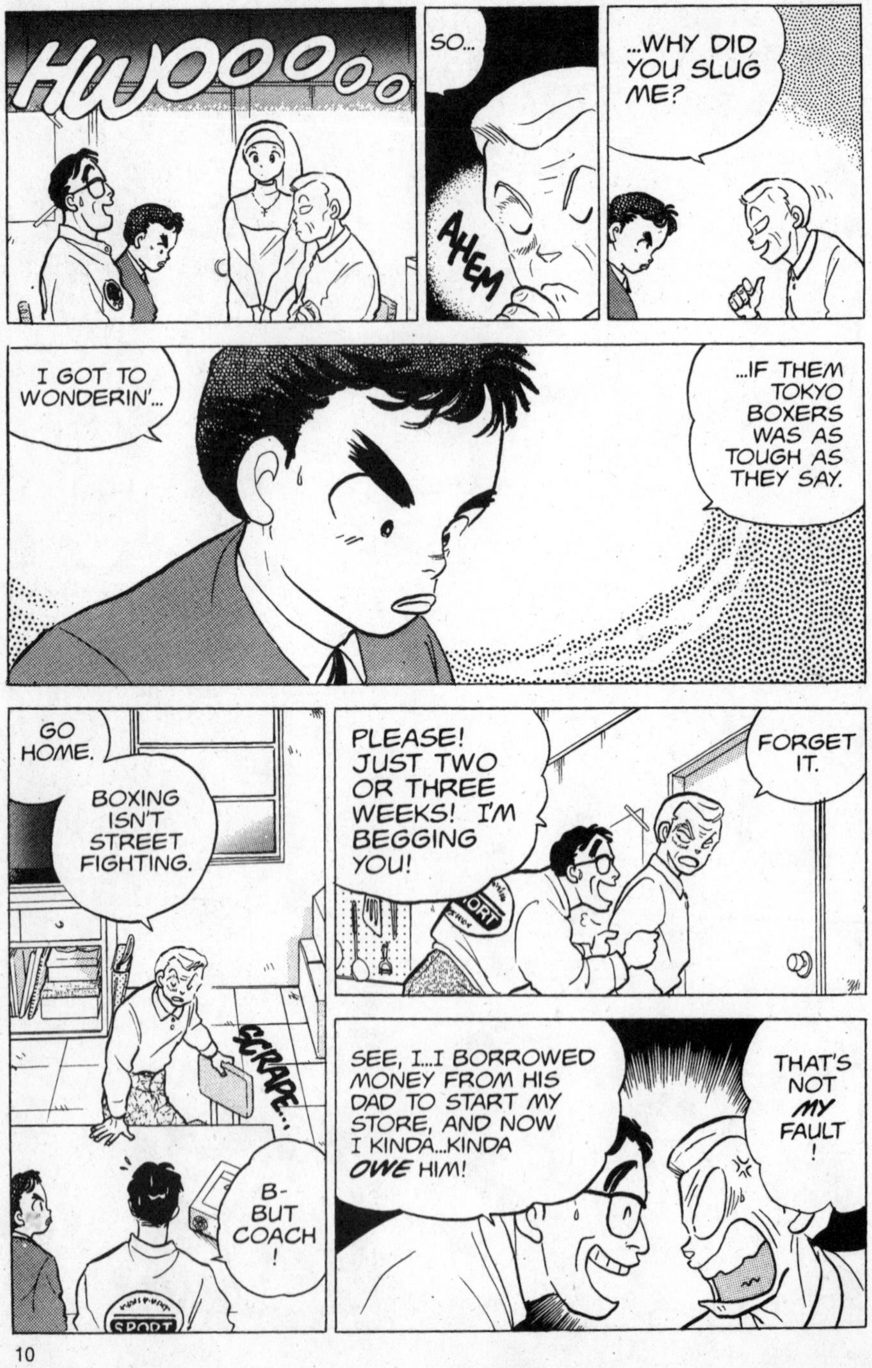
HWOOOooo
SO...
AHEM
...WHY DID YOU SLUG ME?
I GOT TO WONDERIN'...
...IF THEM TOKYO BOXERS WAS AS TOUGH AS THEY SAY.
GO HOME.
BOXING ISN'T STREET FIGHTING.
SCRAPE...
B-BUT COACH!
PLEASE! JUST TWO OR THREE WEEKS! I'M BEGGING YOU!
FORGET IT.
SEE, I...I BORROWED MONEY FROM HIS DAD TO START MY STORE, AND NOW I KINDA...KINDA OWE HIM!
THAT'S NOT MY FAULT!

THIS MUKAIDA'S GYM? DELIVERY!

WHOA! GASP!

HUH ?!

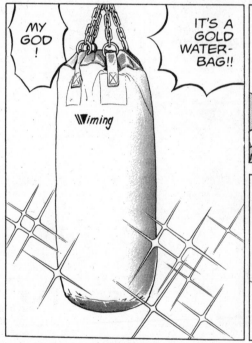

MY GOD!

IT'S A GOLD WATER-BAG!!

Wiming

AN ACTUAL... WATER-BAG...?!

WOW! MAN!

THESE THINGS DON'T MESS UP YOUR FISTS LIKE A SANDBAG DOES, RIGHT? AND HITTIN' 'EM FEELS JUST LIKE HITTIN' A REAL GUY!

I'VE BEEN DYIN' TO TRY ONE!

WHOA!

I DIDN'T ORDER THIS!

JUST A *SMALL* TOKEN OF APPRECIATION... COURTESY OF MY STORE.

HEY, MY DAD PAID FOR IT!

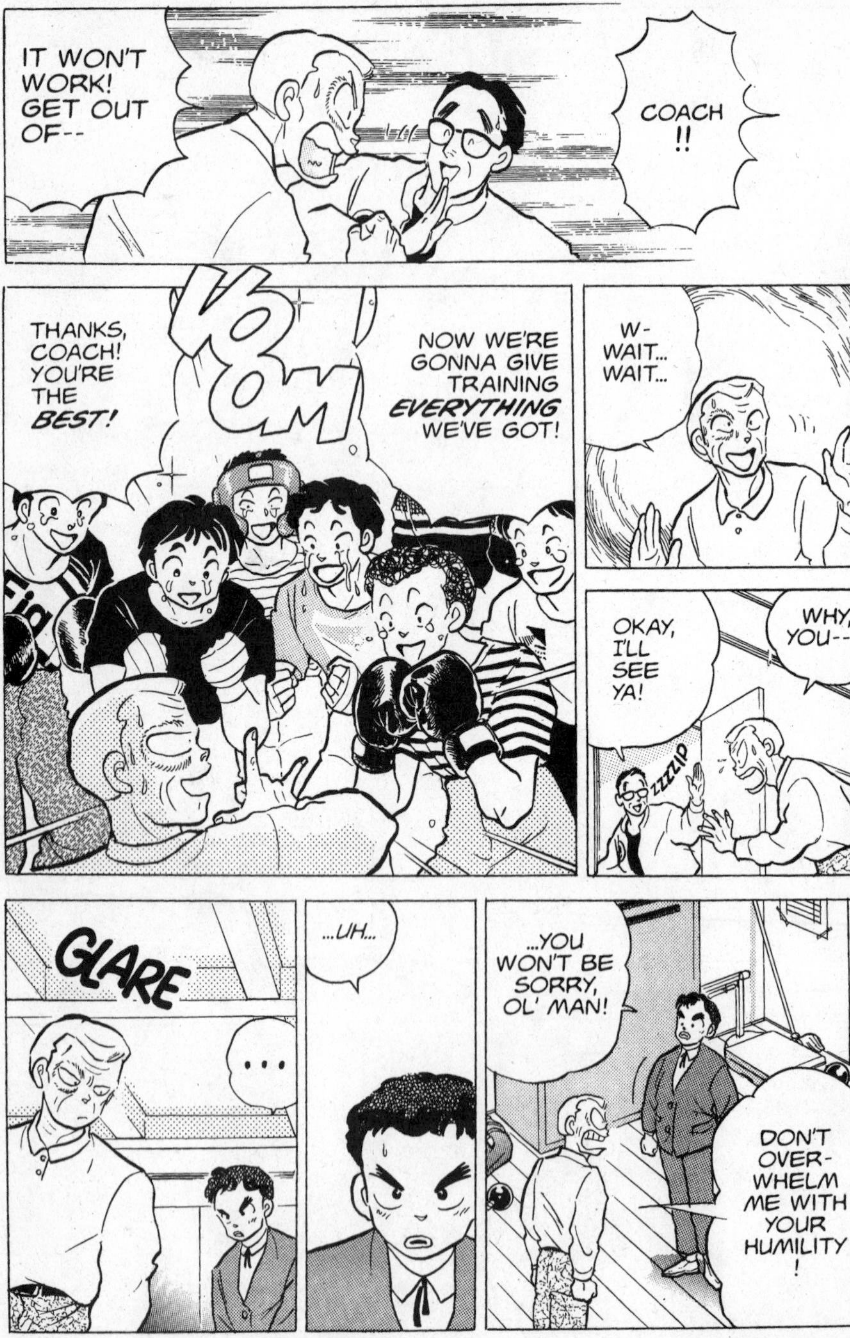
IT WON'T WORK! GET OUT OF--
COACH !!
THANKS, COACH! YOU'RE THE BEST!
VOOM
NOW WE'RE GONNA GIVE TRAINING EVERYTHING WE'VE GOT!
W- WAIT... WAIT...
OKAY, I'LL SEE YA!
ZZZZIP
WHY, YOU--
GLARE
...
...UH...
...YOU WON'T BE SORRY, OL' MAN!
DON'T OVER-WHELM ME WITH YOUR HUMILITY !

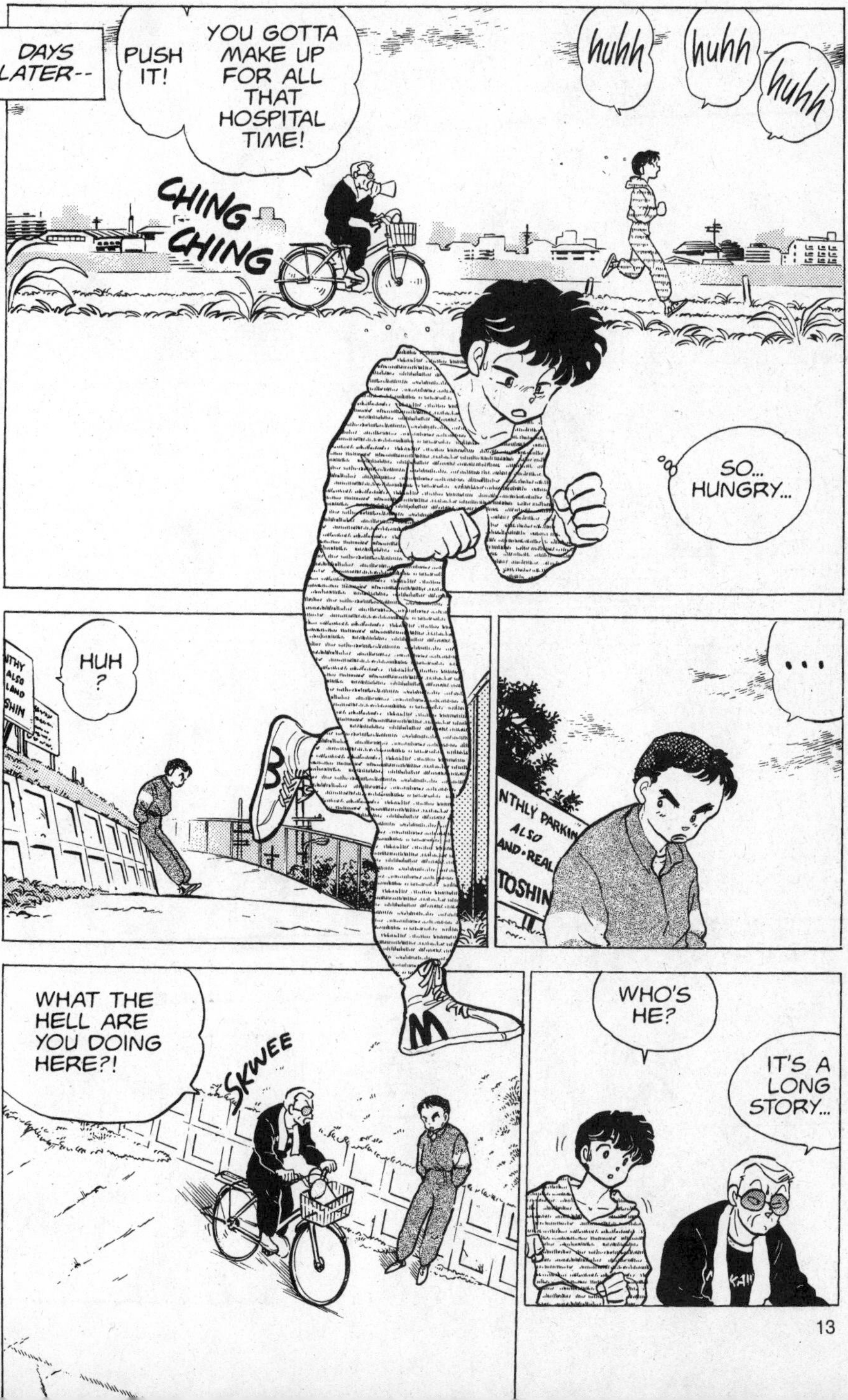
DAYS LATER--
PUSH IT!
YOU GOTTA MAKE UP FOR ALL THAT HOSPITAL TIME!
huhh
huhh
huhh
CHING CHING
SO... HUNGRY...
HUH?
...
WHAT THE HELL ARE YOU DOING HERE?!
SKWEE
WHO'S HE?
IT'S A LONG STORY...

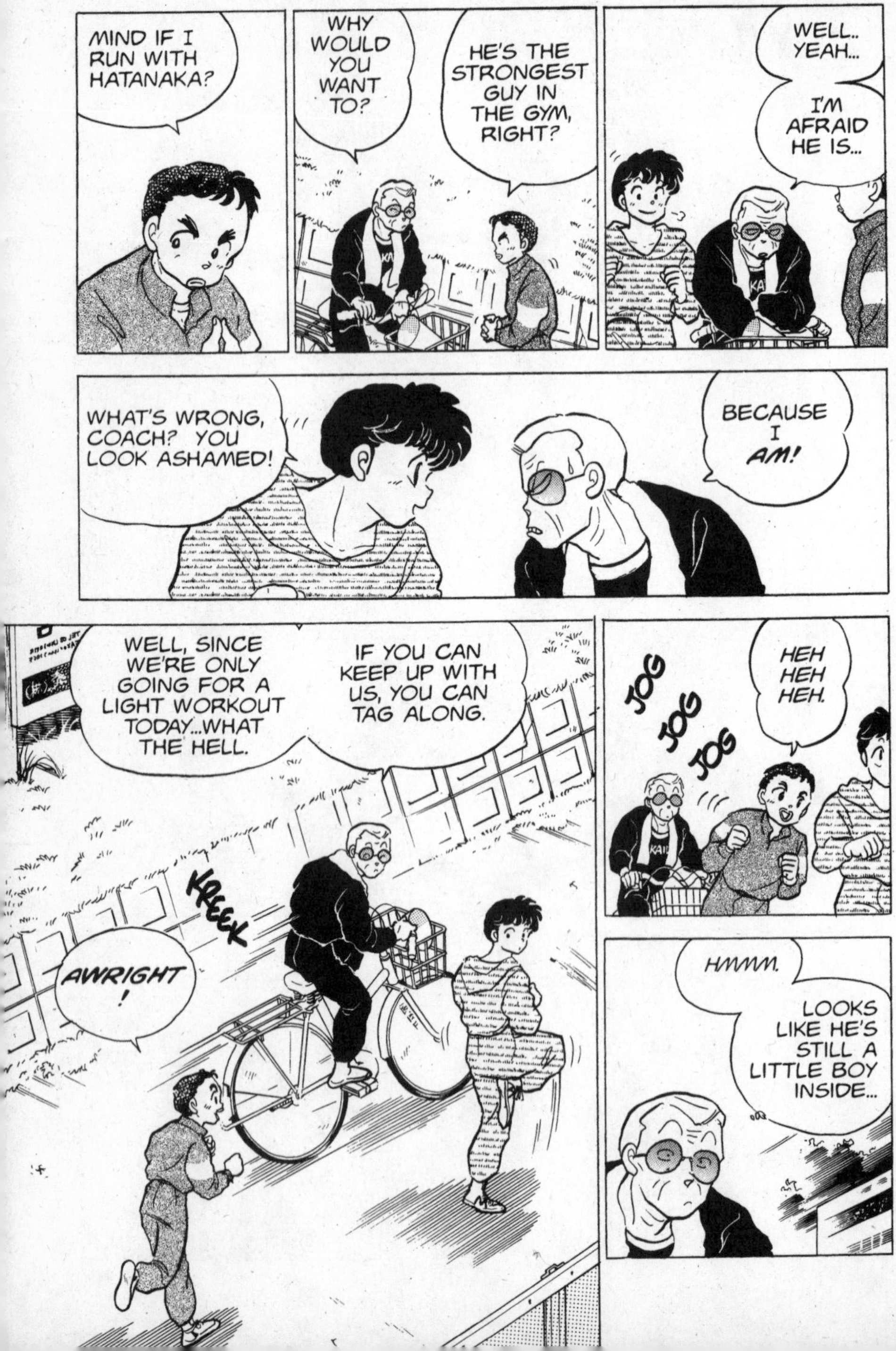
MIND IF I RUN WITH HATANAKA?
WHY WOULD YOU WANT TO?
HE'S THE STRONGEST GUY IN THE GYM, RIGHT?
WELL.. YEAH...
I'M AFRAID HE IS...
WHAT'S WRONG, COACH? YOU LOOK ASHAMED!
BECAUSE I *AM!*
WELL, SINCE WE'RE ONLY GOING FOR A LIGHT WORKOUT TODAY...WHAT THE HELL.
IF YOU CAN KEEP UP WITH US, YOU CAN TAG ALONG.
KREEEK
AWRIGHT!
JOG JOG JOG
HEH HEH HEH.
HMMM.
LOOKS LIKE HE'S STILL A LITTLE BOY INSIDE...

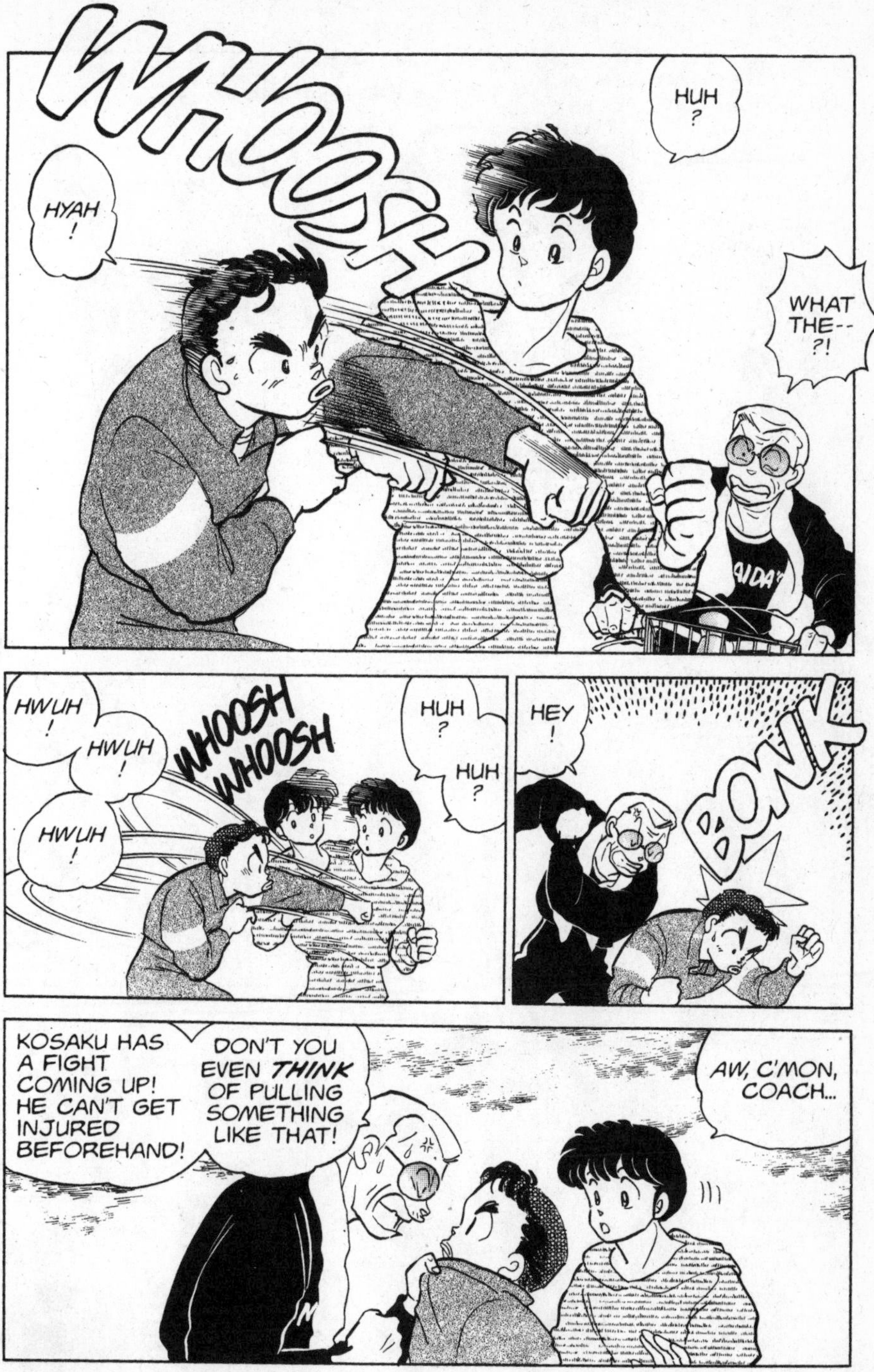
WHOOSH
HYAH!
HUH?
WHAT THE--?!
HWUH!
HWUH!
HWUH!
WHOOSH WHOOSH
HUH?
HUH?
HEY!
BONK
KOSAKU HAS A FIGHT COMING UP! HE CAN'T GET INJURED BEFOREHAND!
DON'T YOU EVEN *THINK* OF PULLING SOMETHING LIKE THAT!
AW, C'MON, COACH...

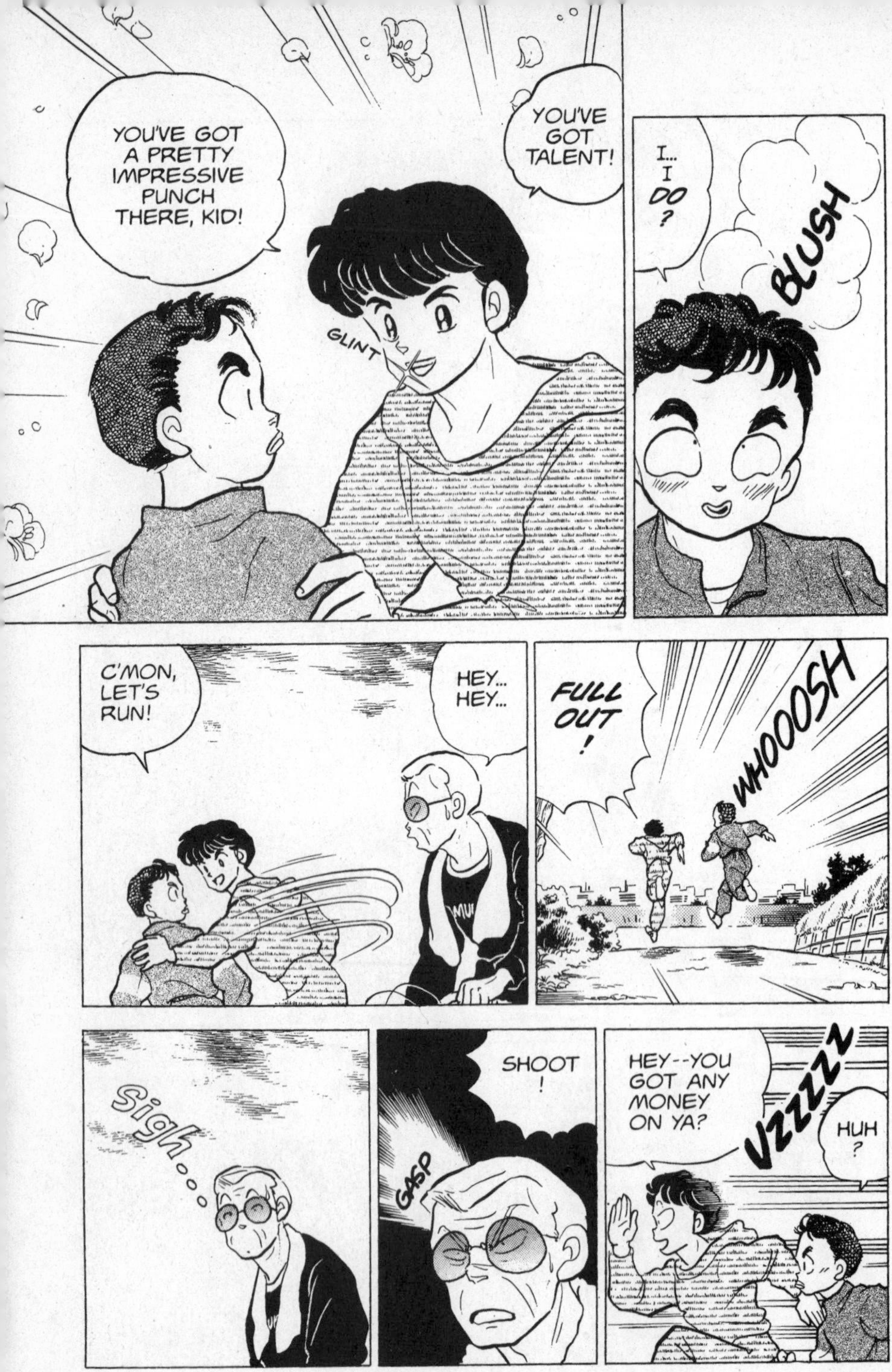
YOU'VE GOT A PRETTY IMPRESSIVE PUNCH THERE, KID!
GLINT
YOU'VE GOT TALENT!
I... I DO?
BLUSH
C'MON, LET'S RUN!
HEY... HEY...
FULL OUT!
WHOOOSH
Sigh...
GASP
SHOOT!
HEY--YOU GOT ANY MONEY ON YA?
VZZZZZ
HUH?

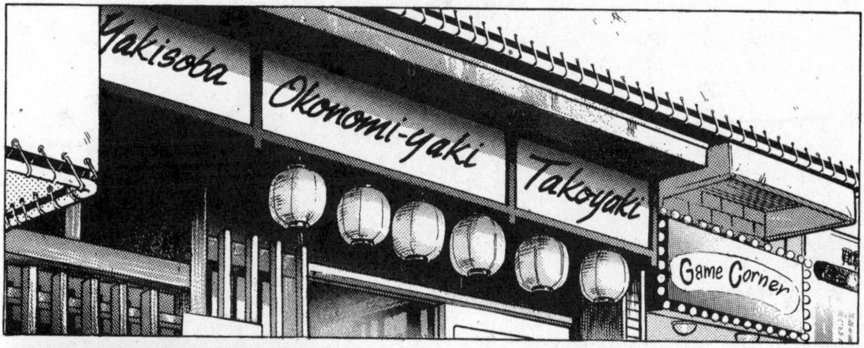
Yakisoba
Okonomi-yaki
Takoyaki
Game Corner
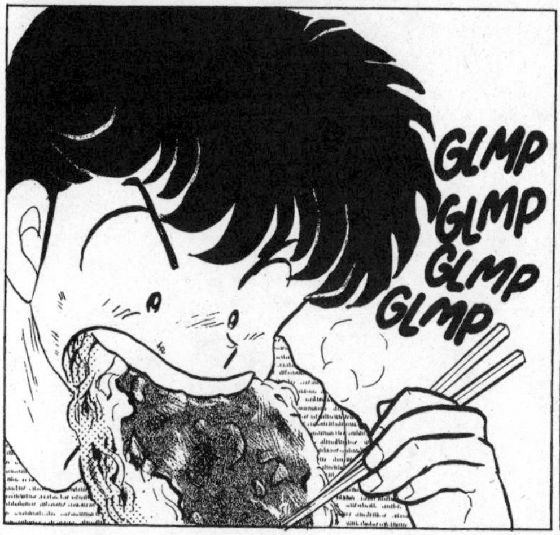
GLMP GLMP GLMP GLMP
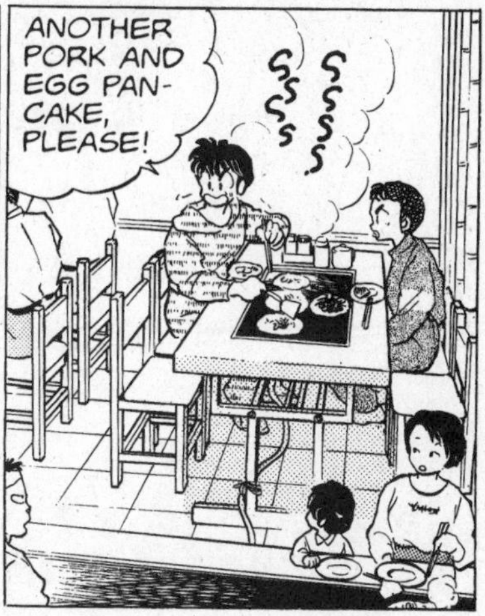
ANOTHER PORK AND EGG PAN-CAKE, PLEASE!
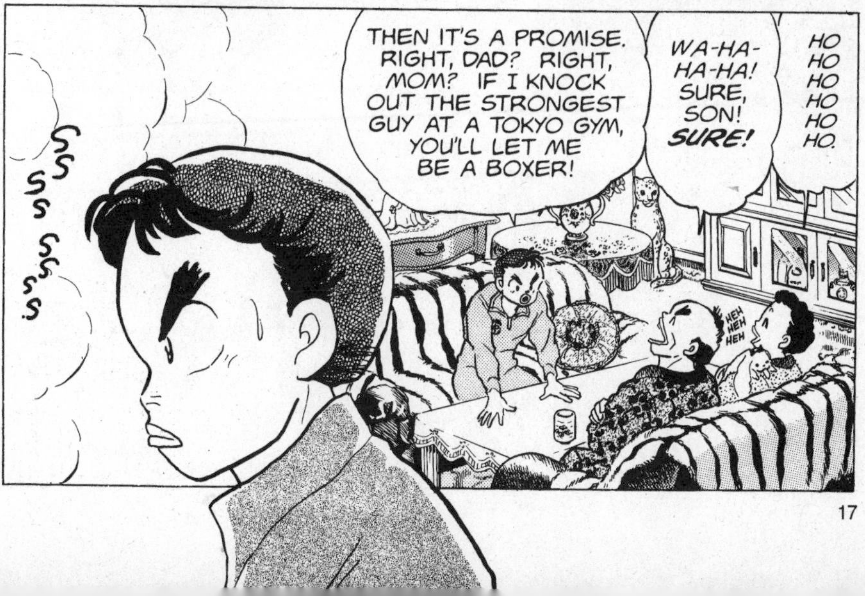
THEN IT'S A PROMISE. RIGHT, DAD? RIGHT, MOM? IF I KNOCK OUT THE STRONGEST GUY AT A TOKYO GYM, YOU'LL LET ME BE A BOXER!
WA-HA-HA-HA! SURE, SON! ***SURE!***
HO HO HO HO HO HO.
HEH HEH HEH

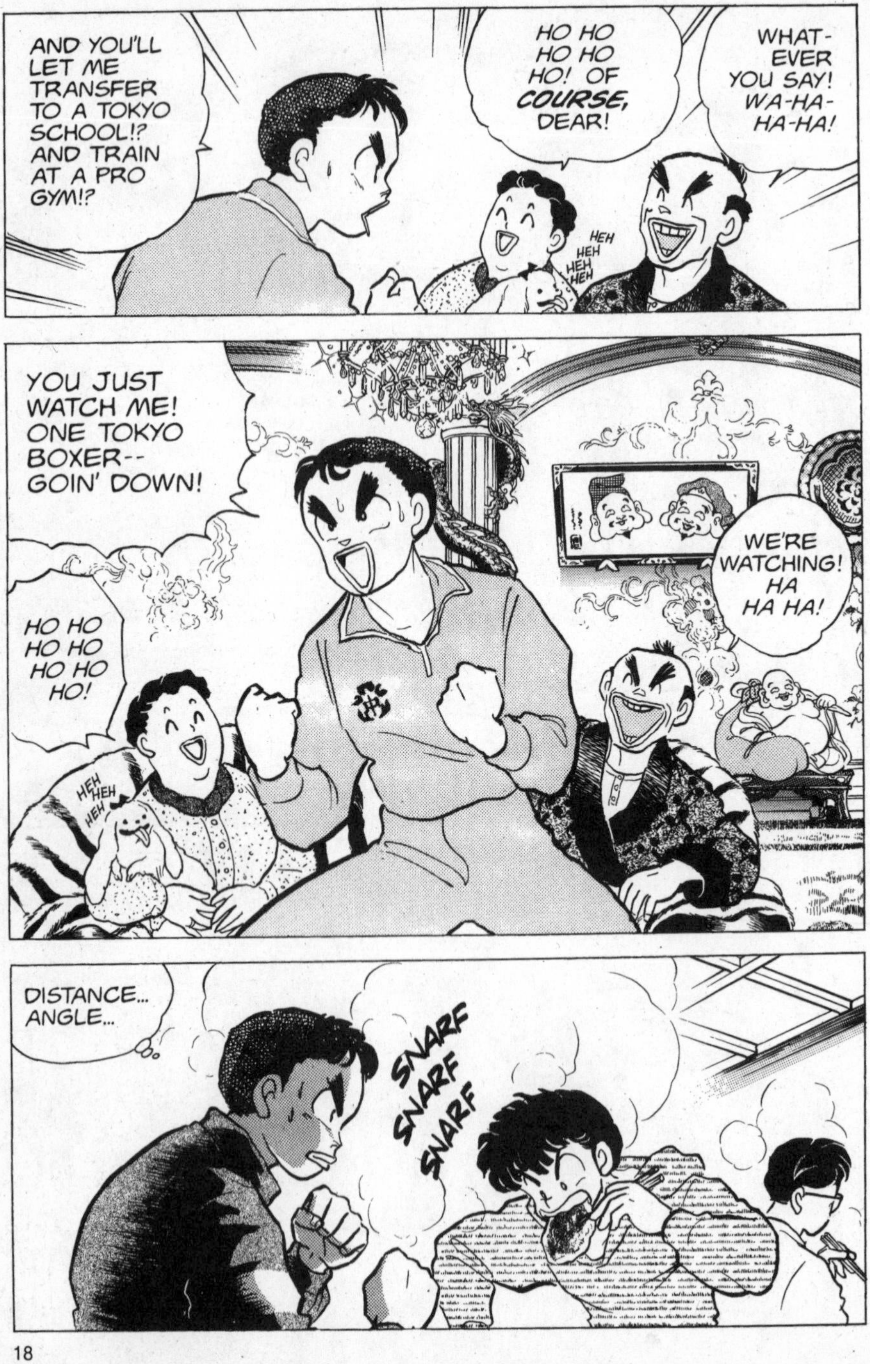
AND YOU'LL LET ME TRANSFER TO A TOKYO SCHOOL!? AND TRAIN AT A PRO GYM!?
HO HO HO HO HO! OF COURSE, DEAR!
WHAT-EVER YOU SAY! WA-HA-HA-HA!
HEH HEH HEH HEH
YOU JUST WATCH ME! ONE TOKYO BOXER-- GOIN' DOWN!
WE'RE WATCHING! HA HA HA!
HO HO HO HO HO HO HO!
HEH HEH HEH
DISTANCE... ANGLE...
SNARF SNARF SNARF

HYAH!

WHOOSH

HYOI

YOU GONNA EAT THAT?

....

JUST SHADOW-BOXING! HEH, HEH...

WHISH WHISH

KOSAKU ESCAPED?

THAT IDIOT'S SNEAKIN' A MEAL AGAIN, I BET.

HE CAN'T BE! HE WAS JUST RELEASED FROM THE HOSPITAL YESTERDAY!

KREEK

CRAB CUISINE
KANIMARO

....

CUH- CUH-

COACH!

KLAK KLAK KLAK KLAK

OKONOMI

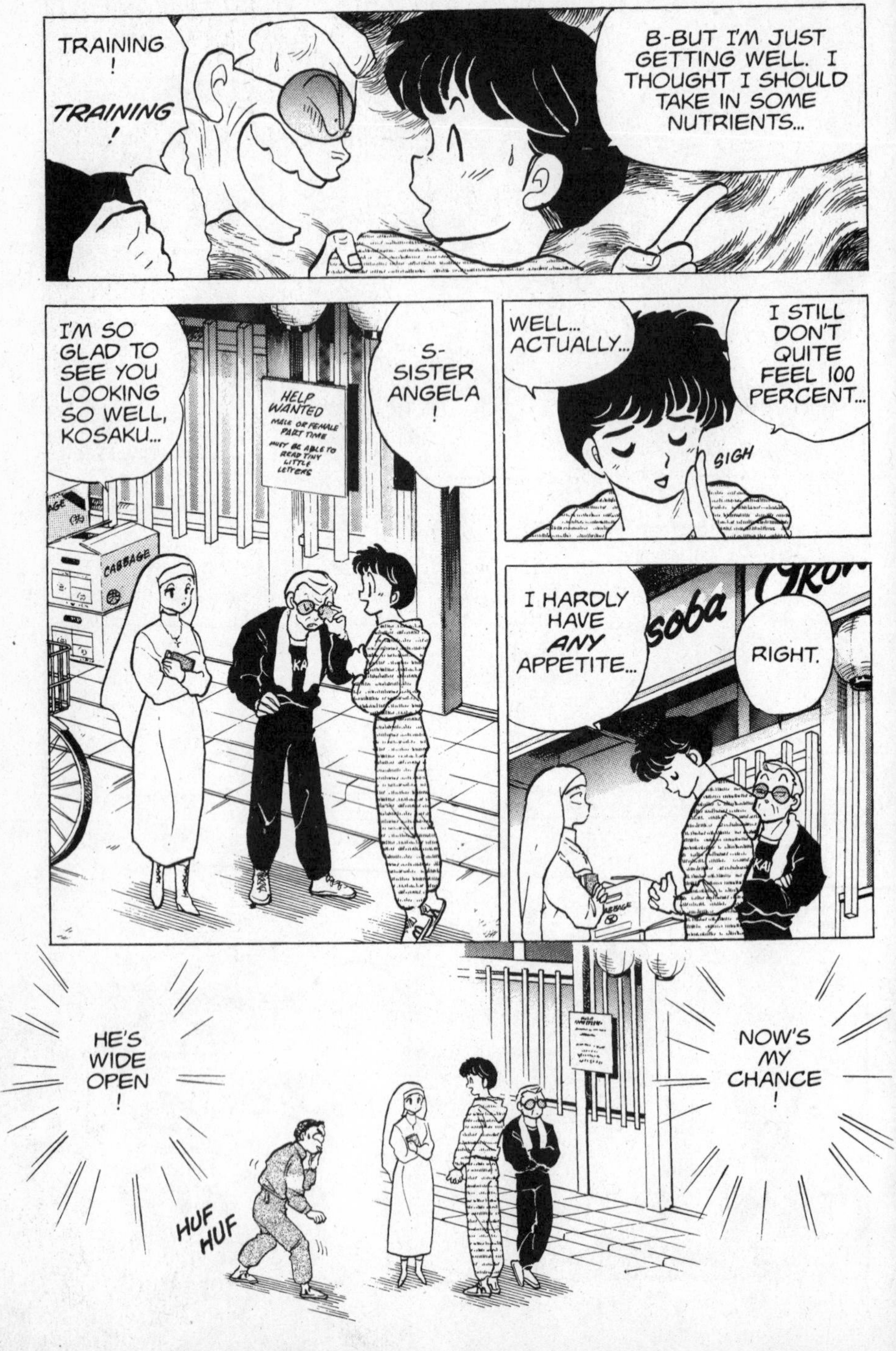
TRAINING!
TRAINING!
B-BUT I'M JUST GETTING WELL. I THOUGHT I SHOULD TAKE IN SOME NUTRIENTS...
I'M SO GLAD TO SEE YOU LOOKING SO WELL, KOSAKU...
S-SISTER ANGELA!
HELP WANTED
MALE OR FEMALE
PART TIME
MUST BE ABLE TO READ TINY LITTLE LETTERS
CABBAGE
WELL... ACTUALLY...
I STILL DON'T QUITE FEEL 100 PERCENT...
SIGH
I HARDLY HAVE *ANY* APPETITE...
soba
RIGHT.
HE'S WIDE OPEN!
HUF HUF
NOW'S MY CHANCE!

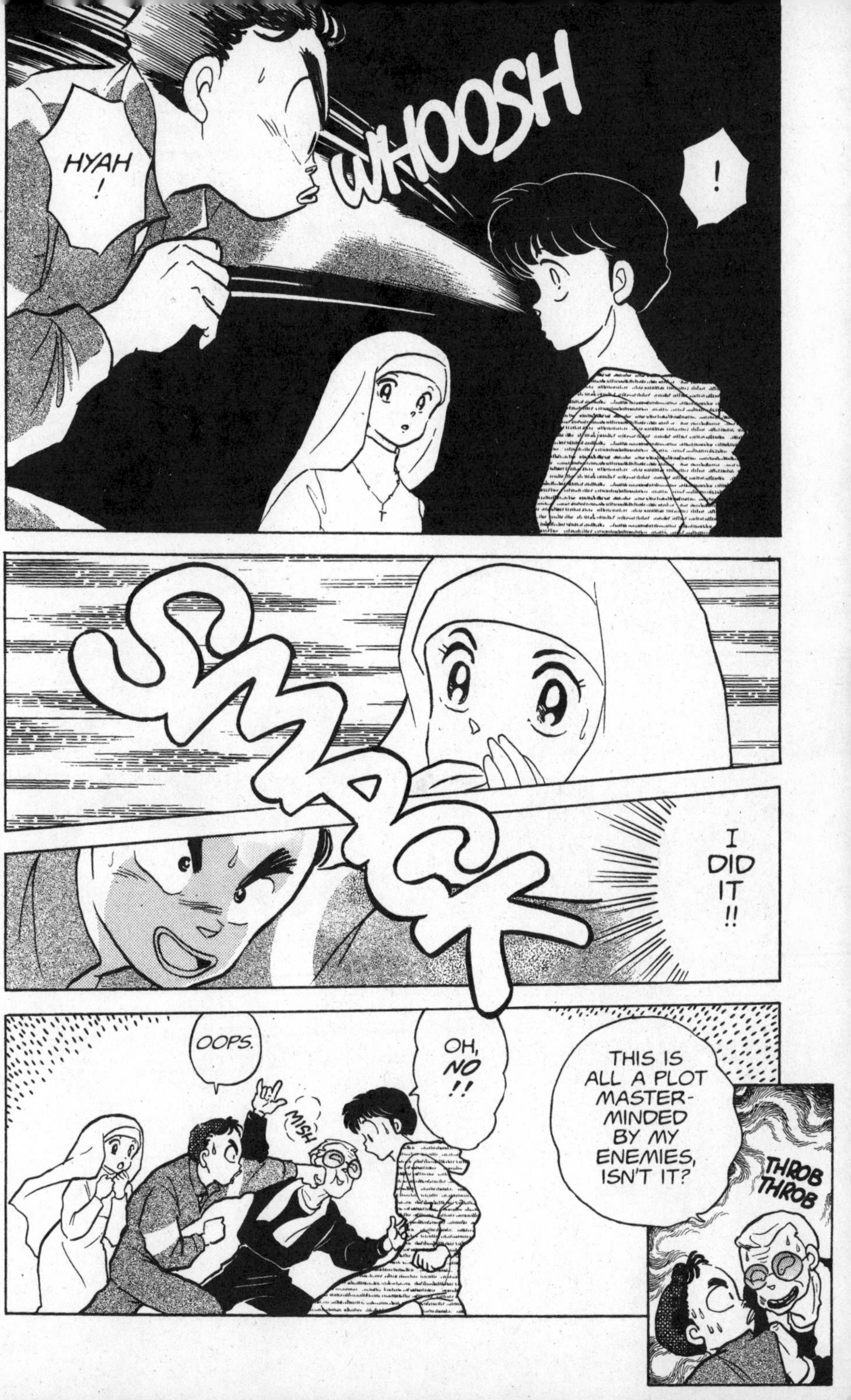
HYAH!
WHOOSH
!
SMACK
I DID IT!!
OOPS.
MISH
OH, NO!!
THIS IS ALL A PLOT MASTER-MINDED BY MY ENEMIES, ISN'T IT?
THROB THROB

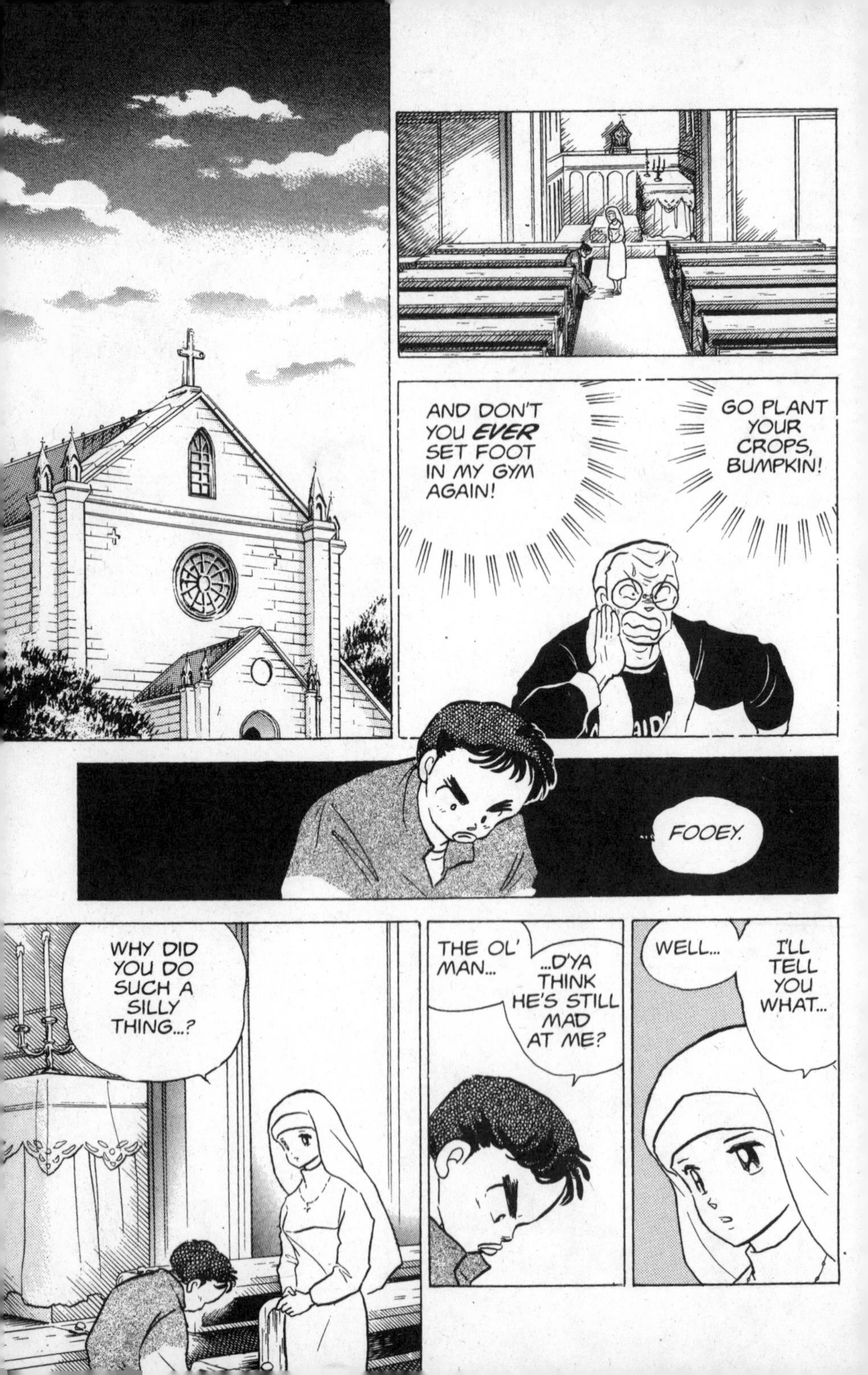
AND DON'T YOU EVER SET FOOT IN MY GYM AGAIN!
GO PLANT YOUR CROPS, BUMPKIN!
AIDO
...FOOEY.
WHY DID YOU DO SUCH A SILLY THING...?
THE OL' MAN...
...D'YA THINK HE'S STILL MAD AT ME?
WELL...
I'LL TELL YOU WHAT...

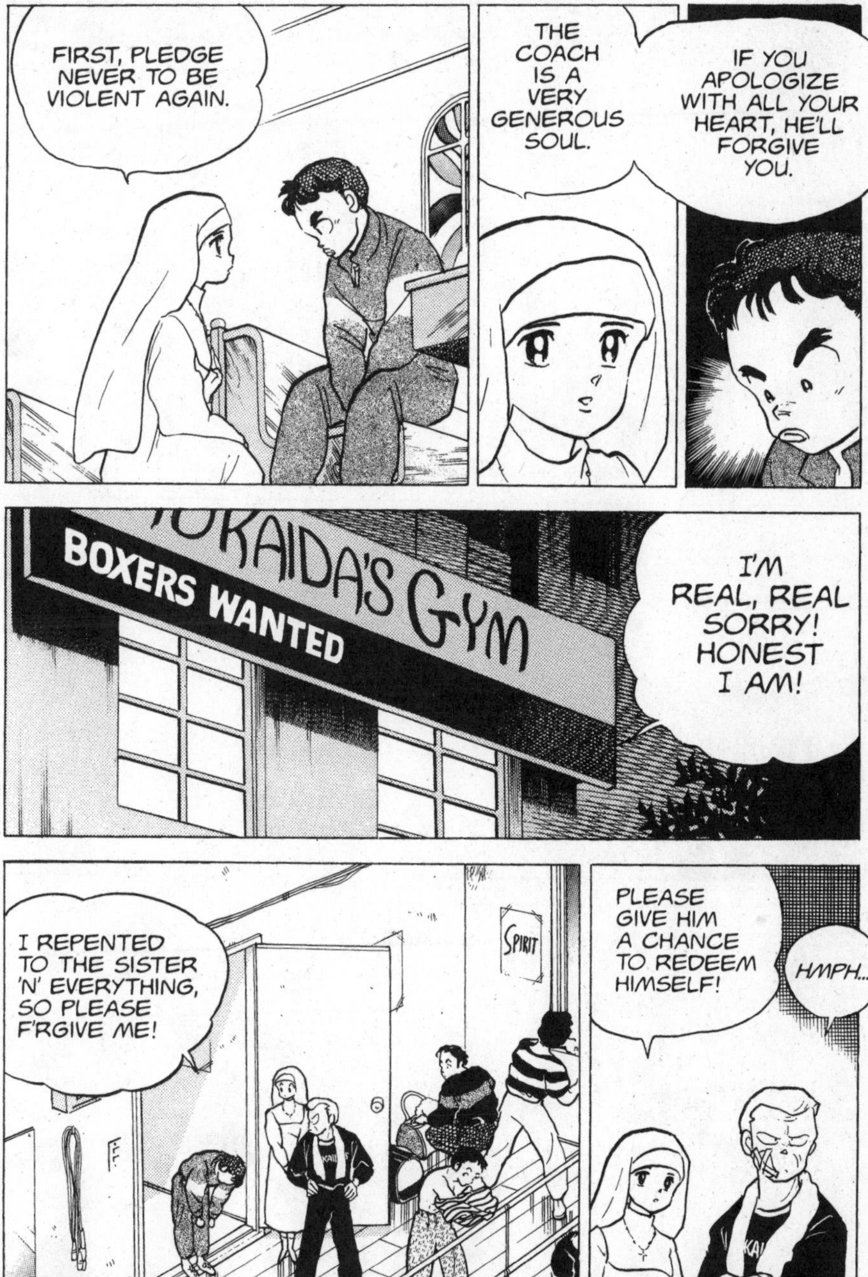
FIRST, PLEDGE NEVER TO BE VIOLENT AGAIN.
THE COACH IS A VERY GENEROUS SOUL.
IF YOU APOLOGIZE WITH ALL YOUR HEART, HE'LL FORGIVE YOU.
BOXERS WANTED
I'M REAL, REAL SORRY! HONEST I AM!
I REPENTED TO THE SISTER 'N' EVERYTHING, SO PLEASE F'RGIVE ME!
SPIRIT
PLEASE GIVE HIM A CHANCE TO REDEEM HIMSELF!
HMPH...

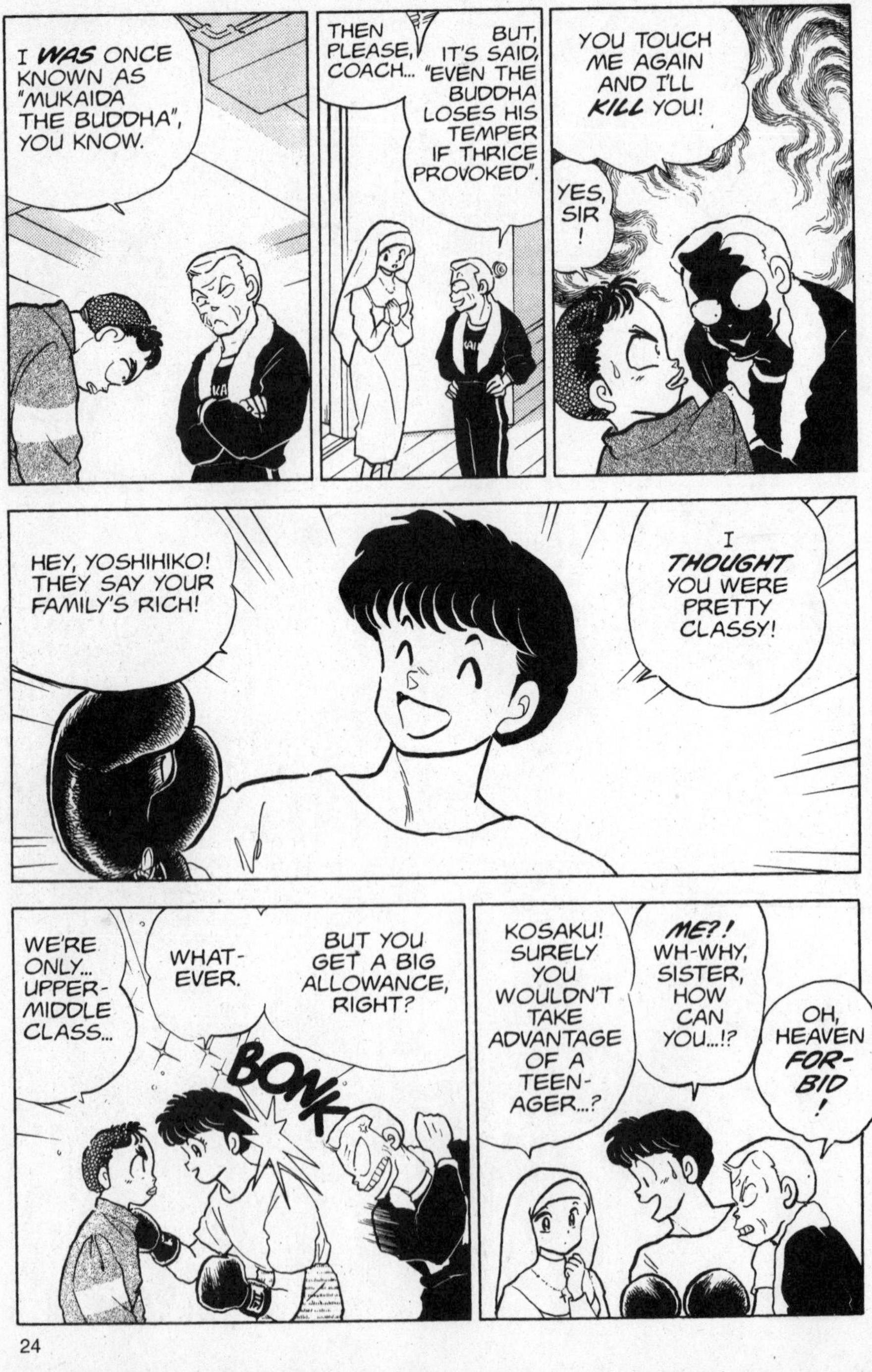

I WAS ONCE KNOWN AS "MUKAIDA THE BUDDHA", YOU KNOW.
THEN PLEASE, COACH...
BUT, IT'S SAID, "EVEN THE BUDDHA LOSES HIS TEMPER IF THRICE PROVOKED".
YOU TOUCH ME AGAIN AND I'LL KILL YOU!
YES, SIR!
HEY, YOSHIHIKO! THEY SAY YOUR FAMILY'S RICH!
I THOUGHT YOU WERE PRETTY CLASSY!
WE'RE ONLY... UPPER-MIDDLE CLASS...
WHAT-EVER.
BUT YOU GET A BIG ALLOWANCE, RIGHT?
BONK
KOSAKU! SURELY YOU WOULDN'T TAKE ADVANTAGE OF A TEEN-AGER...?
ME?! WH-WHY, SISTER, HOW CAN YOU...!?
OH, HEAVEN FOR-BID!

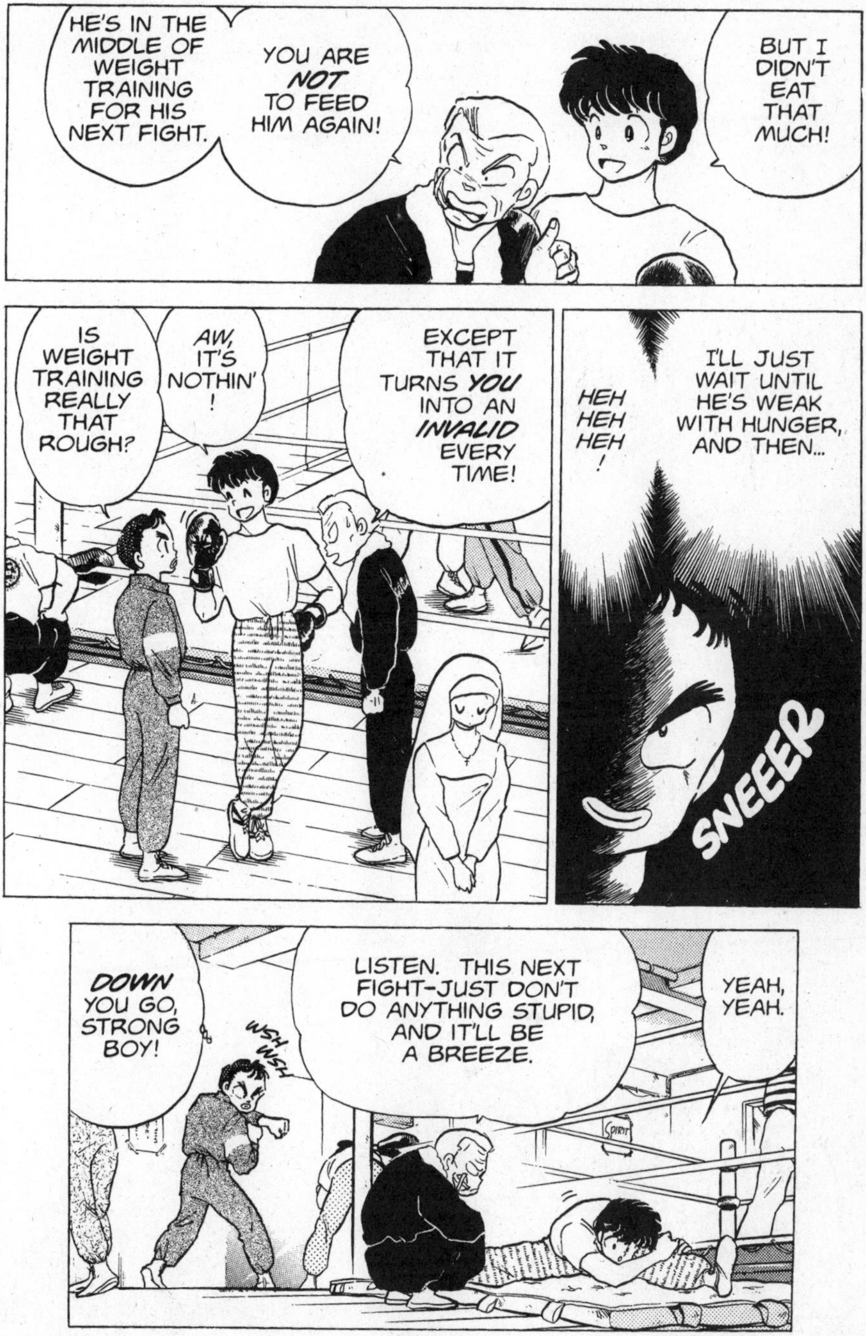
HE'S IN THE MIDDLE OF WEIGHT TRAINING FOR HIS NEXT FIGHT.
YOU ARE NOT TO FEED HIM AGAIN!
BUT I DIDN'T EAT THAT MUCH!
IS WEIGHT TRAINING REALLY THAT ROUGH?
AW, IT'S NOTHIN'!
EXCEPT THAT IT TURNS YOU INTO AN INVALID EVERY TIME!
HEH HEH HEH!
I'LL JUST WAIT UNTIL HE'S WEAK WITH HUNGER, AND THEN...
SNEEER
DOWN YOU GO, STRONG BOY!
WSH WSH
LISTEN. THIS NEXT FIGHT–JUST DON'T DO ANYTHING STUPID, AND IT'LL BE A BREEZE.
YEAH, YEAH.
SPIRIT

CHAPTER ONE

LAMB FOR THE SLAUGHTER

PART TWO

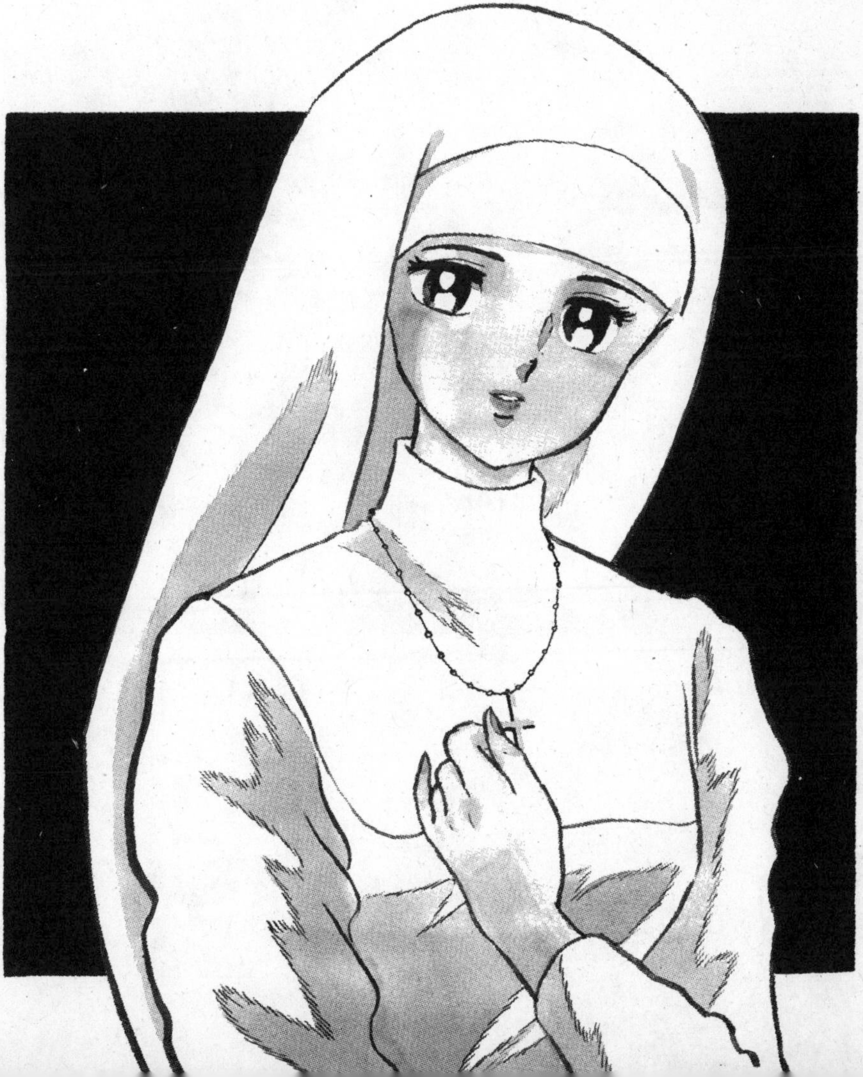

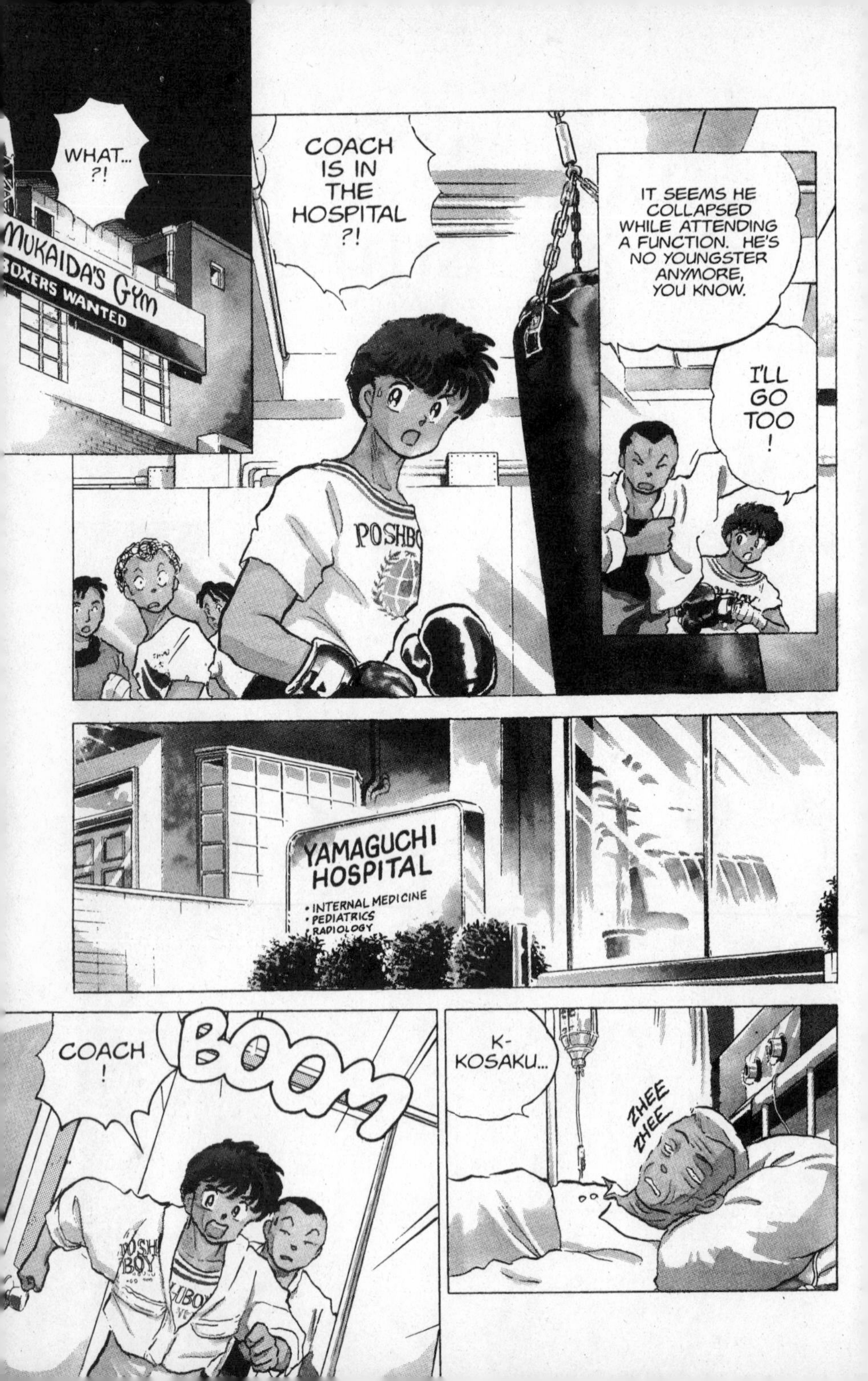
WHAT... ?!
MUKAIDA'S GYM
BOXERS WANTED
COACH IS IN THE HOSPITAL ?!
POSHBO
IT SEEMS HE COLLAPSED WHILE ATTENDING A FUNCTION. HE'S NO YOUNGSTER ANYMORE, YOU KNOW.
I'LL GO TOO !
YAMAGUCHI HOSPITAL
• INTERNAL MEDICINE
• PEDIATRICS
• RADIOLOGY
COACH !
BOOM
K-KOSAKU...
ZHEE ZHEE

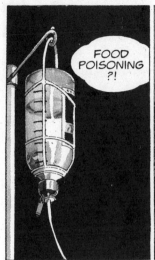

FOOD POISONING ?!

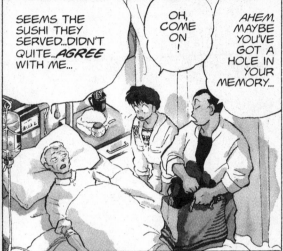

SEEMS THE SUSHI THEY SERVED...DIDN'T QUITE...*AGREE* WITH ME...

OH, COME ON !

AHEM. MAYBE YOU'VE GOT A HOLE IN YOUR MEMORY...

FORGIVE ME, KOSAKU...WITH YOUR FIGHT COMING UP AND ALL...

WHAT ARE YOU TALKING ABOUT, COACH ?!

'TAKE YOUR TIME! GET BETTER!

DON'T WORRY ABOUT MY TRAINING! I CAN TAKE CARE OF MYSELF!

SORRY TO DUMP THIS ON YOU, ISHIDA, BUT YOU'RE GOING TO HAVE TO STAY AT THE GYM WITH KOSAKU--STARTING *TONIGHT*.

SIGH...

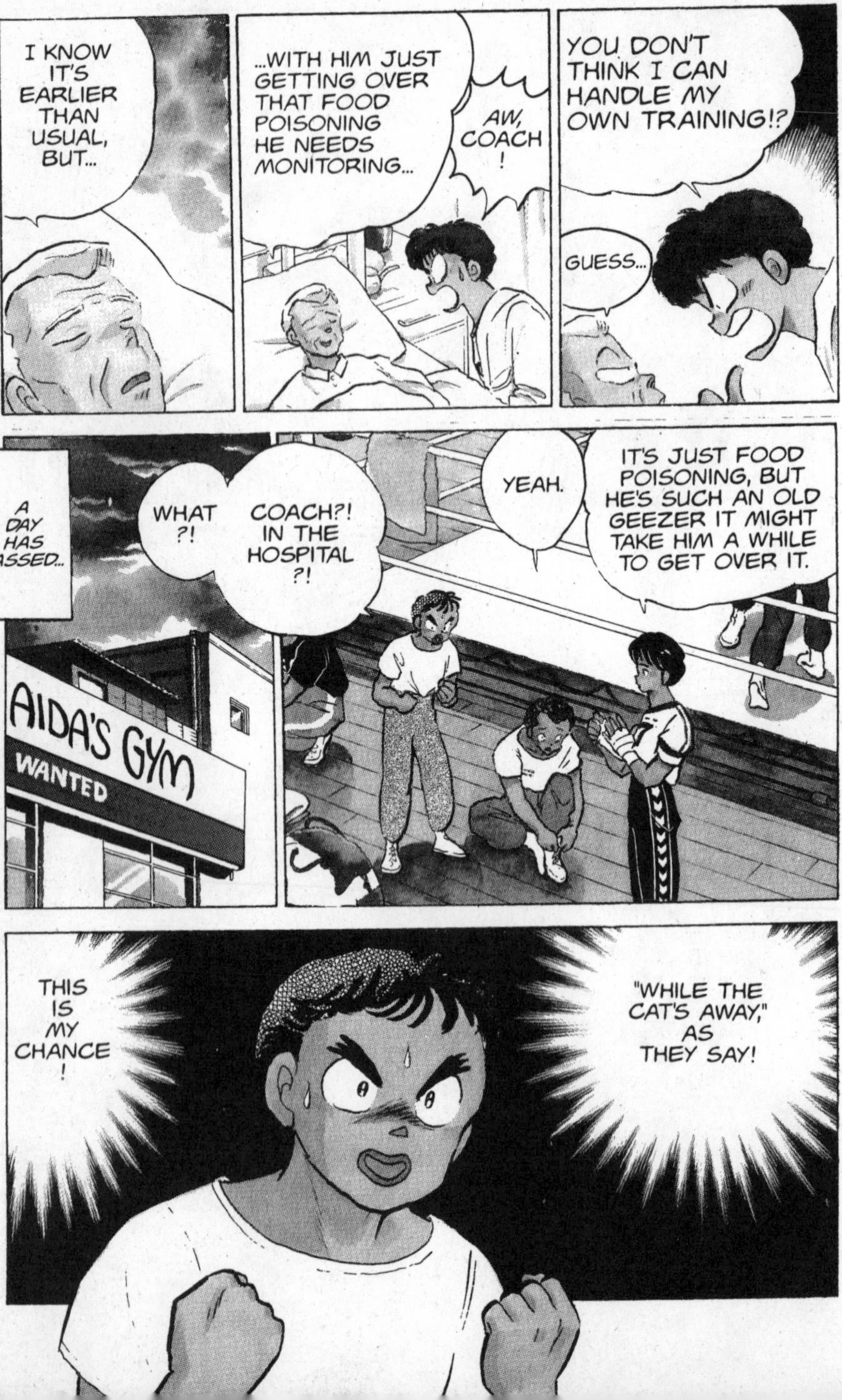
I KNOW IT'S EARLIER THAN USUAL, BUT...
...WITH HIM JUST GETTING OVER THAT FOOD POISONING HE NEEDS MONITORING...
AW, COACH!
YOU DON'T THINK I CAN HANDLE MY OWN TRAINING!?
GUESS...
A DAY HAS PASSED...
AIDA'S GYM
WANTED
WHAT?!
COACH?! IN THE HOSPITAL?!
YEAH.
IT'S JUST FOOD POISONING, BUT HE'S SUCH AN OLD GEEZER IT MIGHT TAKE HIM A WHILE TO GET OVER IT.
THIS IS MY CHANCE!
"WHILE THE CAT'S AWAY," AS THEY SAY!

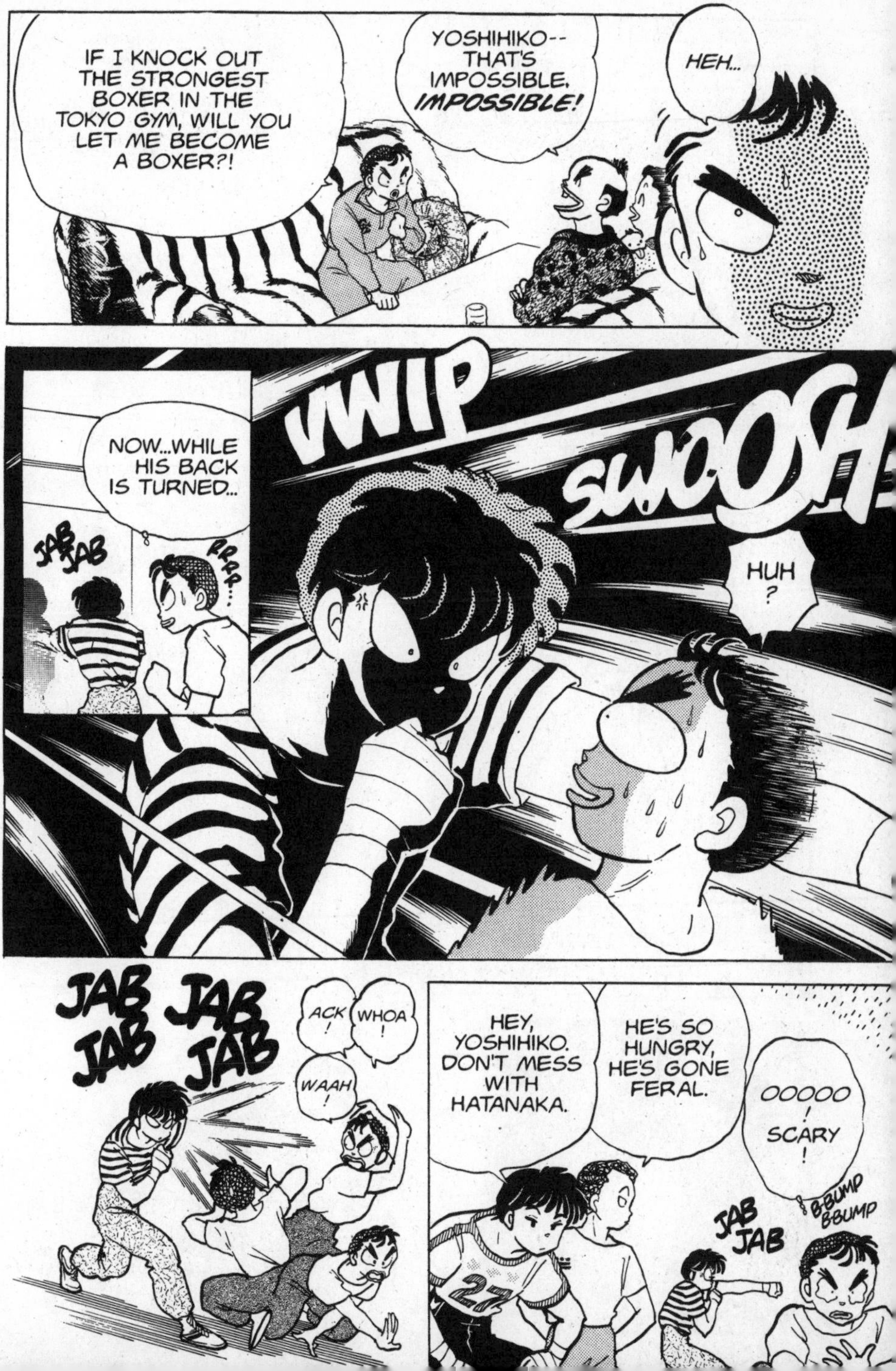
IF I KNOCK OUT THE STRONGEST BOXER IN THE TOKYO GYM, WILL YOU LET ME BECOME A BOXER?!
YOSHIHIKO-- THAT'S IMPOSSIBLE. IMPOSSIBLE!
HEH...
NOW...WHILE HIS BACK IS TURNED...
JAB JAB
RRRR...
VWIP
SWOOSH
HUH?
JAB JAB JAB JAB
ACK!
WHOA!
WAAH!
HEY, YOSHIHIKO. DON'T MESS WITH HATANAKA.
HE'S SO HUNGRY, HE'S GONE FERAL.
OOOOO! SCARY!
B-BUMP B-BUMP
JAB JAB

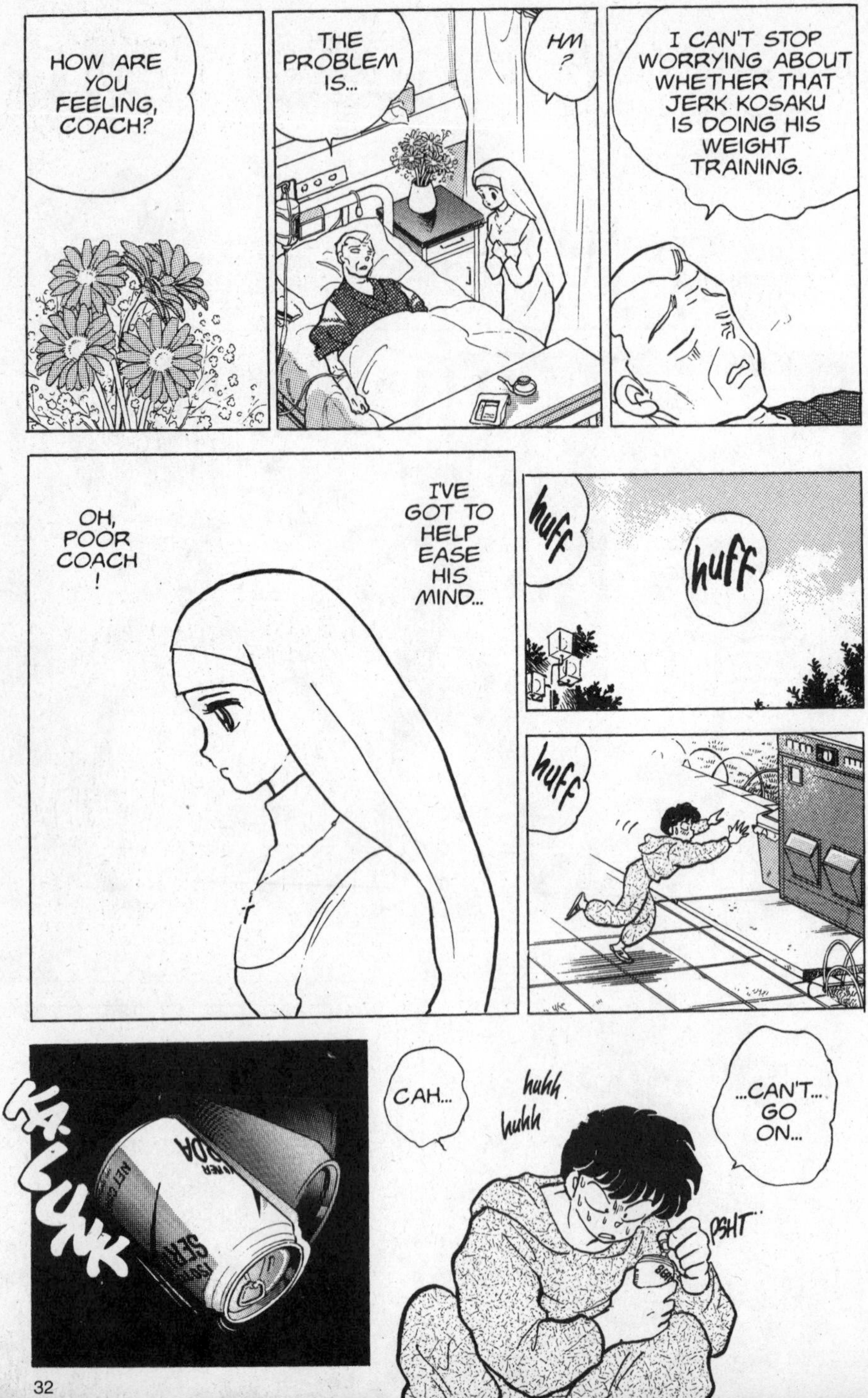
HOW ARE YOU FEELING, COACH?
THE PROBLEM IS...
HM ?
I CAN'T STOP WORRYING ABOUT WHETHER THAT JERK KOSAKU IS DOING HIS WEIGHT TRAINING.
OH, POOR COACH !
I'VE GOT TO HELP EASE HIS MIND...
huff
huff
huff
KA-LUNK
CAH...
huhh
huhh
...CAN'T... GO ON...
PSHT

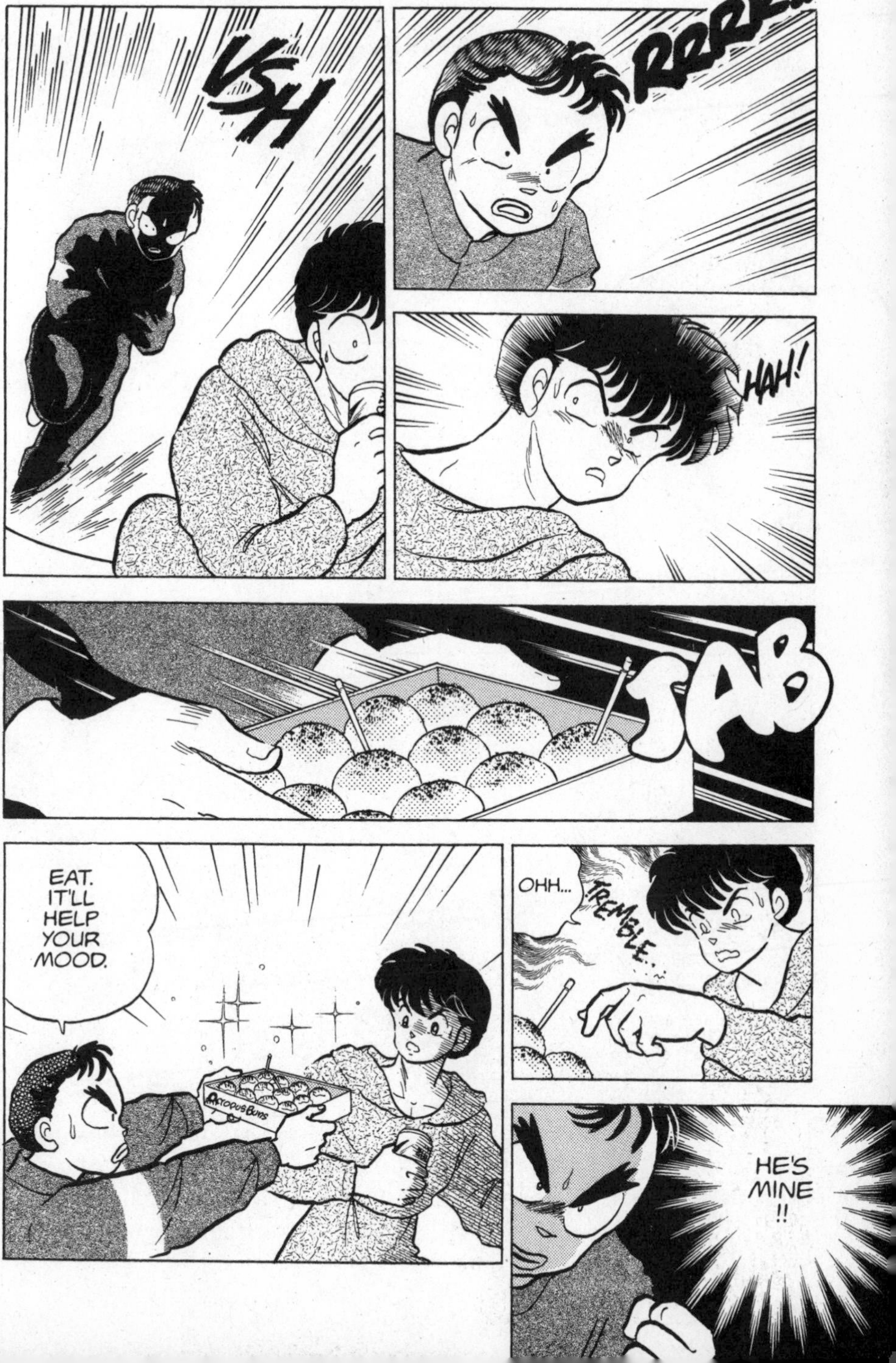
VSH
RRRR...
HAH!
JAB
EAT. IT'LL HELP YOUR MOOD.
OCTOPUS BUNS
OHH...
TREMBLE...
HE'S MINE !!

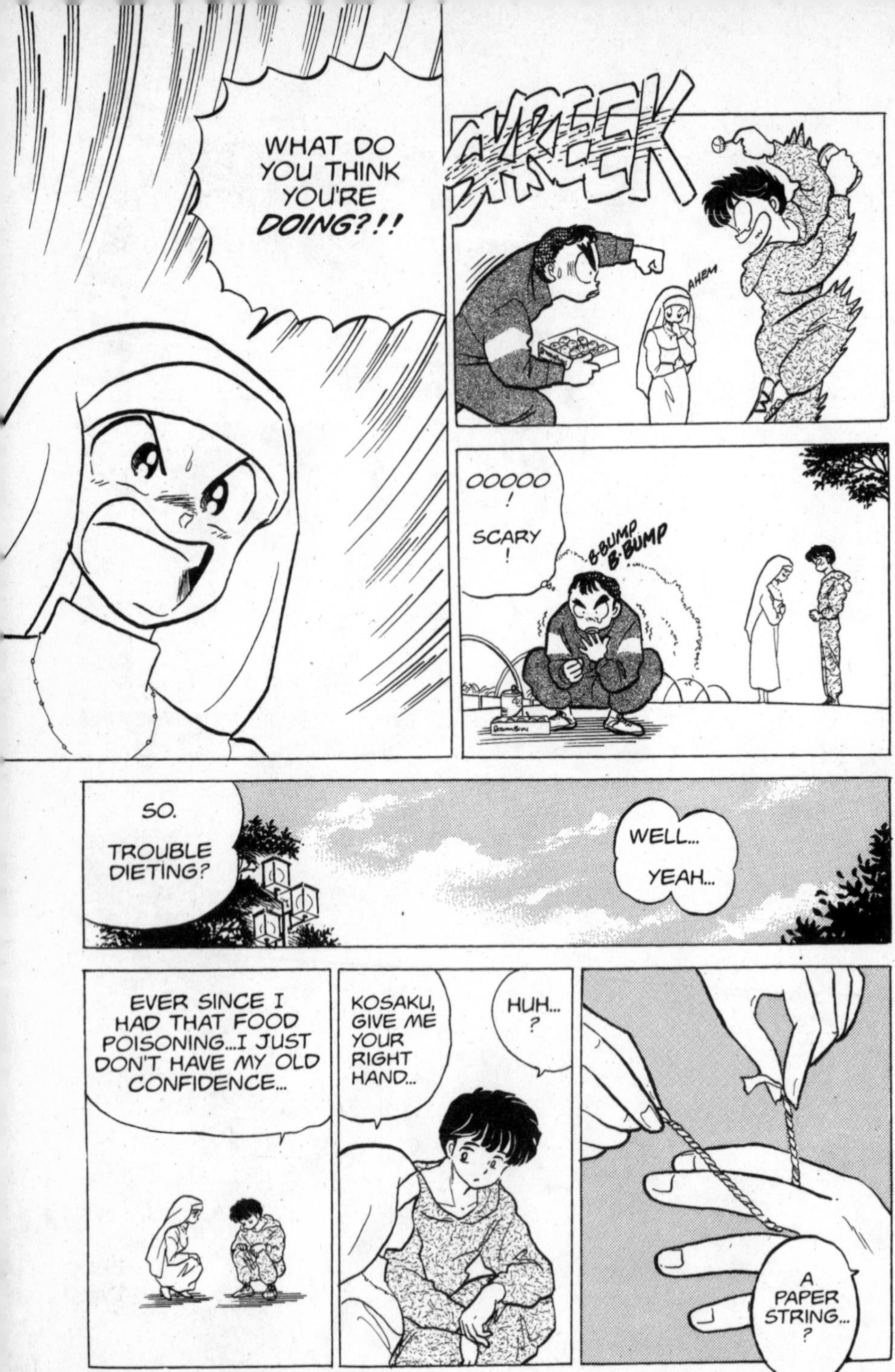
WHAT DO YOU THINK YOU'RE DOING?!!
SKREEK
AHEM
OOOOO! SCARY!
B-BUMP B-BUMP
SO. TROUBLE DIETING?
WELL... YEAH...
EVER SINCE I HAD THAT FOOD POISONING...I JUST DON'T HAVE MY OLD CONFIDENCE...
KOSAKU, GIVE ME YOUR RIGHT HAND...
HUH...?
A PAPER STRING...?

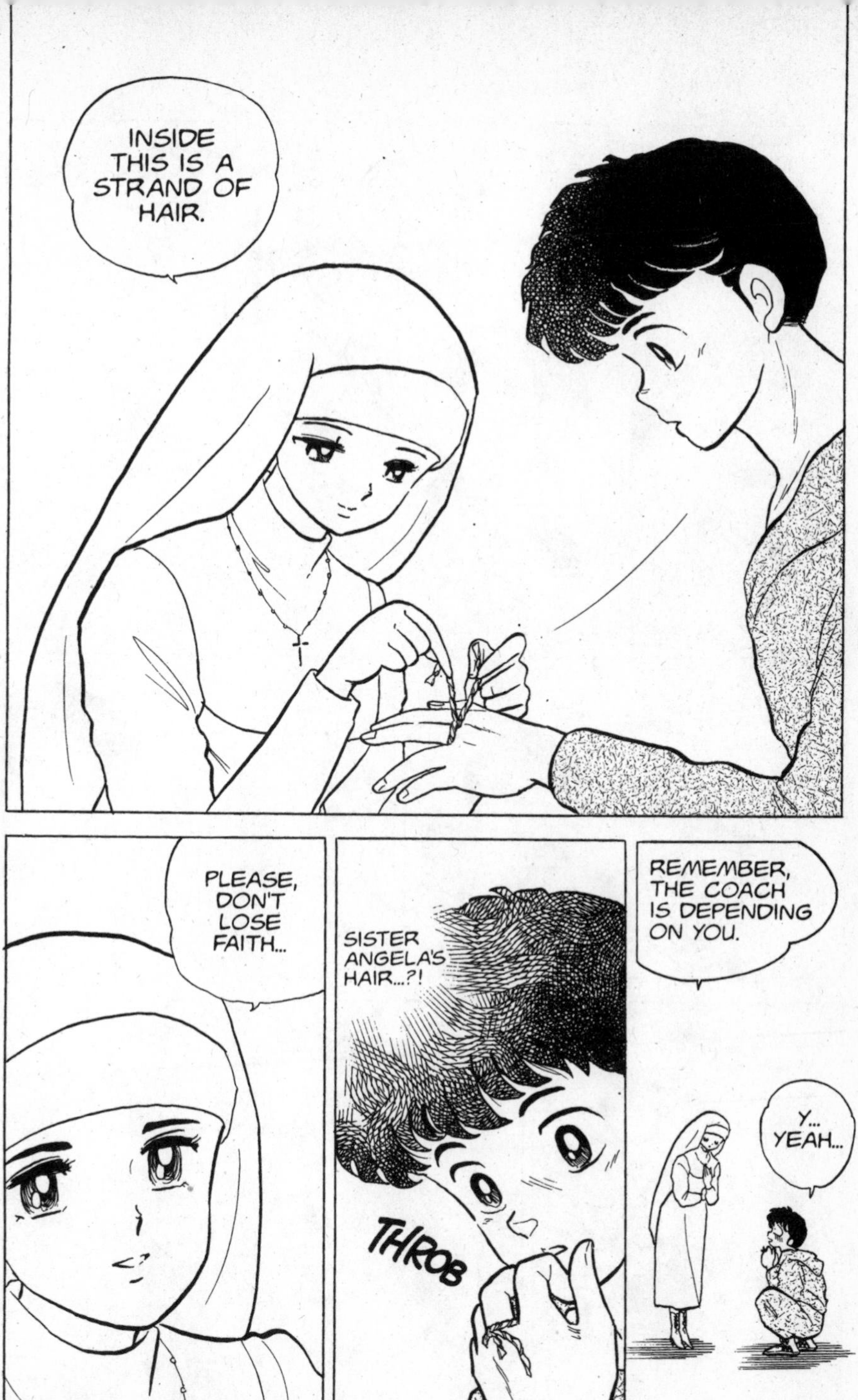
INSIDE THIS IS A STRAND OF HAIR.
PLEASE, DON'T LOSE FAITH...
SISTER ANGELA'S HAIR...?!
THROB
REMEMBER, THE COACH IS DEPENDING ON YOU.
Y... YEAH...

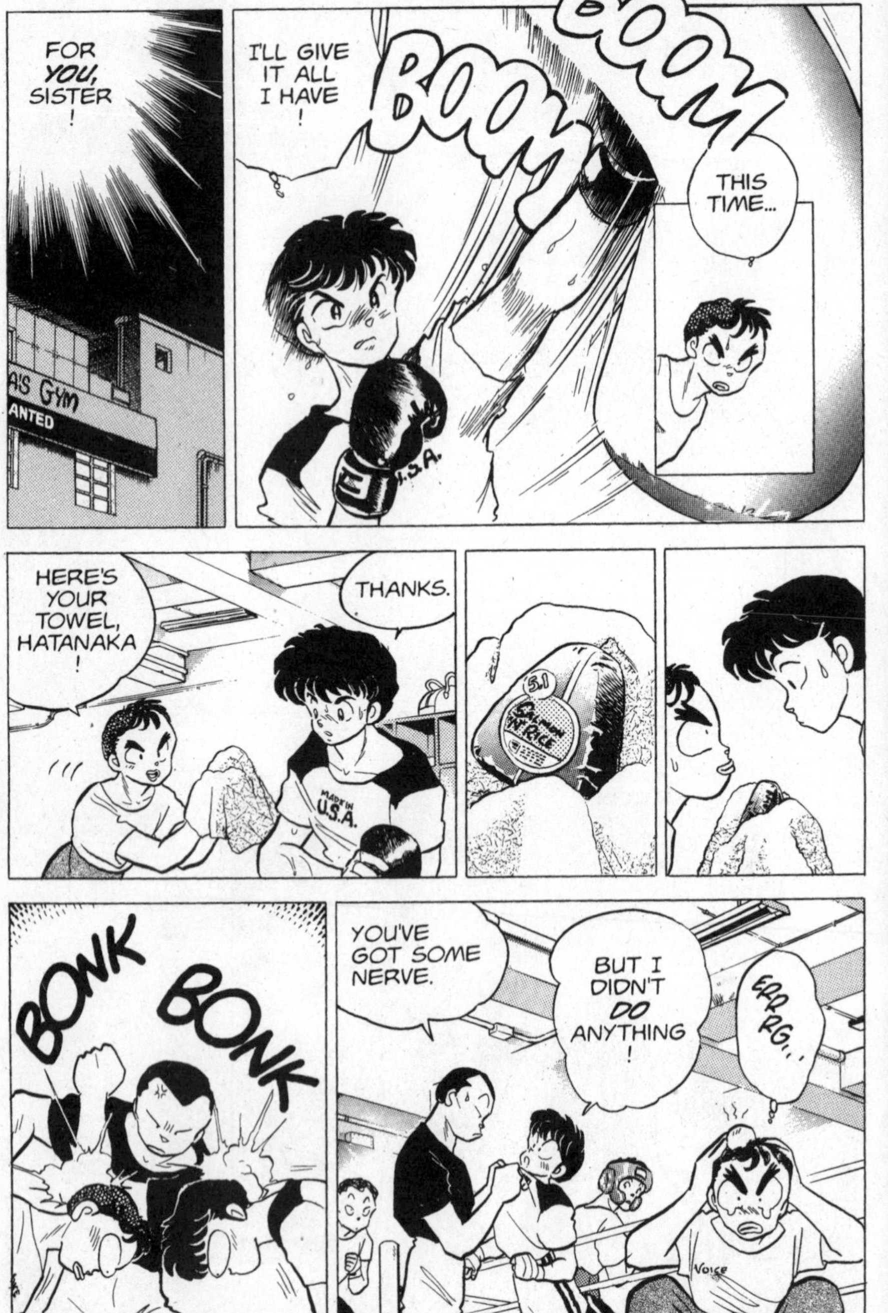
FOR *YOU,* SISTER!
A'S GYM
ANTED
I'LL GIVE IT ALL I HAVE!
BOOM
BOOM
U.S.A.
THIS TIME...
HERE'S YOUR TOWEL, HATANAKA!
THANKS.
MADE IN U.S.A.
5.1
SALMON 'N' RICE
BONK
BONK
YOU'VE GOT SOME NERVE.
BUT I DIDN'T *DO* ANYTHING!
ERRRG...
VOICE

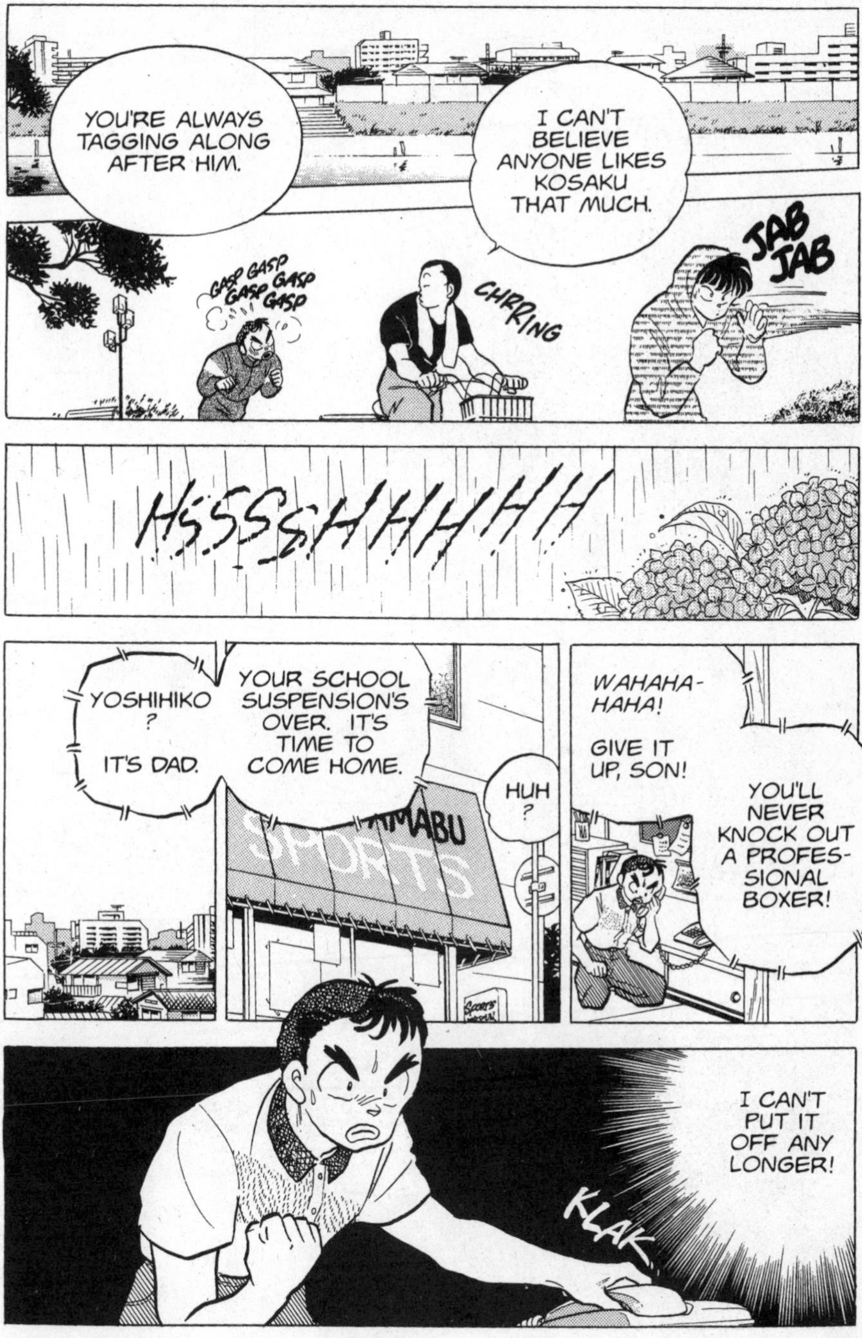

YOU'RE ALWAYS TAGGING ALONG AFTER HIM.
I CAN'T BELIEVE ANYONE LIKES KOSAKU THAT MUCH.
GASP GASP GASP GASP GASP GASP
CHRRING
JAB JAB
HSSSSHHHHH
YOSHIHIKO? IT'S DAD.
YOUR SCHOOL SUSPENSION'S OVER. IT'S TIME TO COME HOME.
HUH?
SPORTS
WAHAHA-HAHA!
GIVE IT UP, SON!
YOU'LL NEVER KNOCK OUT A PROFES-SIONAL BOXER!
I CAN'T PUT IT OFF ANY LONGER!
KLAK

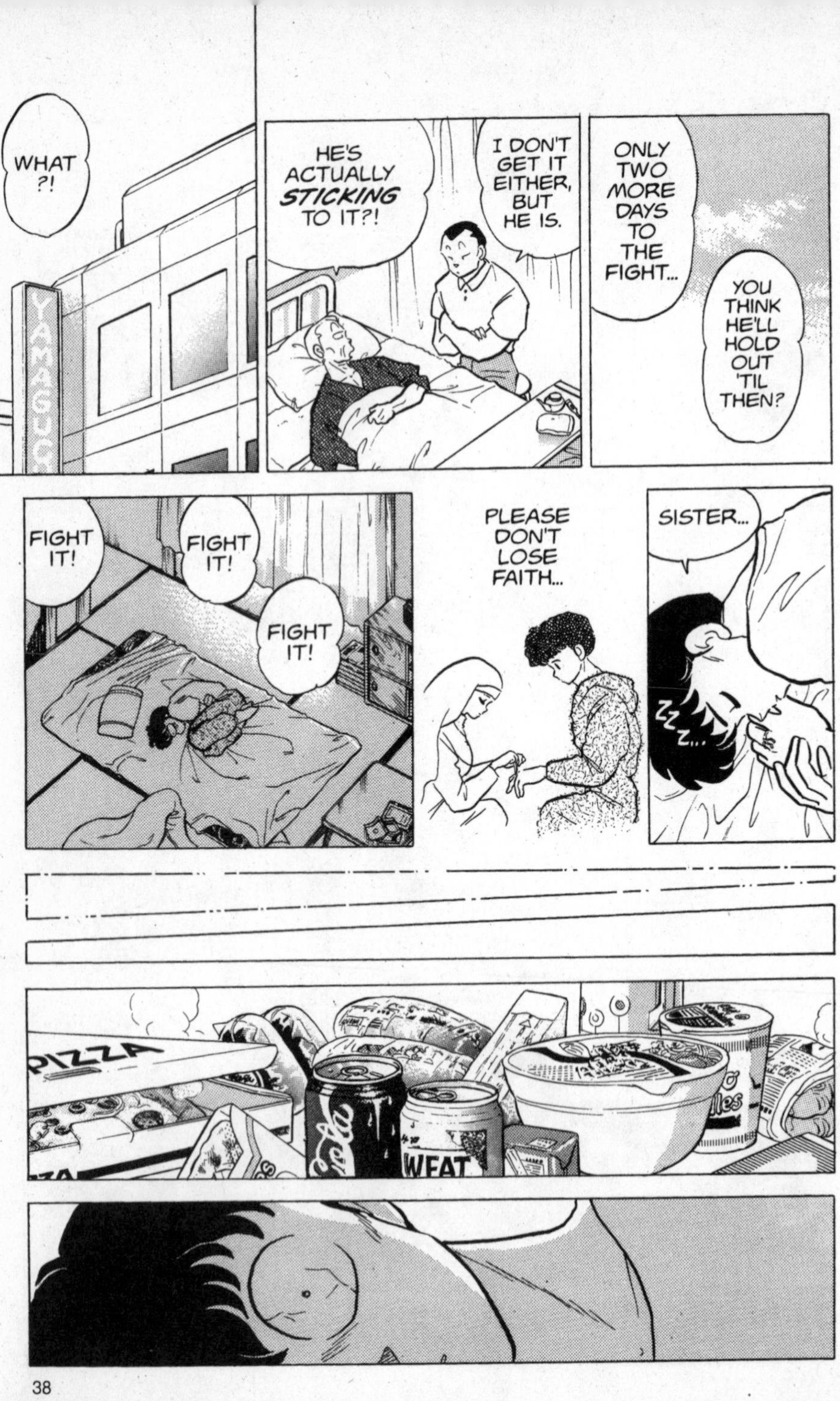
WHAT?!
HE'S ACTUALLY STICKING TO IT?!
I DON'T GET IT EITHER, BUT HE IS.
ONLY TWO MORE DAYS TO THE FIGHT...
YOU THINK HE'LL HOLD OUT 'TIL THEN?
FIGHT IT!
FIGHT IT!
FIGHT IT!
PLEASE DON'T LOSE FAITH...
SISTER...
ZZZ...
PIZZA

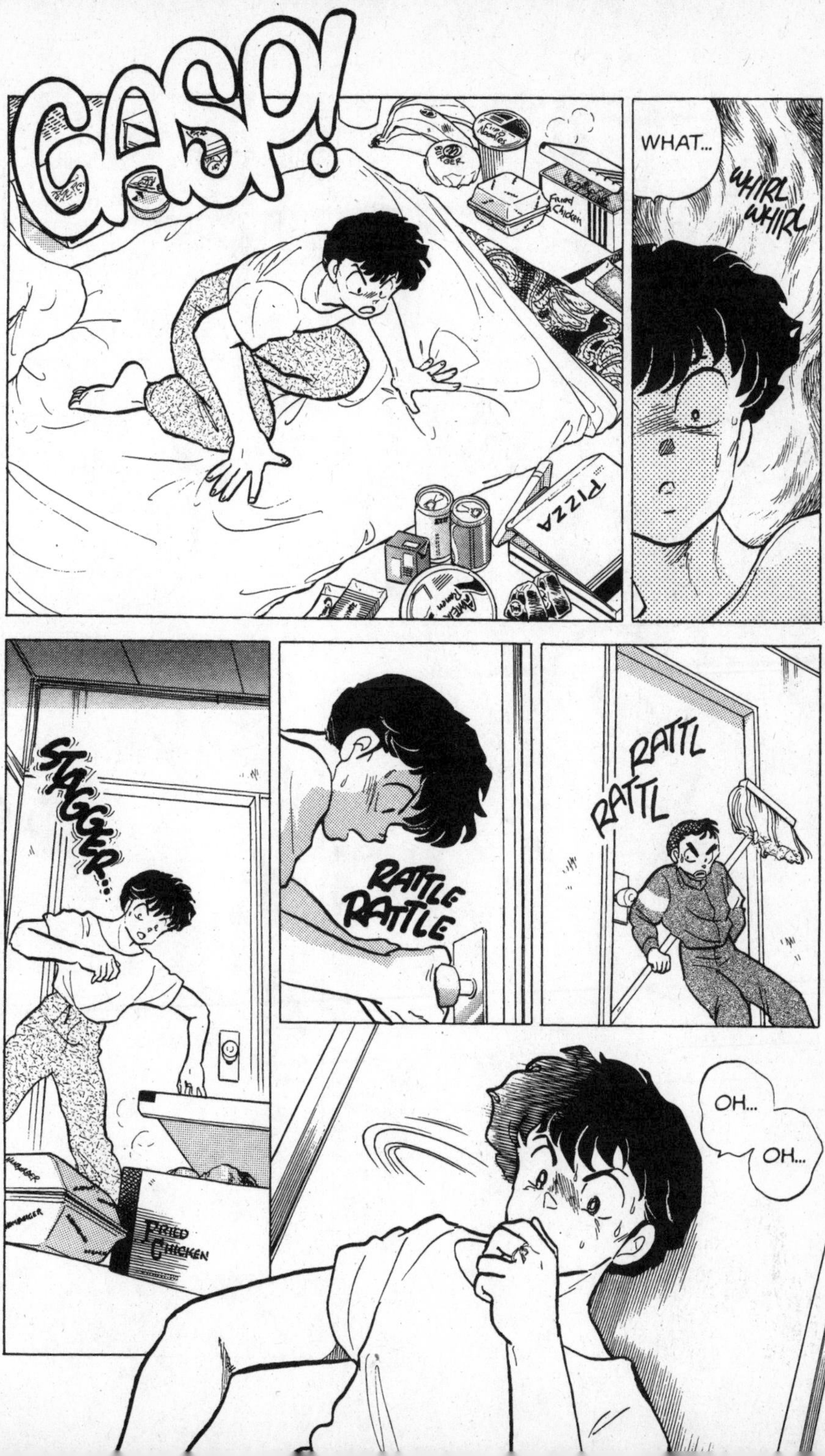
GASP!
Fried Chicken
PIZZA
WHAT...
WHIRL WHIRL
STAGGER...
FRIED CHICKEN
RATTLE RATTLE
RATTL RATTL
OH... OH...

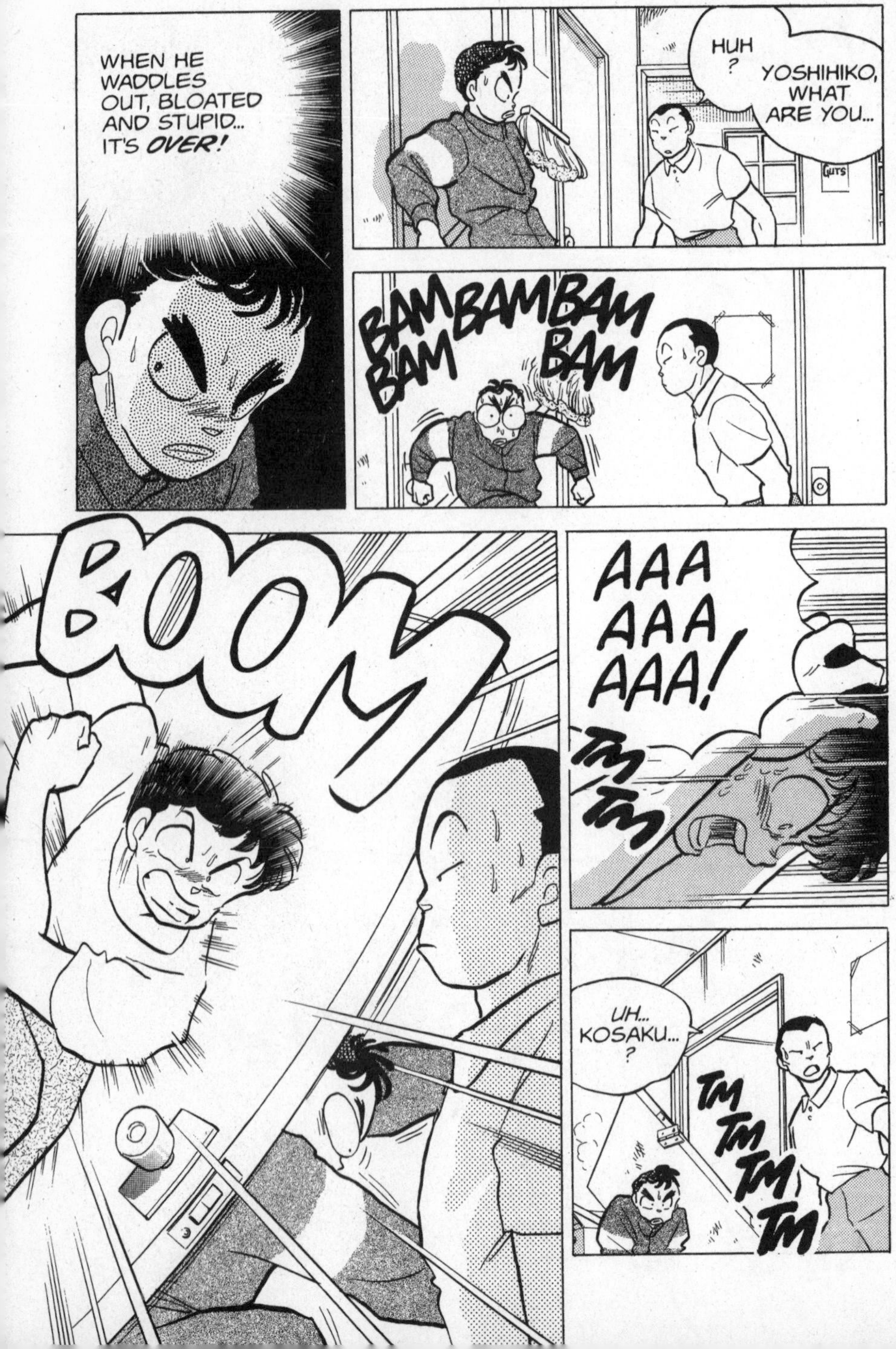
WHEN HE WADDLES OUT, BLOATED AND STUPID... IT'S OVER!
HUH ?
YOSHIHIKO, WHAT ARE YOU...
GUTS
BAM BAM BAM BAM BAM BAM
BOOM
AAA AAA AAA!
TM TM TM
UH... KOSAKU... ?
TM TM TM TM TM

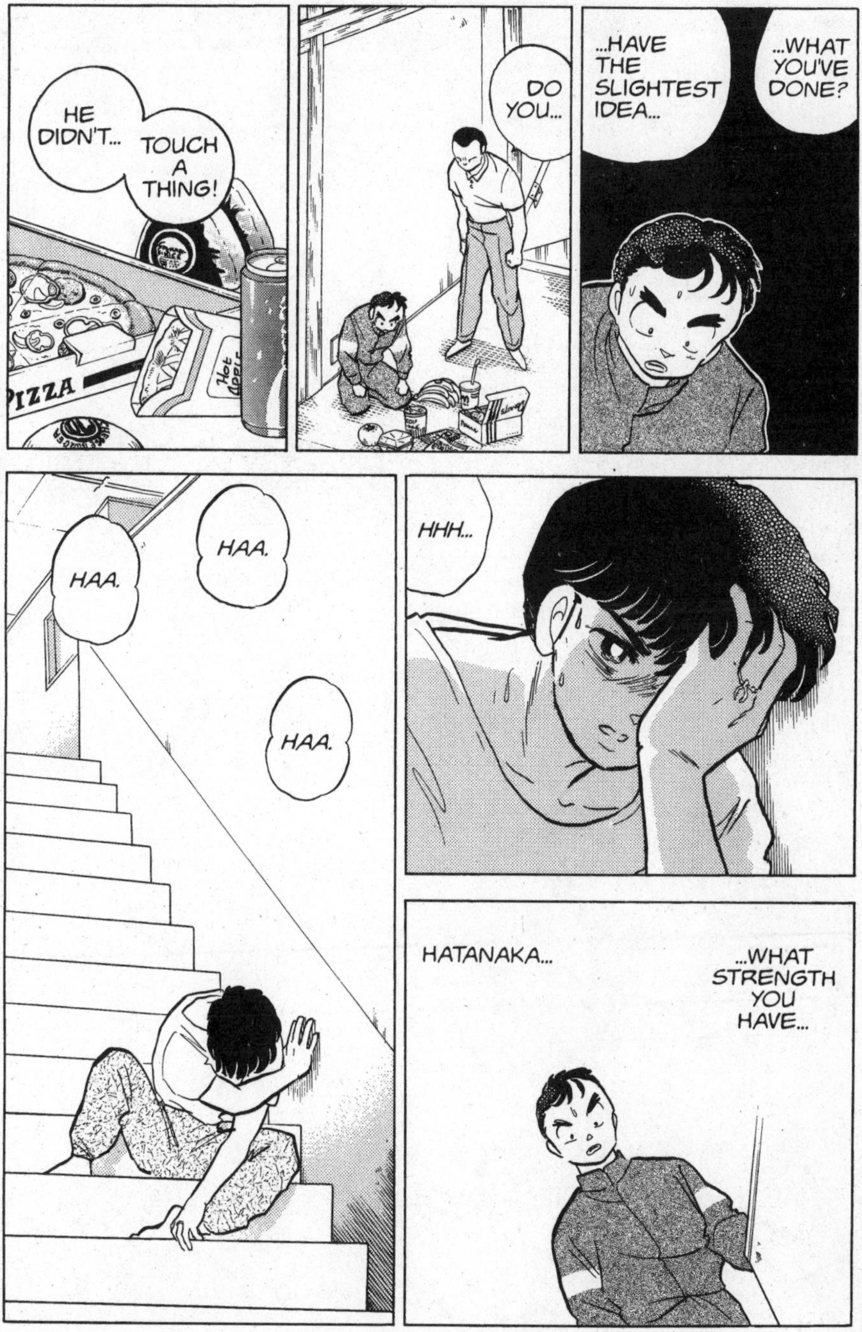
HE DIDN'T...
TOUCH A THING!
DO YOU...
...HAVE THE SLIGHTEST IDEA...
...WHAT YOU'VE DONE?
HAA.
HAA.
HAA.
HHH...
HATANAKA...
...WHAT STRENGTH YOU HAVE...

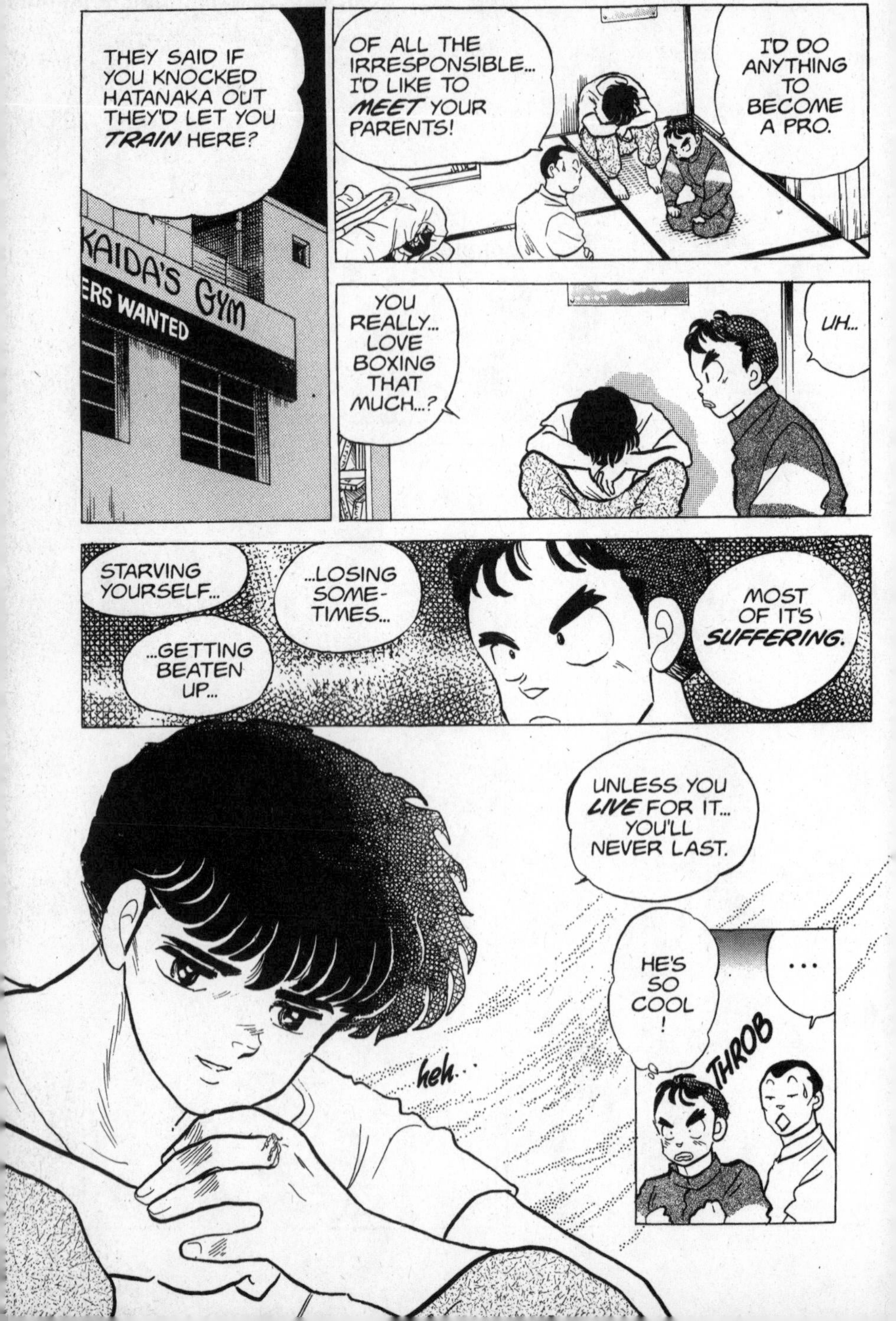
THEY SAID IF YOU KNOCKED HATANAKA OUT THEY'D LET YOU TRAIN HERE?
KAIDA'S GYM
ERS WANTED
OF ALL THE IRRESPONSIBLE... I'D LIKE TO MEET YOUR PARENTS!
I'D DO ANYTHING TO BECOME A PRO.
YOU REALLY... LOVE BOXING THAT MUCH...?
UH...
STARVING YOURSELF...
...GETTING BEATEN UP...
...LOSING SOME-TIMES...
MOST OF IT'S SUFFERING.
UNLESS YOU LIVE FOR IT... YOU'LL NEVER LAST.
heh...
HE'S SO COOL!
...
THROB

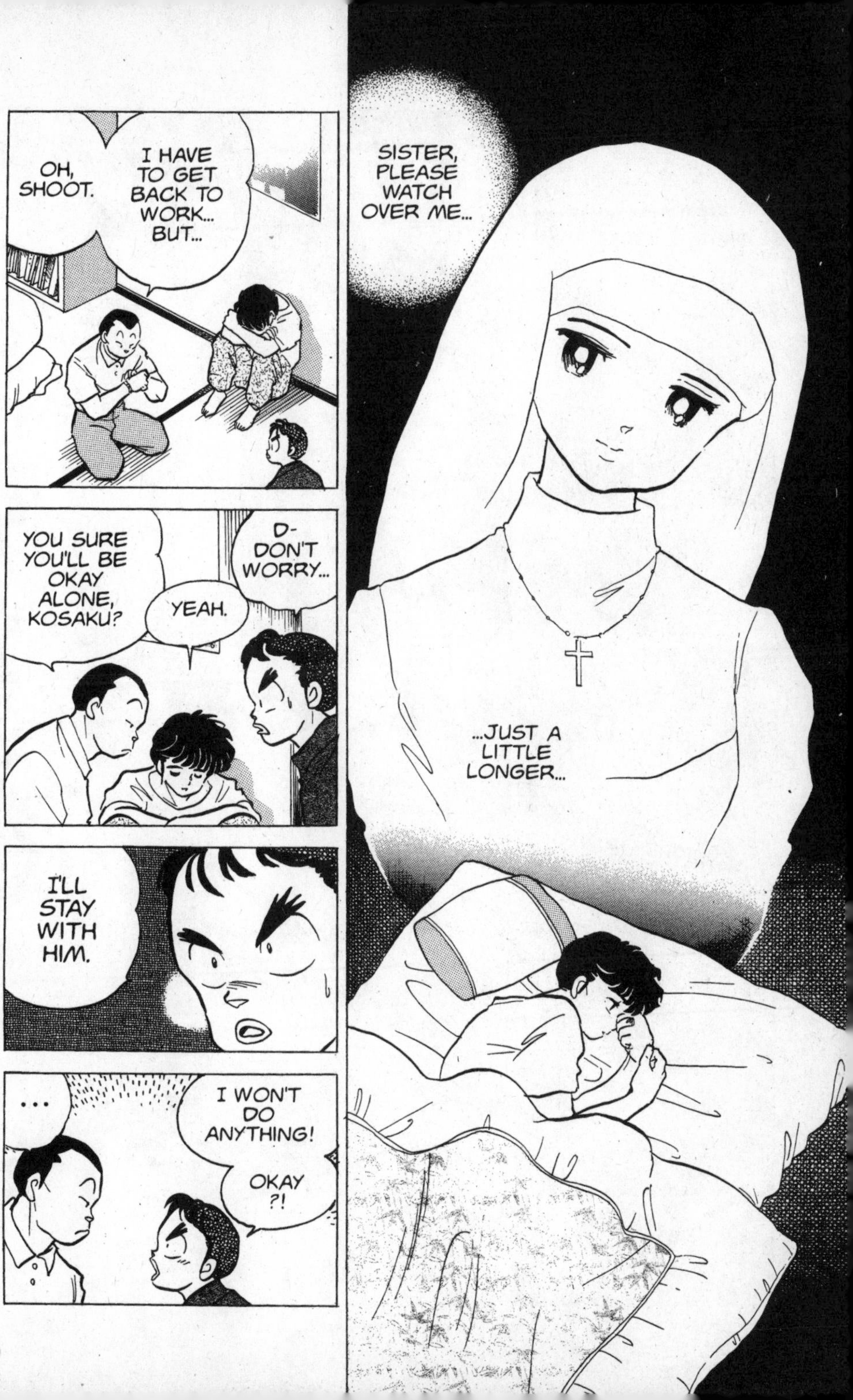
OH, SHOOT.
I HAVE TO GET BACK TO WORK... BUT...
YOU SURE YOU'LL BE OKAY ALONE, KOSAKU?
YEAH.
D-DON'T WORRY...
I'LL STAY WITH HIM.
...
I WON'T DO ANYTHING!
OKAY ?!
SISTER, PLEASE WATCH OVER ME...
...JUST A LITTLE LONGER...

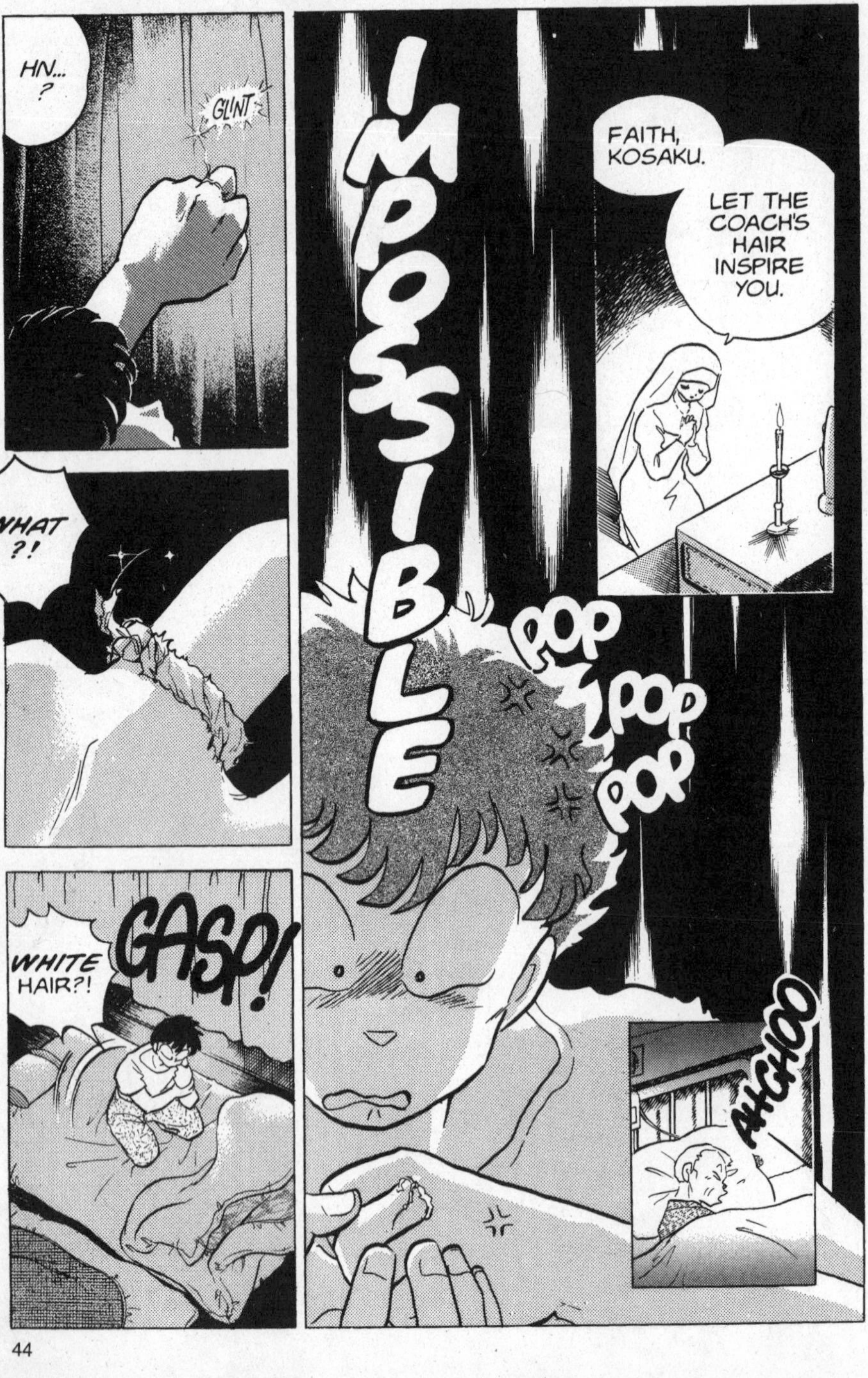
HN... ?
GLINT
WHAT?!
WHITE HAIR?!
GASP!
IMPOSSIBLE
FAITH, KOSAKU.
LET THE COACH'S HAIR INSPIRE YOU.
POP POP POP
AHCHOO

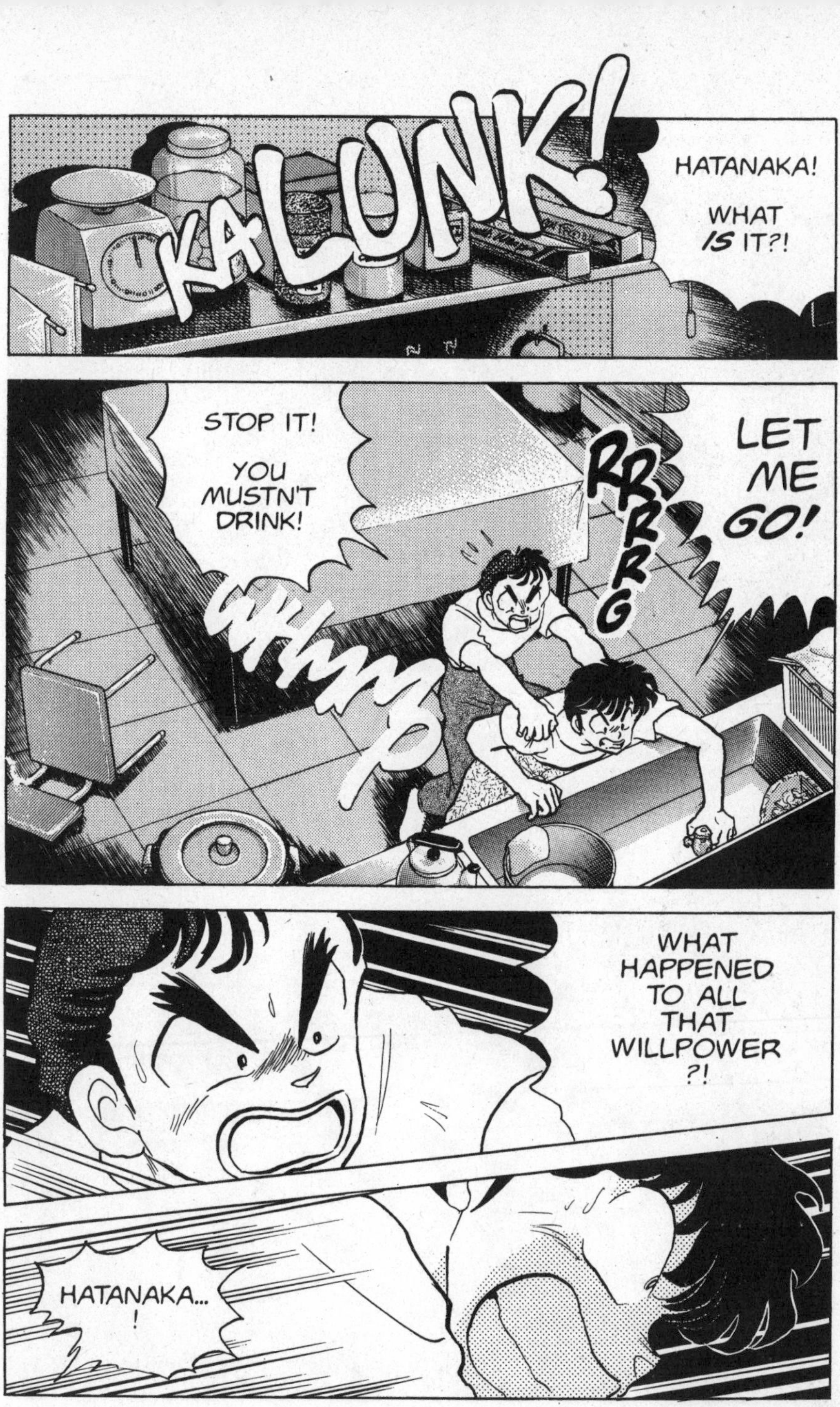
KALUNK!
HATANAKA!
WHAT *IS* IT?!
STOP IT!
YOU MUSTN'T DRINK!
WHMMP
RRRRRG
LET ME GO!
WHAT HAPPENED TO ALL THAT WILLPOWER ?!
HATANAKA... !

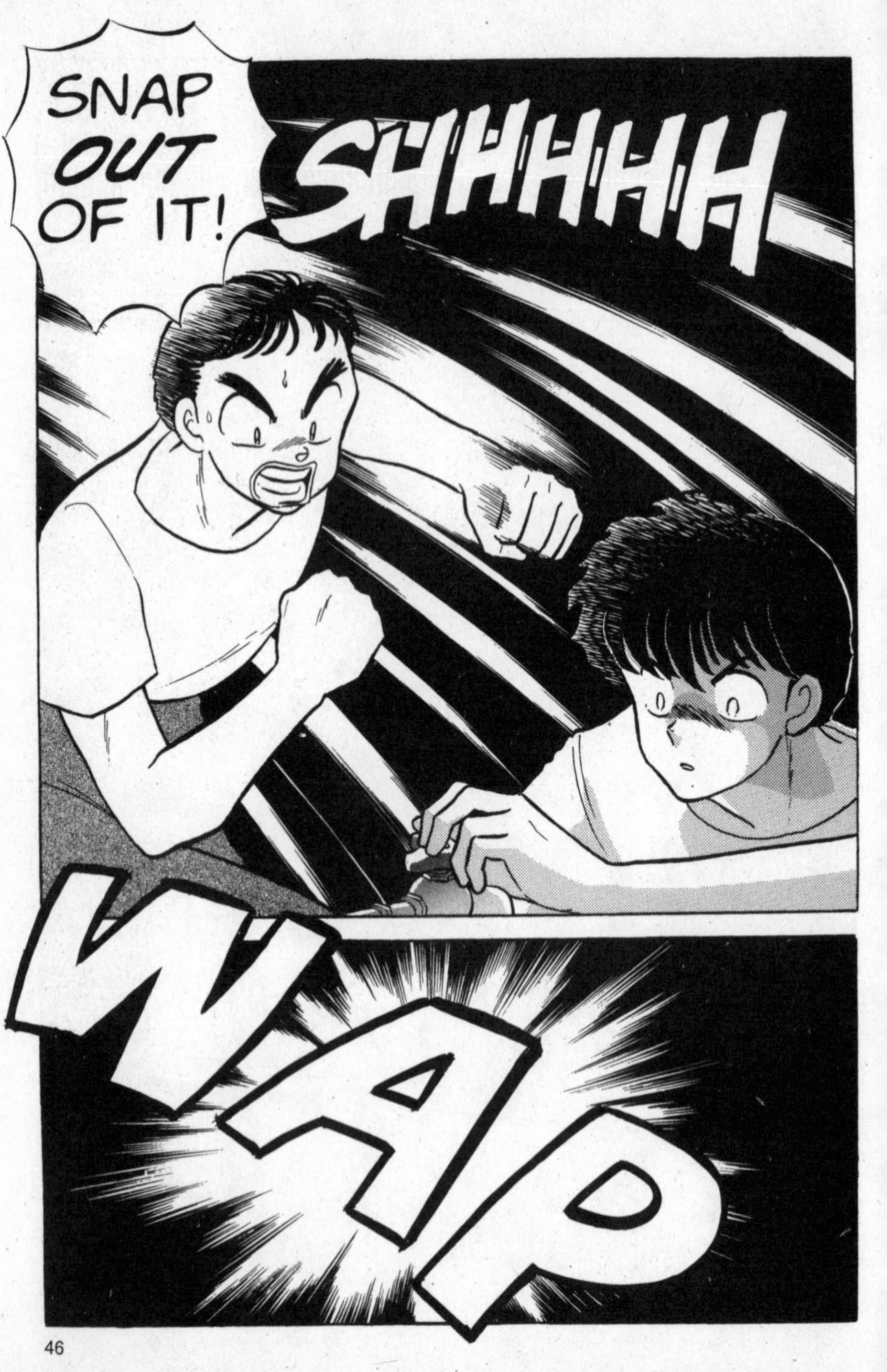
SNAP OUT OF IT!
SHHHHH
WAP

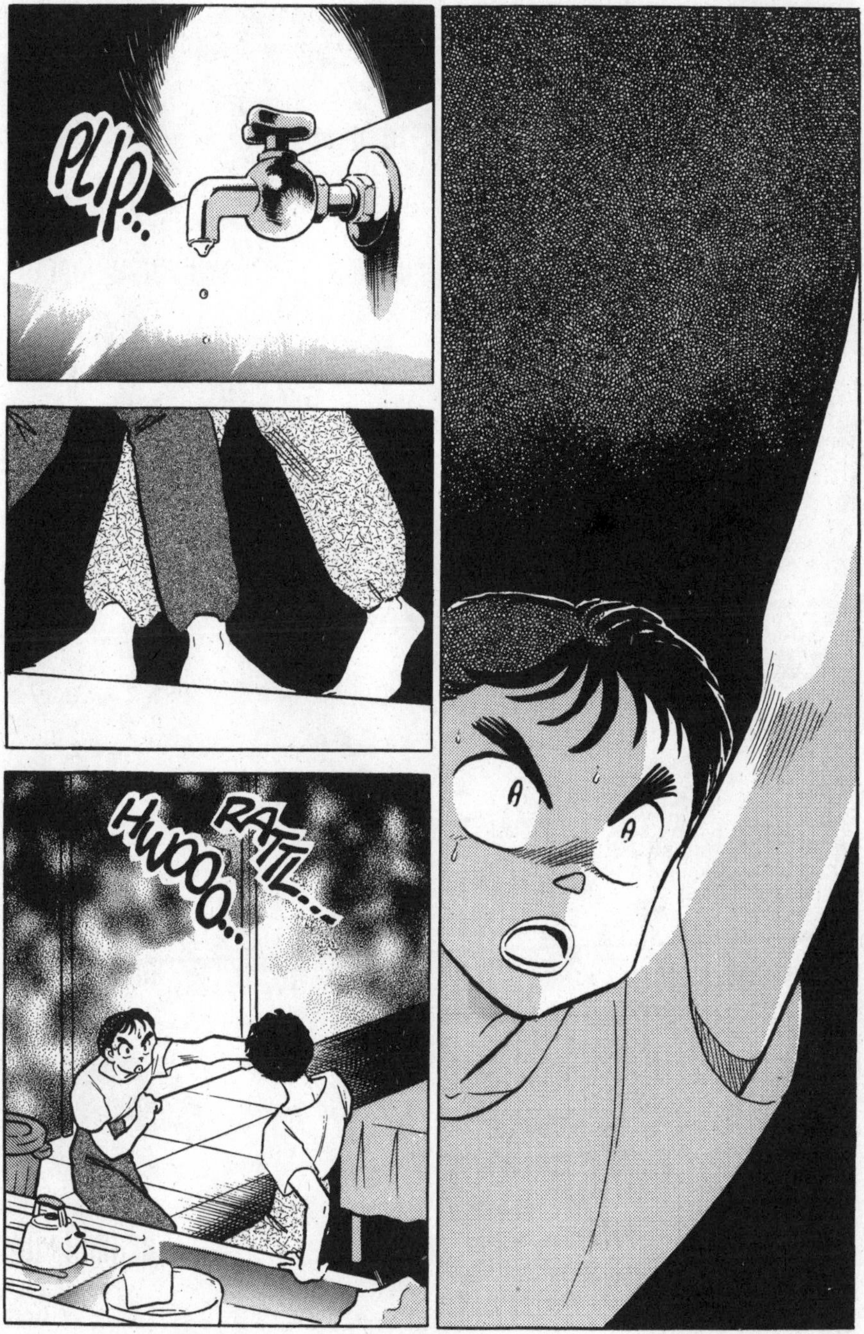
PLIP...
HWOOO...
RATTL...

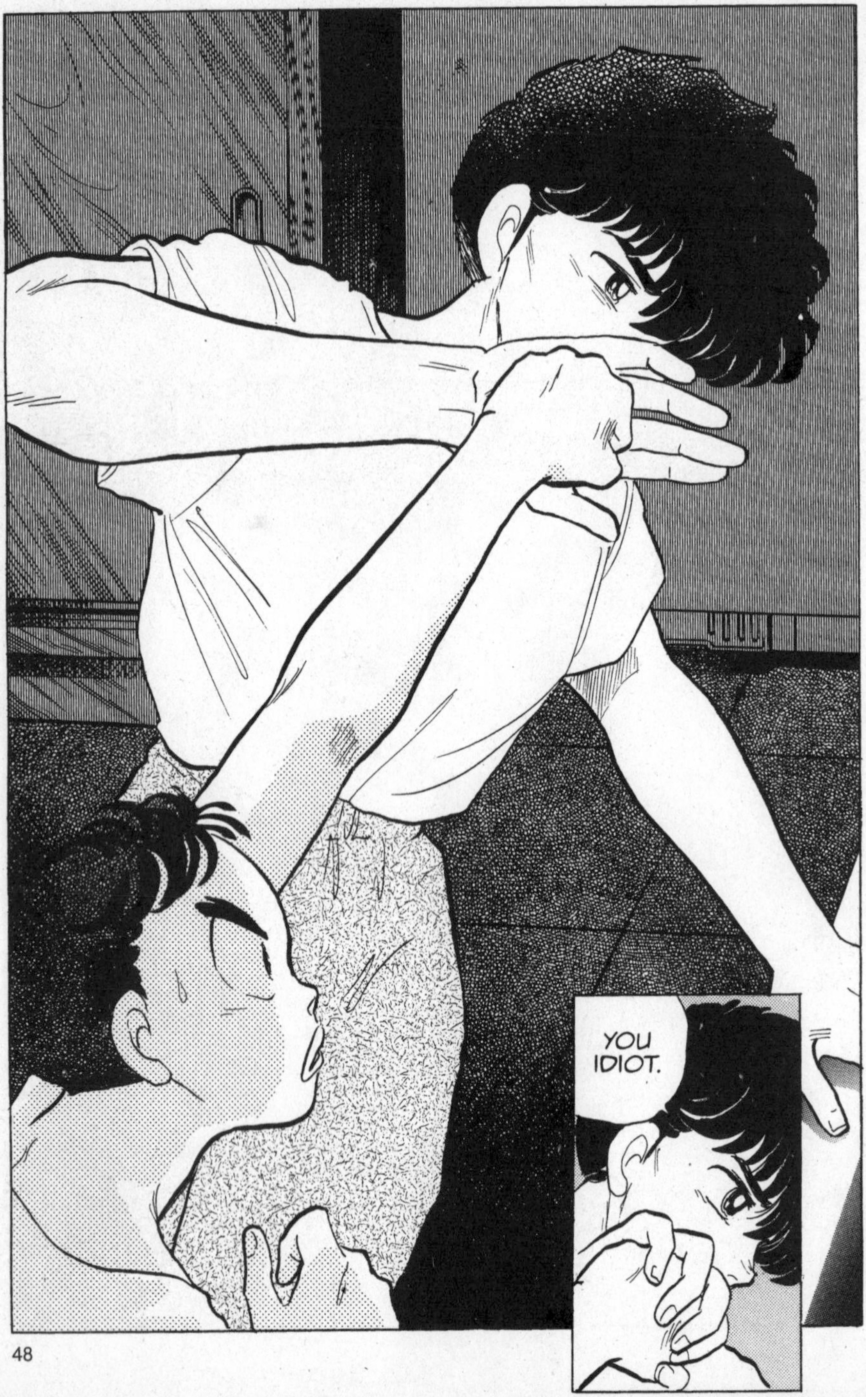
YOU IDIOT.

HATANAKA...

YOU'RE STILL YEARS... FROM KNOCKING ME OUT...

SIGH...

OH, SISTER... YOU DOPE...

SNIF

IS WEIGHT TRAINING REALLY THAT HARD?

SHUT UP.

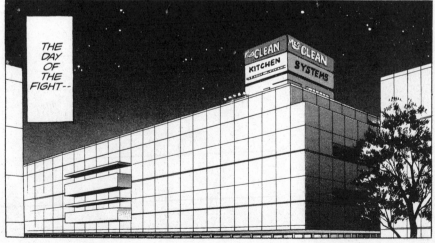

THE DAY OF THE FIGHT--

Mr. CLEAN KITCHEN

Mr. CLEAN SYSTEMS

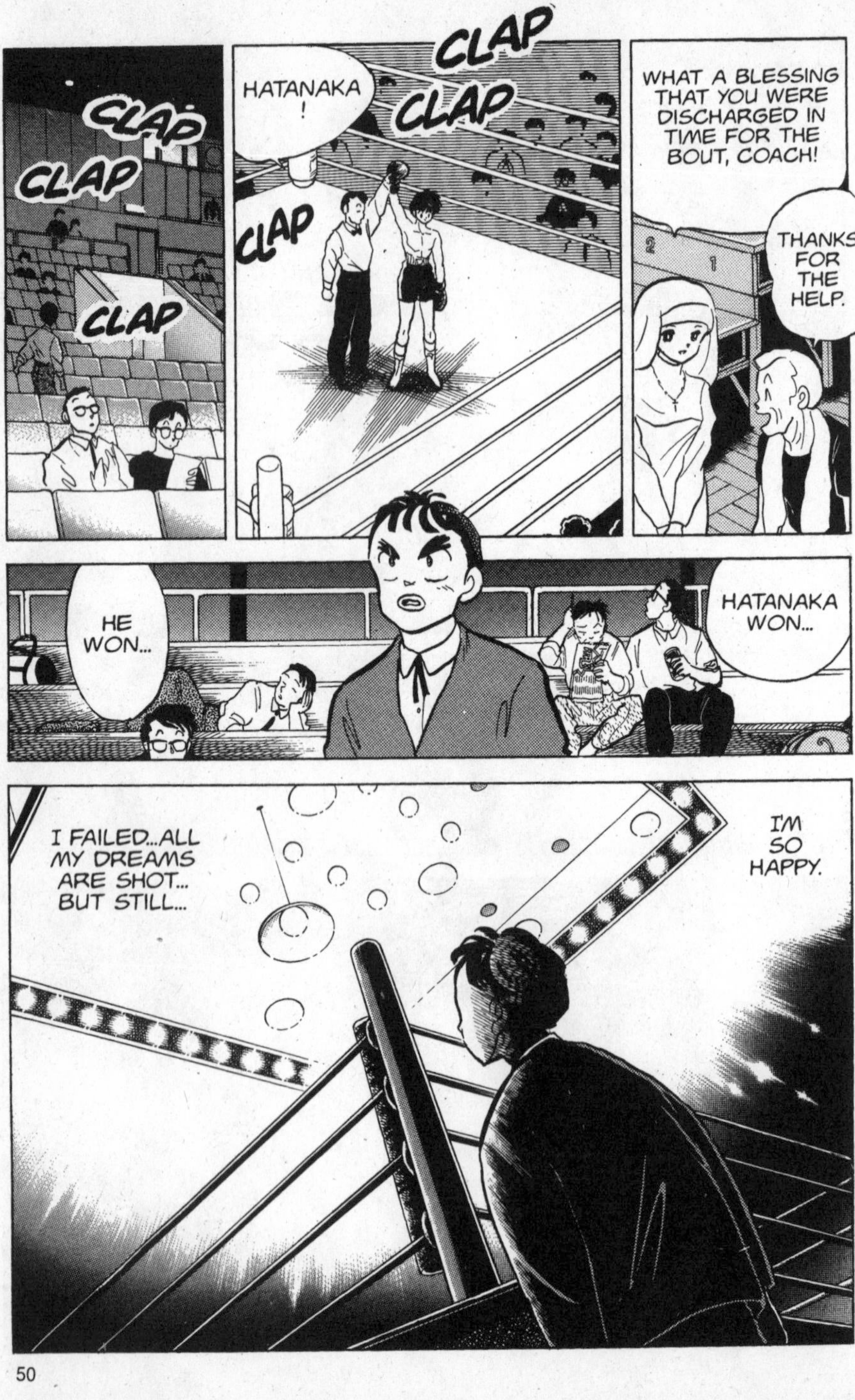
CLAP
CLAP
CLAP
HATANAKA!
CLAP
CLAP
CLAP
WHAT A BLESSING THAT YOU WERE DISCHARGED IN TIME FOR THE BOUT, COACH!
THANKS FOR THE HELP.
HE WON...
HATANAKA WON...
I FAILED...ALL MY DREAMS ARE SHOT... BUT STILL...
I'M SO HAPPY.

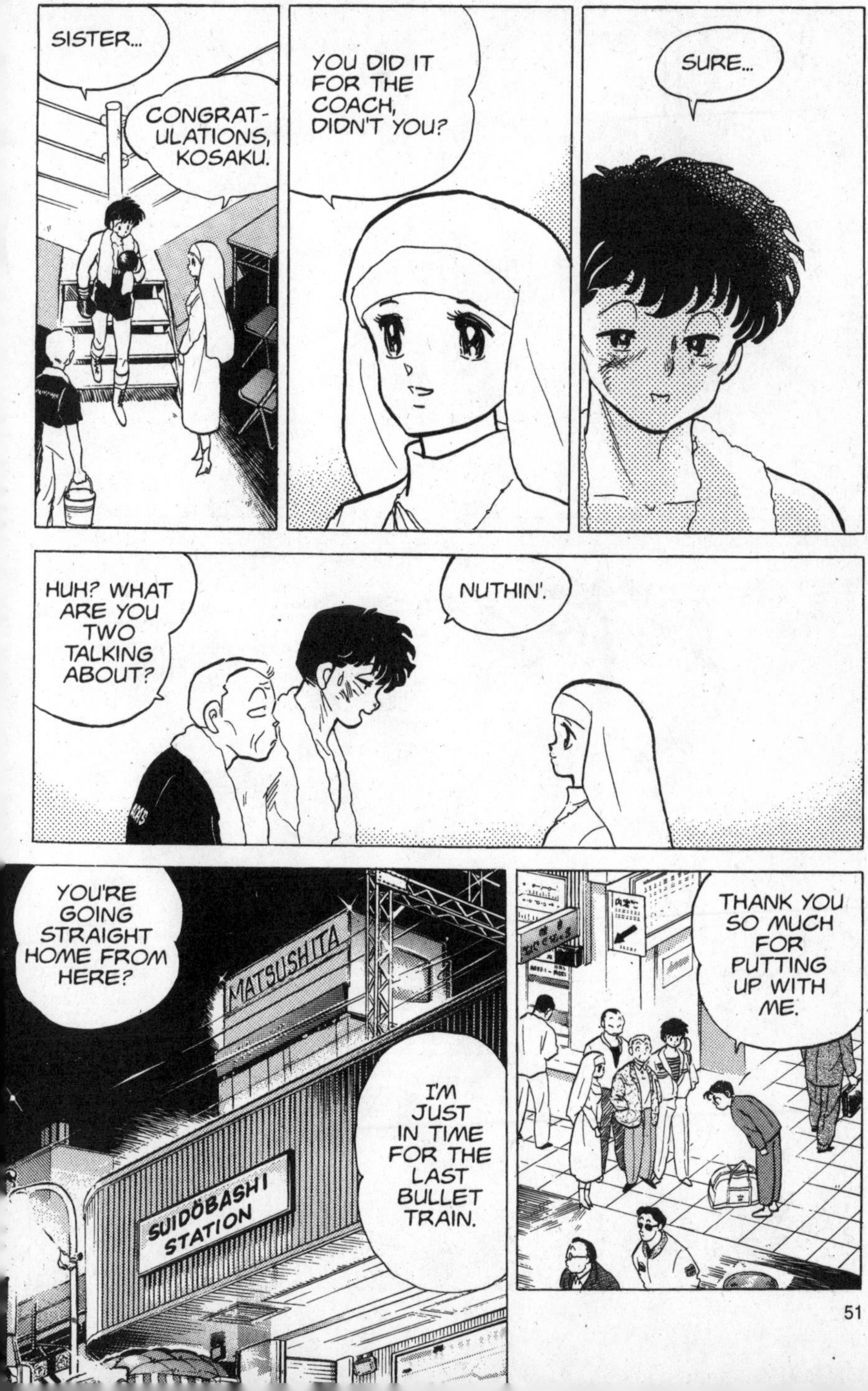
SISTER...
CONGRAT-ULATIONS, KOSAKU.
YOU DID IT FOR THE COACH, DIDN'T YOU?
SURE...
HUH? WHAT ARE YOU TWO TALKING ABOUT?
NUTHIN'.
YOU'RE GOING STRAIGHT HOME FROM HERE?
MATSUSHITA
SUIDŌBASHI STATION
I'M JUST IN TIME FOR THE LAST BULLET TRAIN.
THANK YOU SO MUCH FOR PUTTING UP WITH ME.

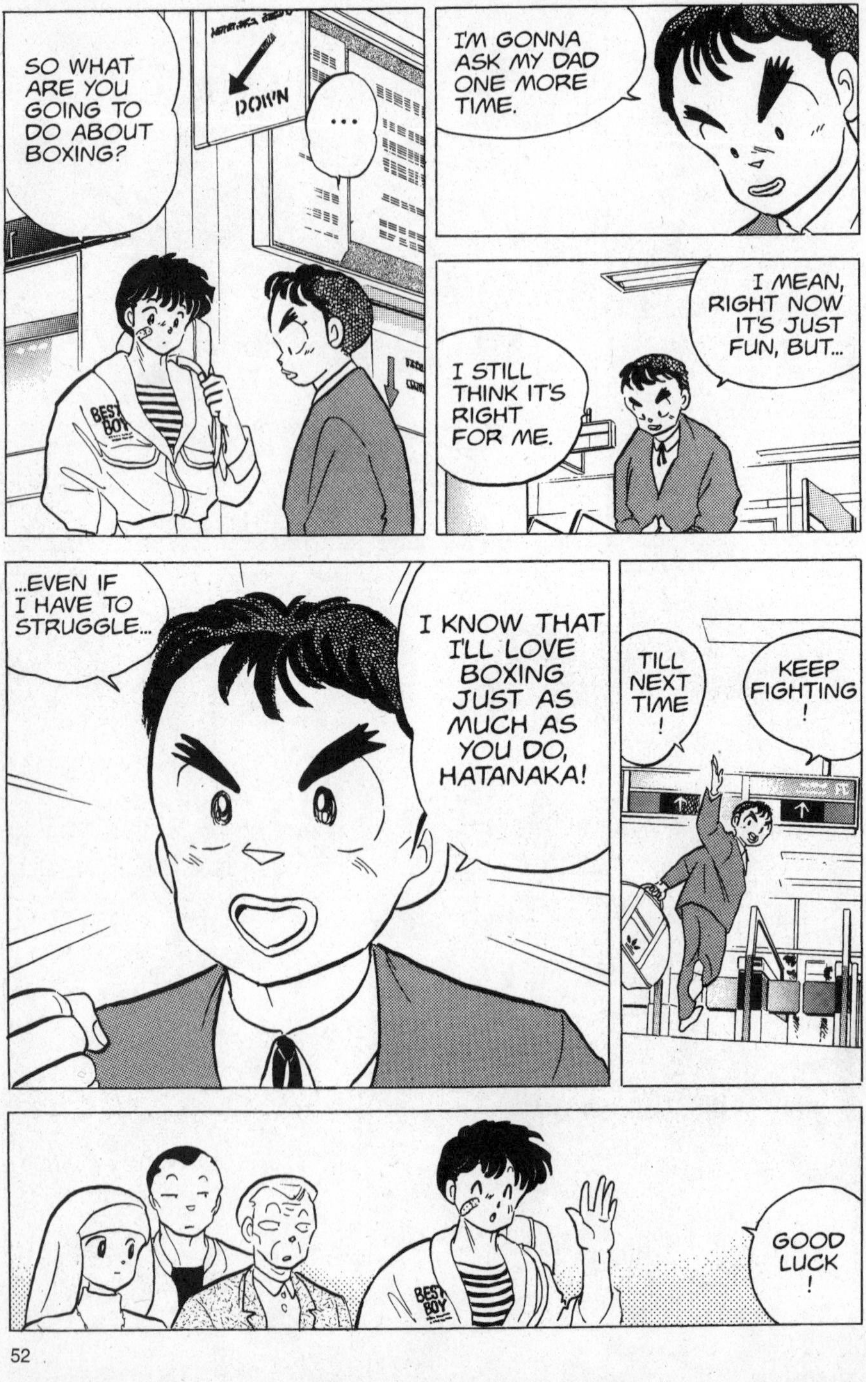
SO WHAT ARE YOU GOING TO DO ABOUT BOXING?
DOWN
...
I'M GONNA ASK MY DAD ONE MORE TIME.
I MEAN, RIGHT NOW IT'S JUST FUN, BUT...
I STILL THINK IT'S RIGHT FOR ME.
...EVEN IF I HAVE TO STRUGGLE...
I KNOW THAT I'LL LOVE BOXING JUST AS MUCH AS YOU DO, HATANAKA!
TILL NEXT TIME!
KEEP FIGHTING!
GOOD LUCK!

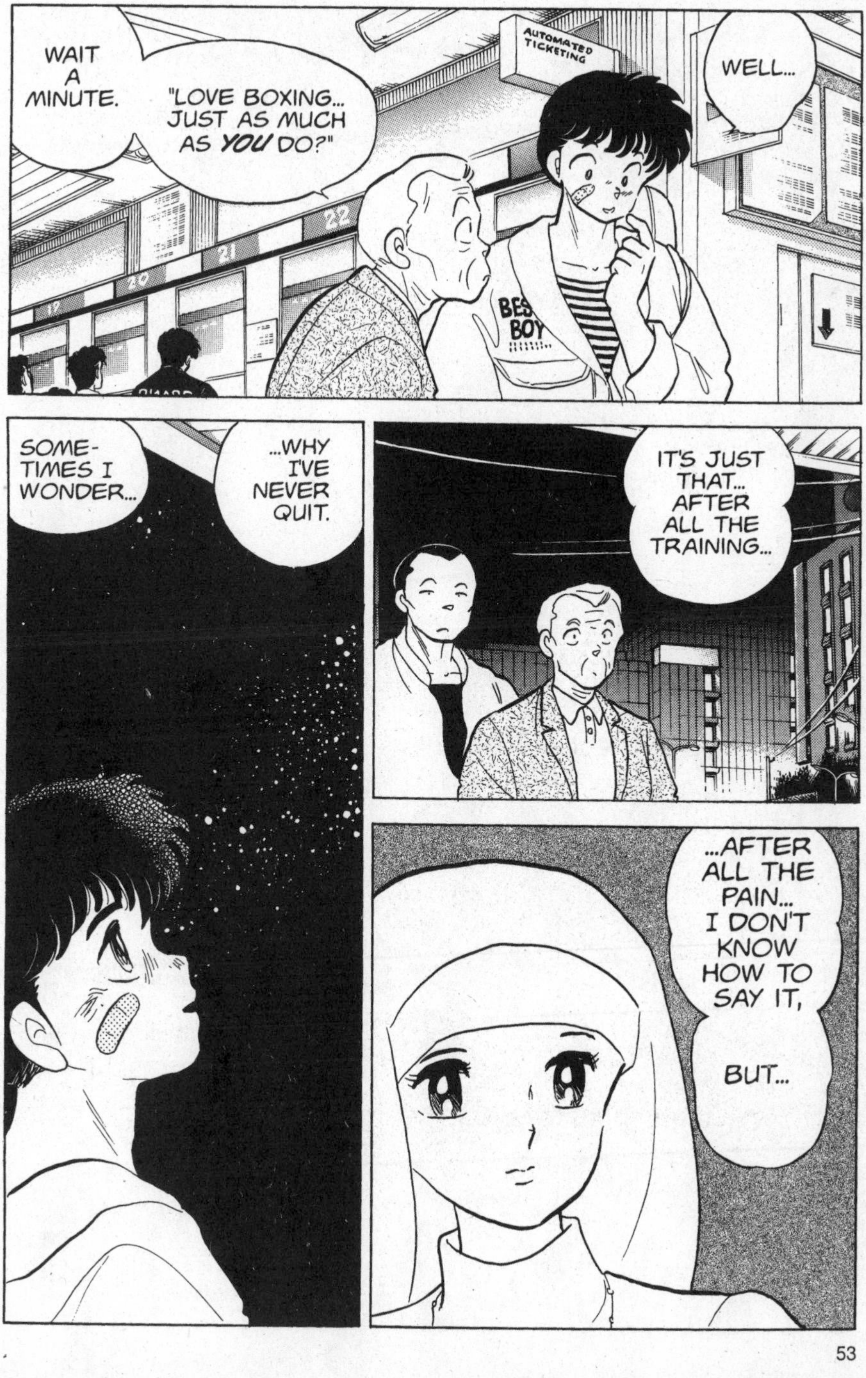
WAIT A MINUTE.
"LOVE BOXING... JUST AS MUCH AS *YOU* DO?"
AUTOMATED TICKETING
WELL...
SOME-TIMES I WONDER...
...WHY I'VE NEVER QUIT.
IT'S JUST THAT... AFTER ALL THE TRAINING...
...AFTER ALL THE PAIN... I DON'T KNOW HOW TO SAY IT,
BUT...

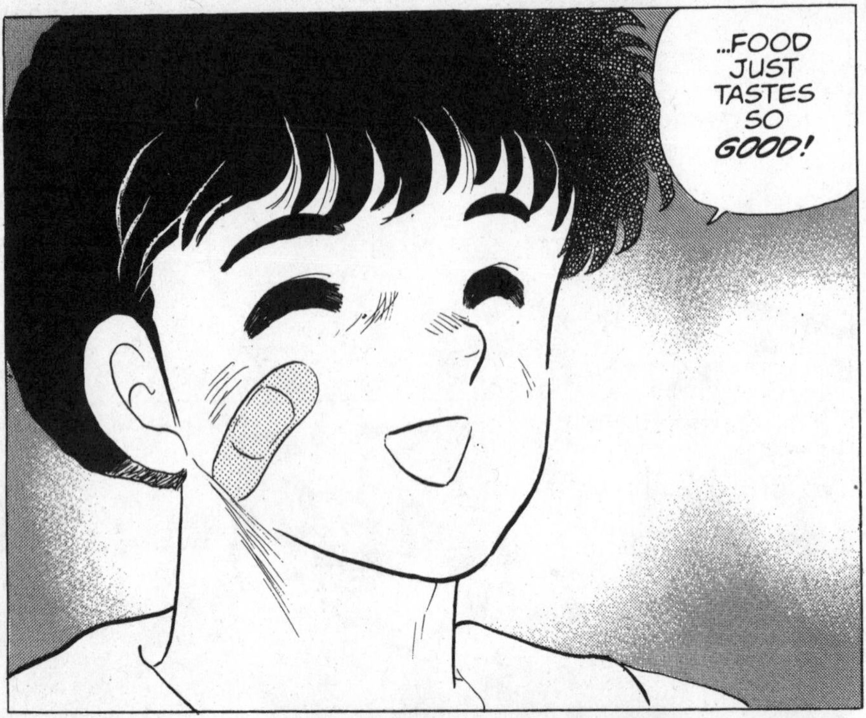
...FOOD JUST TASTES SO GOOD!

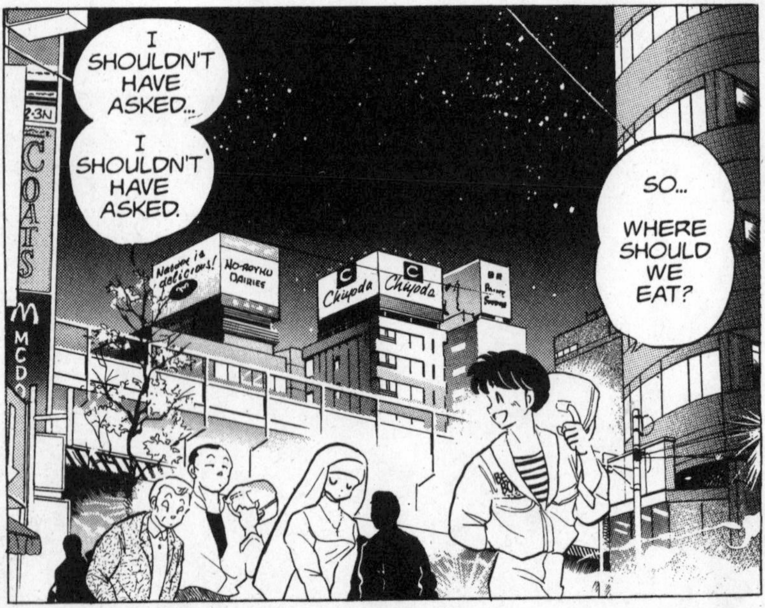
I SHOULDN'T HAVE ASKED...
I SHOULDN'T HAVE ASKED.
COATS
Chiyoda
Chiyoda
SO...
WHERE SHOULD WE EAT?

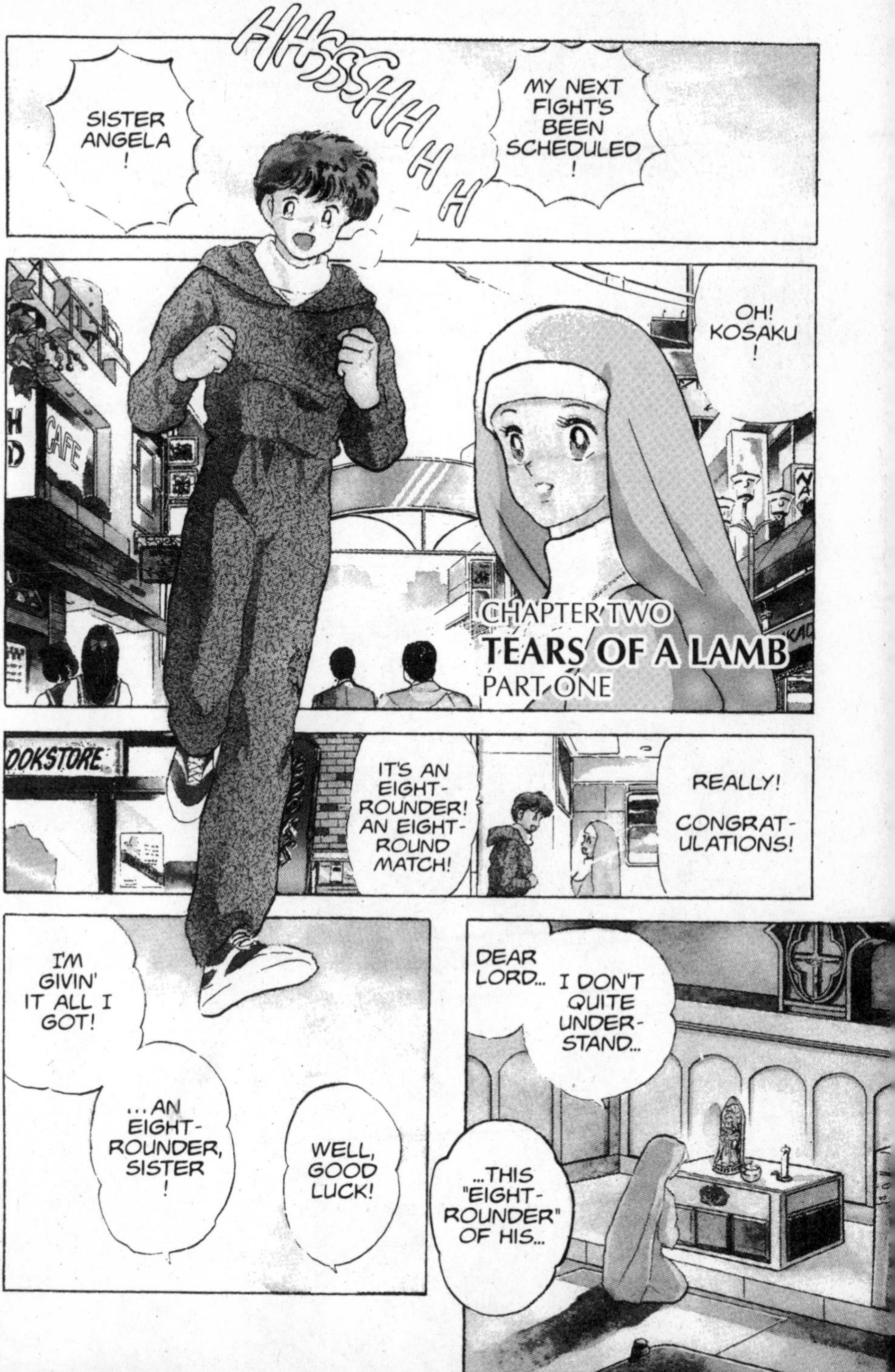
HHSSSHHHHH
SISTER ANGELA!
MY NEXT FIGHT'S BEEN SCHEDULED!
CAFE
OH! KOSAKU!
CHAPTER TWO
TEARS OF A LAMB
PART ONE
OOKSTORE
IT'S AN EIGHT-ROUNDER! AN EIGHT-ROUND MATCH!
REALLY!
CONGRATULATIONS!
I'M GIVIN' IT ALL I GOT!
...AN EIGHT-ROUNDER, SISTER!
WELL, GOOD LUCK!
DEAR LORD...
I DON'T QUITE UNDERSTAND...
...THIS "EIGHT-ROUNDER" OF HIS...

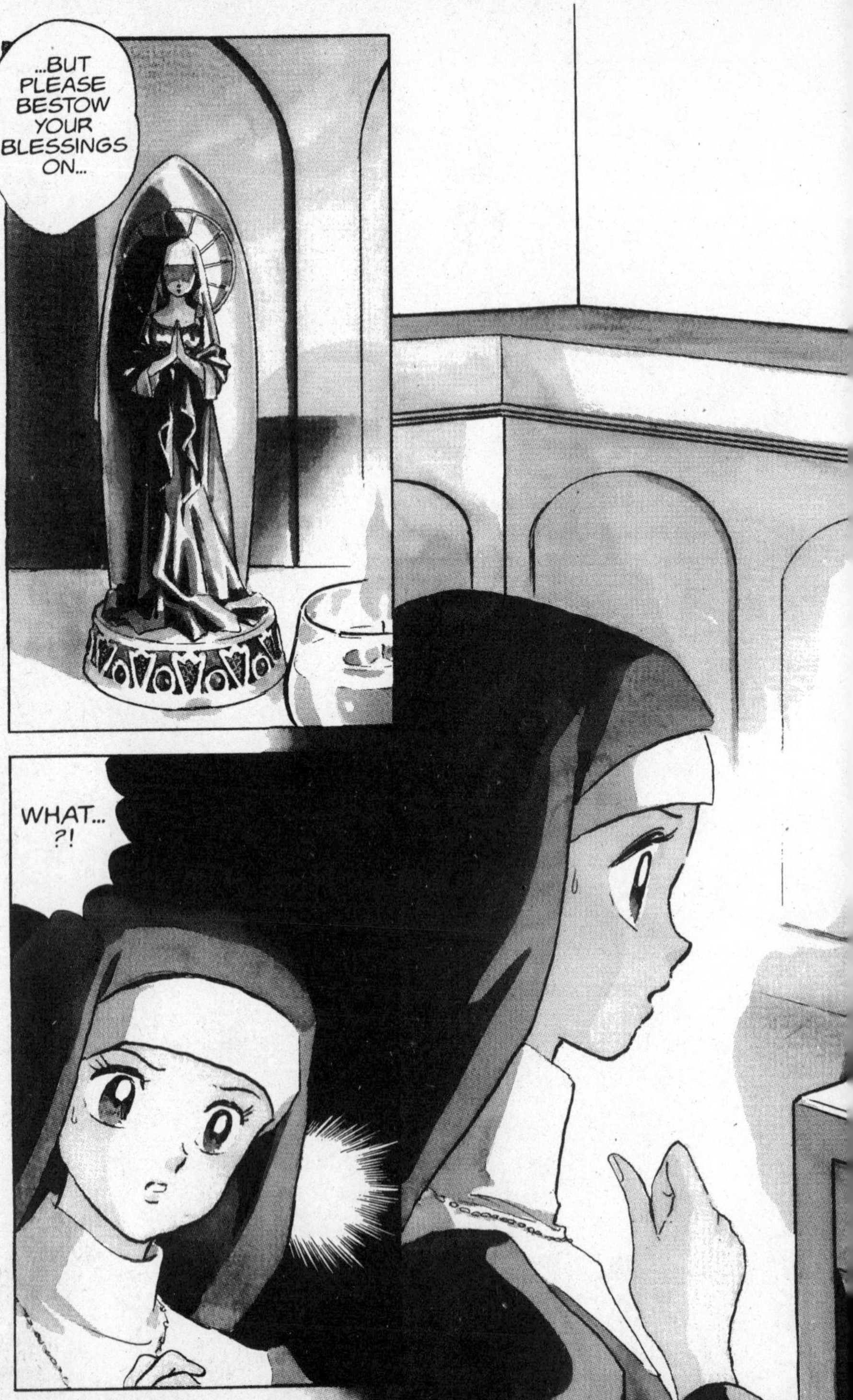
...BUT PLEASE BESTOW YOUR BLESSINGS ON...
WHAT... ?!

CHAPTER TWO

TEARS OF A LAMB

PART ONE

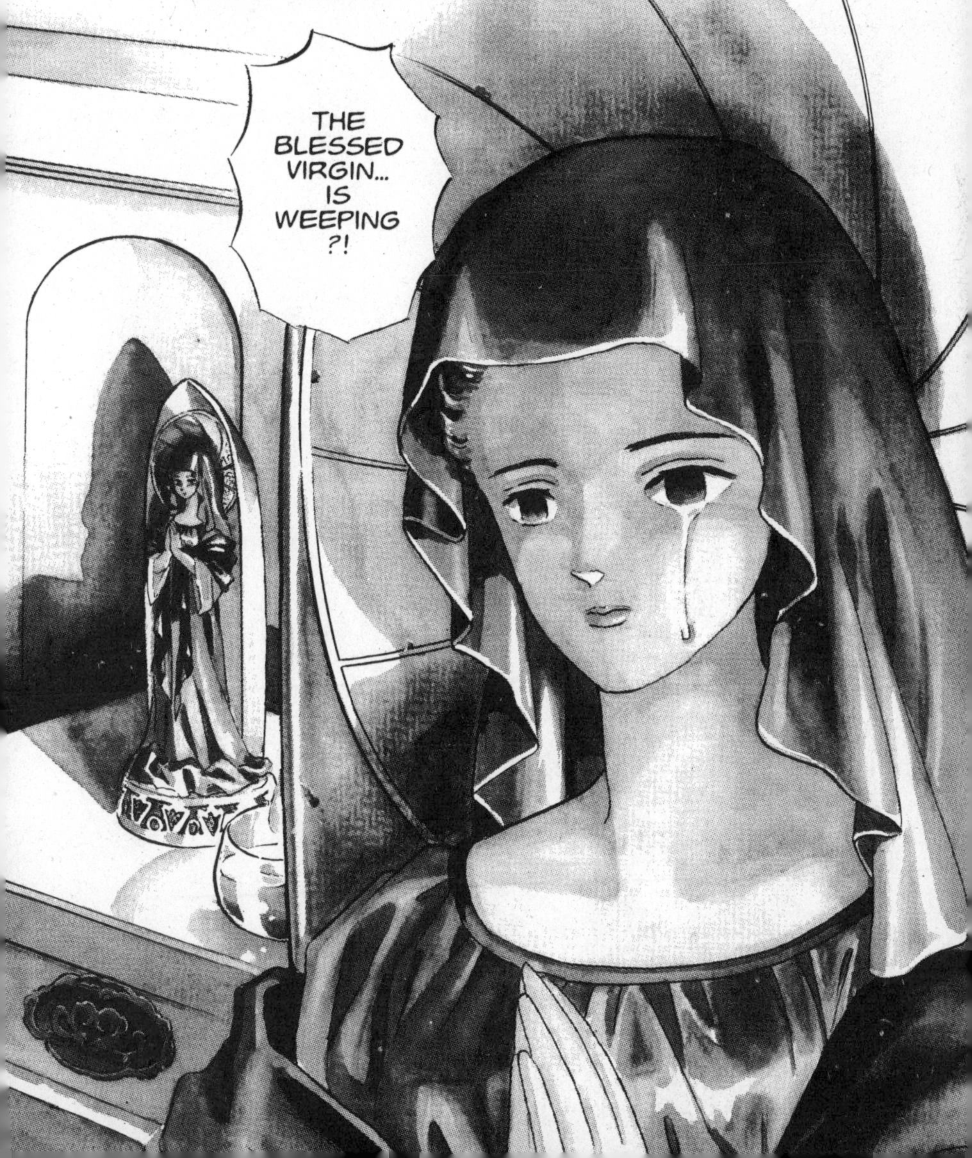
THE BLESSED VIRGIN... IS WEEPING ?!

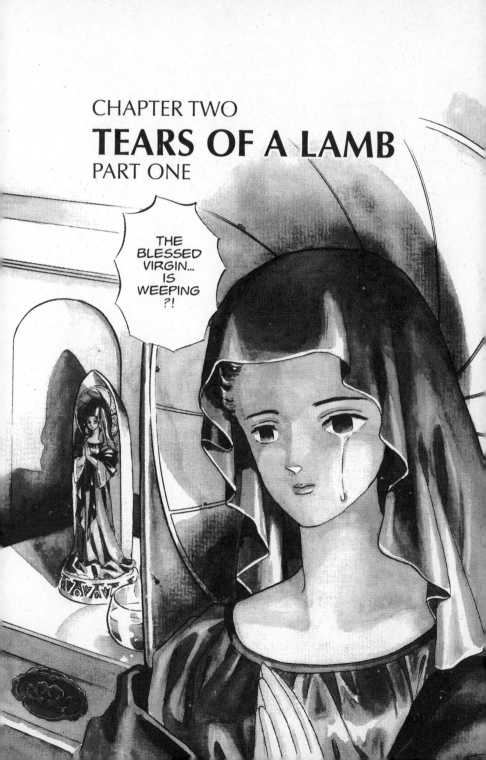

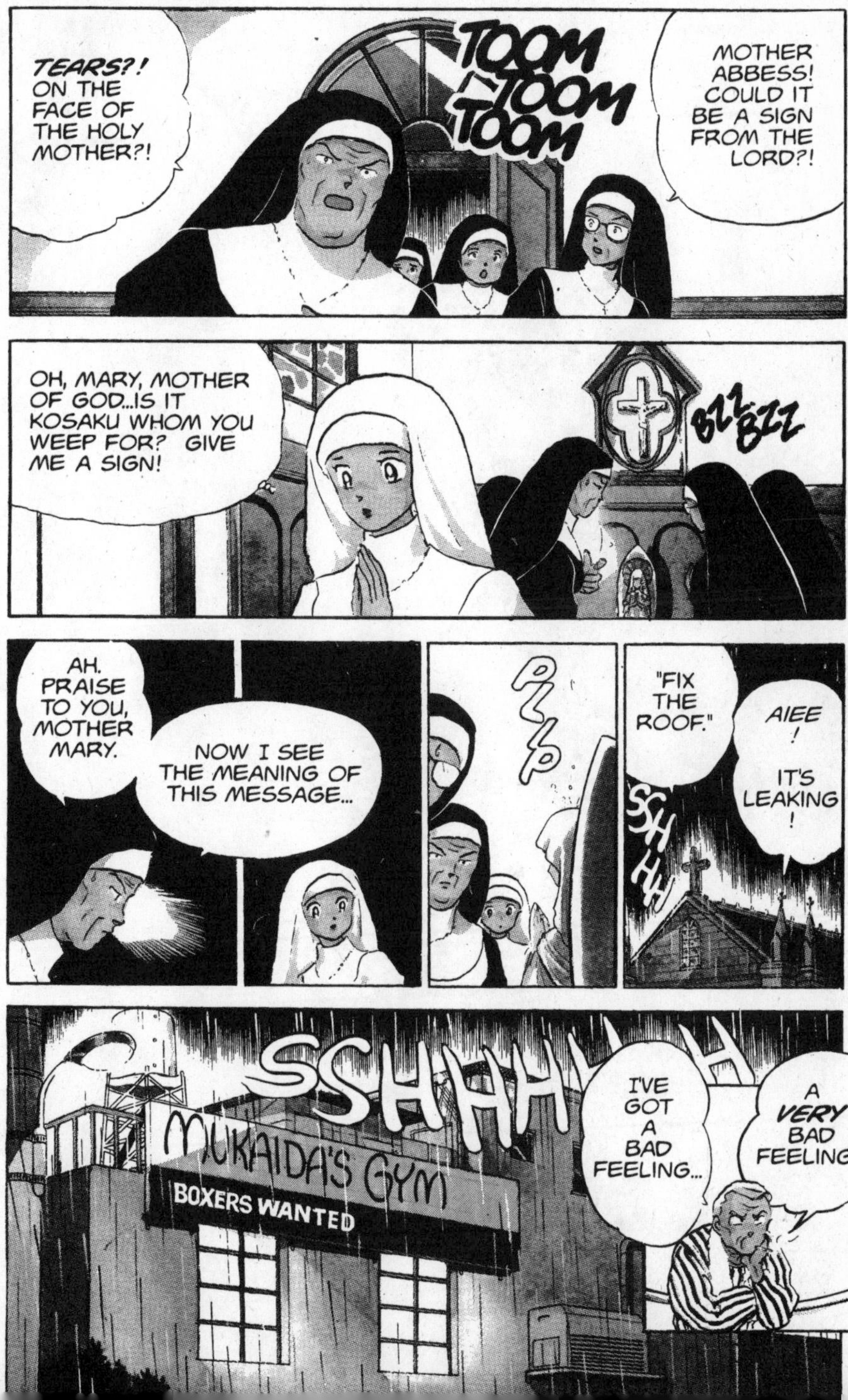
TEARS?! ON THE FACE OF THE HOLY MOTHER?!
TOOM TOOM TOOM
MOTHER ABBESS! COULD IT BE A SIGN FROM THE LORD?!
OH, MARY, MOTHER OF GOD...IS IT KOSAKU WHOM YOU WEEP FOR? GIVE ME A SIGN!
BZZ BZZ
AH. PRAISE TO YOU, MOTHER MARY.
NOW I SEE THE MEANING OF THIS MESSAGE...
"FIX THE ROOF."
SSHHH
AIEE! IT'S LEAKING!
SSHHHHH
MUKAIDA'S GYM
BOXERS WANTED
I'VE GOT A BAD FEELING...
A VERY BAD FEELING...

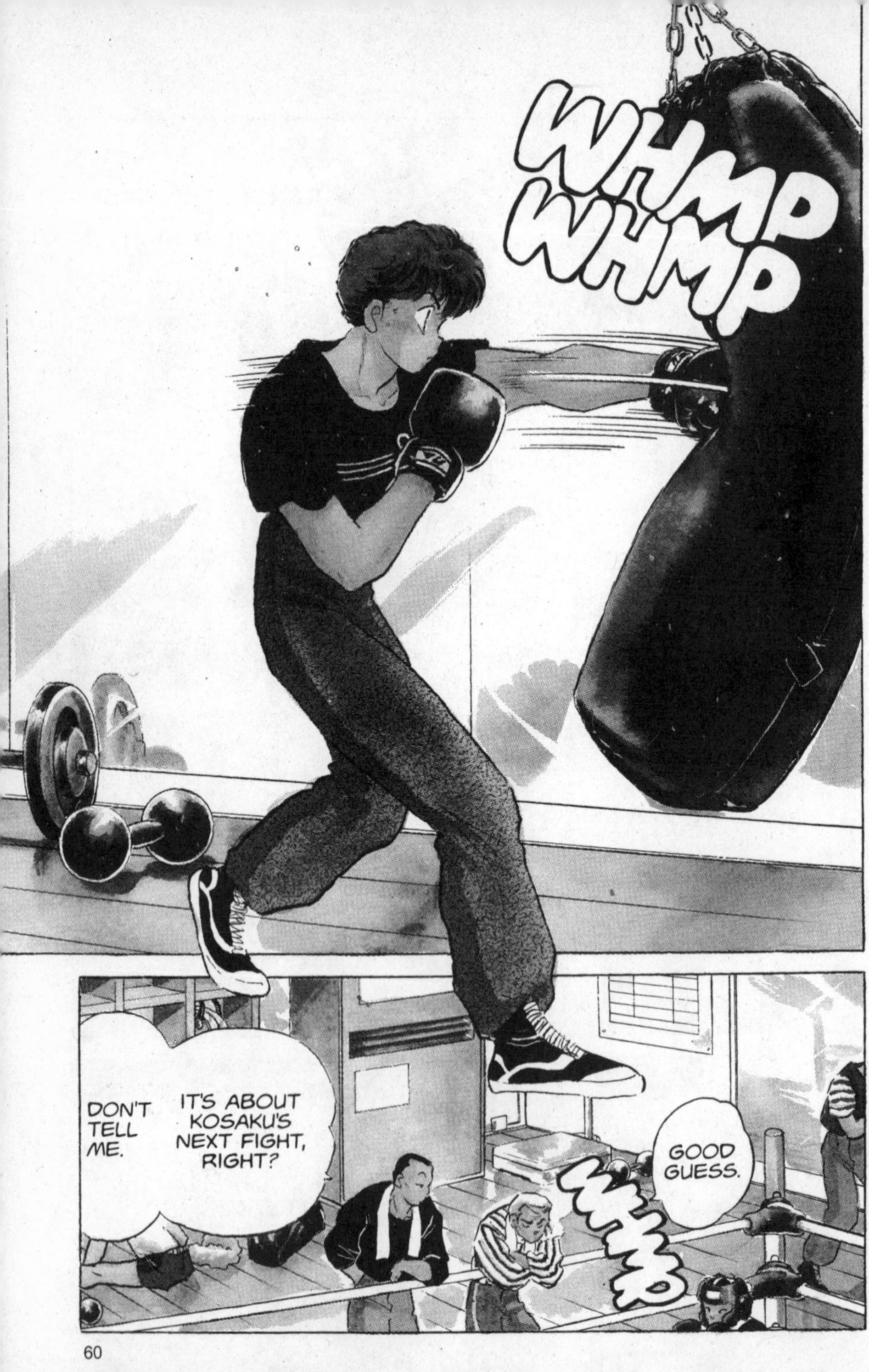
WHMP WHMP
DON'T TELL ME. IT'S ABOUT KOSAKU'S NEXT FIGHT, RIGHT?
WHMP
GOOD GUESS.

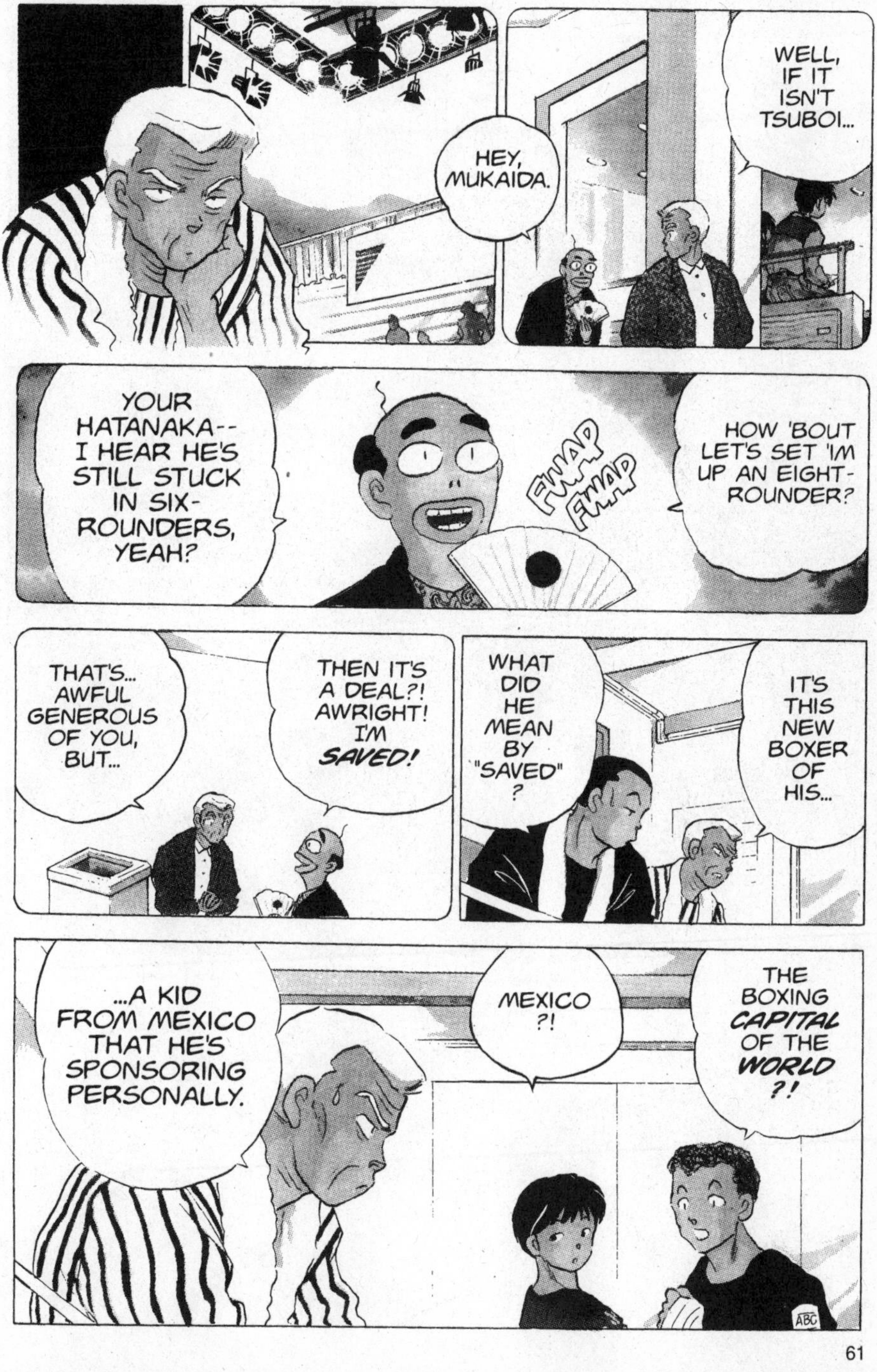
HEY, MUKAIDA.
WELL, IF IT ISN'T TSUBOI...
YOUR HATANAKA-- I HEAR HE'S STILL STUCK IN SIX-ROUNDERS, YEAH?
FWAP FWAP
HOW 'BOUT LET'S SET 'IM UP AN EIGHT-ROUNDER?
THAT'S... AWFUL GENEROUS OF YOU, BUT...
THEN IT'S A DEAL?! AWRIGHT! I'M SAVED!
WHAT DID HE MEAN BY "SAVED"?
IT'S THIS NEW BOXER OF HIS...
...A KID FROM MEXICO THAT HE'S SPONSORING PERSONALLY.
MEXICO?!
THE BOXING CAPITAL OF THE WORLD?!
ABC

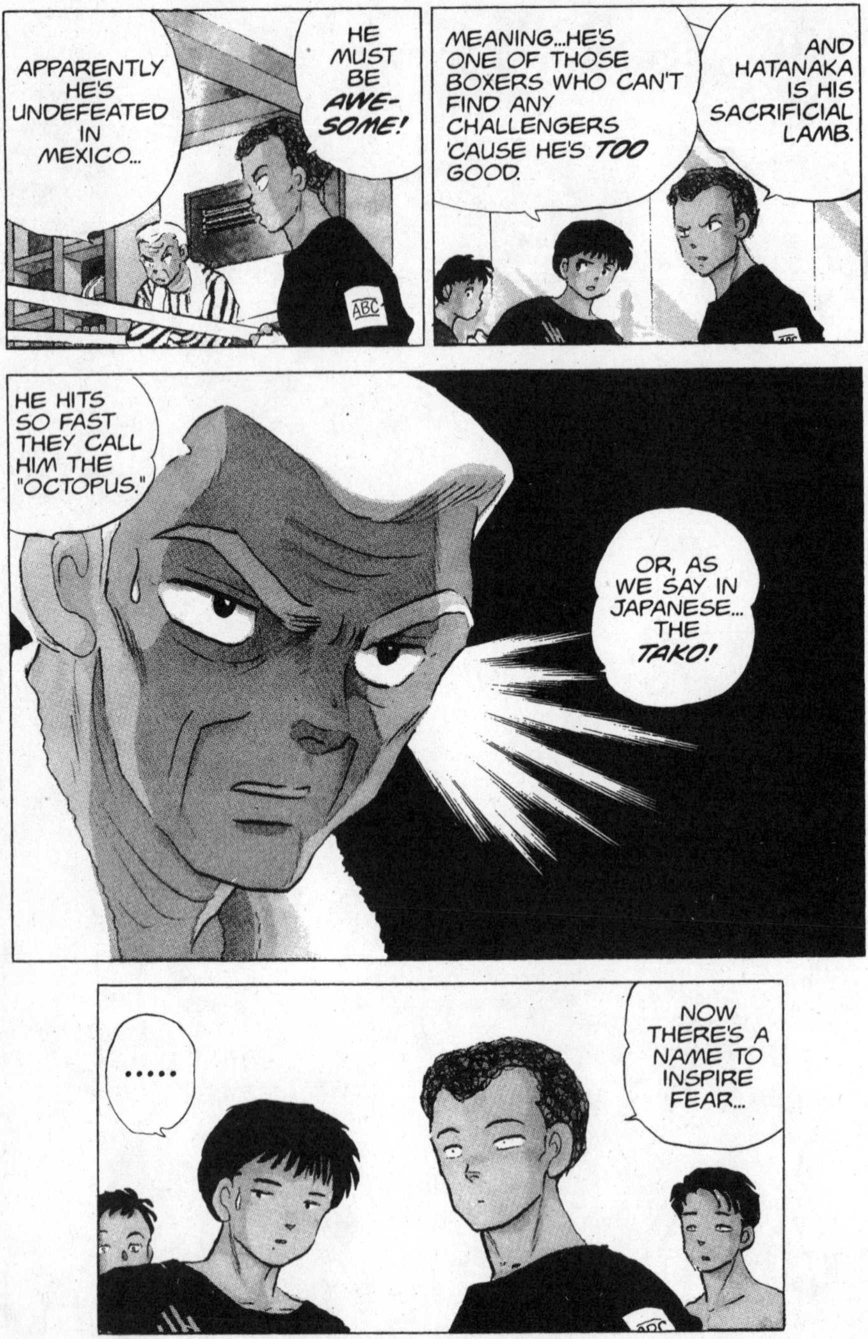
APPARENTLY HE'S UNDEFEATED IN MEXICO...
HE MUST BE AWE-SOME!
ABC
MEANING...HE'S ONE OF THOSE BOXERS WHO CAN'T FIND ANY CHALLENGERS 'CAUSE HE'S TOO GOOD.
AND HATANAKA IS HIS SACRIFICIAL LAMB.
HE HITS SO FAST THEY CALL HIM THE "OCTOPUS."
OR, AS WE SAY IN JAPANESE... THE TAKO!
.....
NOW THERE'S A NAME TO INSPIRE FEAR...

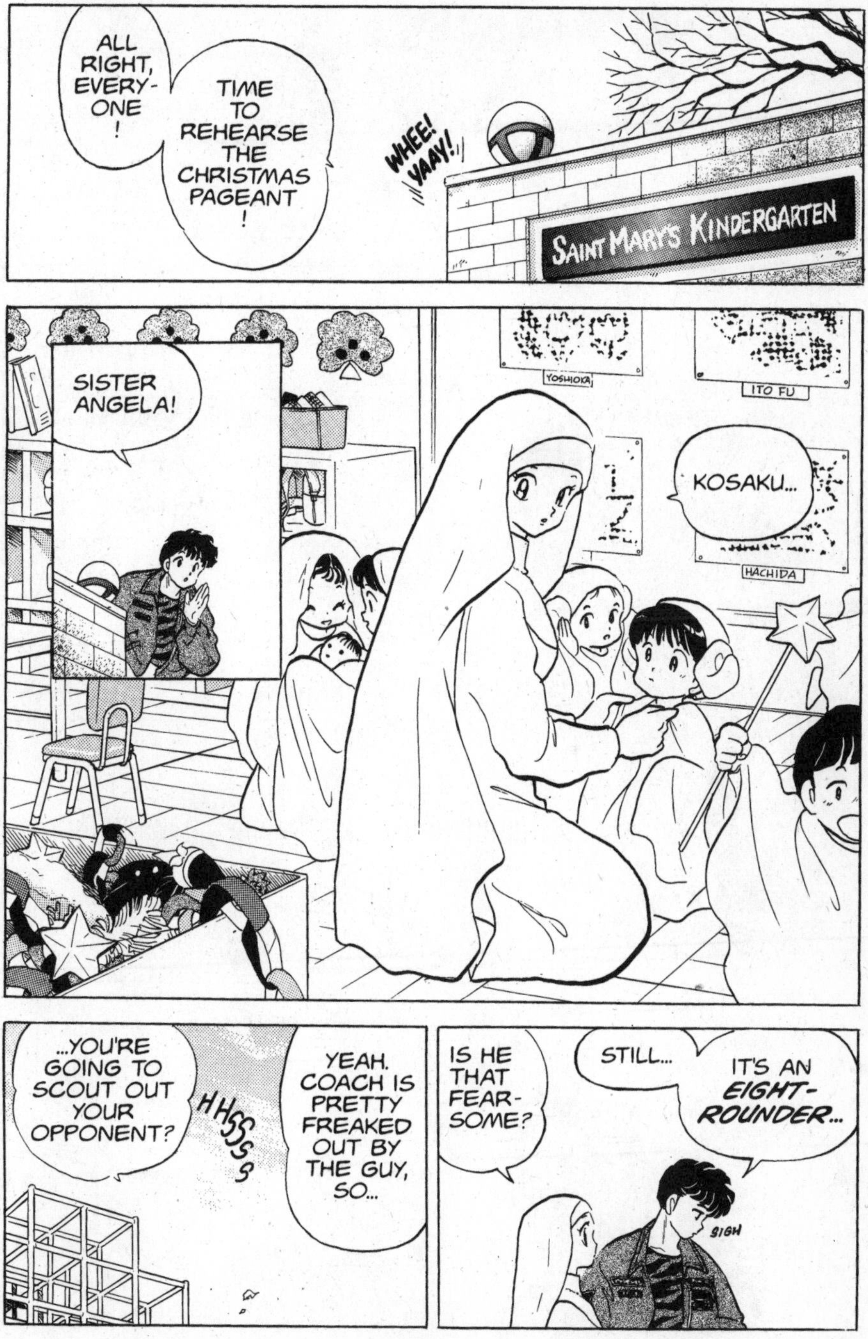

ALL RIGHT, EVERY-ONE!
TIME TO REHEARSE THE CHRISTMAS PAGEANT!
WHEE! YAAY!
SAINT MARY'S KINDERGARTEN
SISTER ANGELA!
YOSHIOKA
ITO FU
KOSAKU...
HACHIDA
...YOU'RE GOING TO SCOUT OUT YOUR OPPONENT?
HHSSSS
YEAH. COACH IS PRETTY FREAKED OUT BY THE GUY, SO...
IS HE THAT FEAR-SOME?
STILL...
IT'S AN EIGHT-ROUNDER...
SIGH

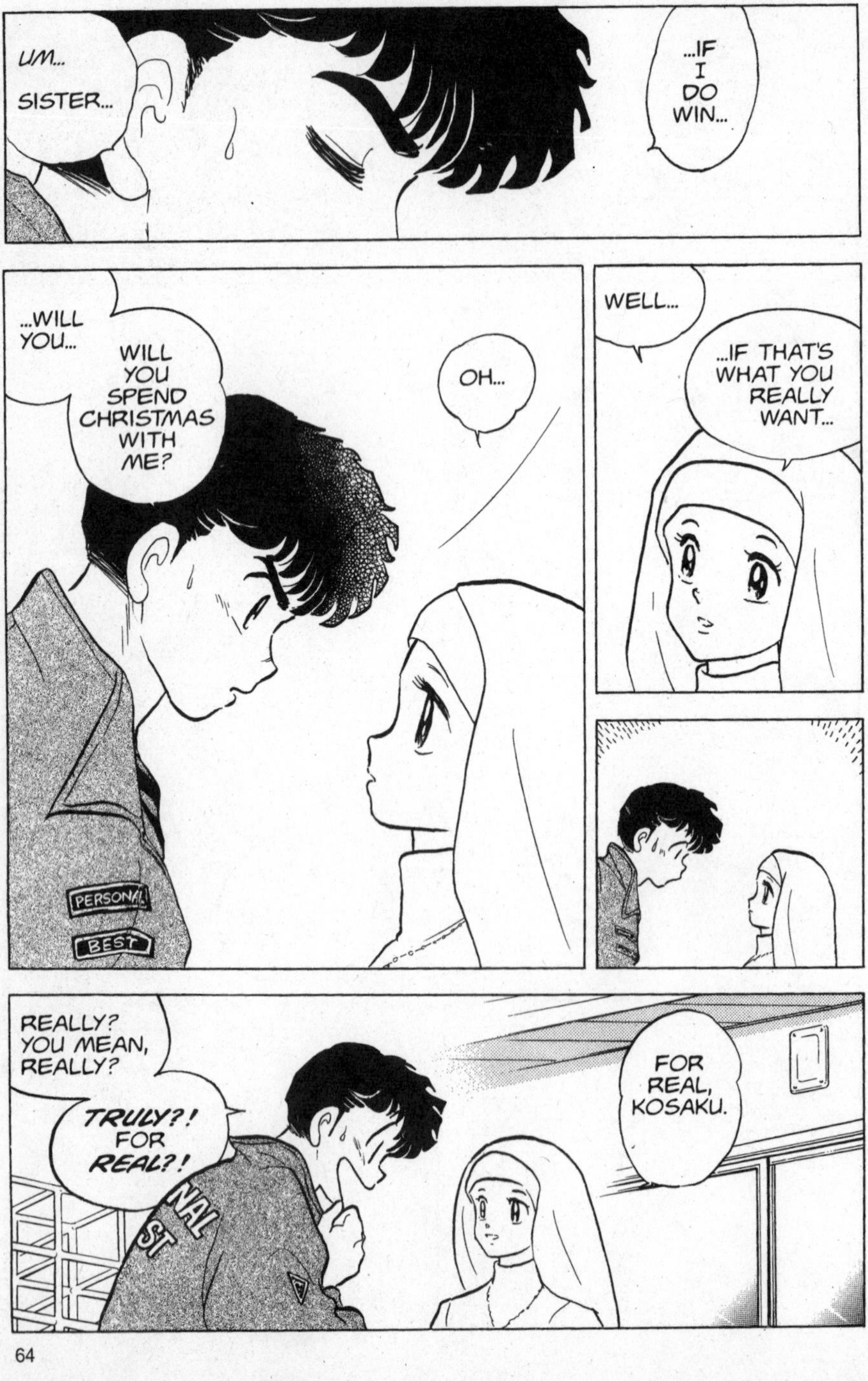
UM...
SISTER...
...IF I DO WIN...
...WILL YOU...
WILL YOU SPEND CHRISTMAS WITH ME?
OH...
PERSONAL
BEST
WELL...
...IF THAT'S WHAT YOU REALLY WANT...
REALLY? YOU MEAN, REALLY?
TRULY?! FOR REAL?!
NAL
ST
FOR REAL, KOSAKU.

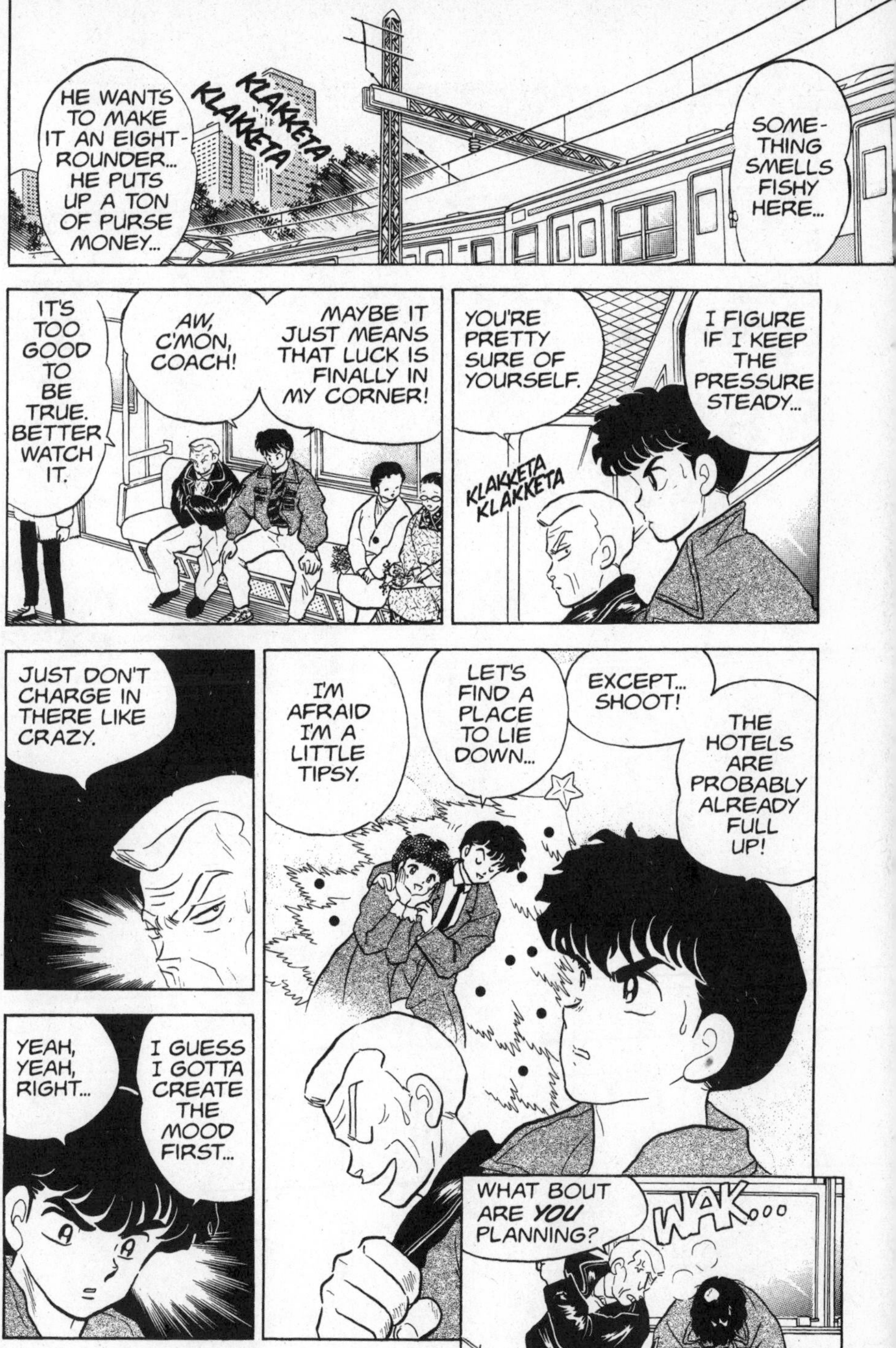
HE WANTS TO MAKE IT AN EIGHT-ROUNDER... HE PUTS UP A TON OF PURSE MONEY...
KLAKKETA KLAKKETA
SOME-THING SMELLS FISHY HERE...
IT'S TOO GOOD TO BE TRUE. BETTER WATCH IT.
AW, C'MON, COACH!
MAYBE IT JUST MEANS THAT LUCK IS FINALLY IN MY CORNER!
YOU'RE PRETTY SURE OF YOURSELF.
I FIGURE IF I KEEP THE PRESSURE STEADY...
KLAKKETA KLAKKETA
JUST DON'T CHARGE IN THERE LIKE CRAZY.
YEAH, YEAH, RIGHT...
I GUESS I GOTTA CREATE THE MOOD FIRST...
I'M AFRAID I'M A LITTLE TIPSY.
LET'S FIND A PLACE TO LIE DOWN...
EXCEPT... SHOOT!
THE HOTELS ARE PROBABLY ALREADY FULL UP!
WHAT BOUT ARE *YOU* PLANNING?
WAK...

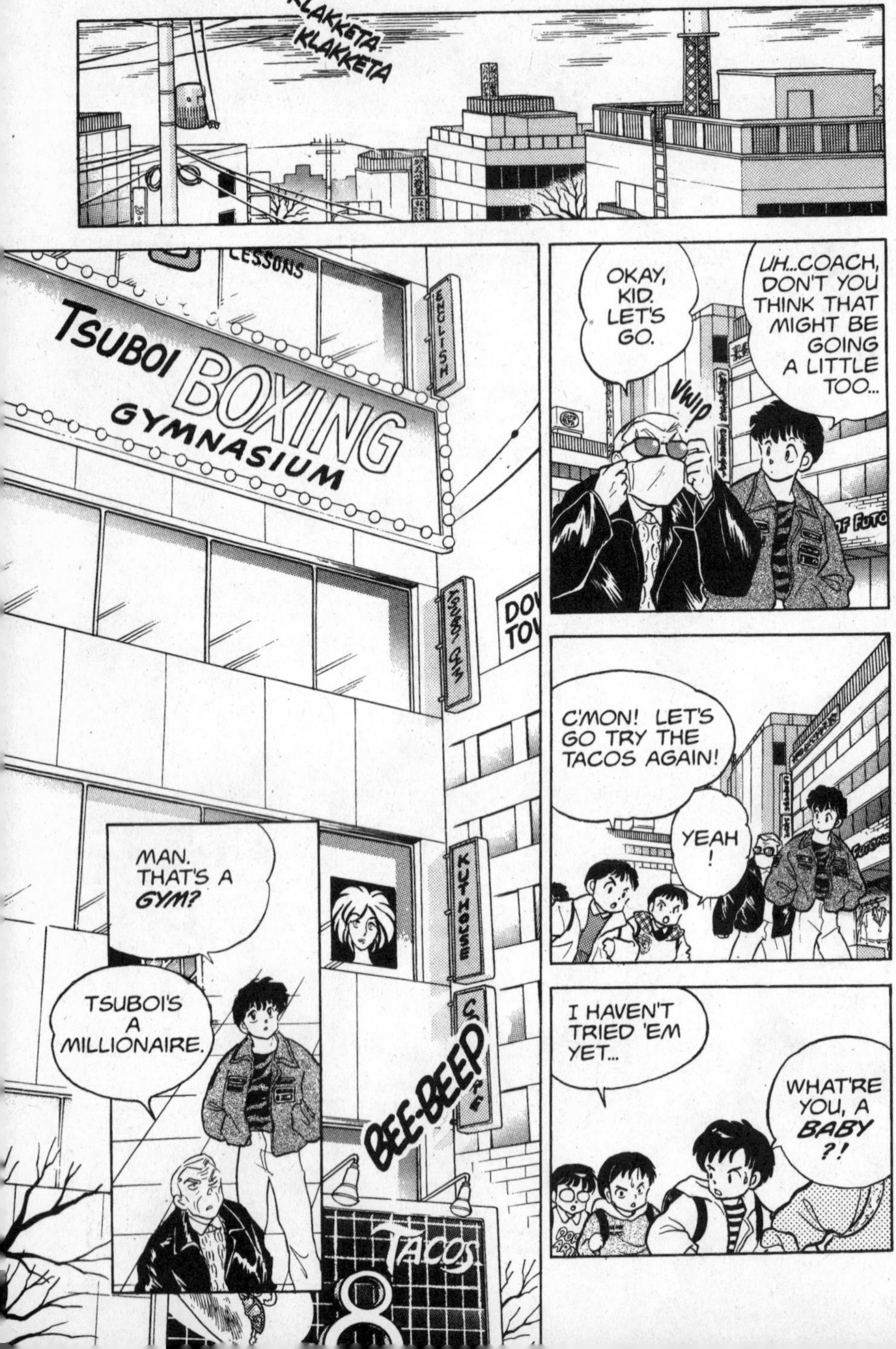
KLAKKETA KLAKKETA
LESSONS
TSUBOI BOXING GYMNASIUM
ENGLISH
MAN. THAT'S A *GYM?*
TSUBOI'S A MILLIONAIRE.
KUT HOUSE
BEE-BEEP
TACOS
8
OKAY, KID. LET'S GO.
UH...COACH, DON'T YOU THINK THAT MIGHT BE GOING A LITTLE TOO...
VWIP!
C'MON! LET'S GO TRY THE TACOS AGAIN!
YEAH!
I HAVEN'T TRIED 'EM YET...
WHAT'RE YOU, A *BABY* ?!

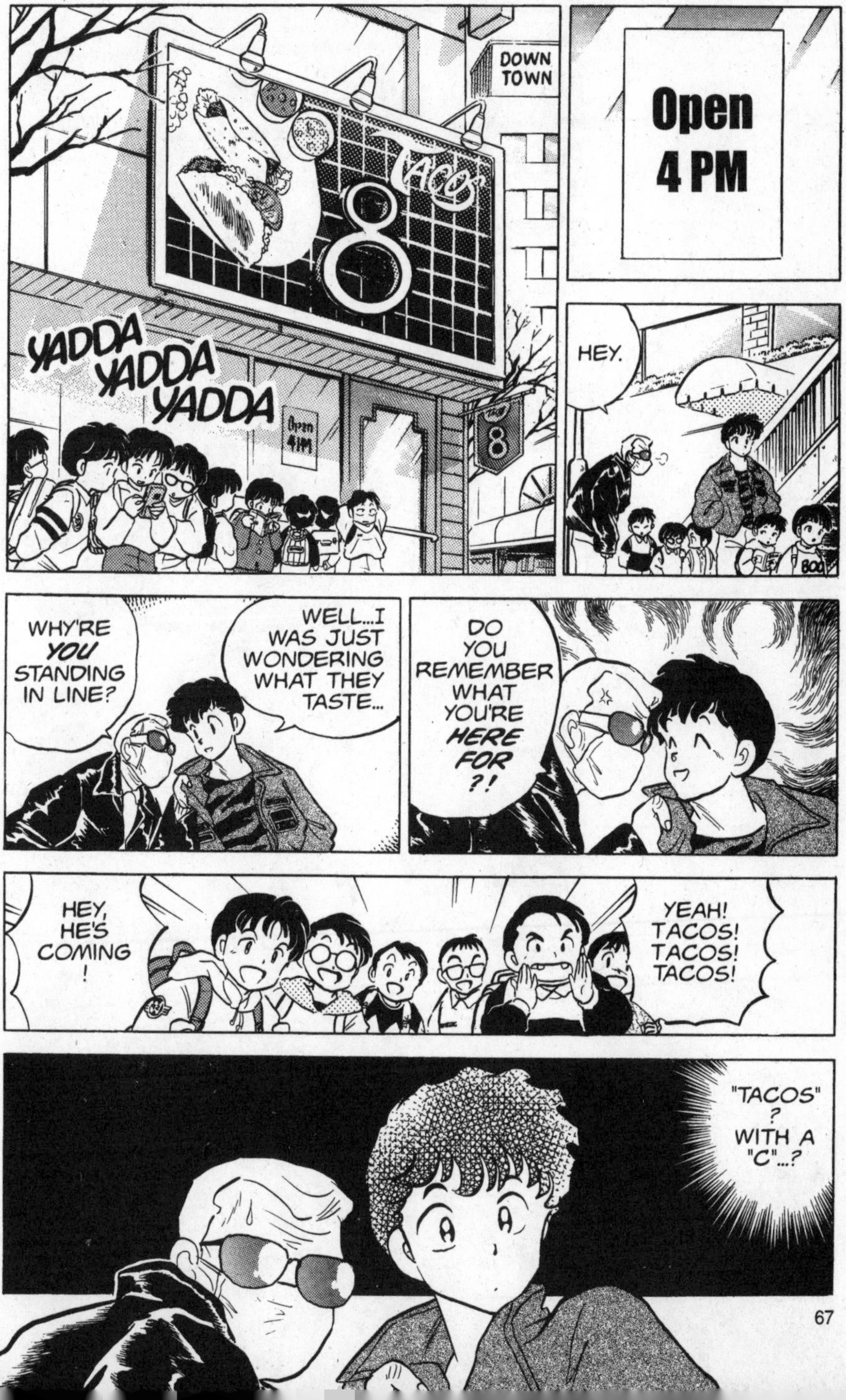
DOWN TOWN
TACOS 8
YADDA YADDA YADDA
Open 4PM
Open 4 PM
HEY.
WHY'RE *YOU* STANDING IN LINE?
WELL...I WAS JUST WONDERING WHAT THEY TASTE...
DO YOU REMEMBER WHAT YOU'RE *HERE FOR* ?!
HEY, HE'S COMING !
YEAH! TACOS! TACOS! TACOS!
"TACOS" ? WITH A "C"...?

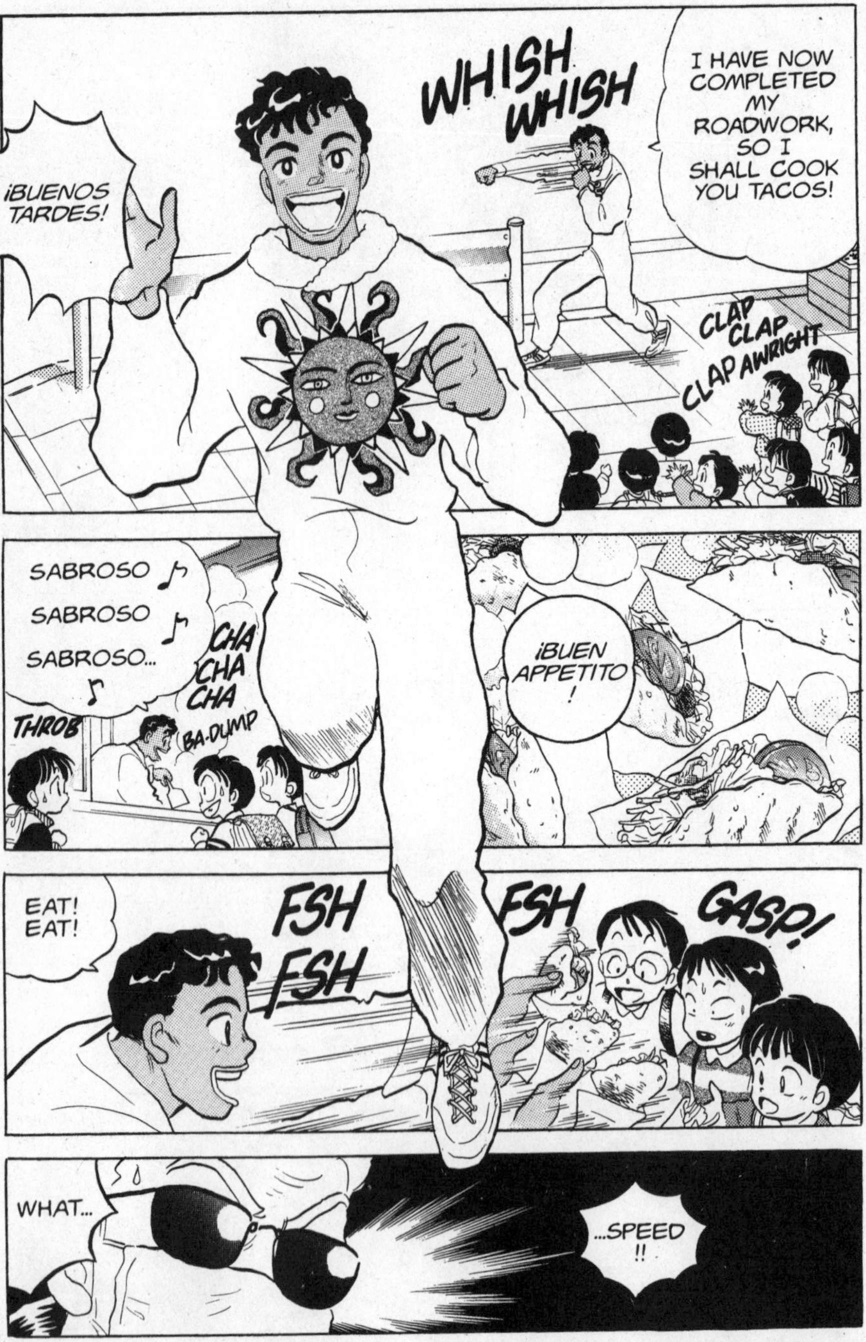
¡BUENOS TARDES!
WHISH WHISH
I HAVE NOW COMPLETED MY ROADWORK, SO I SHALL COOK YOU TACOS!
CLAP CLAP CLAP AWRIGHT
SABROSO ♪ SABROSO ♪ SABROSO... ♪
CHA CHA CHA
THROB
BA-DUMP
¡BUEN APPETITO!
EAT! EAT!
FSH FSH
FSH
GASP!
WHAT...
...SPEED!!

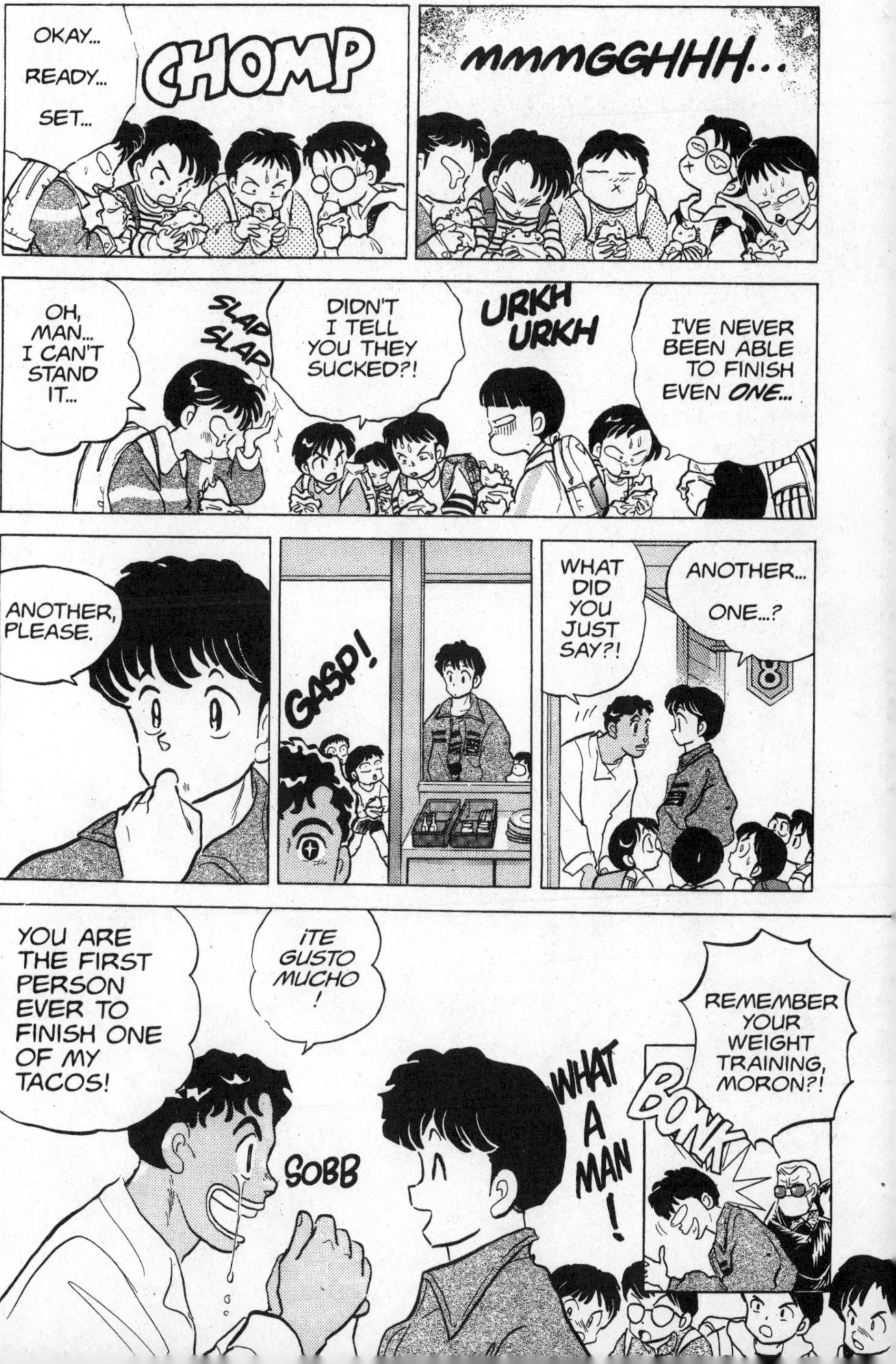
OKAY...
READY...
SET...
CHOMP
MMMGGHHH...
OH, MAN... I CAN'T STAND IT...
SLAP SLAP
DIDN'T I TELL YOU THEY SUCKED?!
URKH URKH
I'VE NEVER BEEN ABLE TO FINISH EVEN *ONE*...
ANOTHER, PLEASE.
GASP!
WHAT DID YOU JUST SAY?!
ANOTHER...
ONE...?
YOU ARE THE FIRST PERSON EVER TO FINISH ONE OF MY TACOS!
¡TE GUSTO MUCHO!
SOBB
WHAT A MAN!
REMEMBER YOUR WEIGHT TRAINING, MORON?!
BONK

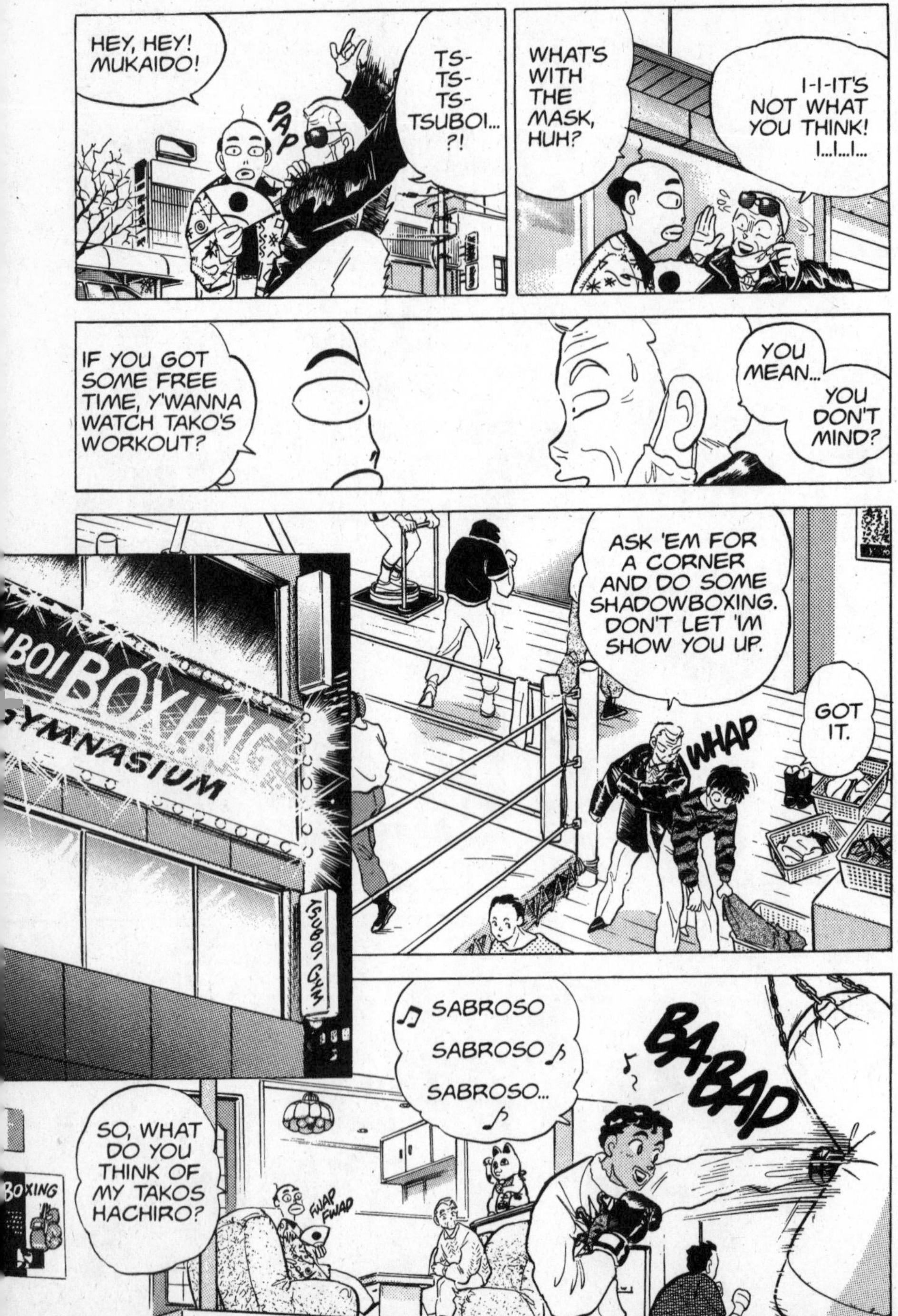
HEY, HEY! MUKAIDO!
PAP
TS-TS-TS-TSUBOI... ?!
WHAT'S WITH THE MASK, HUH?
I-I-IT'S NOT WHAT YOU THINK! I...I...I...
IF YOU GOT SOME FREE TIME, Y'WANNA WATCH TAKO'S WORKOUT?
YOU MEAN... YOU DON'T MIND?
BOXING
GYMNASIUM
TSUBOI GYM
ASK 'EM FOR A CORNER AND DO SOME SHADOWBOXING. DON'T LET 'IM SHOW YOU UP.
GOT IT.
WHAP
BOXING
SO, WHAT DO YOU THINK OF MY TAKOS HACHIRO?
FWAP FWAP
SABROSO SABROSO SABROSO...
BABAP

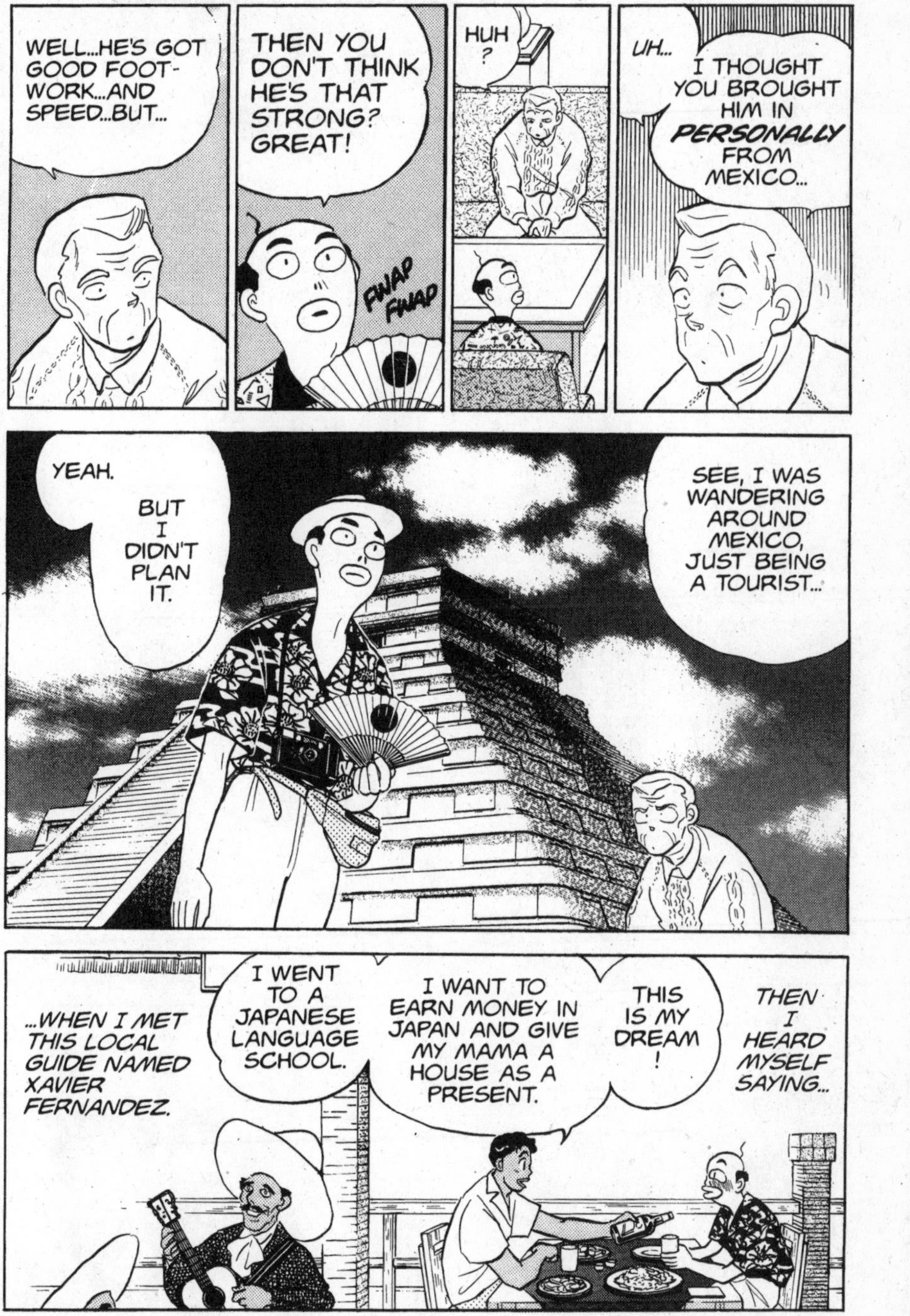
WELL...HE'S GOT GOOD FOOT-WORK...AND SPEED...BUT...
THEN YOU DON'T THINK HE'S THAT STRONG? GREAT!
FWAP FWAP
HUH ?
UH...
I THOUGHT YOU BROUGHT HIM IN **PERSONALLY** FROM MEXICO...
YEAH.
BUT I DIDN'T PLAN IT.
SEE, I WAS WANDERING AROUND MEXICO, JUST BEING A TOURIST...
...WHEN I MET THIS LOCAL GUIDE NAMED XAVIER FERNANDEZ.
I WENT TO A JAPANESE LANGUAGE SCHOOL.
I WANT TO EARN MONEY IN JAPAN AND GIVE MY MAMA A HOUSE AS A PRESENT.
THIS IS MY DREAM !
THEN I HEARD MYSELF SAYING...

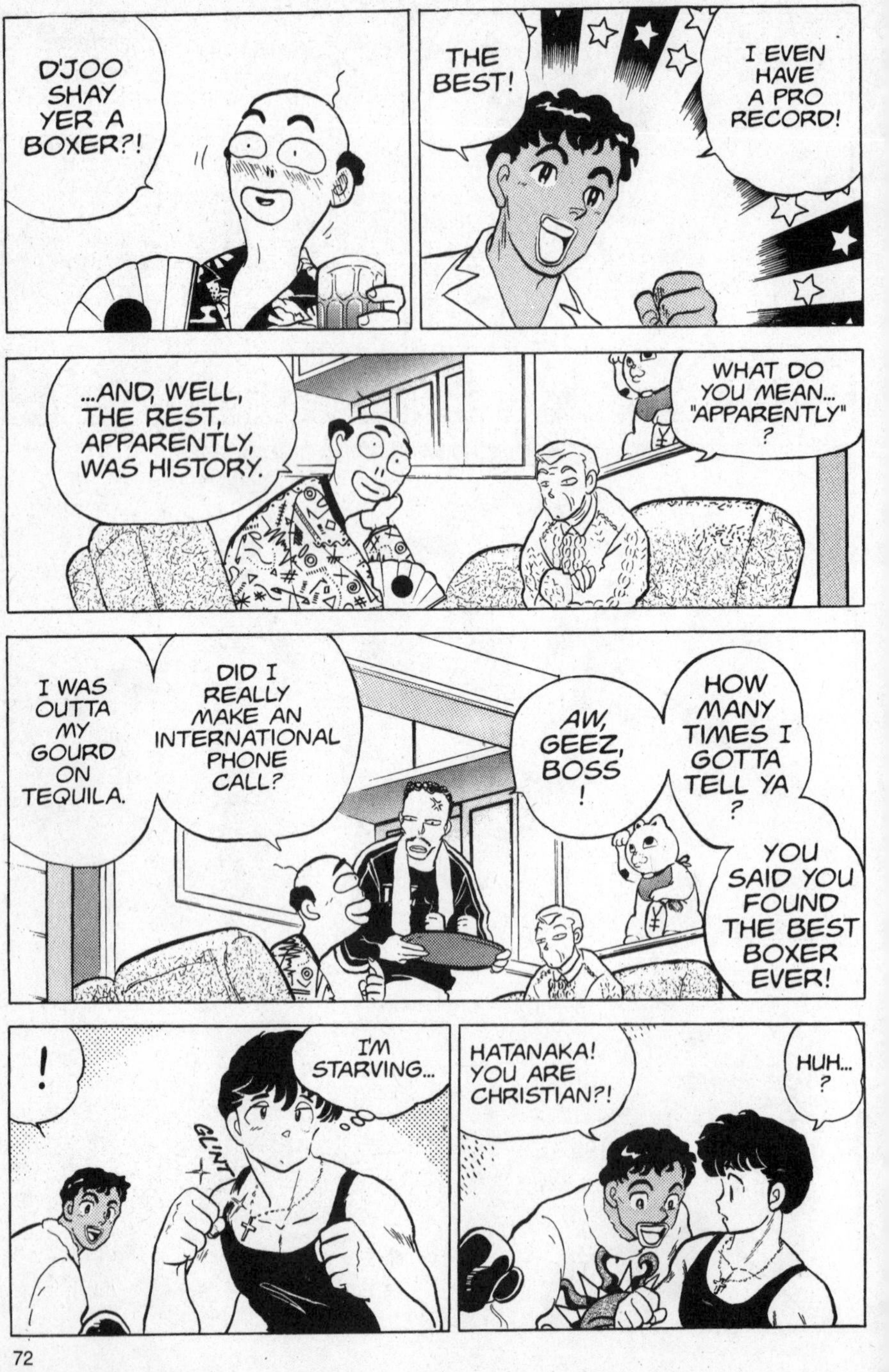

D'JOO SHAY YER A BOXER?!
THE BEST!
I EVEN HAVE A PRO RECORD!
...AND, WELL, THE REST, APPARENTLY, WAS HISTORY.
WHAT DO YOU MEAN... "APPARENTLY" ?
I WAS OUTTA MY GOURD ON TEQUILA.
DID I REALLY MAKE AN INTERNATIONAL PHONE CALL?
AW, GEEZ, BOSS !
HOW MANY TIMES I GOTTA TELL YA ?
YOU SAID YOU FOUND THE BEST BOXER EVER!
!
I'M STARVING...
GLINT
HATANAKA! YOU ARE CHRISTIAN?!
HUH... ?

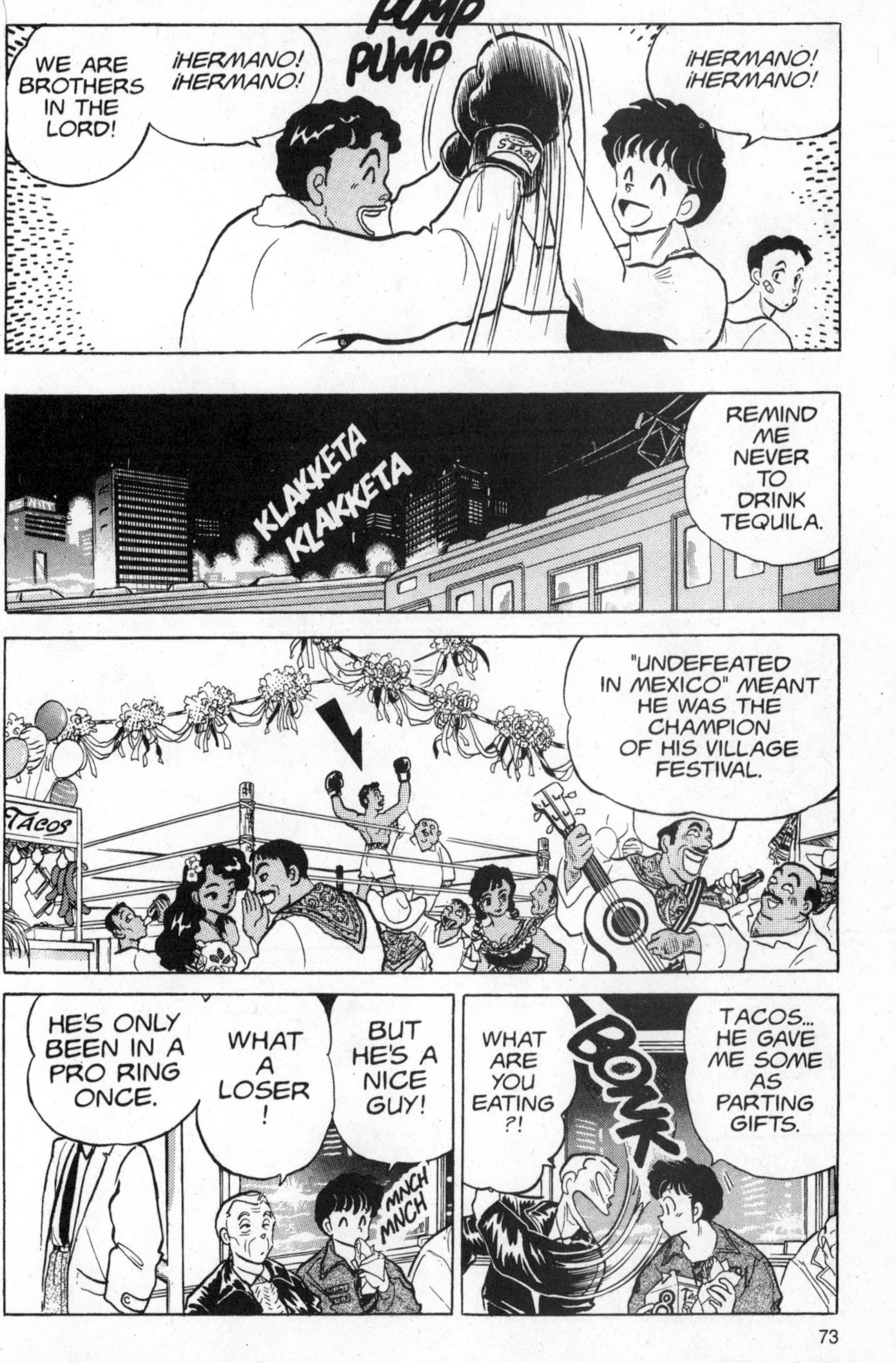

WE ARE BROTHERS IN THE LORD!
¡HERMANO! ¡HERMANO!
PUMP PUMP
¡HERMANO! ¡HERMANO!
KLAKKETA KLAKKETA
REMIND ME NEVER TO DRINK TEQUILA.
"UNDEFEATED IN MEXICO" MEANT HE WAS THE CHAMPION OF HIS VILLAGE FESTIVAL.
TACOS
HE'S ONLY BEEN IN A PRO RING ONCE.
WHAT A LOSER!
BUT HE'S A NICE GUY!
MNCH MNCH
WHAT ARE YOU EATING?!
BONK
TACOS... HE GAVE ME SOME AS PARTING GIFTS.

HE SAID HE WAS A TACO CHEF AND A BOXER.

I TRIED TO TURN THAT INTO A SCARY RING-NAME. "TAKO" FOR OCTOPUS, AND "HACHIRO" FOR EIGHT ARMS.

BUT NOBODY'LL BUY THAT CRAP EXCEPT SCHOOL BOYS TRYING TO PROVE HOW TOUGH THEY ARE!

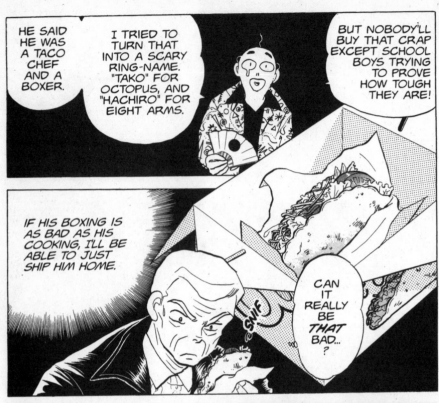

IF HIS BOXING IS AS BAD AS HIS COOKING, I'LL BE ABLE TO JUST SHIP HIM HOME.

SNIF

CAN IT REALLY BE *THAT* BAD...?

CHOMP

AND YOU ASKED FOR *MORE*?

SIGH

EVERYTHING TASTES GOOD DURING WEIGHT TRAINING...

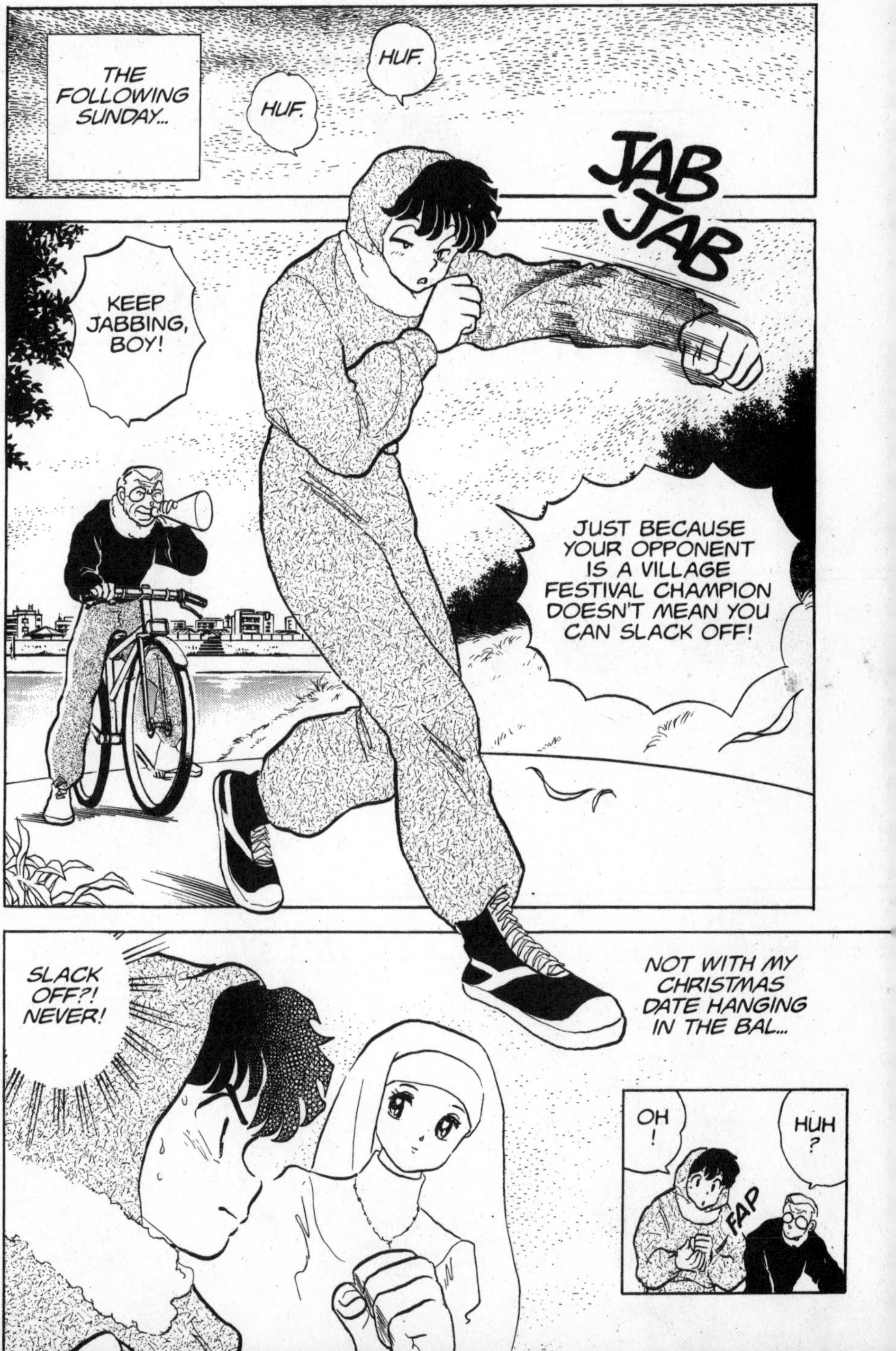
THE FOLLOWING SUNDAY...
HUF.
HUF.
JAB JAB
KEEP JABBING, BOY!
JUST BECAUSE YOUR OPPONENT IS A VILLAGE FESTIVAL CHAMPION DOESN'T MEAN YOU CAN SLACK OFF!
SLACK OFF?! NEVER!
NOT WITH MY CHRISTMAS DATE HANGING IN THE BAL...
OH !
HUH ?
FAP

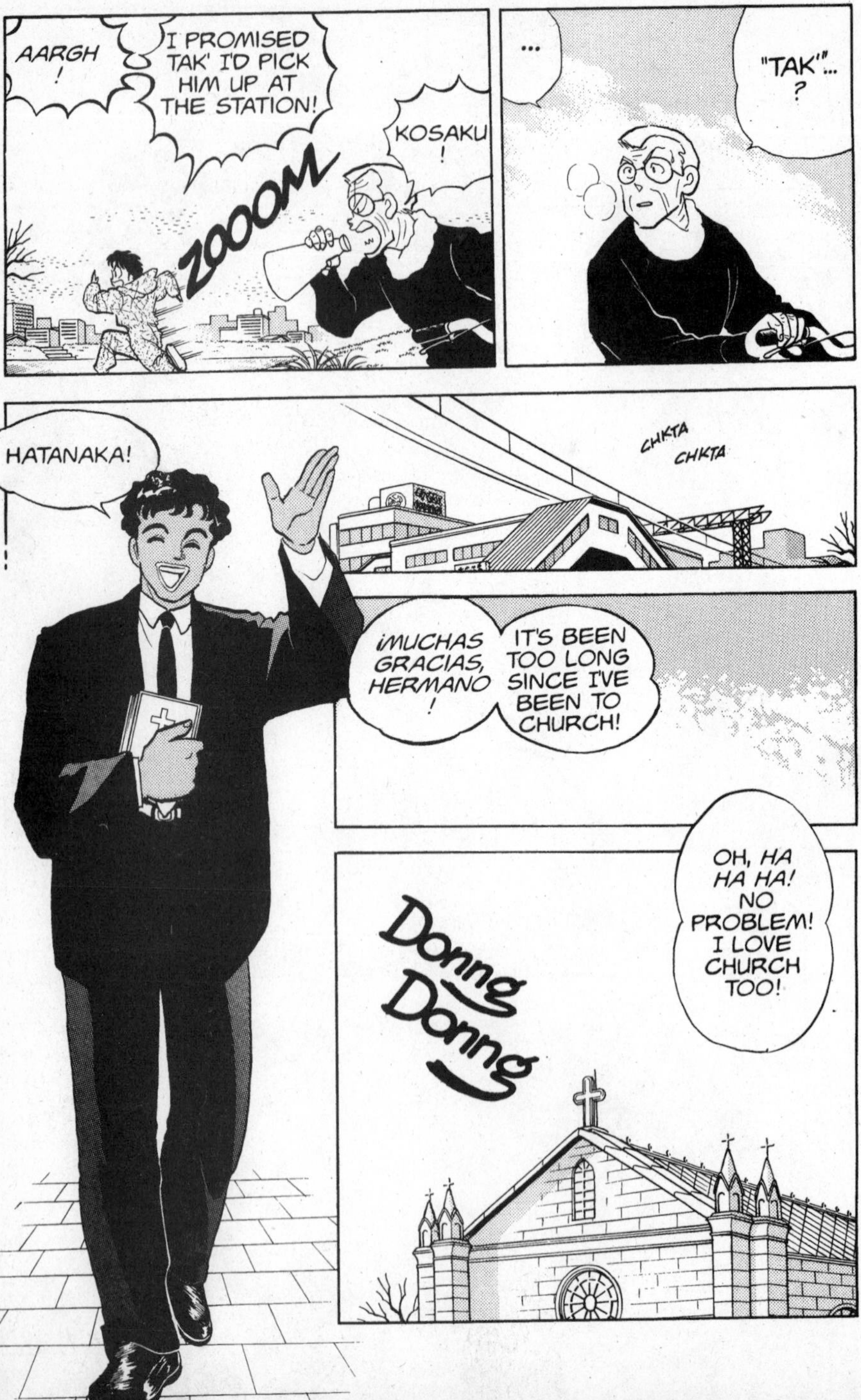

AARGH!
I PROMISED TAK' I'D PICK HIM UP AT THE STATION!
KOSAKU!
ZOOOM
...
"TAK"...?
HATANAKA!
CHKTA
CHKTA
¡MUCHAS GRACIAS, HERMANO!
IT'S BEEN TOO LONG SINCE I'VE BEEN TO CHURCH!
OH, HA HA HA! NO PROBLEM! I LOVE CHURCH TOO!
Donng
Donng

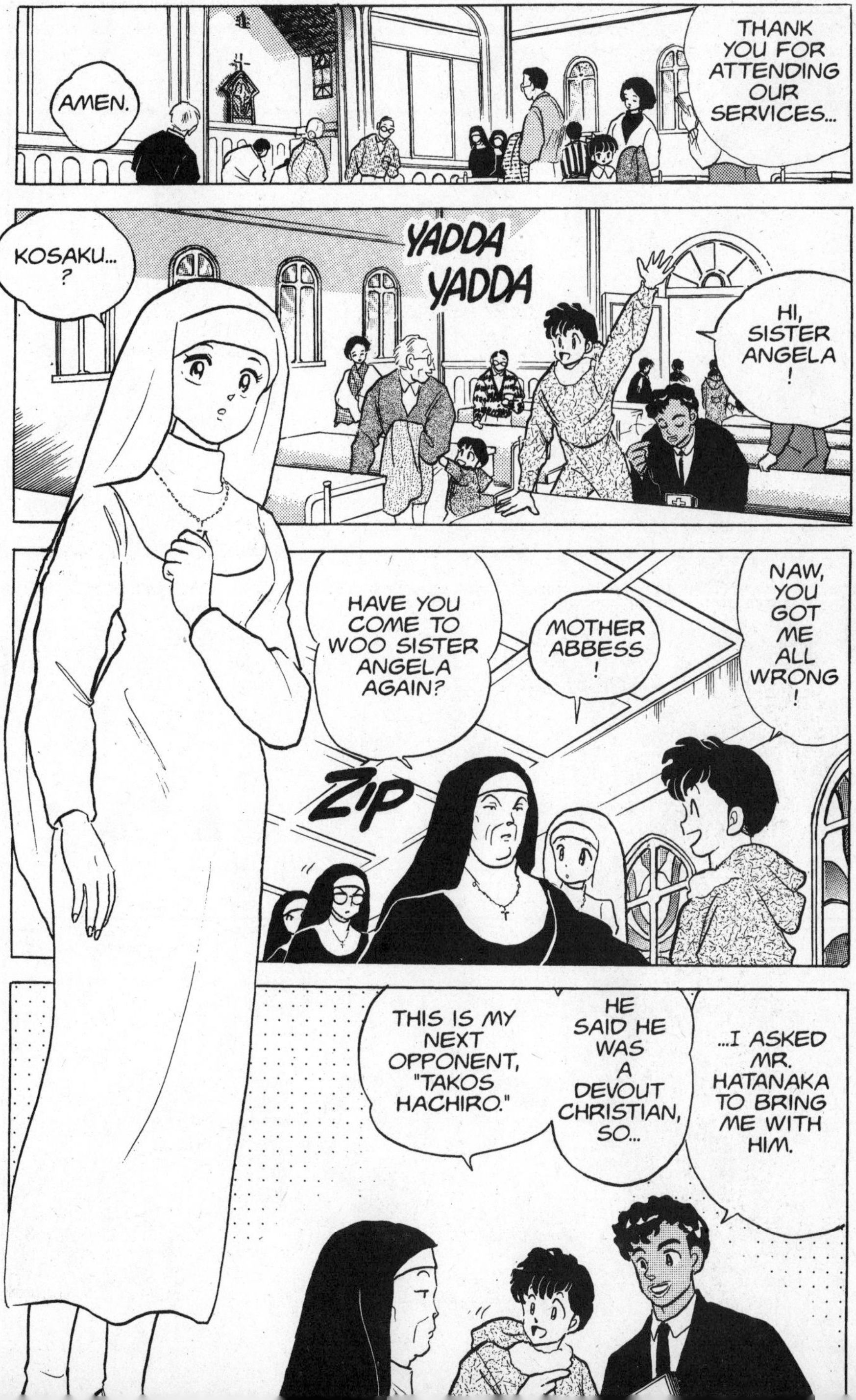
AMEN.
THANK YOU FOR ATTENDING OUR SERVICES...
KOSAKU... ?
YADDA YADDA
HI, SISTER ANGELA !
HAVE YOU COME TO WOO SISTER ANGELA AGAIN?
MOTHER ABBESS !
NAW, YOU GOT ME ALL WRONG !
ZIP
THIS IS MY NEXT OPPONENT, "TAKOS HACHIRO."
HE SAID HE WAS A DEVOUT CHRISTIAN, SO...
...I ASKED MR. HATANAKA TO BRING ME WITH HIM.

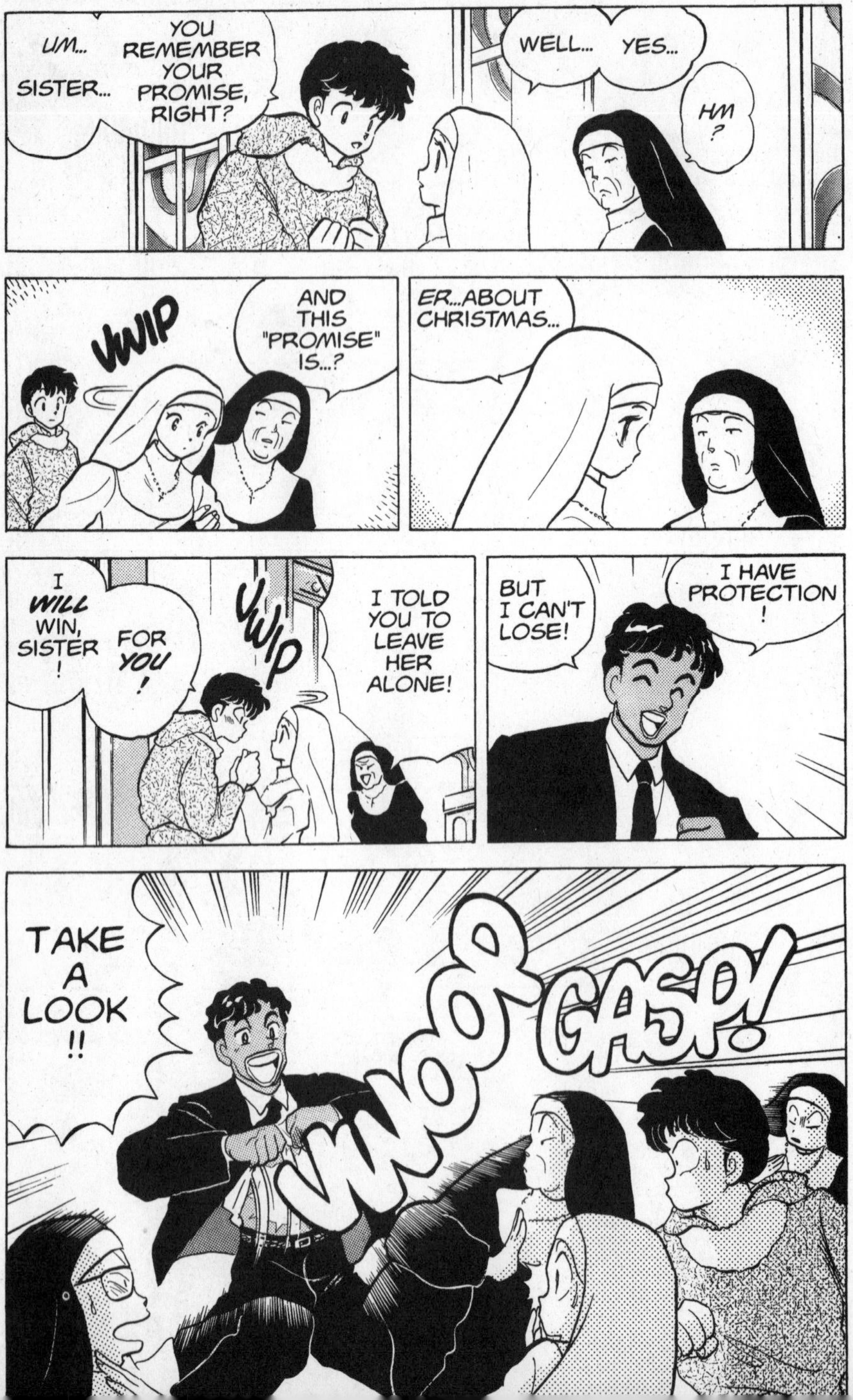
UM... SISTER...
YOU REMEMBER YOUR PROMISE, RIGHT?
WELL... YES...
HM?
VWIP
AND THIS "PROMISE" IS...?
ER...ABOUT CHRISTMAS...
I *WILL* WIN, SISTER!
FOR *YOU*!
VWIP
I TOLD YOU TO LEAVE HER ALONE!
BUT I CAN'T LOSE!
I HAVE PROTECTION!
TAKE A LOOK!!
VWOOP
GASP!

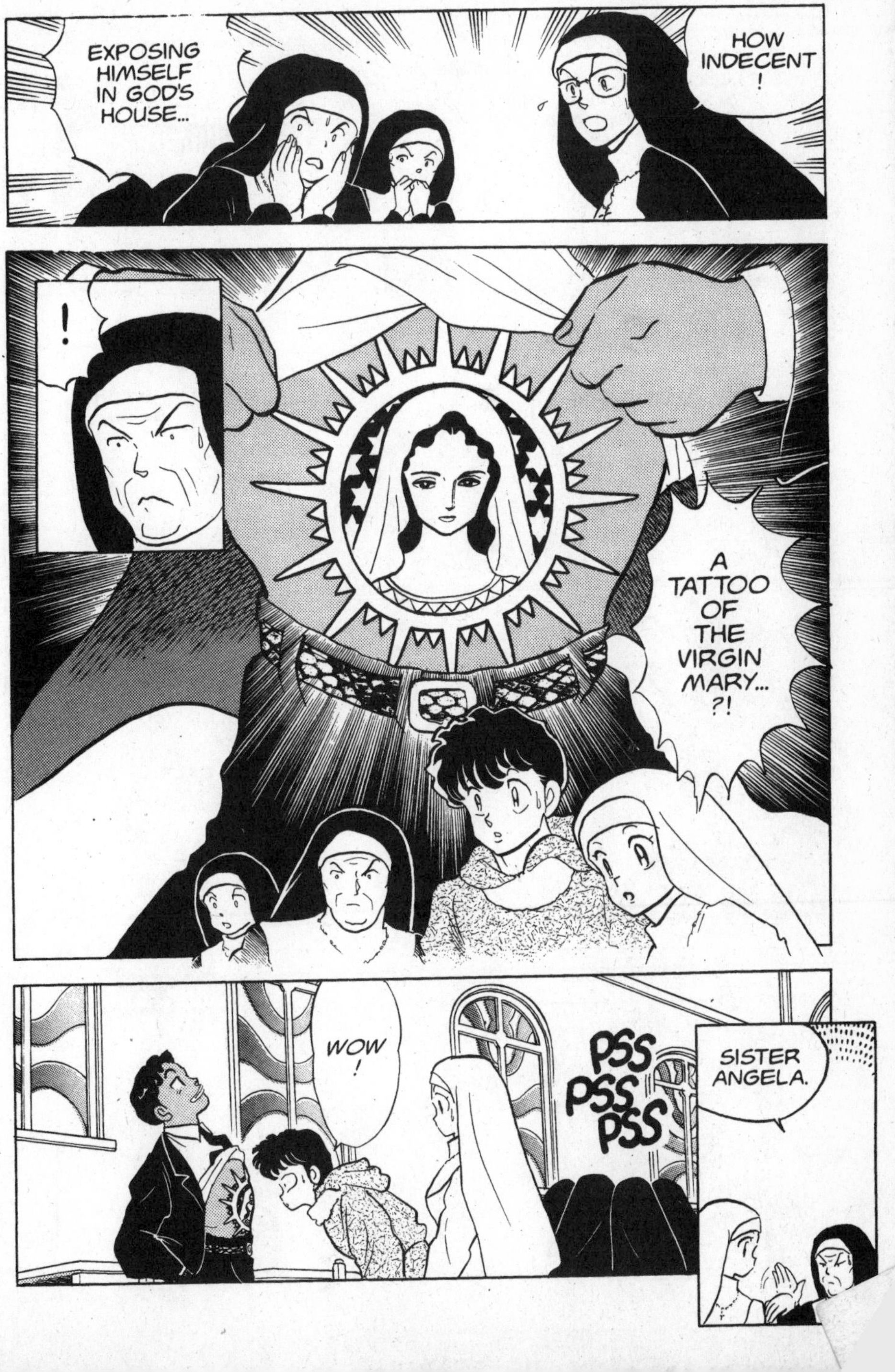
EXPOSING HIMSELF IN GOD'S HOUSE...
HOW INDECENT !
!
A TATTOO OF THE VIRGIN MARY... ?!
WOW !
PSS PSS PSS PSS
SISTER ANGELA.

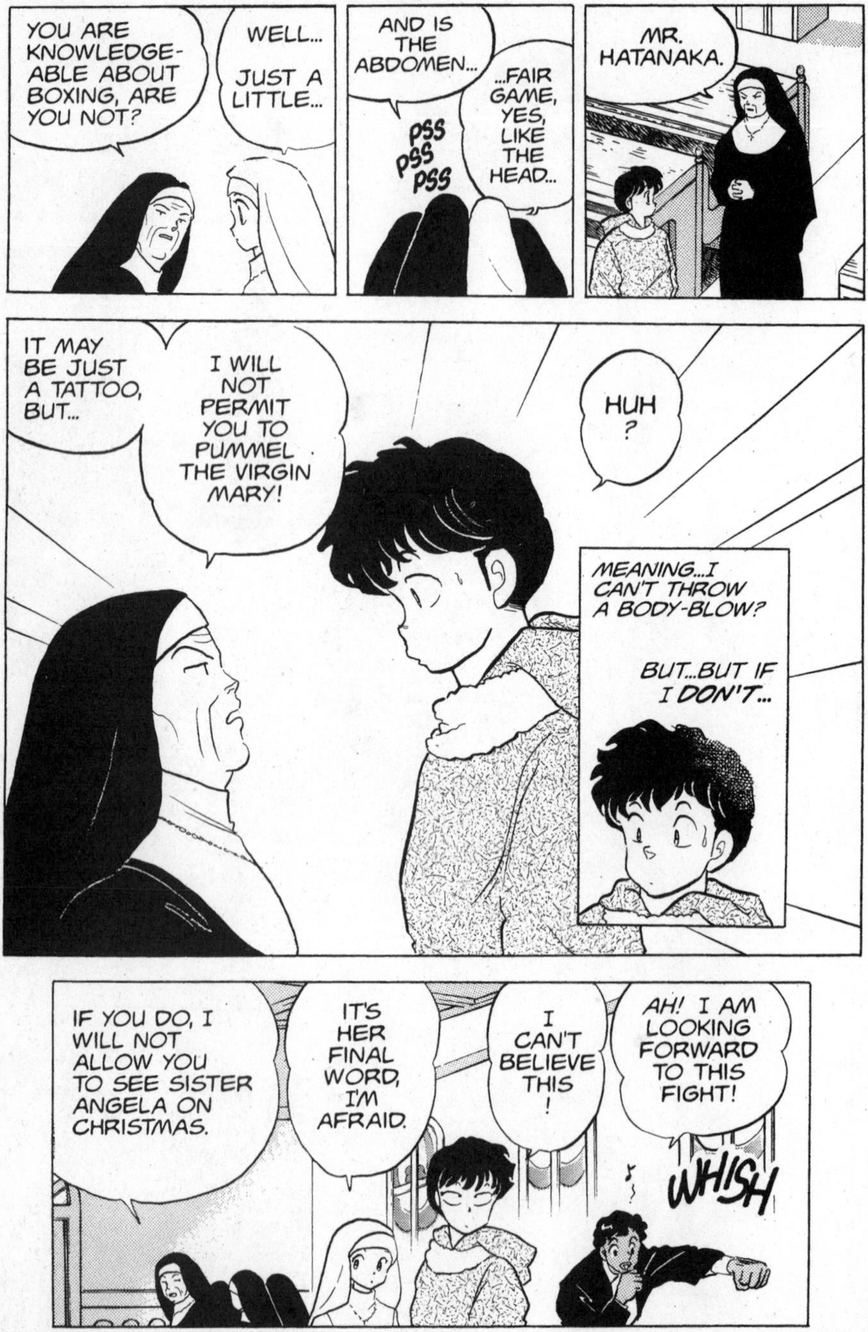
YOU ARE KNOWLEDGE-ABLE ABOUT BOXING, ARE YOU NOT?
WELL... JUST A LITTLE...
AND IS THE ABDOMEN...
PSS PSS PSS
...FAIR GAME, YES, LIKE THE HEAD...
MR. HATANAKA.
IT MAY BE JUST A TATTOO, BUT...
I WILL NOT PERMIT YOU TO PUMMEL THE VIRGIN MARY!
HUH?
MEANING...I CAN'T THROW A BODY-BLOW?
BUT...BUT IF I DON'T...
IF YOU DO, I WILL NOT ALLOW YOU TO SEE SISTER ANGELA ON CHRISTMAS.
IT'S HER FINAL WORD, I'M AFRAID.
I CAN'T BELIEVE THIS!
AH! I AM LOOKING FORWARD TO THIS FIGHT!
WHISH

CHAPTER TWO

TEARS OF A LAMB

PART TWO

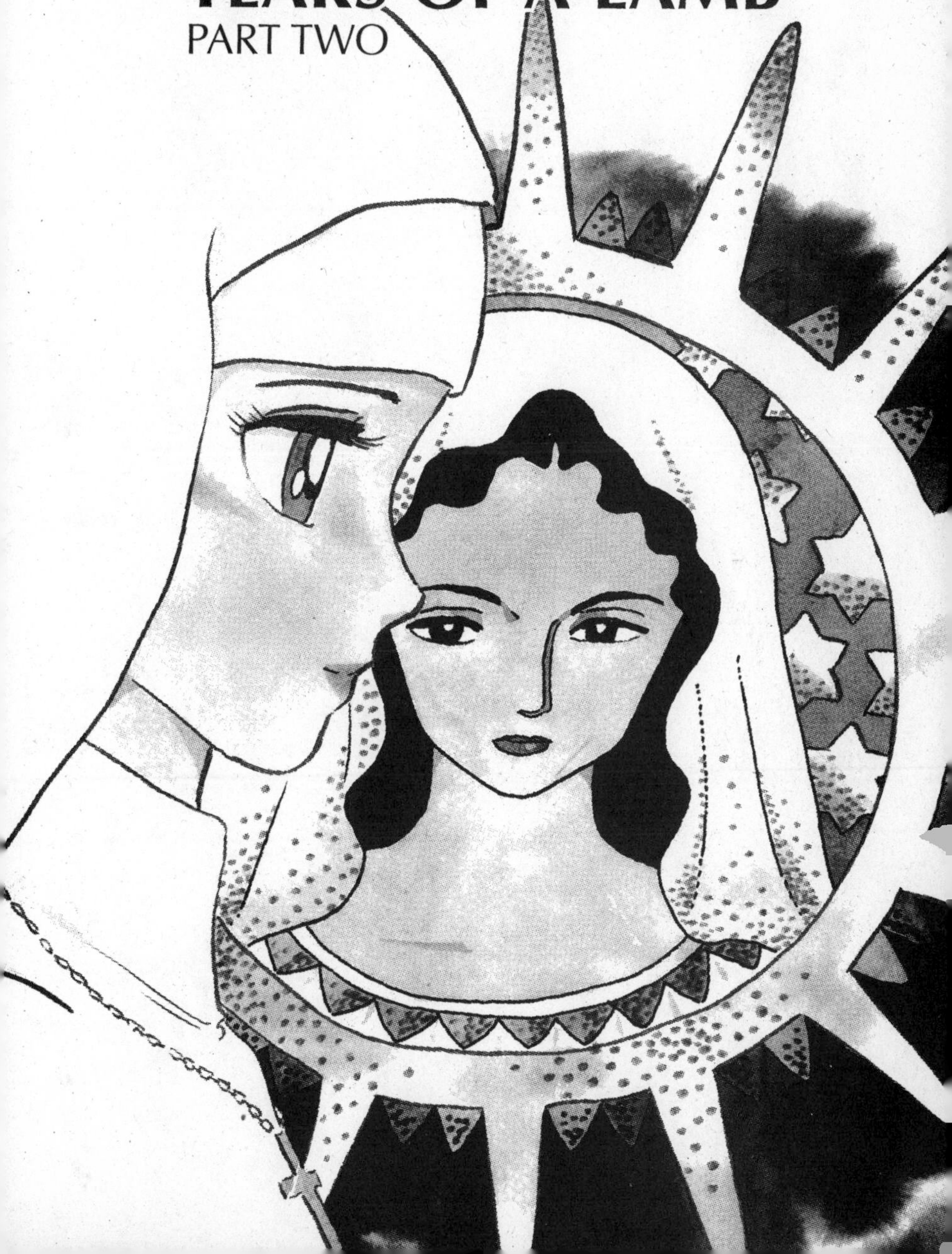

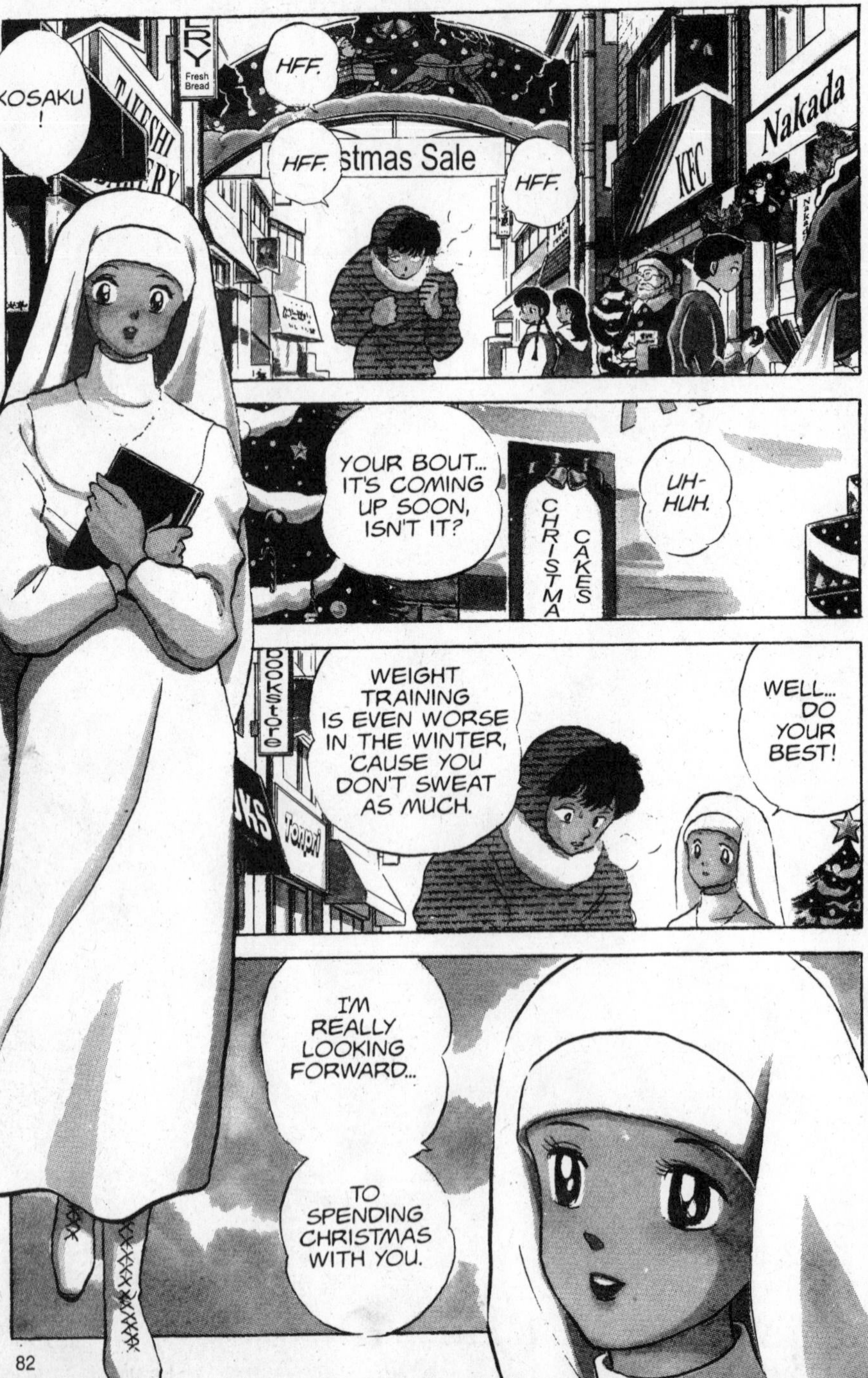

KOSAKU!
LRY
Fresh Bread
HFF.
HFF.
stmas Sale
HFF.
KFC
Nakada
YOUR BOUT... IT'S COMING UP SOON, ISN'T IT?
CHRISTMA CAKES
UH-HUH.
bookstore
Tonpri
WEIGHT TRAINING IS EVEN WORSE IN THE WINTER, 'CAUSE YOU DON'T SWEAT AS MUCH.
WELL... DO YOUR BEST!
I'M REALLY LOOKING FORWARD...
TO SPENDING CHRISTMAS WITH YOU.

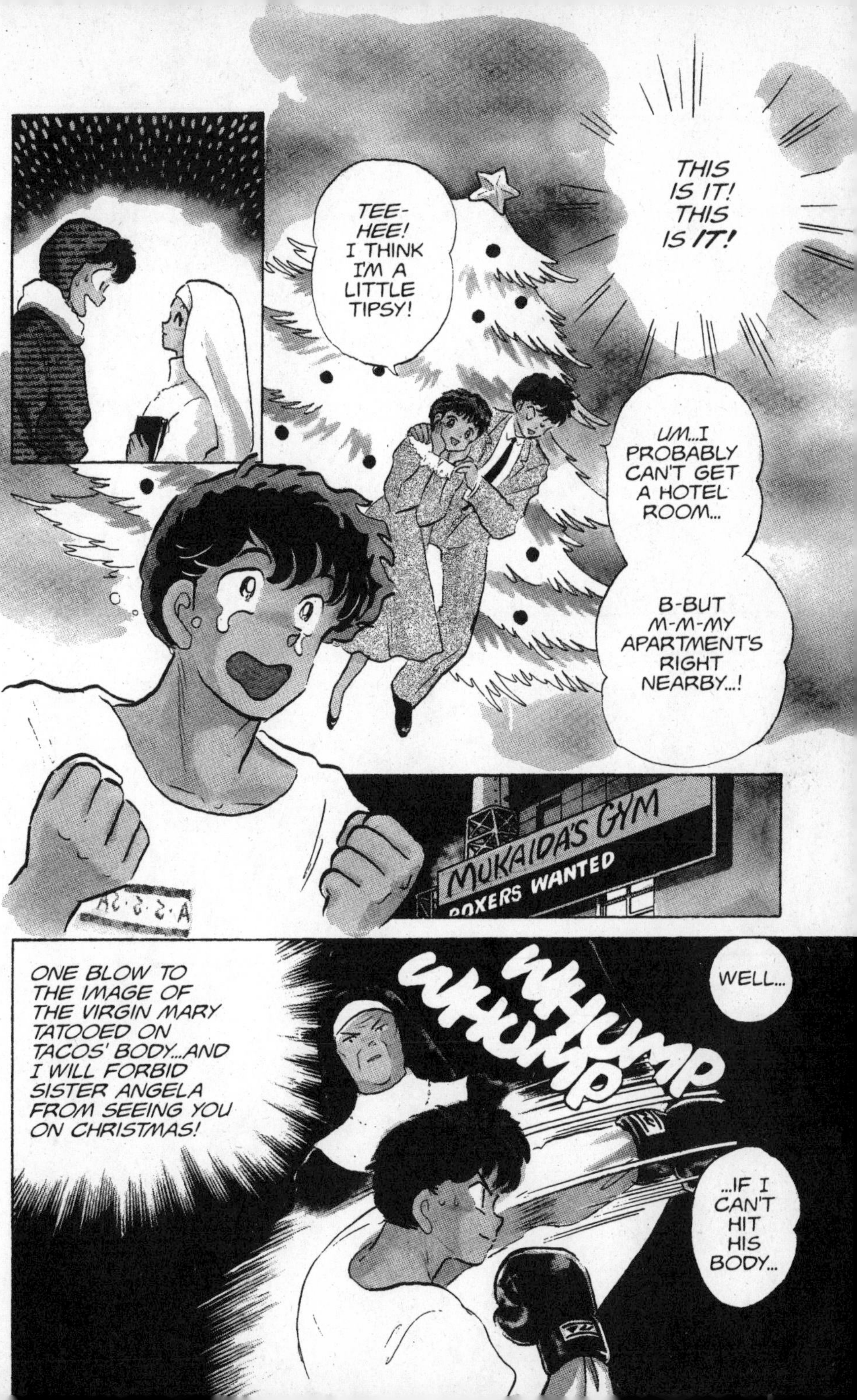
TEE-HEE! I THINK I'M A LITTLE TIPSY!
THIS IS IT! THIS IS IT!
UM...I PROBABLY CAN'T GET A HOTEL ROOM...
B-BUT M-M-MY APARTMENT'S RIGHT NEARBY...!
MUKAIDA'S GYM
BOXERS WANTED
ONE BLOW TO THE IMAGE OF THE VIRGIN MARY TATOOED ON TACOS' BODY...AND I WILL FORBID SISTER ANGELA FROM SEEING YOU ON CHRISTMAS!
WHUMP WHUMP
WELL...
...IF I CAN'T HIT HIS BODY...

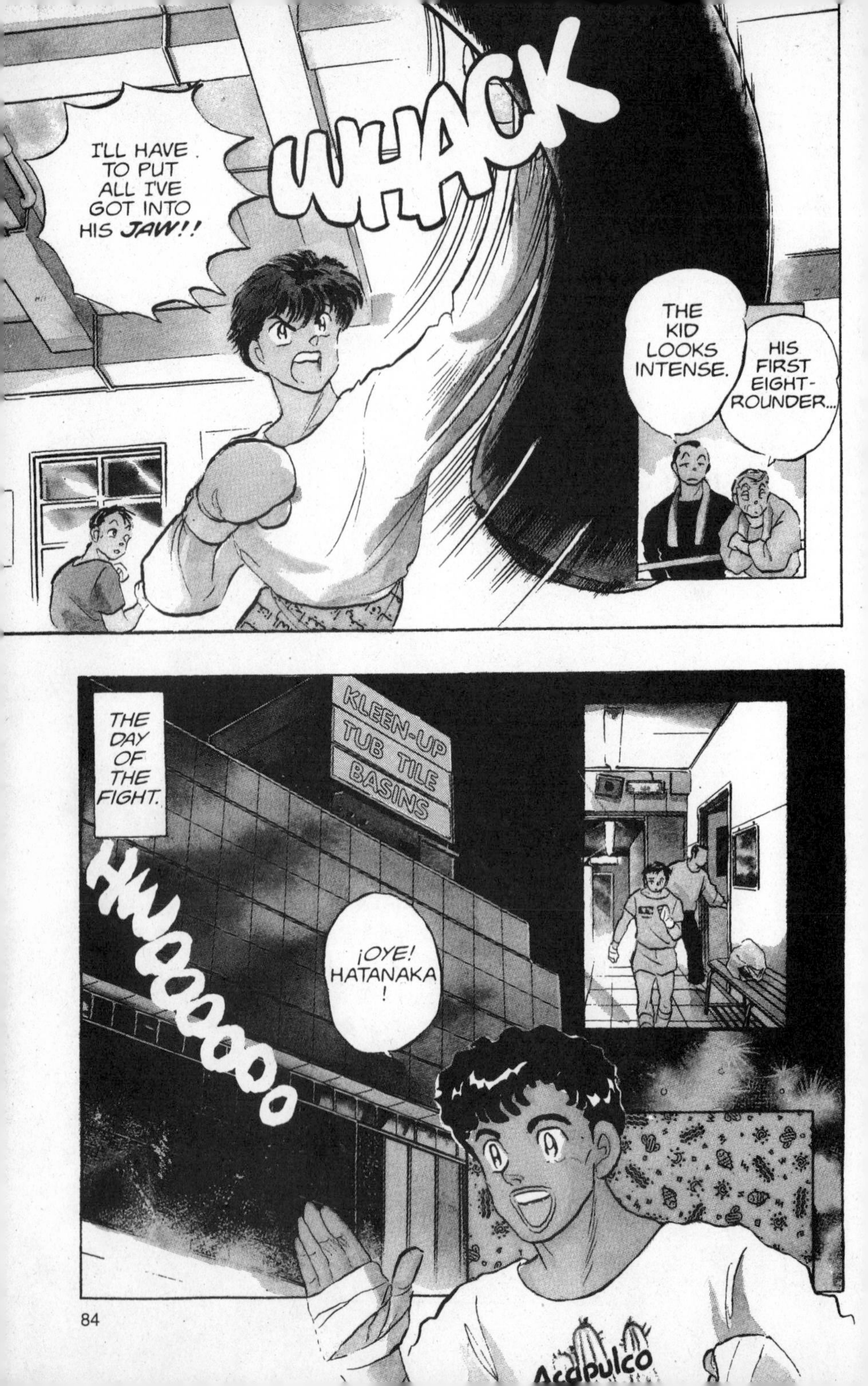
I'LL HAVE TO PUT ALL I'VE GOT INTO HIS JAW!!
WHACK
THE KID LOOKS INTENSE.
HIS FIRST EIGHT-ROUNDER...
THE DAY OF THE FIGHT.
KLEEN-UP TUB TILE BASINS
HWOOOOOOO
¡OYE! HATANAKA!
Acapulco

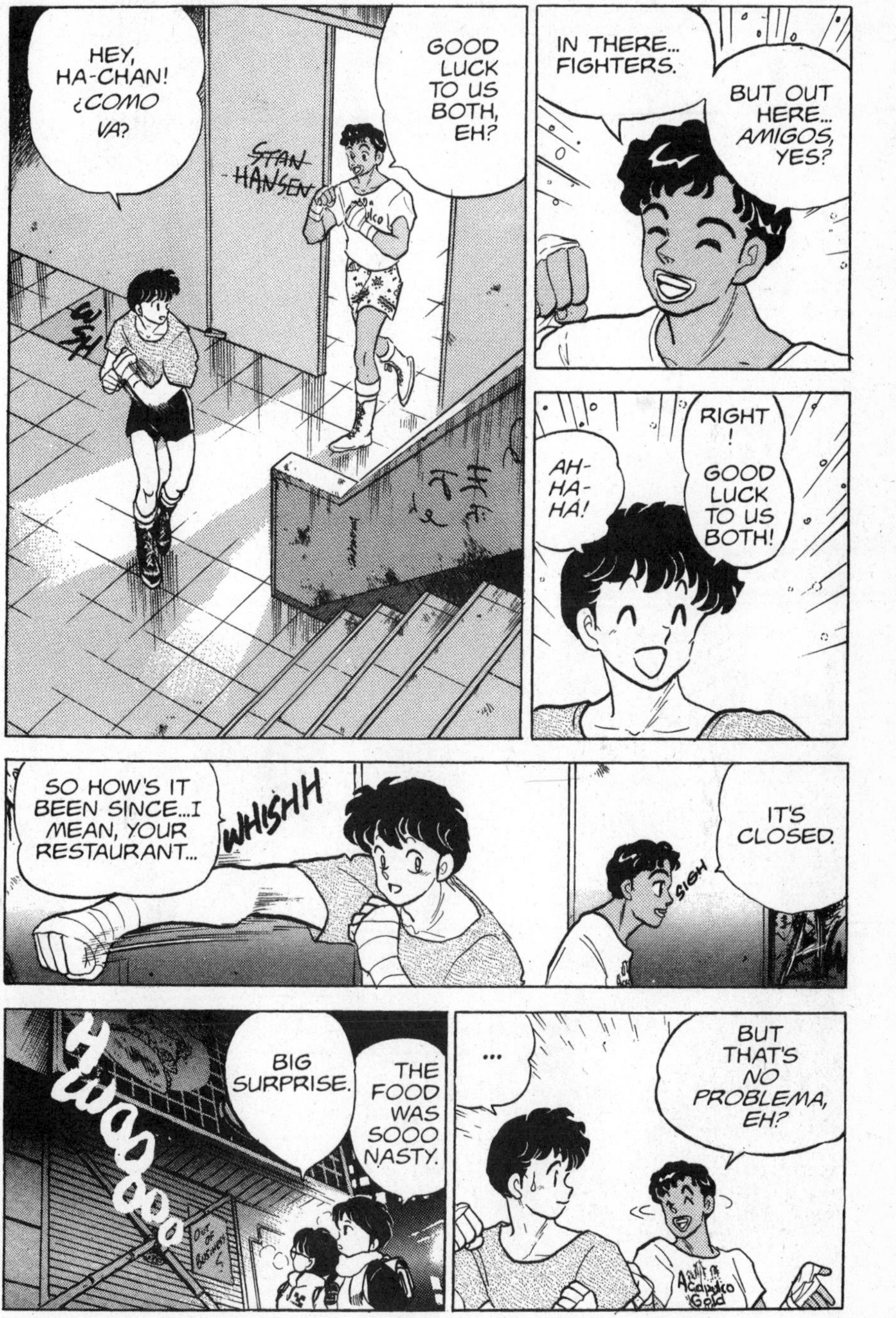
HEY, HA-CHAN! ¿COMO VA?
GOOD LUCK TO US BOTH, EH?
STAN HANSEN
IN THERE... FIGHTERS.
BUT OUT HERE... AMIGOS, YES?
AH-HA-HA!
RIGHT! GOOD LUCK TO US BOTH!
SO HOW'S IT BEEN SINCE...I MEAN, YOUR RESTAURANT...
WHISHH
SIGH
IT'S CLOSED.
HWOOOOO
BIG SURPRISE.
THE FOOD WAS SOOOO NASTY.
...
BUT THAT'S NO PROBLEMA, EH?
Acapulco Gold

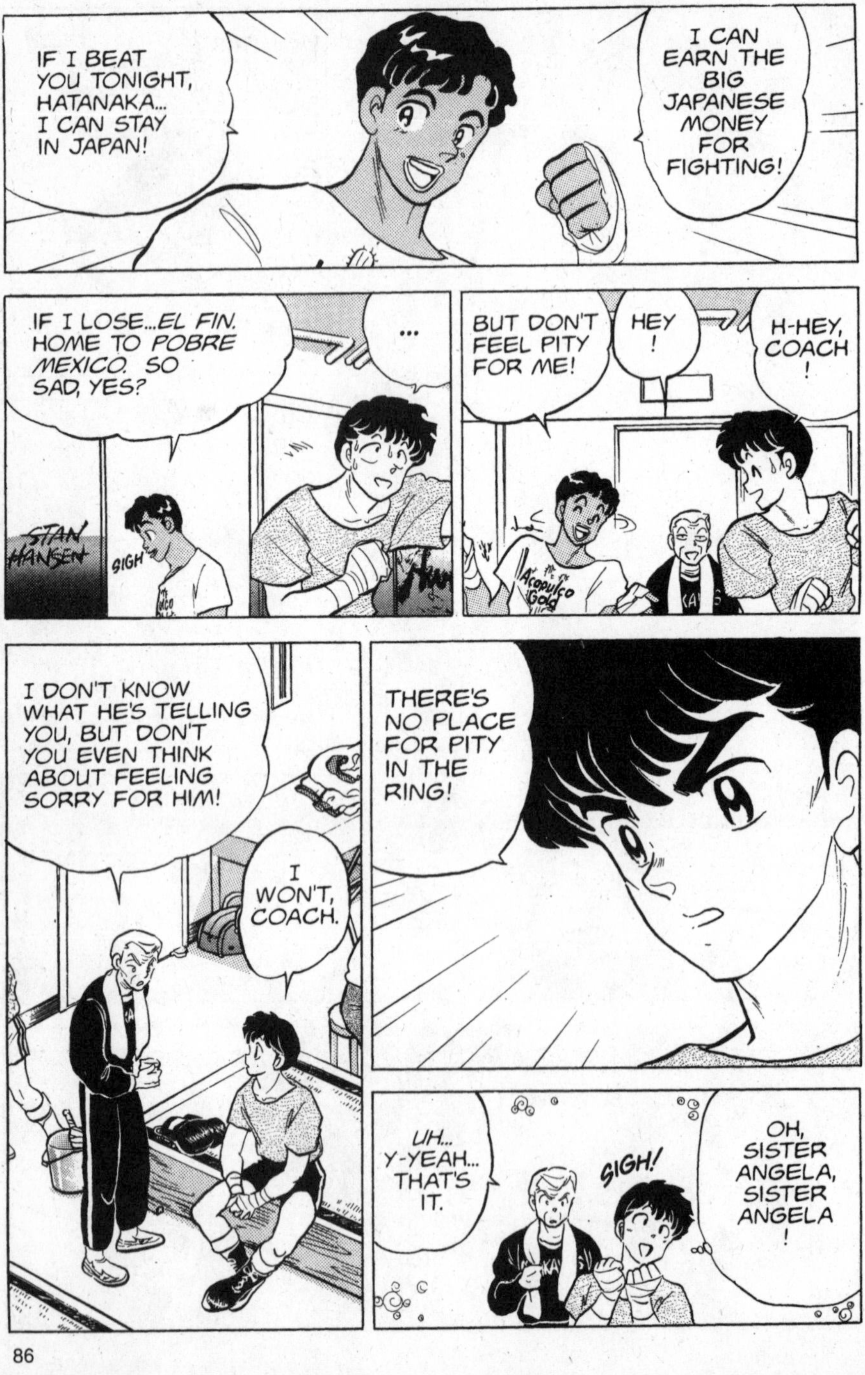
IF I BEAT YOU TONIGHT, HATANAKA... I CAN STAY IN JAPAN!
I CAN EARN THE BIG JAPANESE MONEY FOR FIGHTING!
IF I LOSE...EL FIN. HOME TO POBRE MEXICO. SO SAD, YES?
STAN HANSEN
SIGH
...
BUT DON'T FEEL PITY FOR ME!
HEY!
H-HEY, COACH!
Acapulco Gold
I DON'T KNOW WHAT HE'S TELLING YOU, BUT DON'T YOU EVEN THINK ABOUT FEELING SORRY FOR HIM!
I WON'T, COACH.
THERE'S NO PLACE FOR PITY IN THE RING!
UH... Y-YEAH... THAT'S IT.
SIGH!
OH, SISTER ANGELA, SISTER ANGELA!

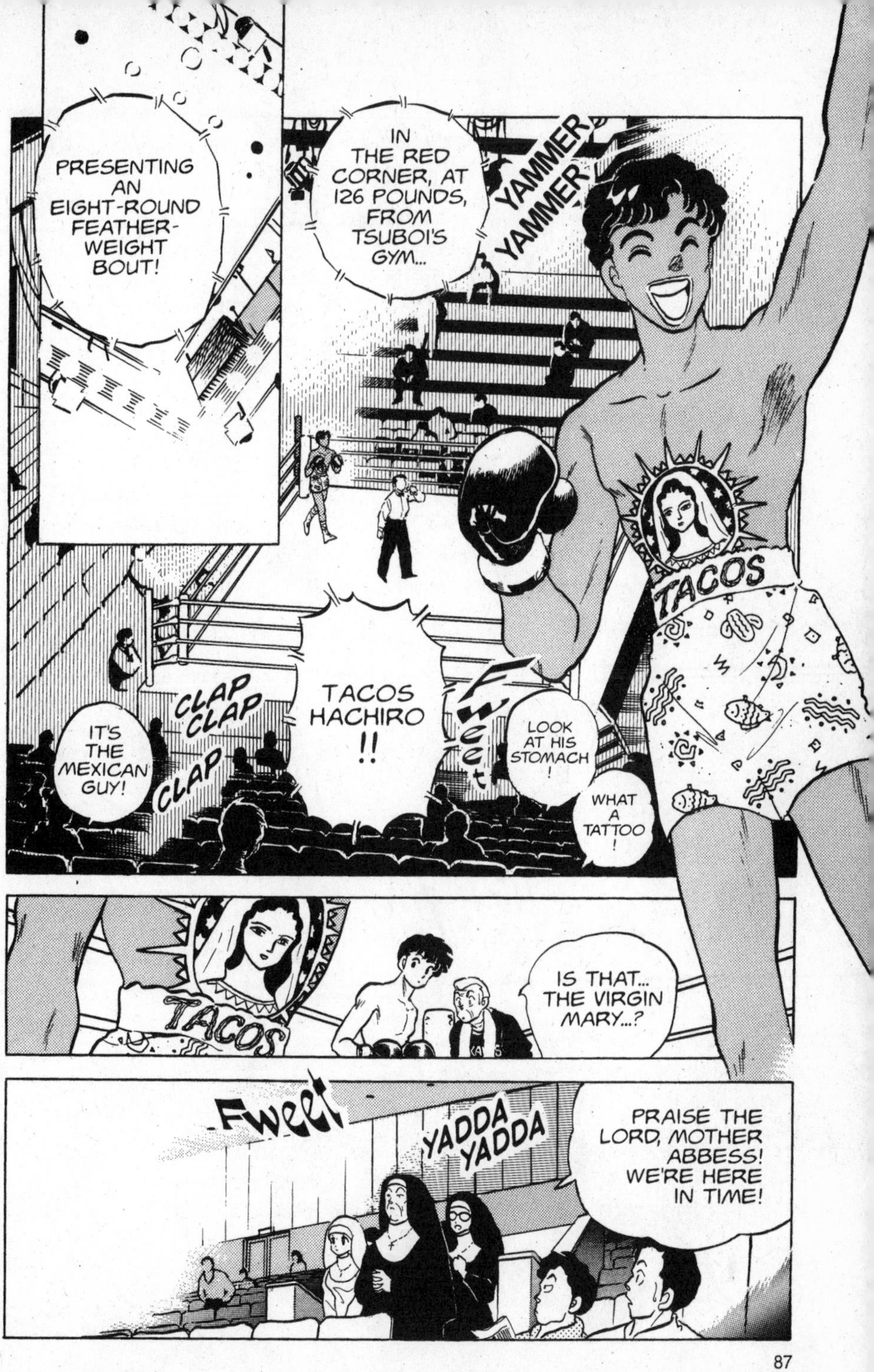
PRESENTING AN EIGHT-ROUND FEATHER-WEIGHT BOUT!
IN THE RED CORNER, AT 126 POUNDS, FROM TSUBOI'S GYM...
YAMMER YAMMER
IT'S THE MEXICAN GUY!
CLAP CLAP CLAP
TACOS HACHIRO !!
Fweet
LOOK AT HIS STOMACH!
WHAT A TATTOO!
TACOS
TACOS
IS THAT... THE VIRGIN MARY...?
Fweet
YADDA YADDA
PRAISE THE LORD, MOTHER ABBESS! WE'RE HERE IN TIME!

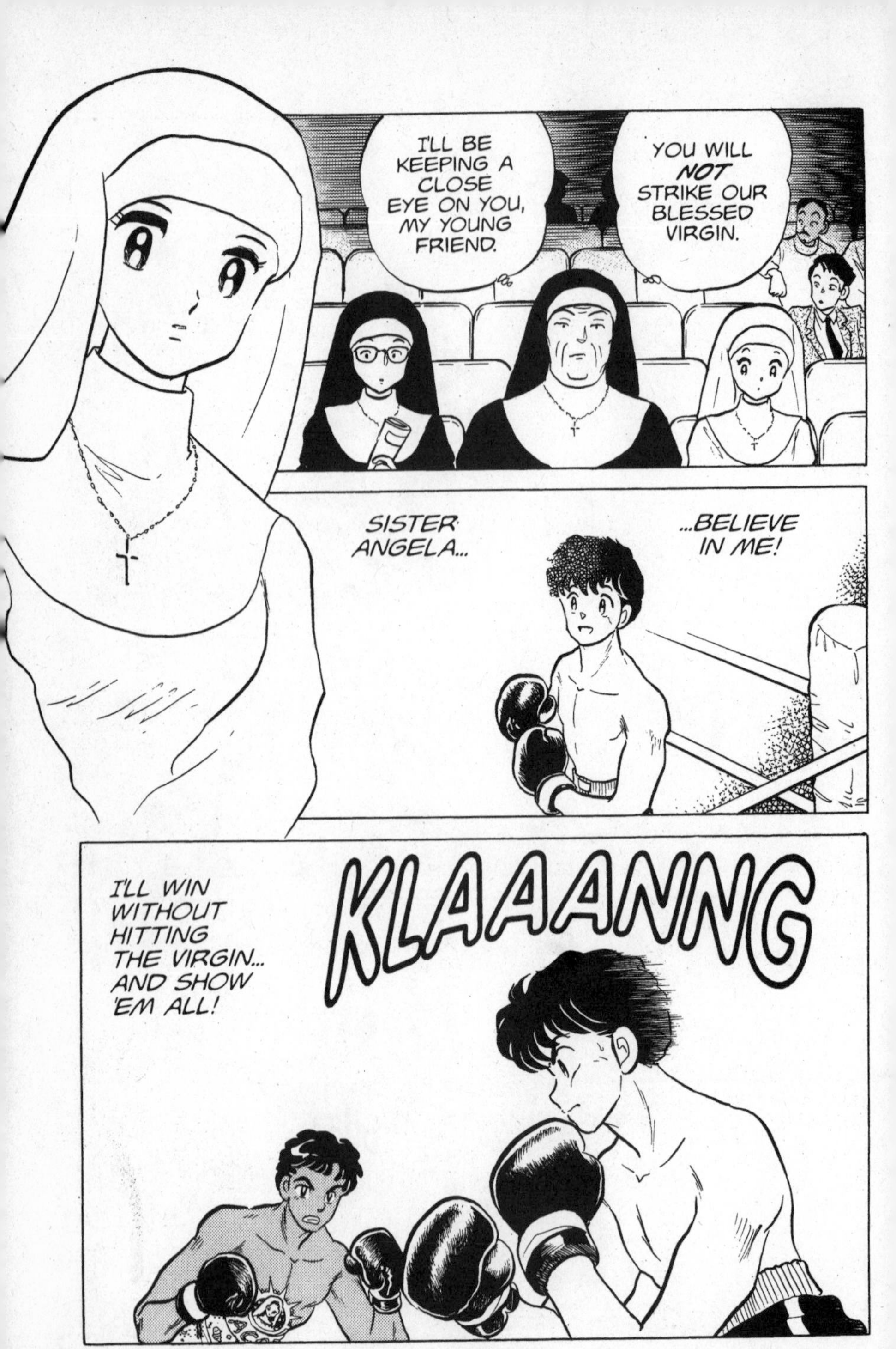
I'LL BE KEEPING A CLOSE EYE ON YOU, MY YOUNG FRIEND.
YOU WILL NOT STRIKE OUR BLESSED VIRGIN.
SISTER ANGELA...
...BELIEVE IN ME!
I'LL WIN WITHOUT HITTING THE VIRGIN... AND SHOW 'EM ALL!
KLAAANNG

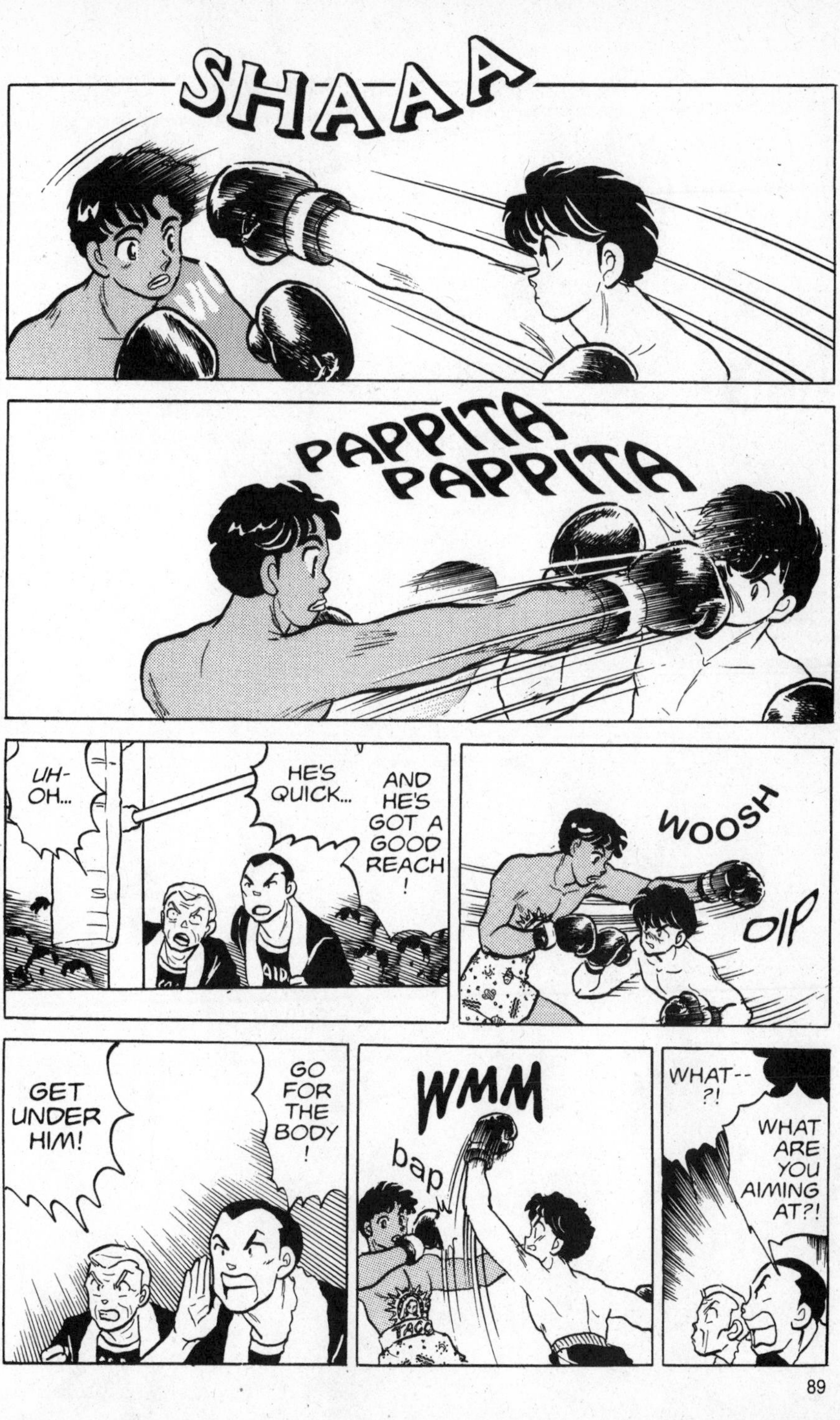
SHAAA
PAPPITA PAPPITA
UH-OH...
HE'S QUICK...
AND HE'S GOT A GOOD REACH!
WOOSH
OIP
GET UNDER HIM!
GO FOR THE BODY!
WMM
bap
WHAT--?!
WHAT ARE YOU AIMING AT?!

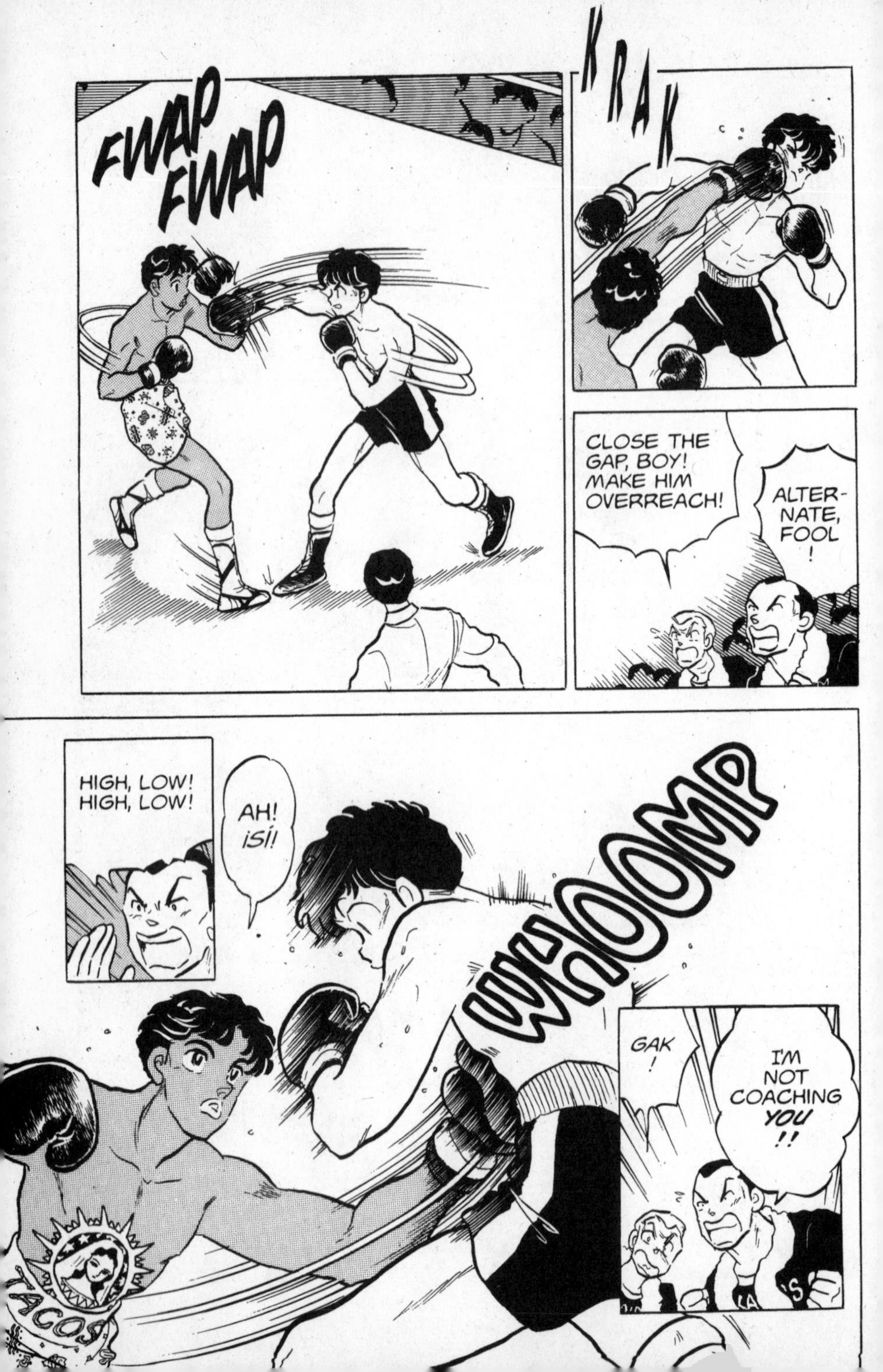
FWAP FWAP
KRAK
CLOSE THE GAP, BOY! MAKE HIM OVERREACH!
ALTER-NATE, FOOL!
HIGH, LOW! HIGH, LOW!
AH! ¡SÍ!
WHOOMP
GAK!
I'M NOT COACHING YOU!!

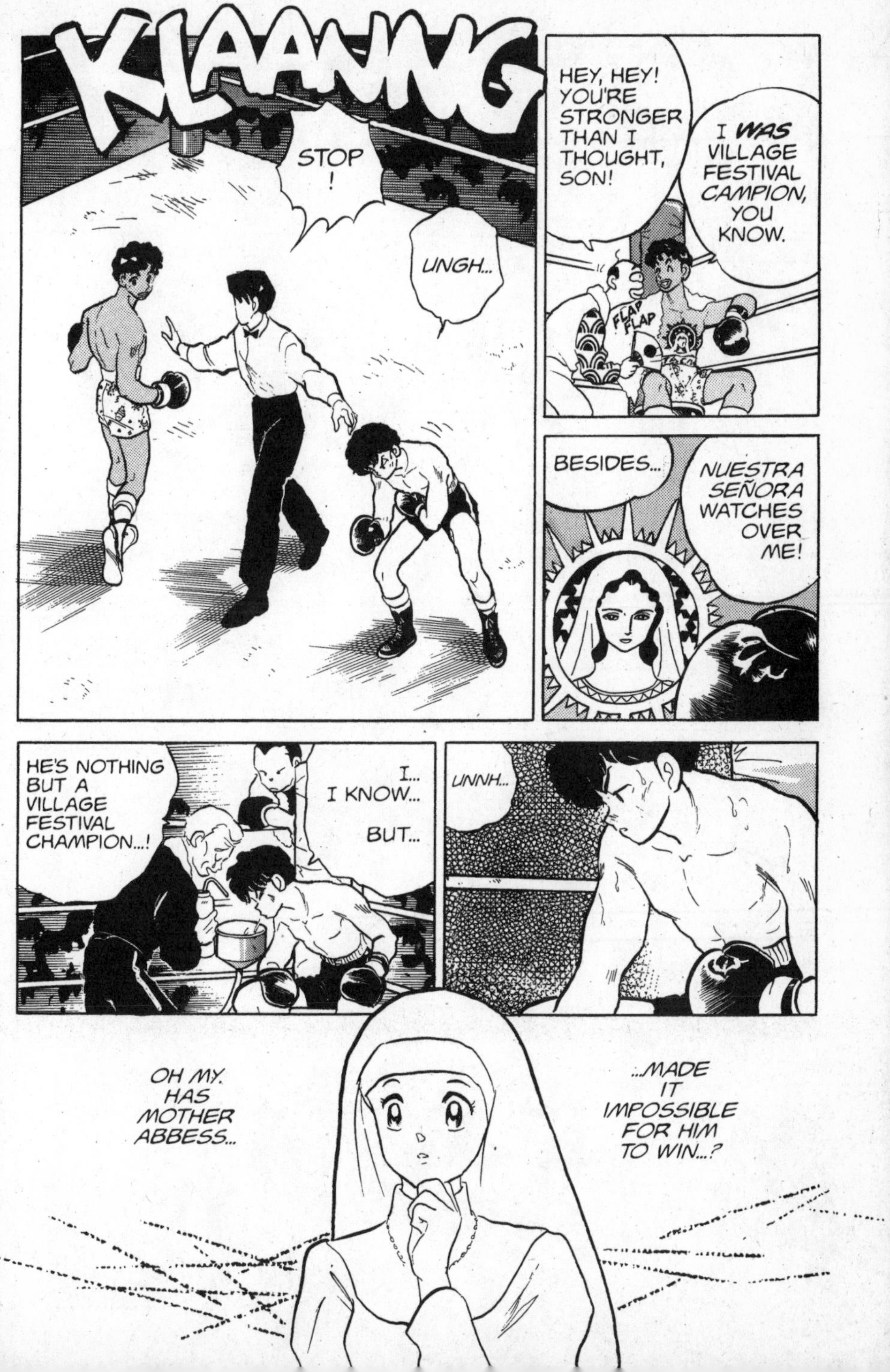
KLAANNG
STOP!
UNGH...
HEY, HEY! YOU'RE STRONGER THAN I THOUGHT, SON!
I WAS VILLAGE FESTIVAL CAMPION, YOU KNOW.
FLAP FLAP
BESIDES...
NUESTRA SEÑORA WATCHES OVER ME!
HE'S NOTHING BUT A VILLAGE FESTIVAL CHAMPION...!
I... I KNOW... BUT...
UNNH...
OH MY. HAS MOTHER ABBESS...
...MADE IT IMPOSSIBLE FOR HIM TO WIN...?

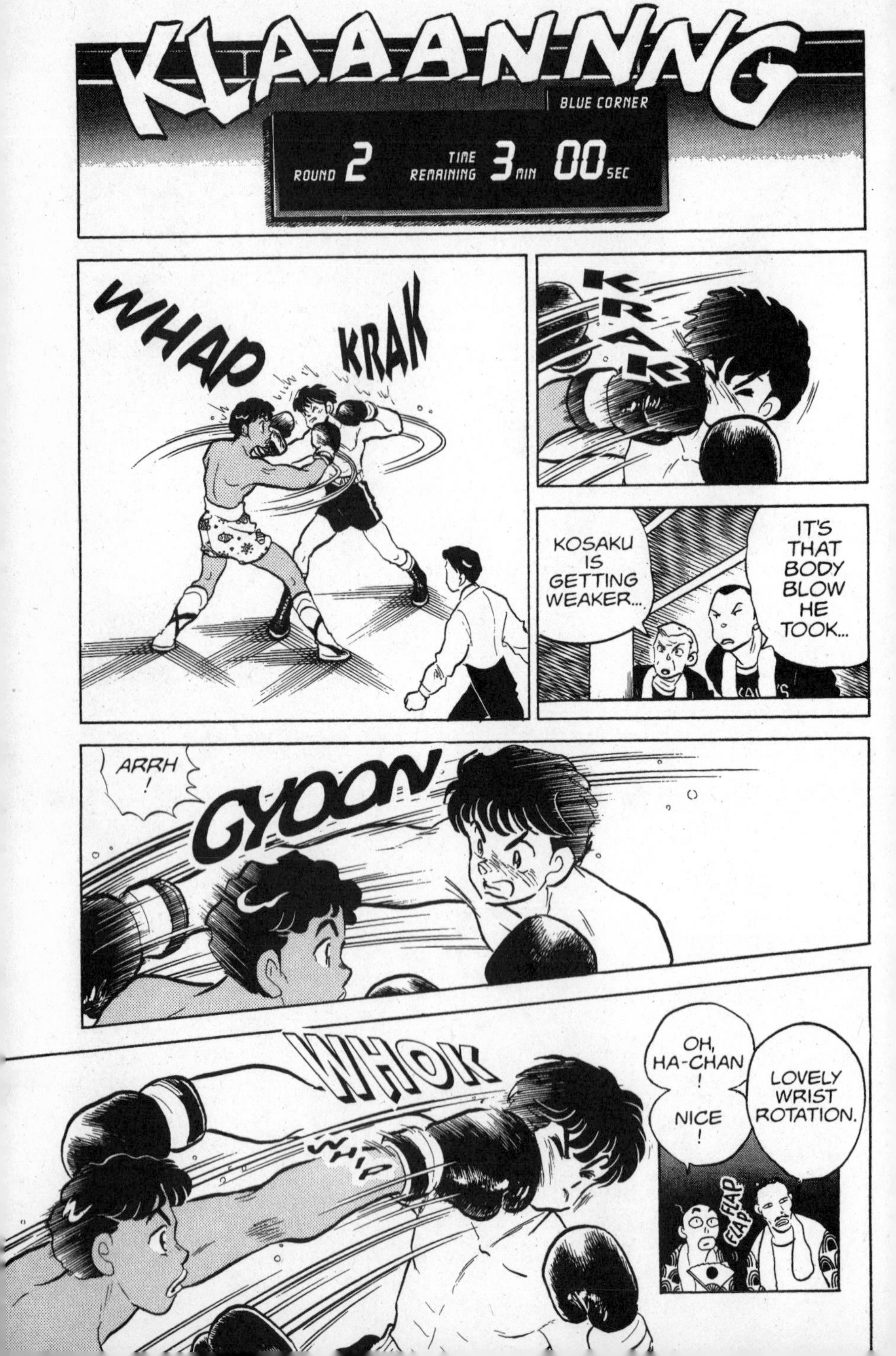
KLAAANNNG
BLUE CORNER
ROUND 2 TIME REMAINING 3 MIN 00 SEC
WHAP
KRAK
KRAB
KOSAKU IS GETTING WEAKER...
IT'S THAT BODY BLOW HE TOOK...
ARRH!
GYOON
WHOK
WHIP
OH, HA-CHAN!
NICE!
LOVELY WRIST ROTATION.
FLAP FLAP

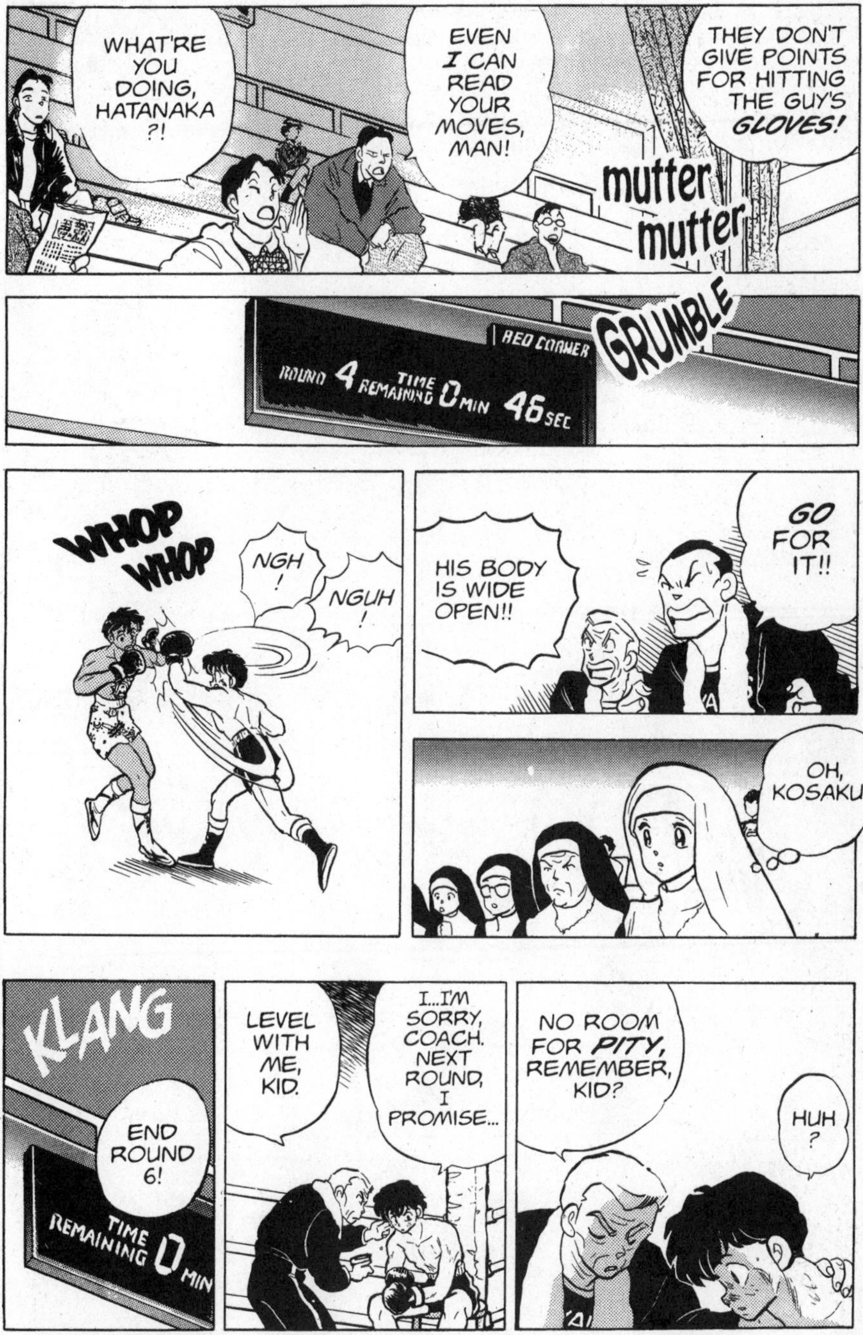
WHAT'RE YOU DOING, HATANAKA?!
EVEN I CAN READ YOUR MOVES, MAN!
THEY DON'T GIVE POINTS FOR HITTING THE GUY'S GLOVES!
mutter mutter
RED CORNER
ROUND 4 TIME REMAINING 0 MIN 46 SEC
GRUMBLE
WHOP WHOP
NGH!
NGUH!
HIS BODY IS WIDE OPEN!!
GO FOR IT!!
OH, KOSAKU...
KLANG
END ROUND 6!
TIME REMAINING 0 MIN
LEVEL WITH ME, KID.
I...I'M SORRY, COACH. NEXT ROUND, I PROMISE...
NO ROOM FOR PITY, REMEMBER, KID?
HUH?

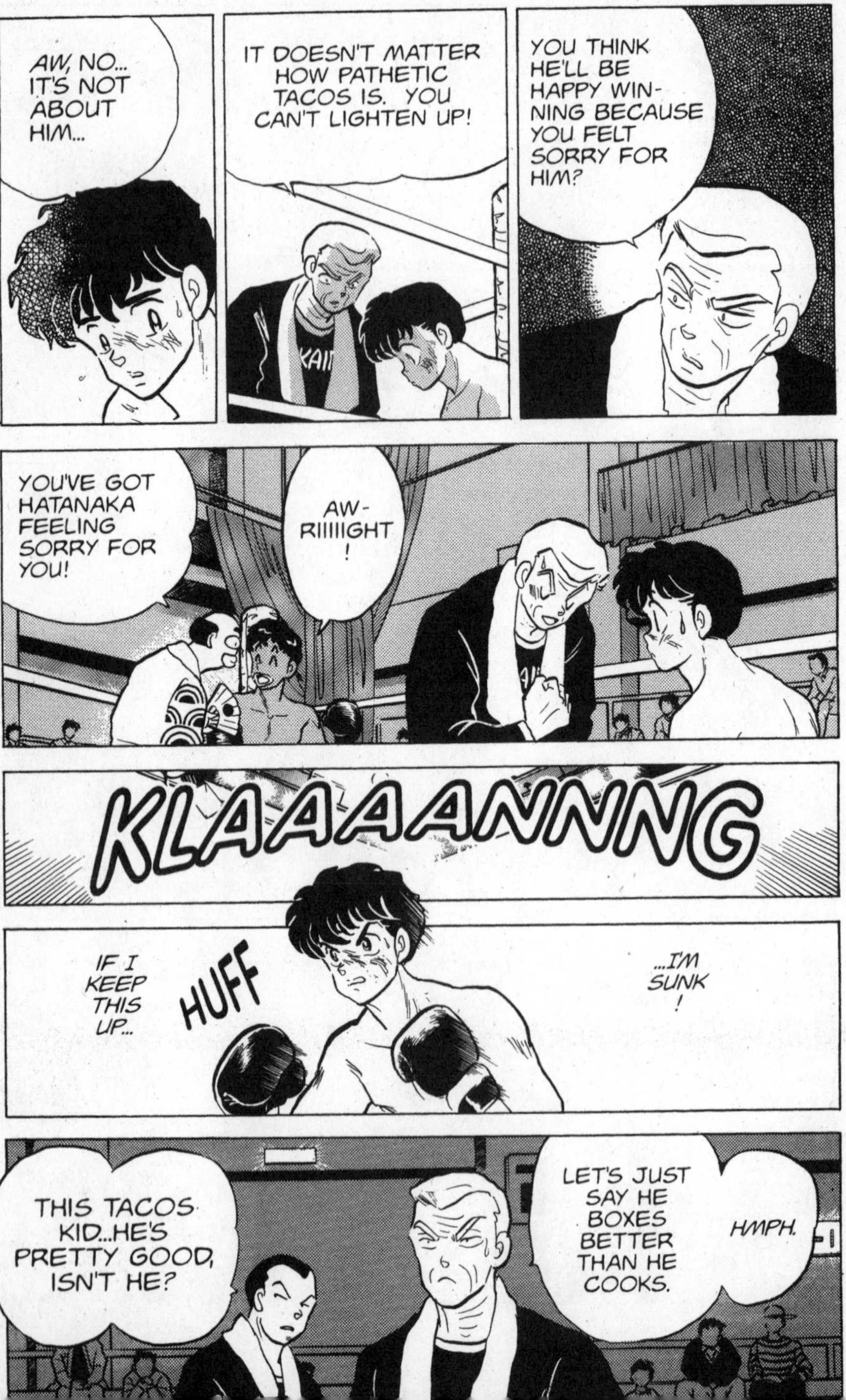
AW, NO... IT'S NOT ABOUT HIM...
IT DOESN'T MATTER HOW PATHETIC TACOS IS. YOU CAN'T LIGHTEN UP!
YOU THINK HE'LL BE HAPPY WIN-NING BECAUSE YOU FELT SORRY FOR HIM?
YOU'VE GOT HATANAKA FEELING SORRY FOR YOU!
AW-RIIIIIGHT!
KLAAAANNNG
IF I KEEP THIS UP...
HUFF
...I'M SUNK!
THIS TACOS KID...HE'S PRETTY GOOD, ISN'T HE?
LET'S JUST SAY HE BOXES BETTER THAN HE COOKS.
HMPH.

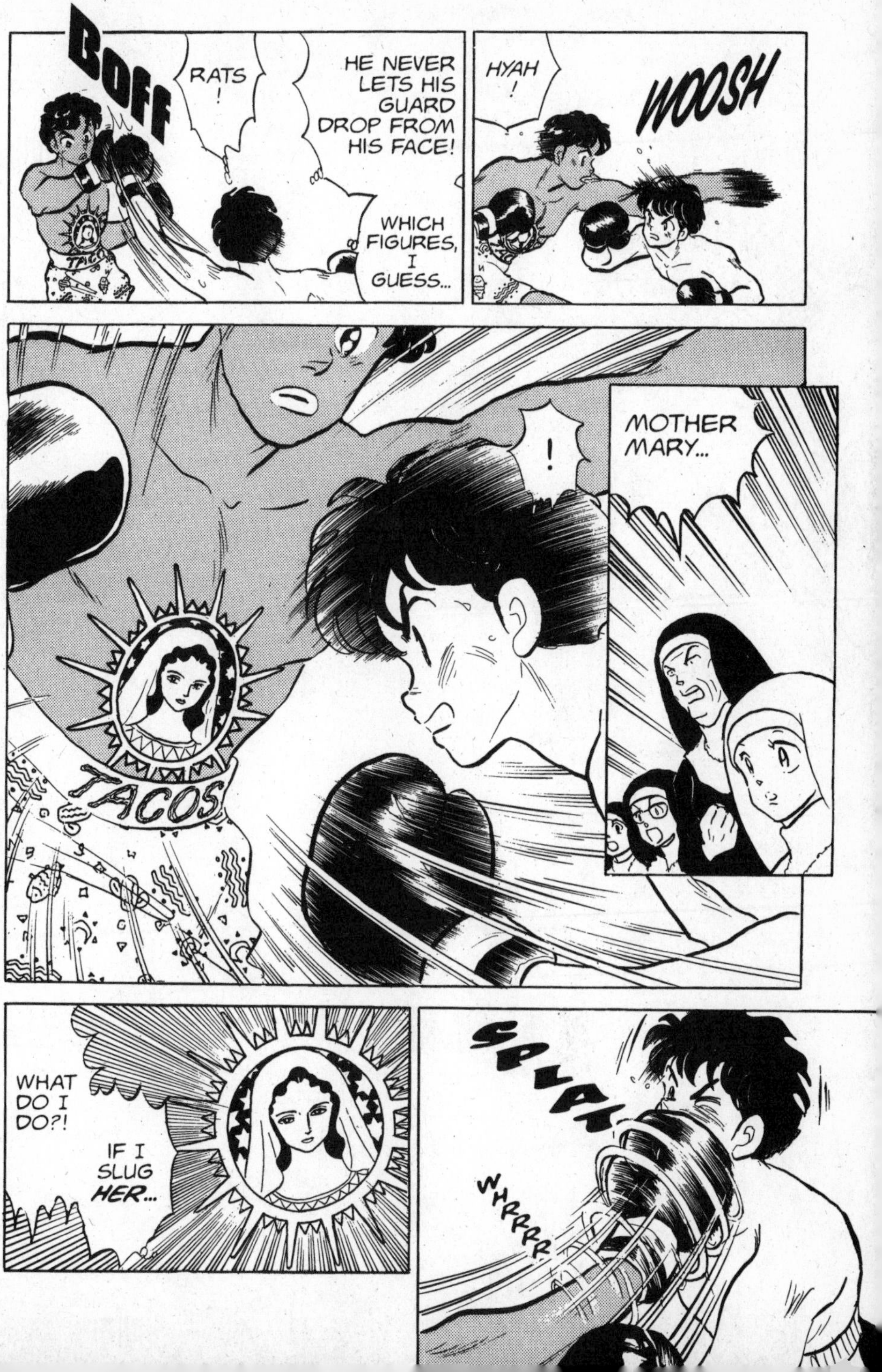
BOFF
RATS!
HE NEVER LETS HIS GUARD DROP FROM HIS FACE!
WHICH FIGURES, I GUESS...
HYAH!
WOOSH
TACOS
!
MOTHER MARY...
WHAT DO I DO?!
IF I SLUG *HER*...
SPLAK
WHRRRR

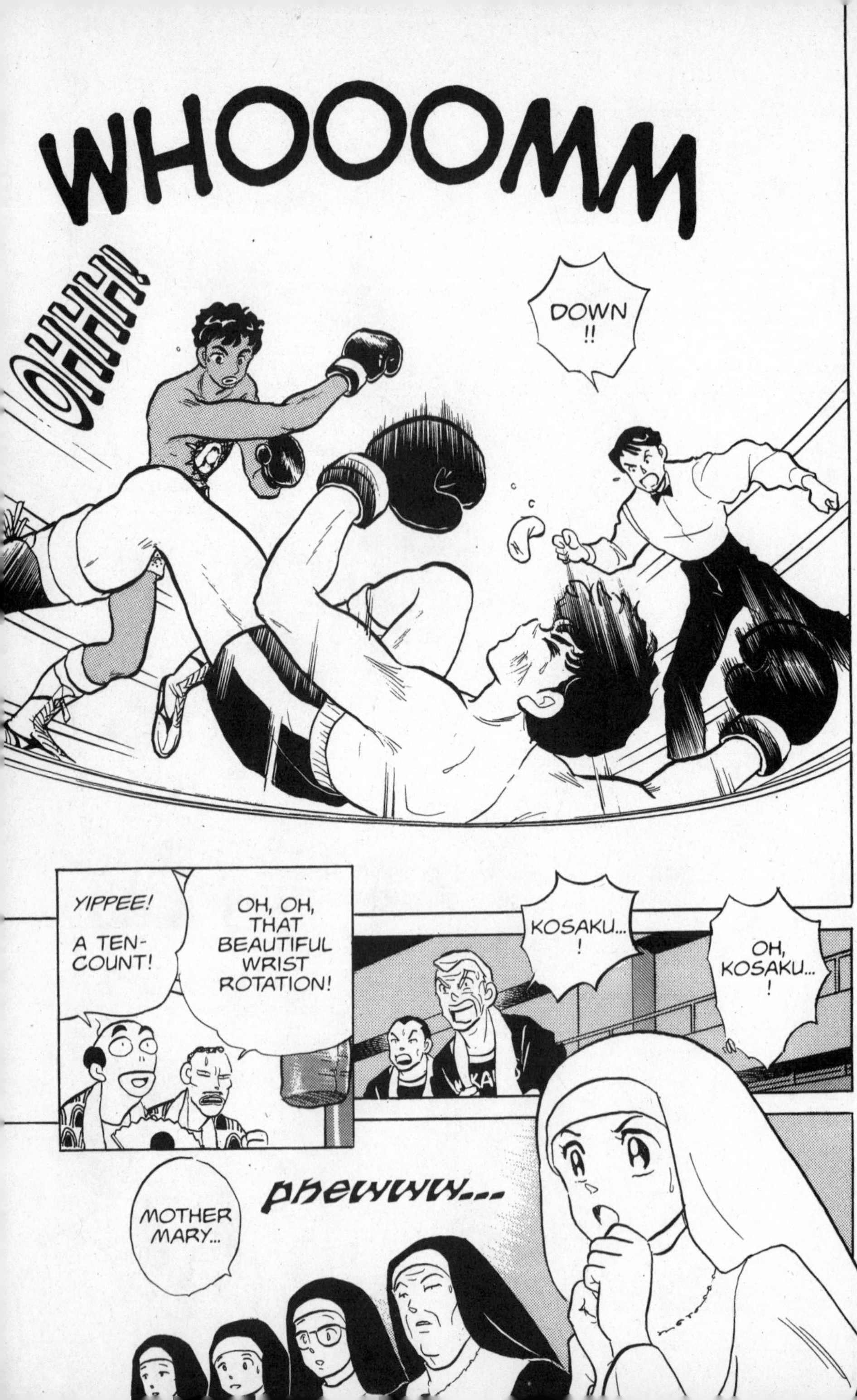
WHOOOMM
DOWN!!
YIPPEE!
A TEN-COUNT!
OH, OH, THAT BEAUTIFUL WRIST ROTATION!
KOSAKU...!
OH, KOSAKU...!
MOTHER MARY...
phewww...

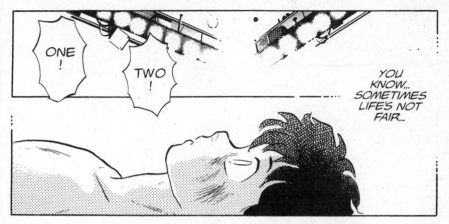

ONE
!

TWO
!

YOU KNOW... SOMETIMES LIFE'S NOT FAIR...

FOUR
!

FIVE
!

SIX
!

SISTER! I'M SORRY!

I HAVE TO RUIN OUR CHRISTMAS
!

WHAT...?

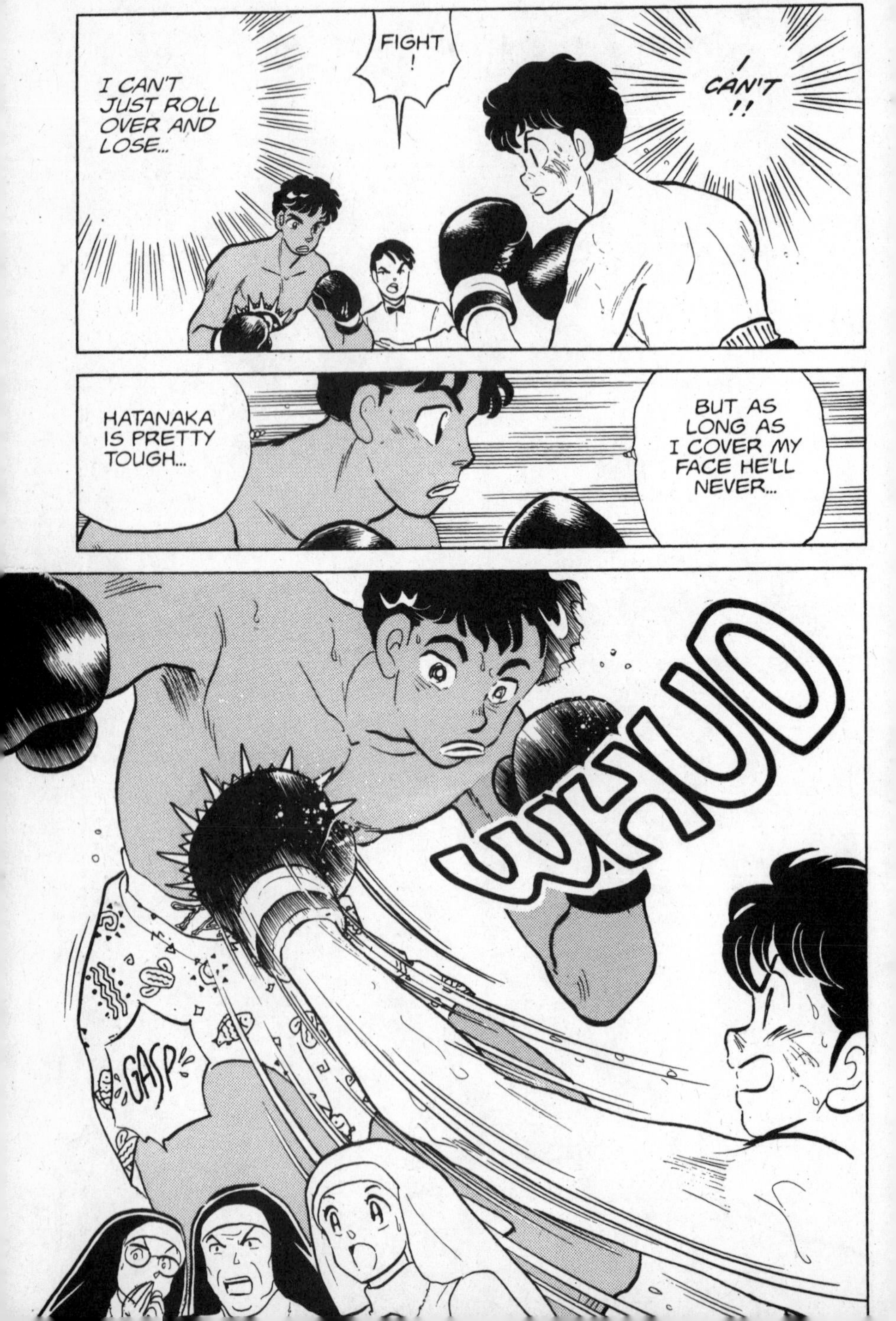
I CAN'T JUST ROLL OVER AND LOSE...
FIGHT!
I CAN'T!!
HATANAKA IS PRETTY TOUGH...
BUT AS LONG AS I COVER MY FACE HE'LL NEVER...
WHUD
GASP

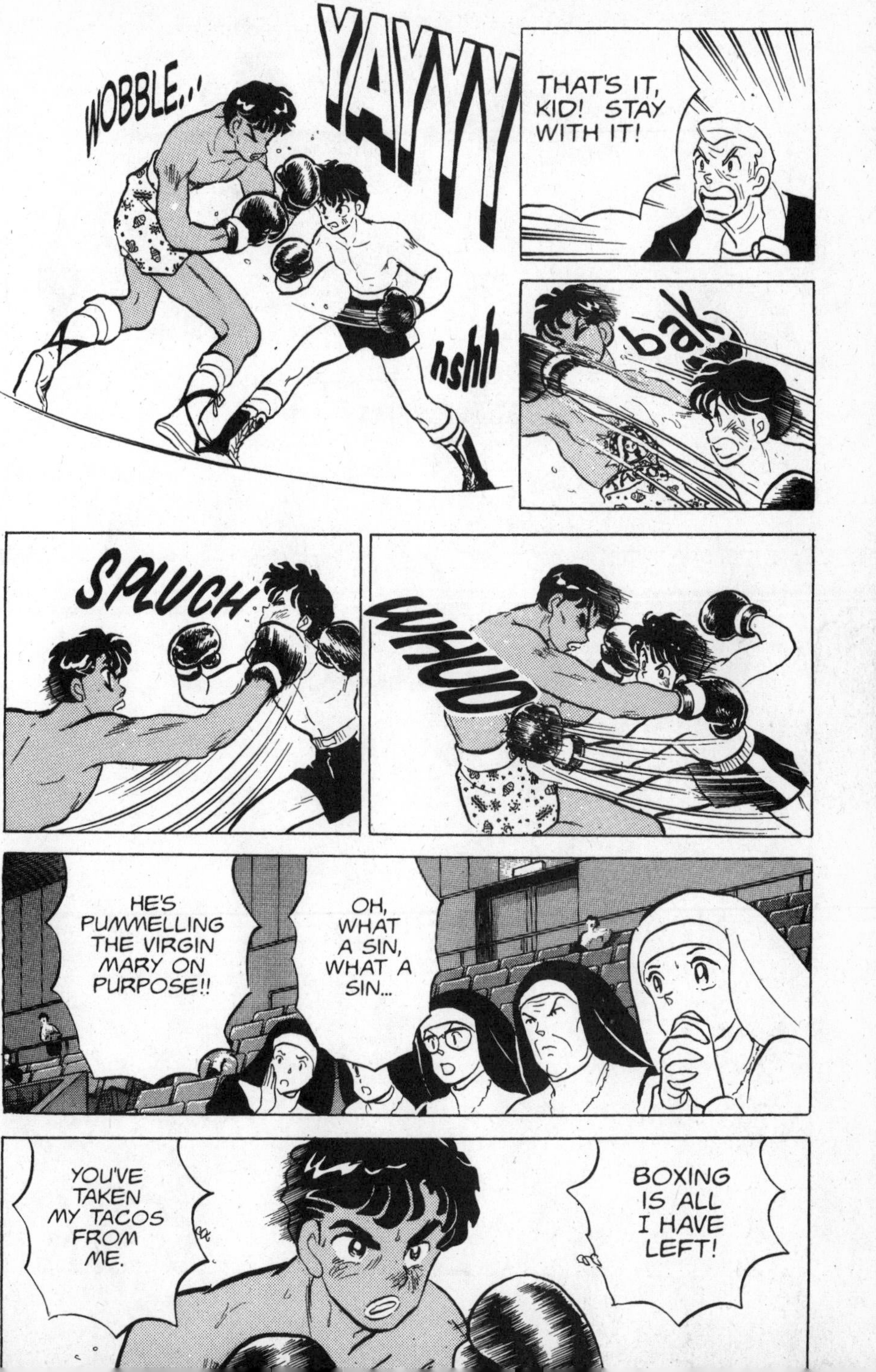
WOBBLE...
YAYYY
THAT'S IT, KID! STAY WITH IT!
hshh
bak
SPLUCH
WHUD
HE'S PUMMELLING THE VIRGIN MARY ON PURPOSE!!
OH, WHAT A SIN, WHAT A SIN...
YOU'VE TAKEN MY TACOS FROM ME.
BOXING IS ALL I HAVE LEFT!

BLACH

I WON'T LOSE THAT!!

WIN OR LOSE...

I'VE GOTTA GIVE IT EVERY-THING...

BWONK

NO MORE HUMILIATING MYSELF...

FOO FOO

AI...

HATANAKA'S PUNCHES...

...THEY HURT!

TATTOO MAN LOOKS FROZEN!

BODY BLOWS AFFECT YOUR LEGS, TOO.

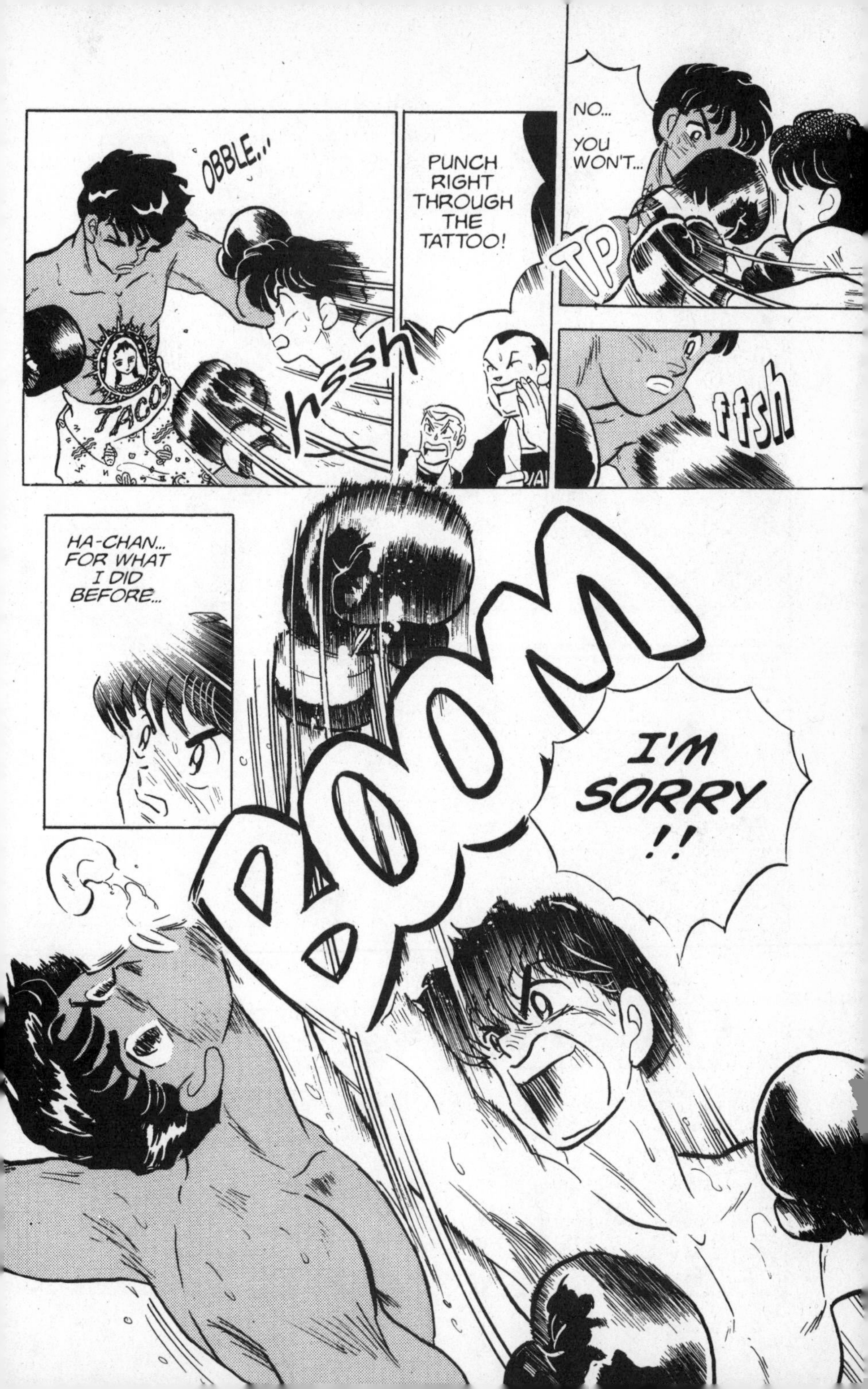
OBBLE...
rssh
PUNCH RIGHT THROUGH THE TATTOO!
NO... YOU WON'T...
TP
ffsh
HA-CHAN... FOR WHAT I DID BEFORE...
BOOM
I'M SORRY !!

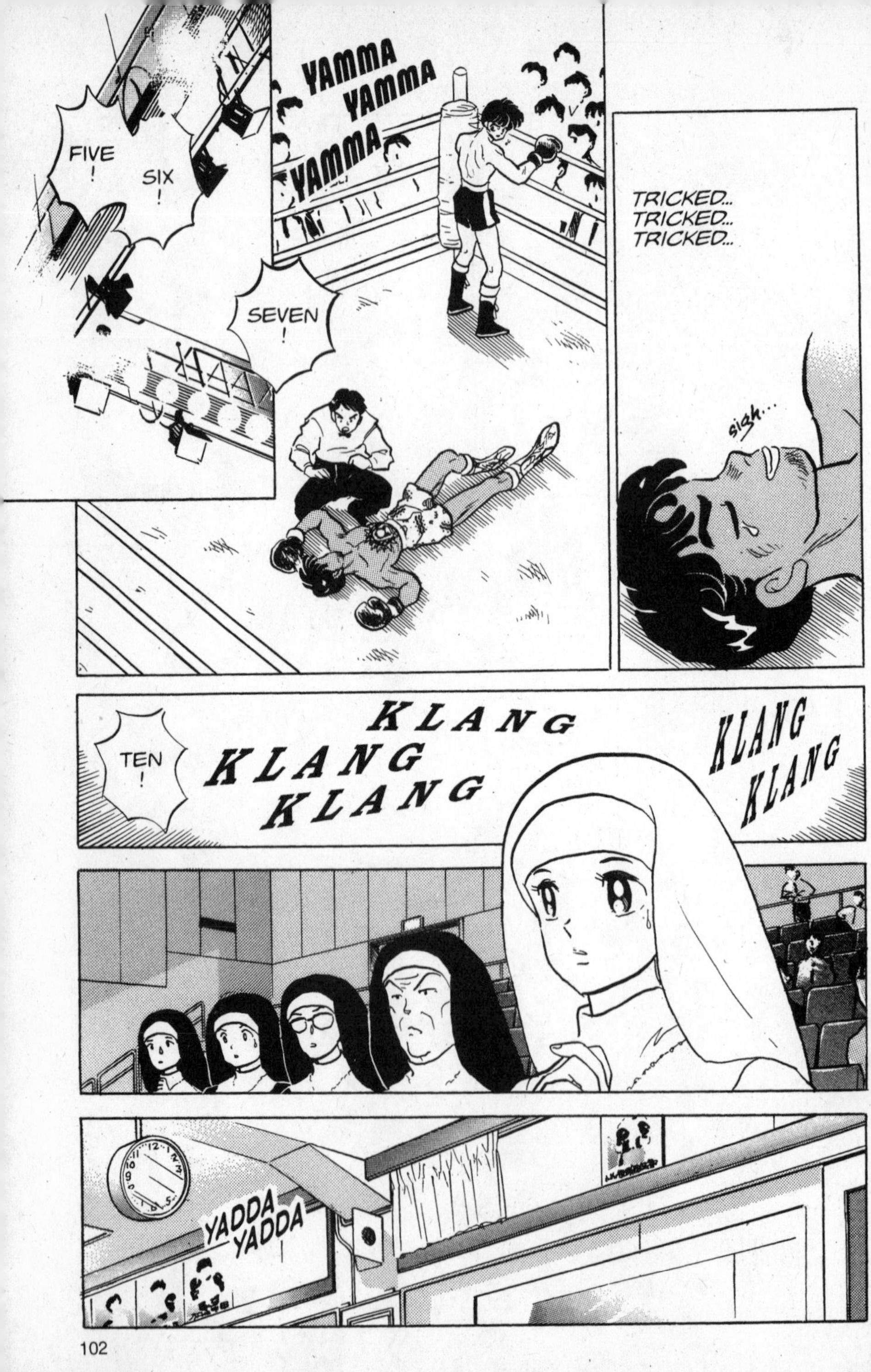

FIVE! SIX!
YAMMA YAMMA YAMMA
SEVEN!
TRICKED... TRICKED... TRICKED...
sigh...
TEN!
KLANG KLANG KLANG
KLANG KLANG
YADDA YADDA!

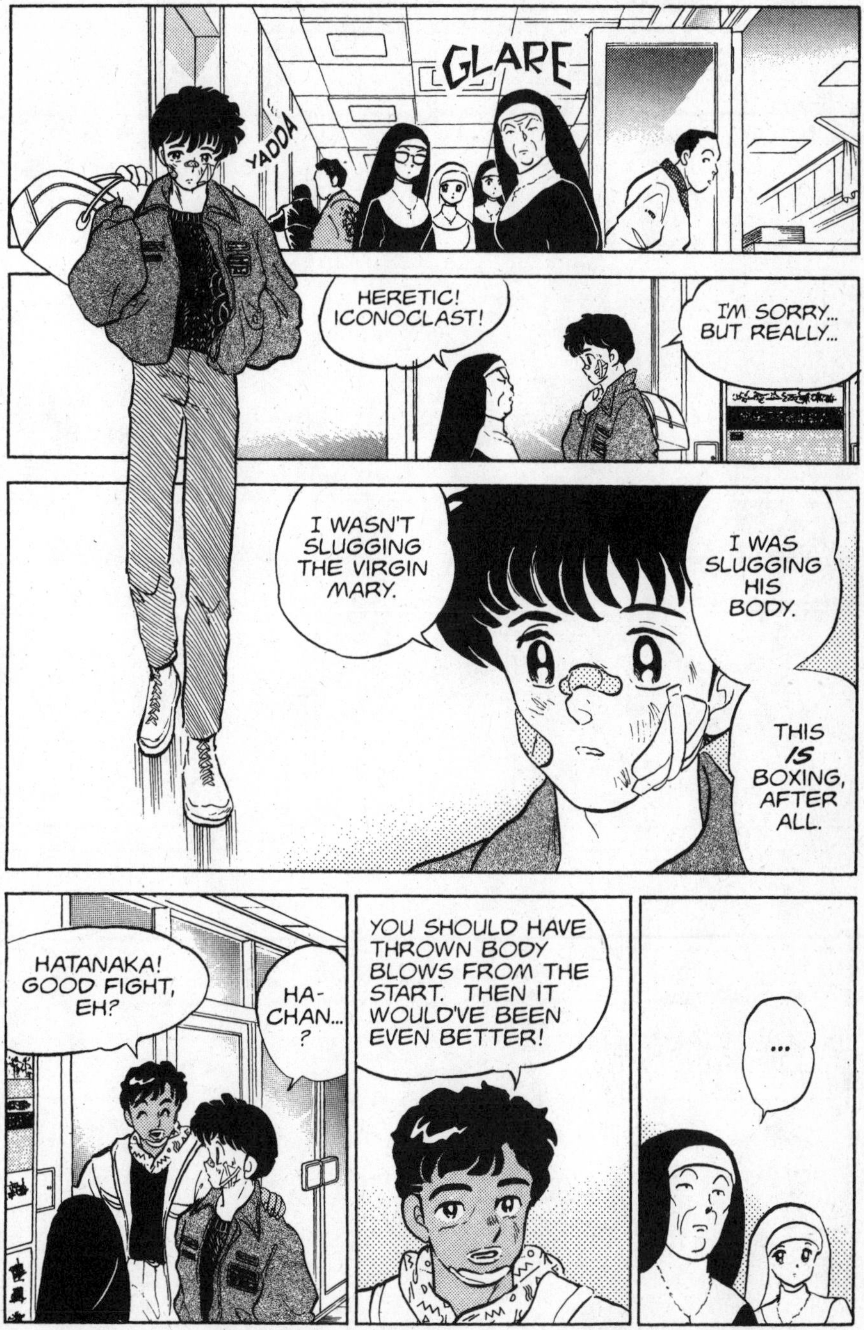
GLARE
YADDA
HERETIC! ICONOCLAST!
I'M SORRY... BUT REALLY...
I WASN'T SLUGGING THE VIRGIN MARY.
I WAS SLUGGING HIS BODY.
THIS IS BOXING, AFTER ALL.
HATANAKA! GOOD FIGHT, EH?
HA-CHAN...?
YOU SHOULD HAVE THROWN BODY BLOWS FROM THE START. THEN IT WOULD'VE BEEN EVEN BETTER!
...

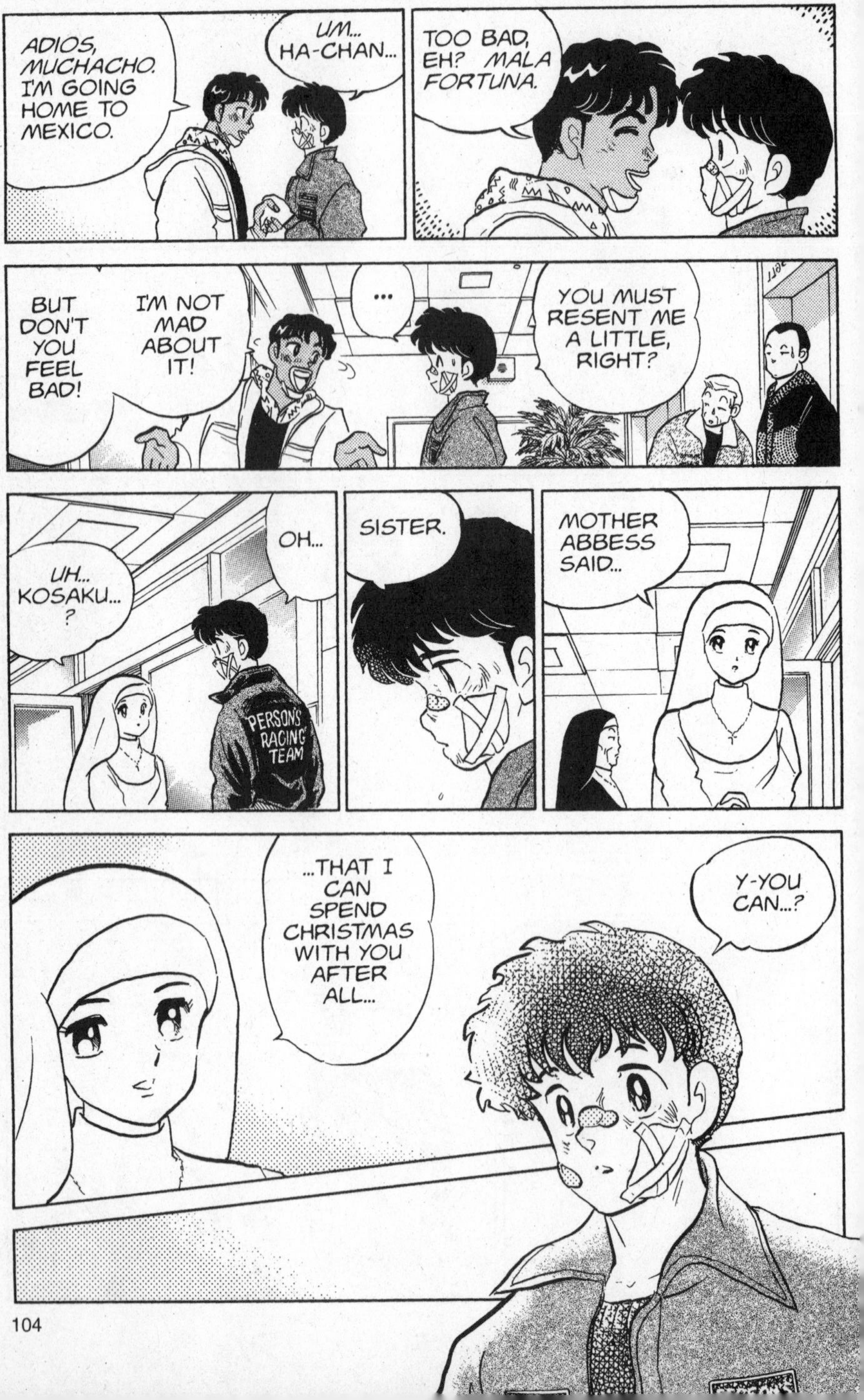
ADIOS, MUCHACHO. I'M GOING HOME TO MEXICO.
UM... HA-CHAN...
TOO BAD, EH? MALA FORTUNA.
BUT DON'T YOU FEEL BAD!
I'M NOT MAD ABOUT IT!
...
YOU MUST RESENT ME A LITTLE, RIGHT?
UH... KOSAKU... ?
OH...
PERSON'S RACING TEAM
SISTER.
MOTHER ABBESS SAID...
...THAT I CAN SPEND CHRISTMAS WITH YOU AFTER ALL...
Y-YOU CAN...?

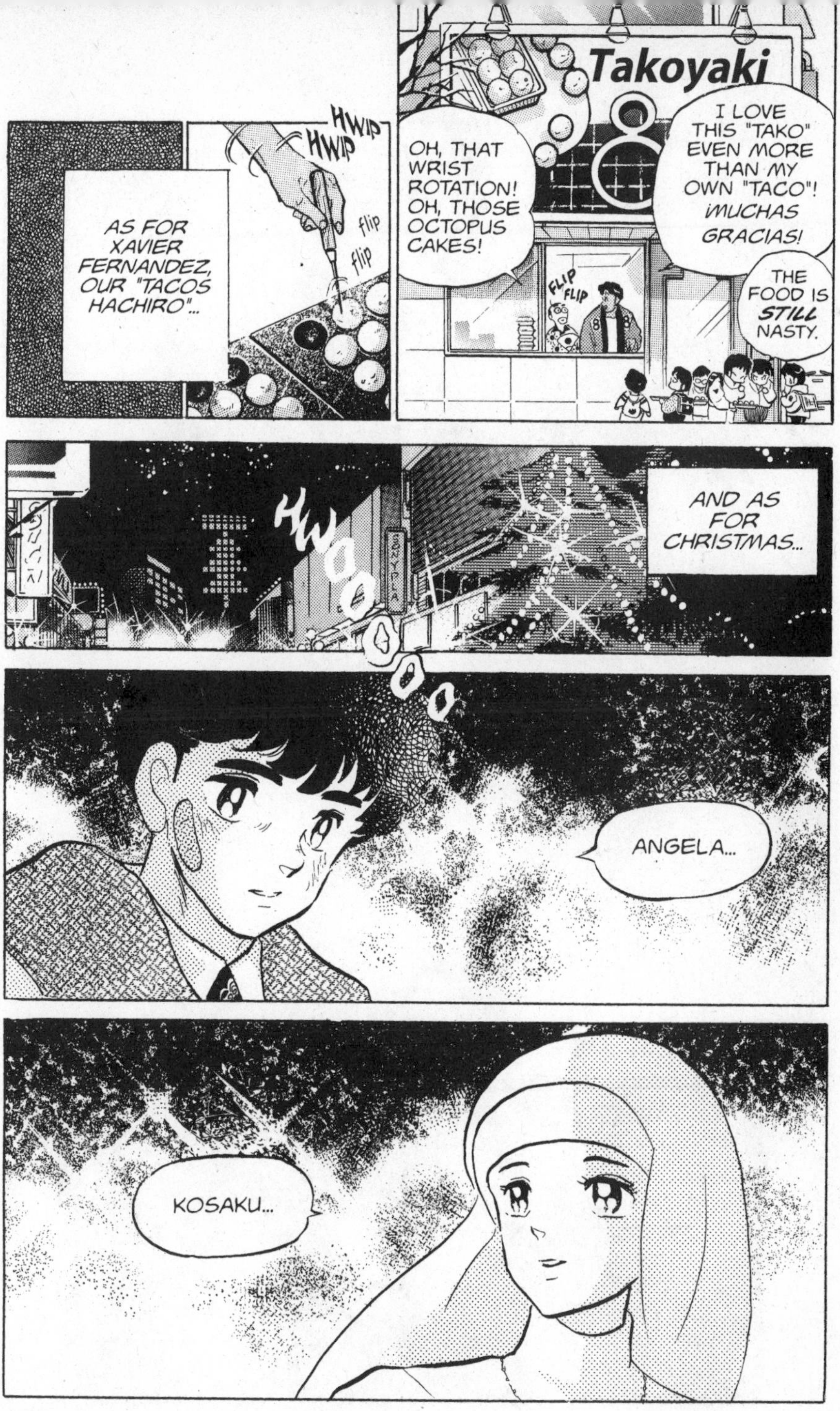
HWIP HWIP
AS FOR XAVIER FERNANDEZ, OUR "TACOS HACHIRO"...
flip flip
Takoyaki
OH, THAT WRIST ROTATION! OH, THOSE OCTOPUS CAKES!
I LOVE THIS "TAKO" EVEN MORE THAN MY OWN "TACO"! ¡MUCHAS GRACIAS!
FLIP FLIP
THE FOOD IS STILL NASTY.
HWOOOOOO
AND AS FOR CHRISTMAS...
ANGELA...
KOSAKU...

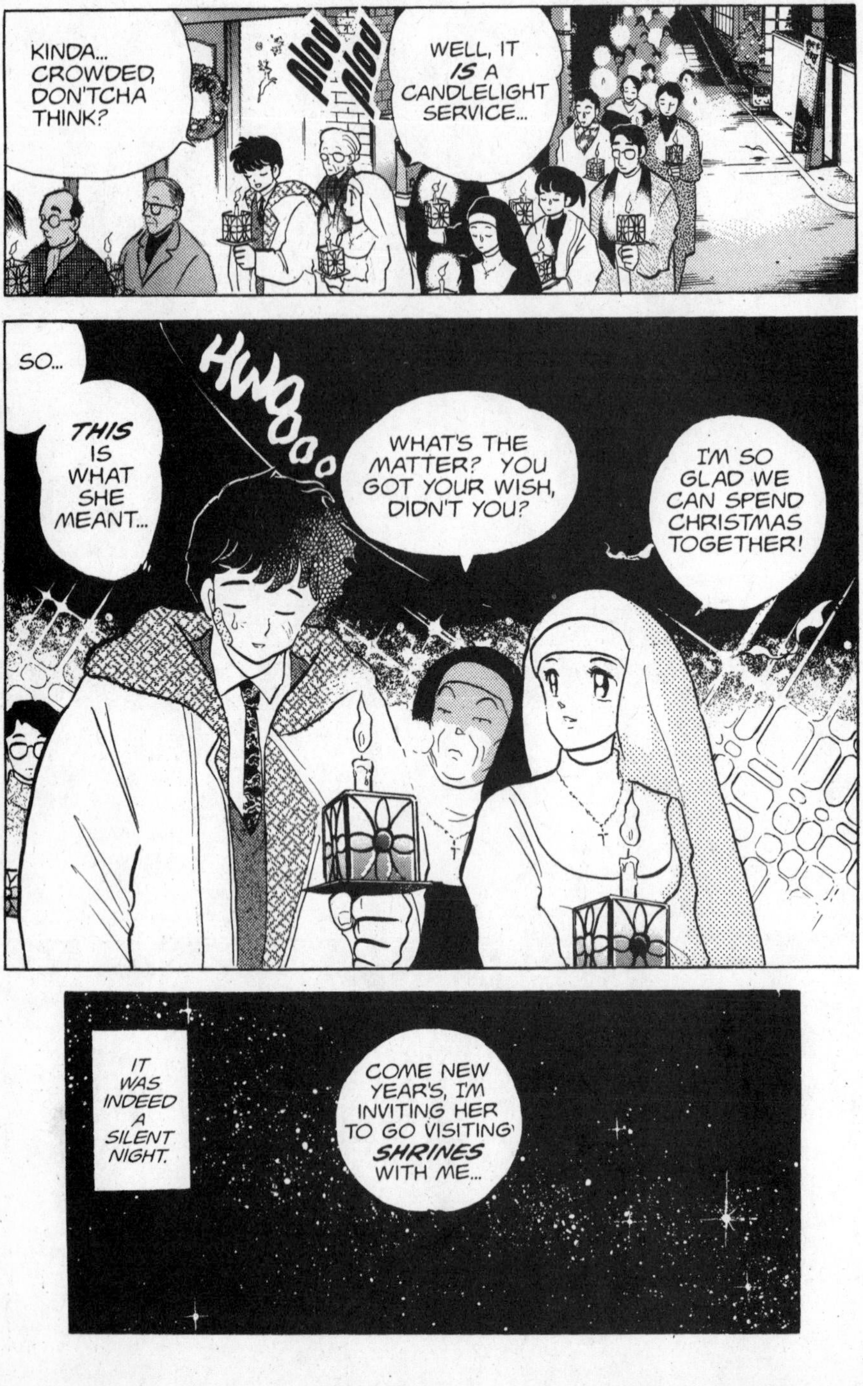
KINDA... CROWDED, DON'TCHA THINK?
plod plod
WELL, IT *IS* A CANDLELIGHT SERVICE...
SO...
THIS IS WHAT SHE MEANT...
HWOOOOO
WHAT'S THE MATTER? YOU GOT YOUR WISH, DIDN'T YOU?
I'M SO GLAD WE CAN SPEND CHRISTMAS TOGETHER!
IT WAS INDEED A SILENT NIGHT.
COME NEW YEAR'S, I'M INVITING HER TO GO VISITING *SHRINES* WITH ME...

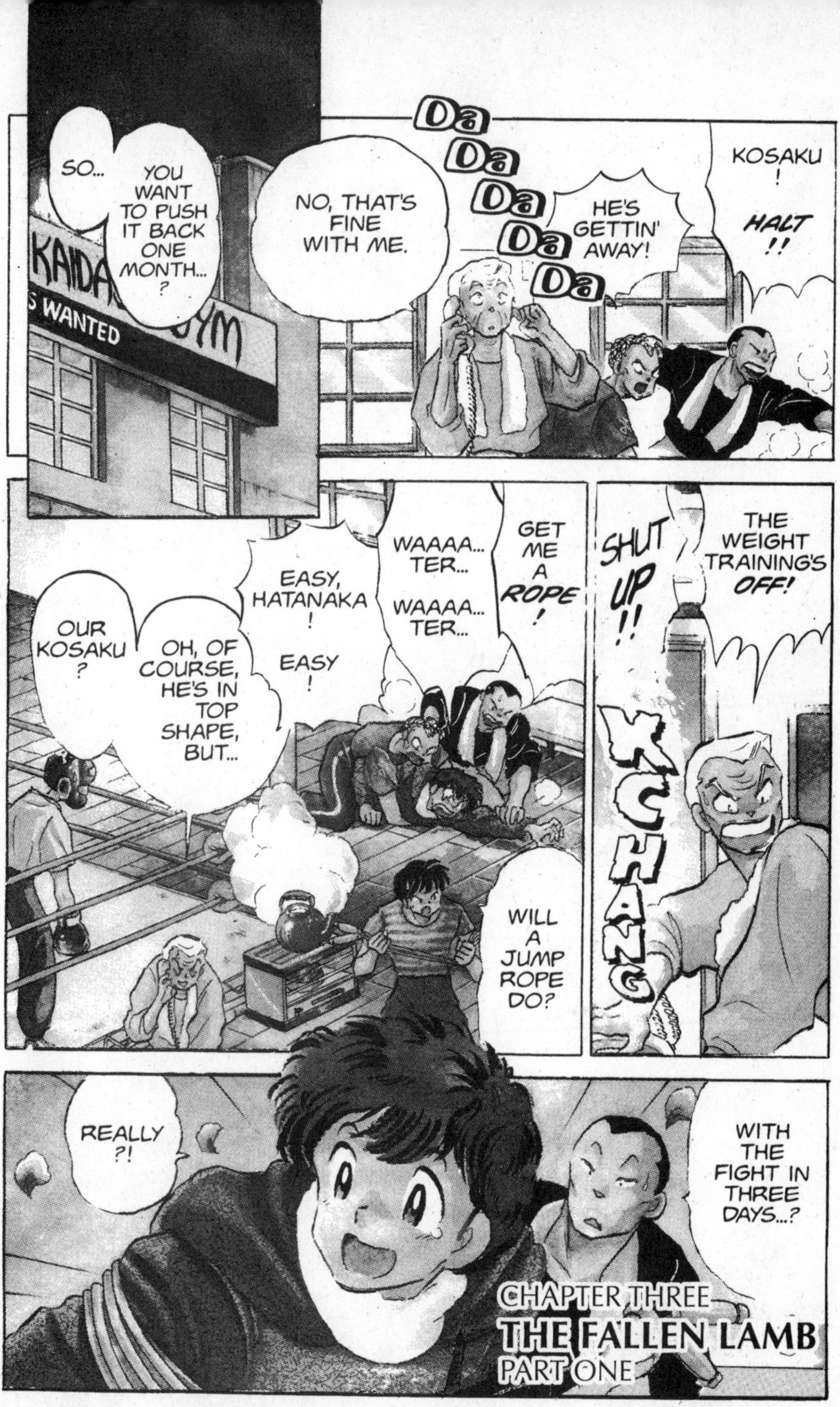
SO...
YOU WANT TO PUSH IT BACK ONE MONTH...?
KAIDA GYM
S WANTED
NO, THAT'S FINE WITH ME.
Da Da Da Da Da
HE'S GETTIN' AWAY!
KOSAKU! HALT!!
OUR KOSAKU?
OH, OF COURSE, HE'S IN TOP SHAPE, BUT...
EASY, HATANAKA! EASY!
WAAAA... TER... WAAAA... TER...
GET ME A ROPE!
WILL A JUMP ROPE DO?
SHUT UP!!
THE WEIGHT TRAINING'S OFF!
KCHANG
REALLY?!
WITH THE FIGHT IN THREE DAYS...?

CHAPTER THREE
THE FALLEN LAMB
PART ONE

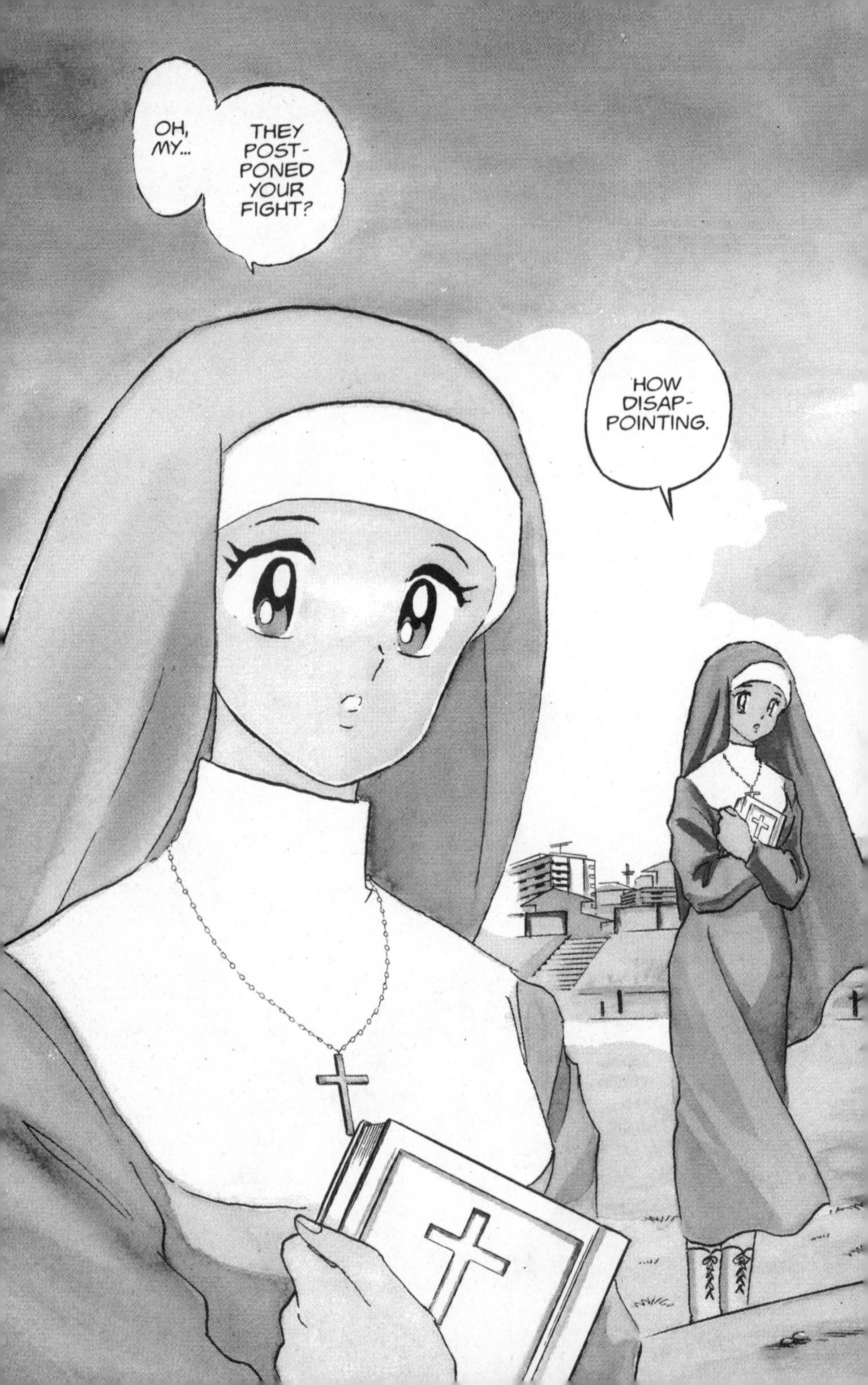
OH, MY...
THEY POST-PONED YOUR FIGHT?
HOW DISAP-POINTING.

CHAPTER THREE

THE FALLEN LAMB

PART ONE

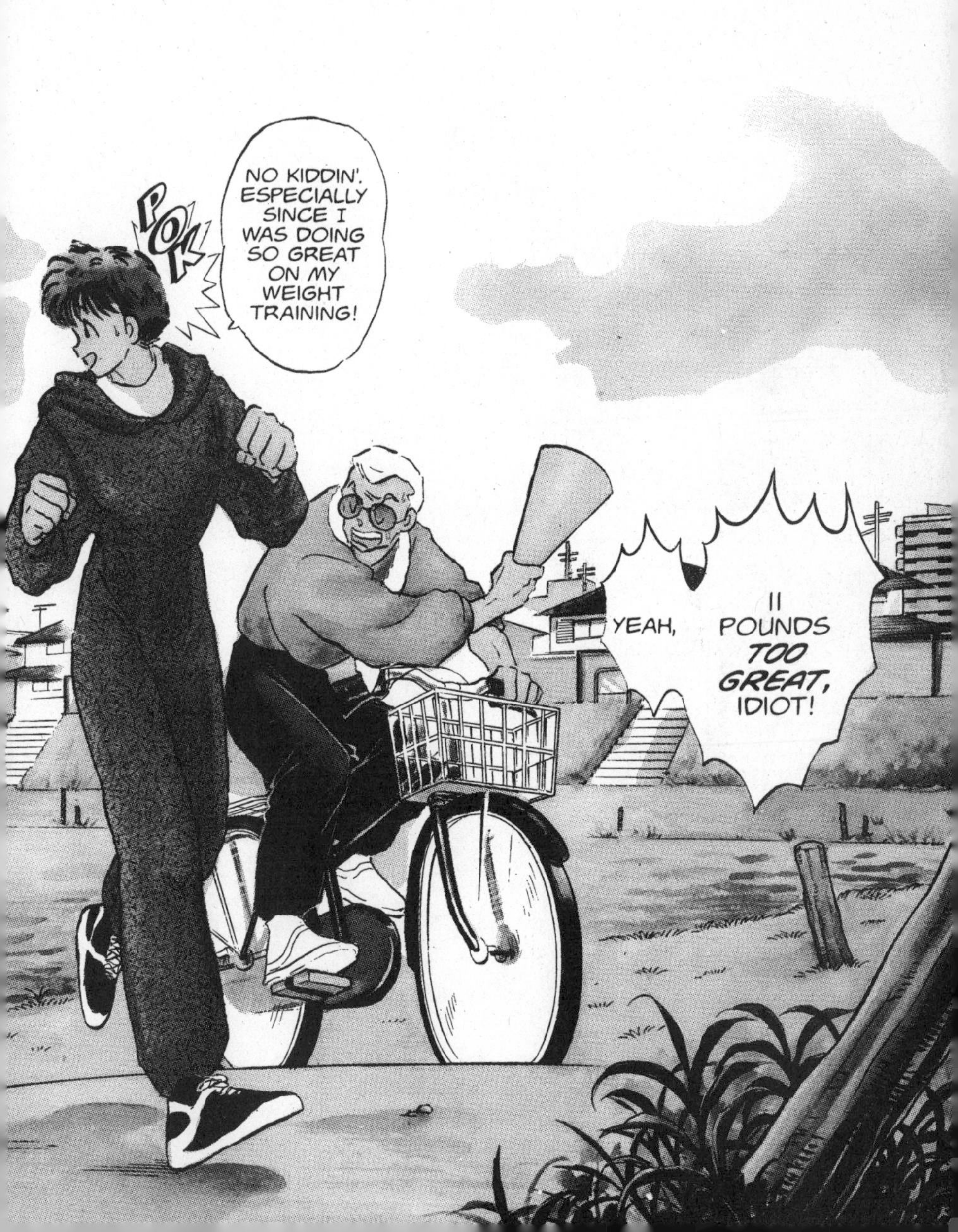
POK
NO KIDDIN'. ESPECIALLY SINCE I WAS DOING SO GREAT ON MY WEIGHT TRAINING!
YEAH,
11 POUNDS *TOO GREAT,* IDIOT!

SO WHAT HAPPENED? THE OTHER GUY-- YASHAMARU--

HE GET INJURED OR SOME- THING?

SOME- THING LIKE THAT...

GASTRITIS ?!

FROM *STRESS* ?!

WHAT THE... ?

IS HE CHICKEN, OR WHAT?

WHO KNOWS ?

I ONLY SAW HIM FIGHT ONCE, SO... WHAT- EVER...

YOU GET THE PICTURE, KOSAKU ?

YOU'VE GOT AN EXTRA MONTH!

GOT IT!!

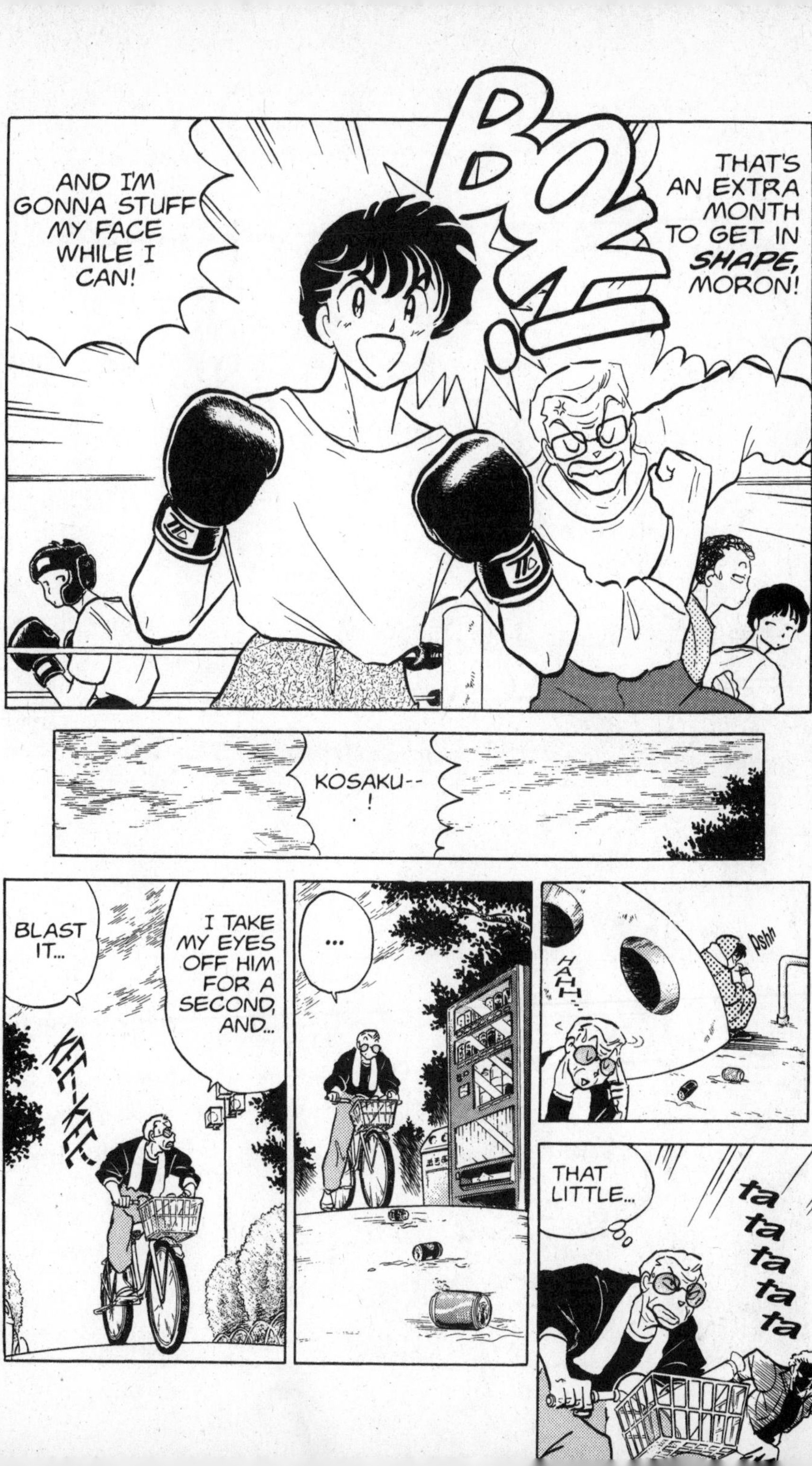
AND I'M GONNA STUFF MY FACE WHILE I CAN!
BOOM!
THAT'S AN EXTRA MONTH TO GET IN SHAPE, MORON!
KOSAKU-- !
BLAST IT...
I TAKE MY EYES OFF HIM FOR A SECOND, AND...
KEE-KEE
...
HAHH
Pshh
THAT LITTLE...
ta ta ta ta ta ta

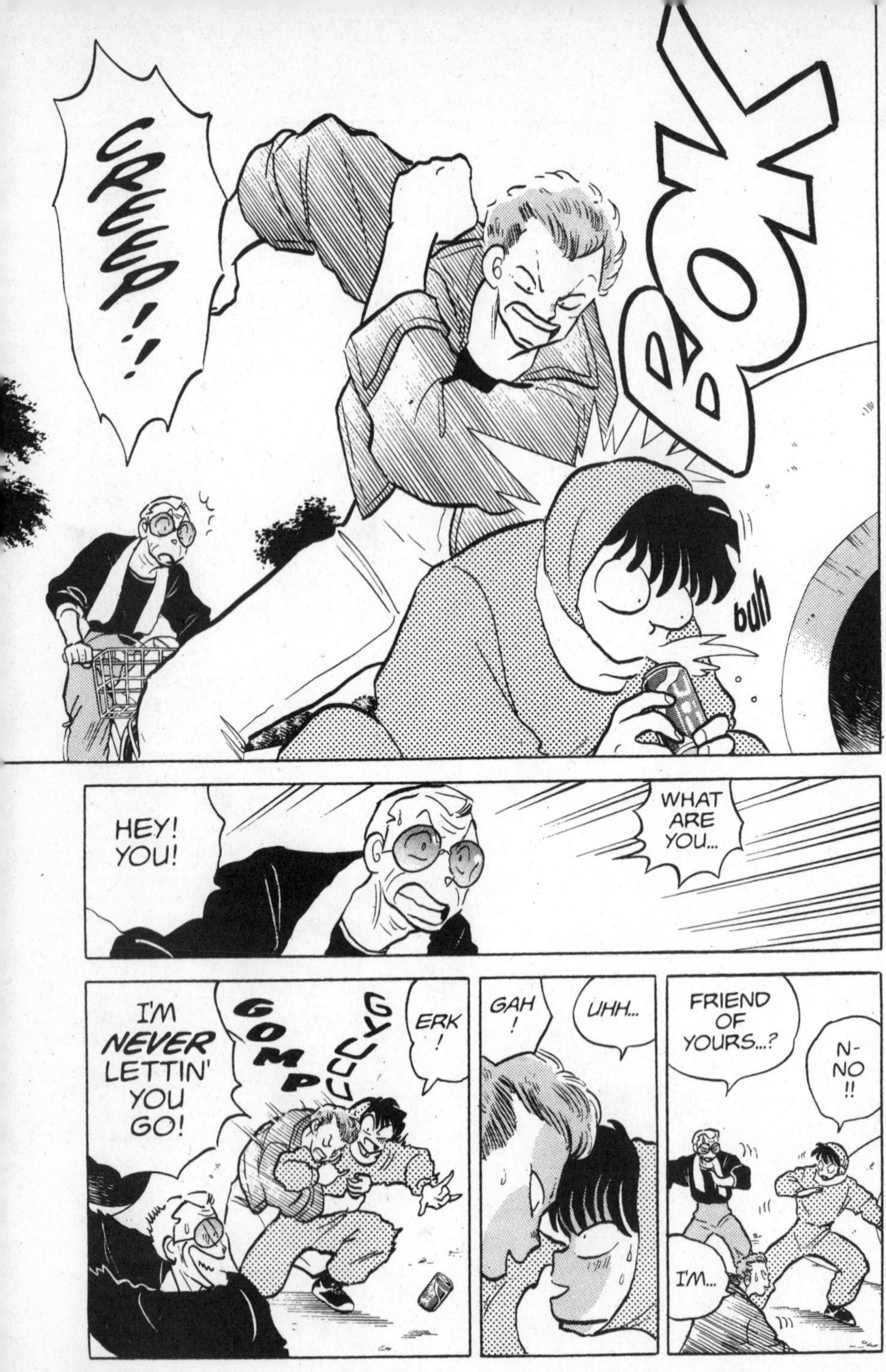
CREEEP!!!
BOK
buh
HEY! YOU!
WHAT ARE YOU...
I'M NEVER LETTIN' YOU GO!
GOMP
GYUUU
ERK!
GAH!
UHH...
FRIEND OF YOURS...?
N-NO!!
I'M...

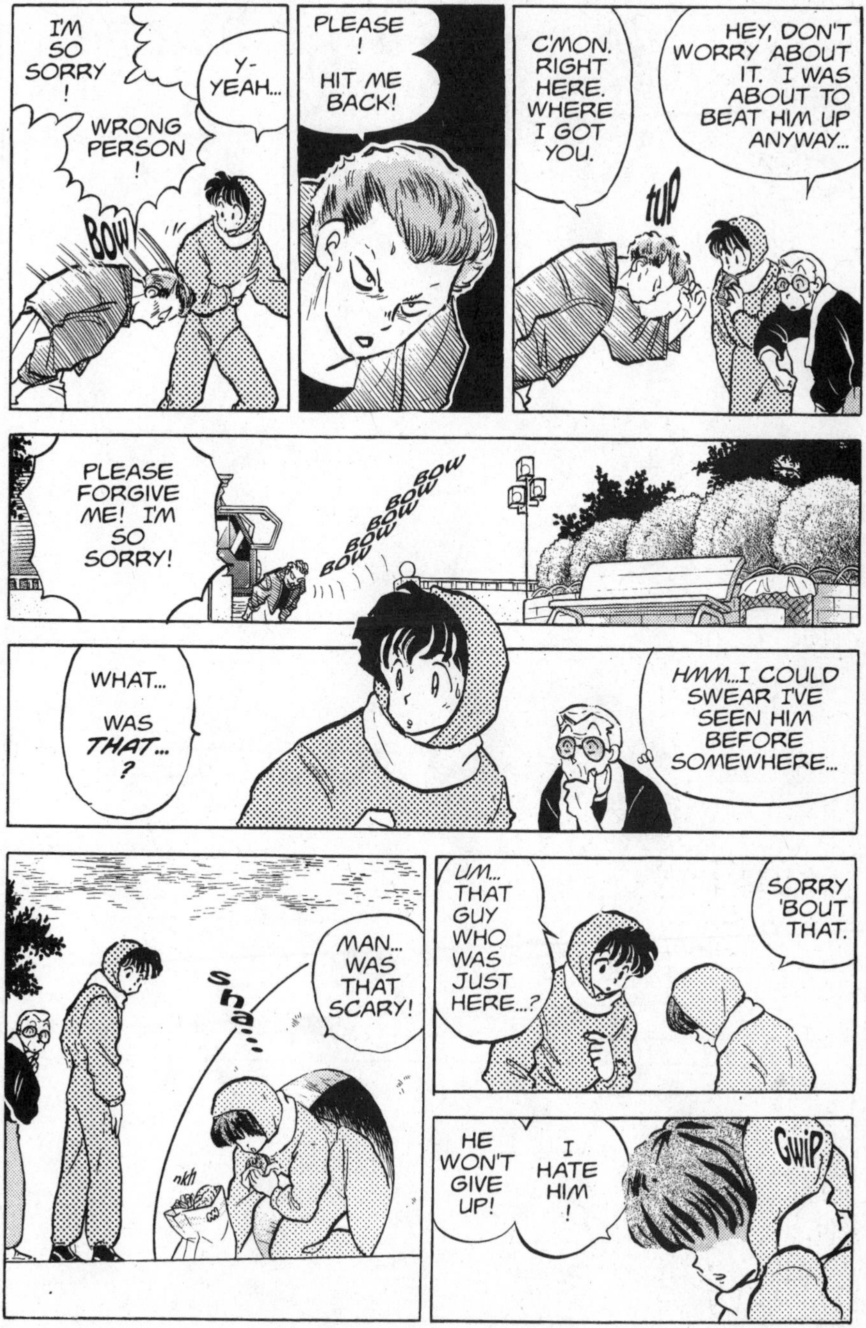
I'M SO SORRY !
WRONG PERSON !
Y-YEAH...
BOW
PLEASE ! HIT ME BACK!
C'MON. RIGHT HERE. WHERE I GOT YOU.
HEY, DON'T WORRY ABOUT IT. I WAS ABOUT TO BEAT HIM UP ANYWAY...
tup
PLEASE FORGIVE ME! I'M SO SORRY!
BOW BOW BOW BOW BOW
WHAT... WAS THAT... ?
HMM...I COULD SWEAR I'VE SEEN HIM BEFORE SOMEWHERE...
MAN... WAS THAT SCARY!
sha...
nkh
UM... THAT GUY WHO WAS JUST HERE...?
SORRY 'BOUT THAT.
HE WON'T GIVE UP!
I HATE HIM !
GWIP

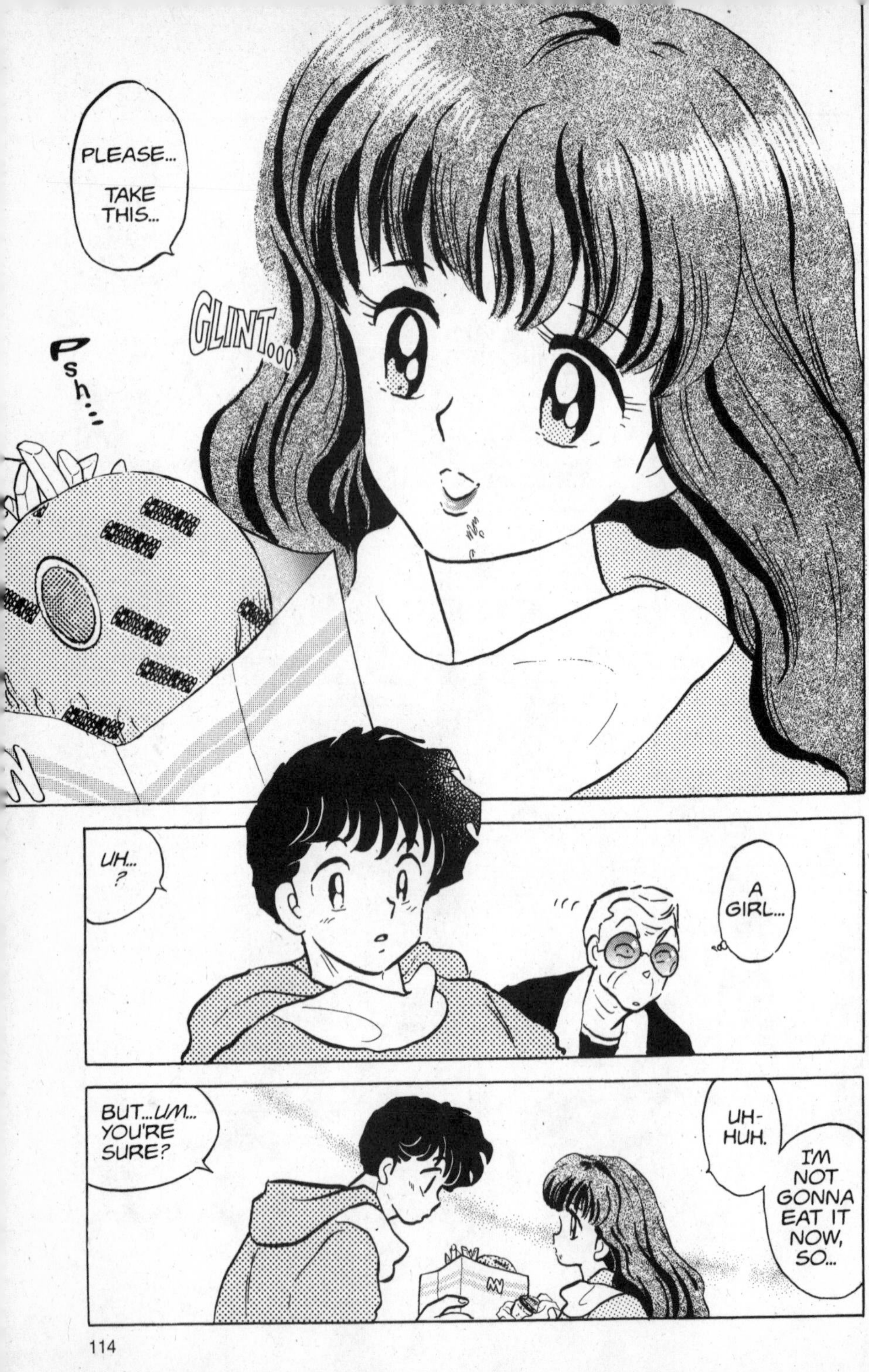
PLEASE... TAKE THIS...
GLINT...
Psh...
UH... ?
A GIRL...
BUT...UM... YOU'RE SURE?
UH-HUH.
I'M NOT GONNA EAT IT NOW, SO...

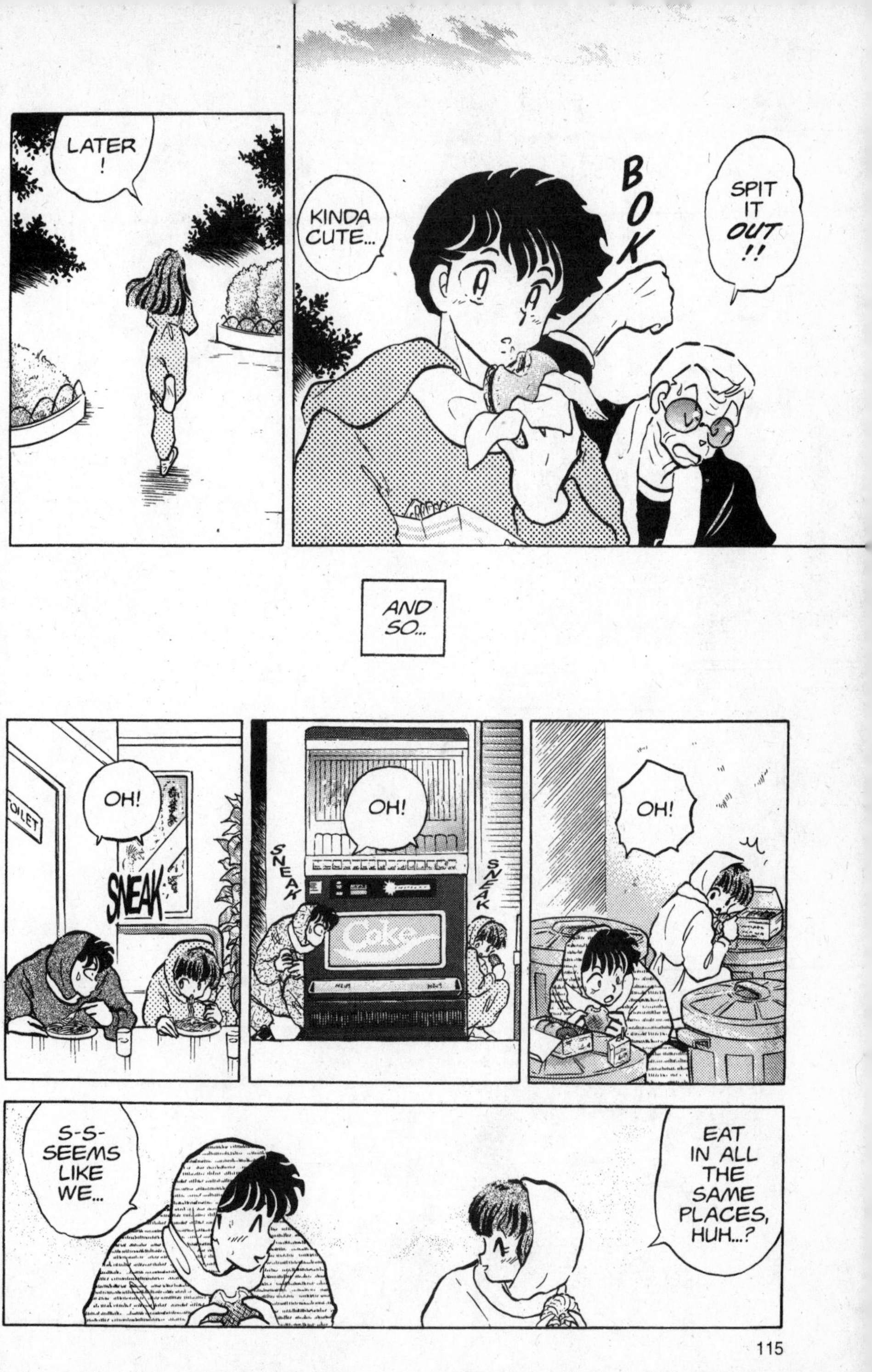
LATER!
KINDA CUTE...
BOK
SPIT IT OUT!!
AND SO...
TOILET
OH!
SNEAK
OH!
SNEAK
SNEAK
Coke
OH!
S-S-SEEMS LIKE WE...
EAT IN ALL THE SAME PLACES, HUH...?

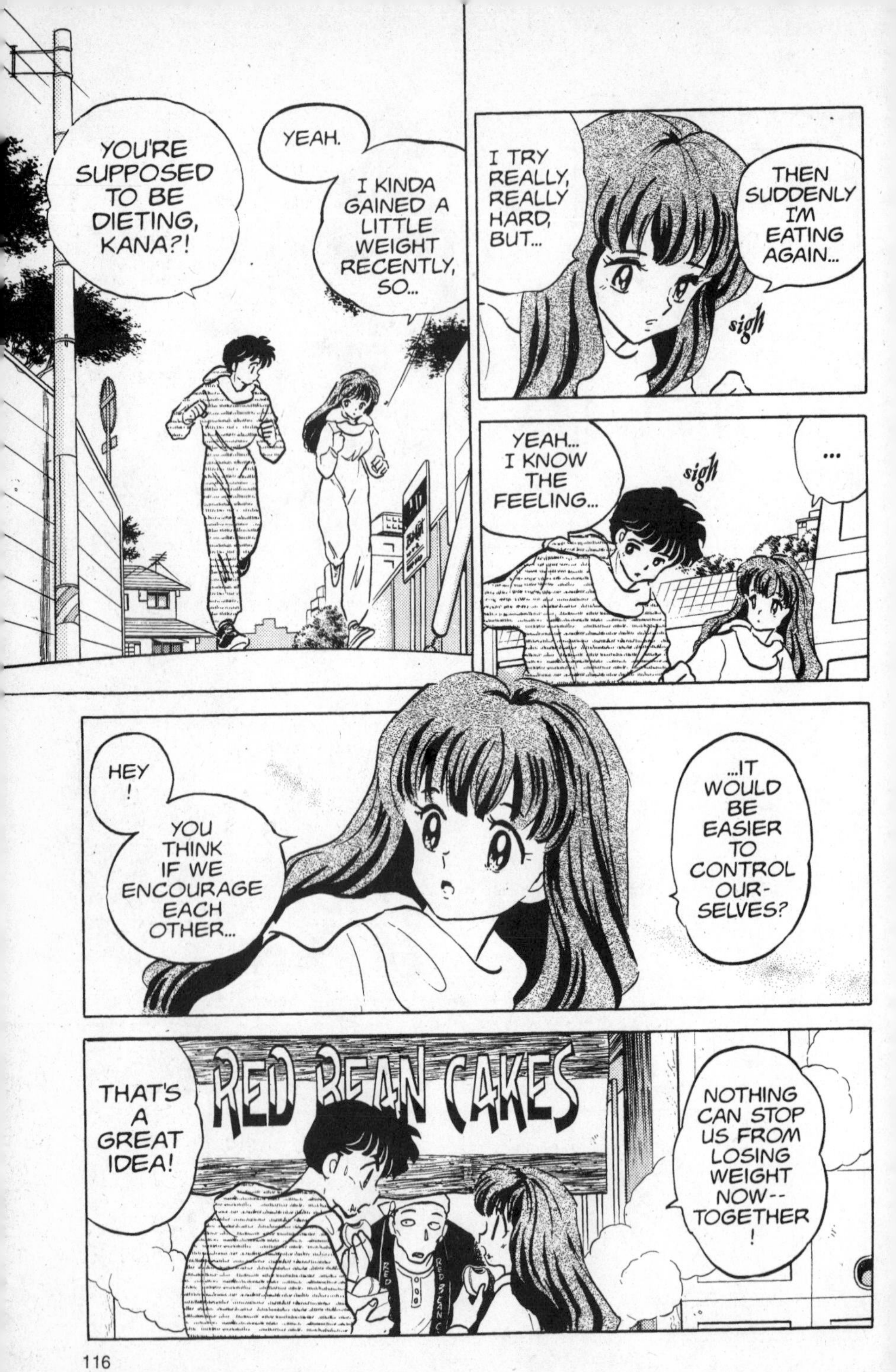
YOU'RE SUPPOSED TO BE DIETING, KANA?!
YEAH.
I KINDA GAINED A LITTLE WEIGHT RECENTLY, SO...
I TRY REALLY, REALLY HARD, BUT...
THEN SUDDENLY I'M EATING AGAIN...
sigh
YEAH... I KNOW THE FEELING...
sigh
...
HEY!
YOU THINK IF WE ENCOURAGE EACH OTHER...
...IT WOULD BE EASIER TO CONTROL OUR-SELVES?
RED BEAN CAKES
THAT'S A GREAT IDEA!
NOTHING CAN STOP US FROM LOSING WEIGHT NOW--TOGETHER!

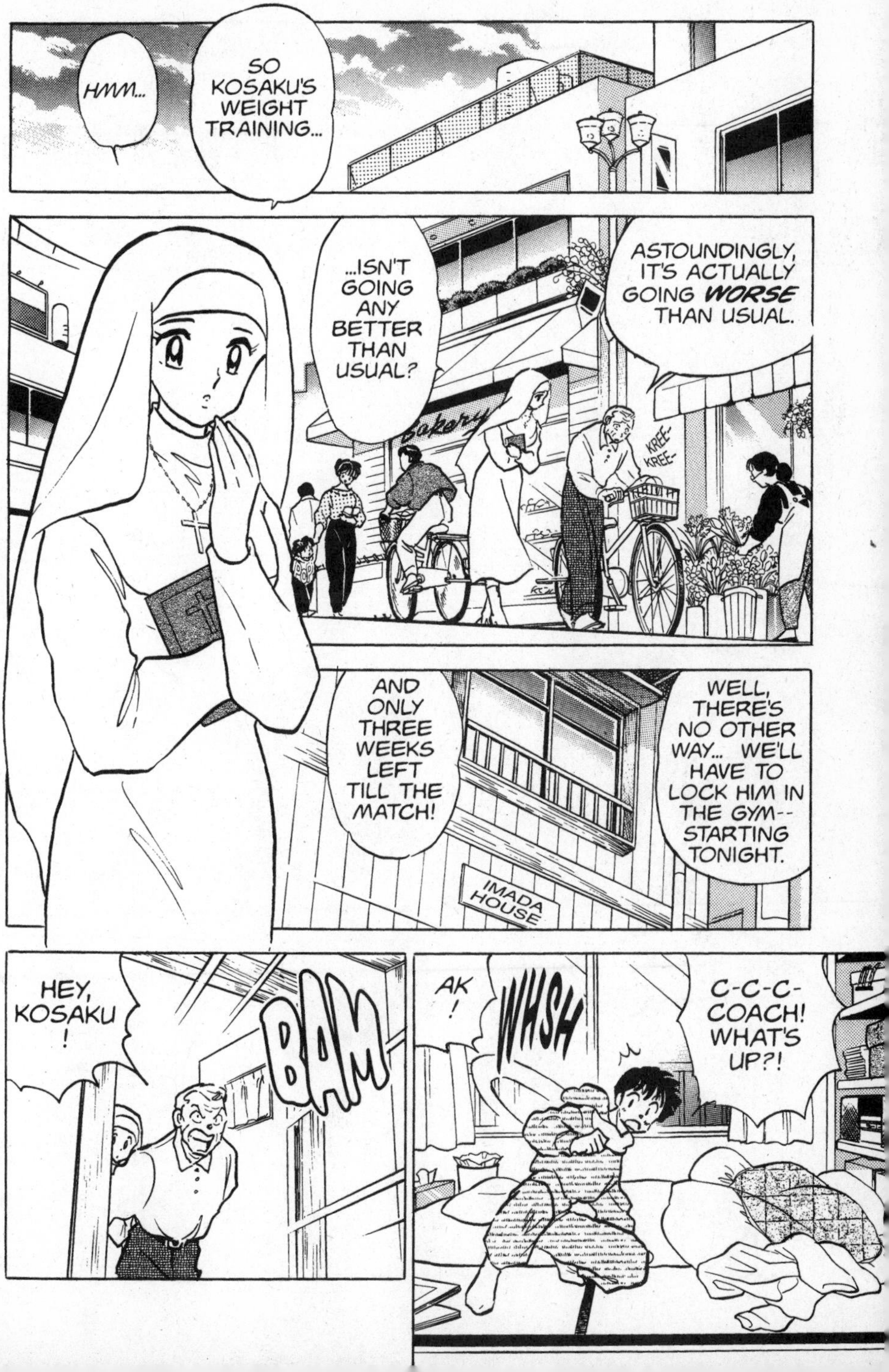
HMM...
SO KOSAKU'S WEIGHT TRAINING...
...ISN'T GOING ANY BETTER THAN USUAL?
Bakery
ASTOUNDINGLY, IT'S ACTUALLY GOING **WORSE** THAN USUAL.
KREE-KREE-
AND ONLY THREE WEEKS LEFT TILL THE MATCH!
WELL, THERE'S NO OTHER WAY... WE'LL HAVE TO LOCK HIM IN THE GYM--STARTING TONIGHT.
IMADA HOUSE
HEY, KOSAKU!
BAM
AK!
WHSH
C-C-C-COACH! WHAT'S UP?!

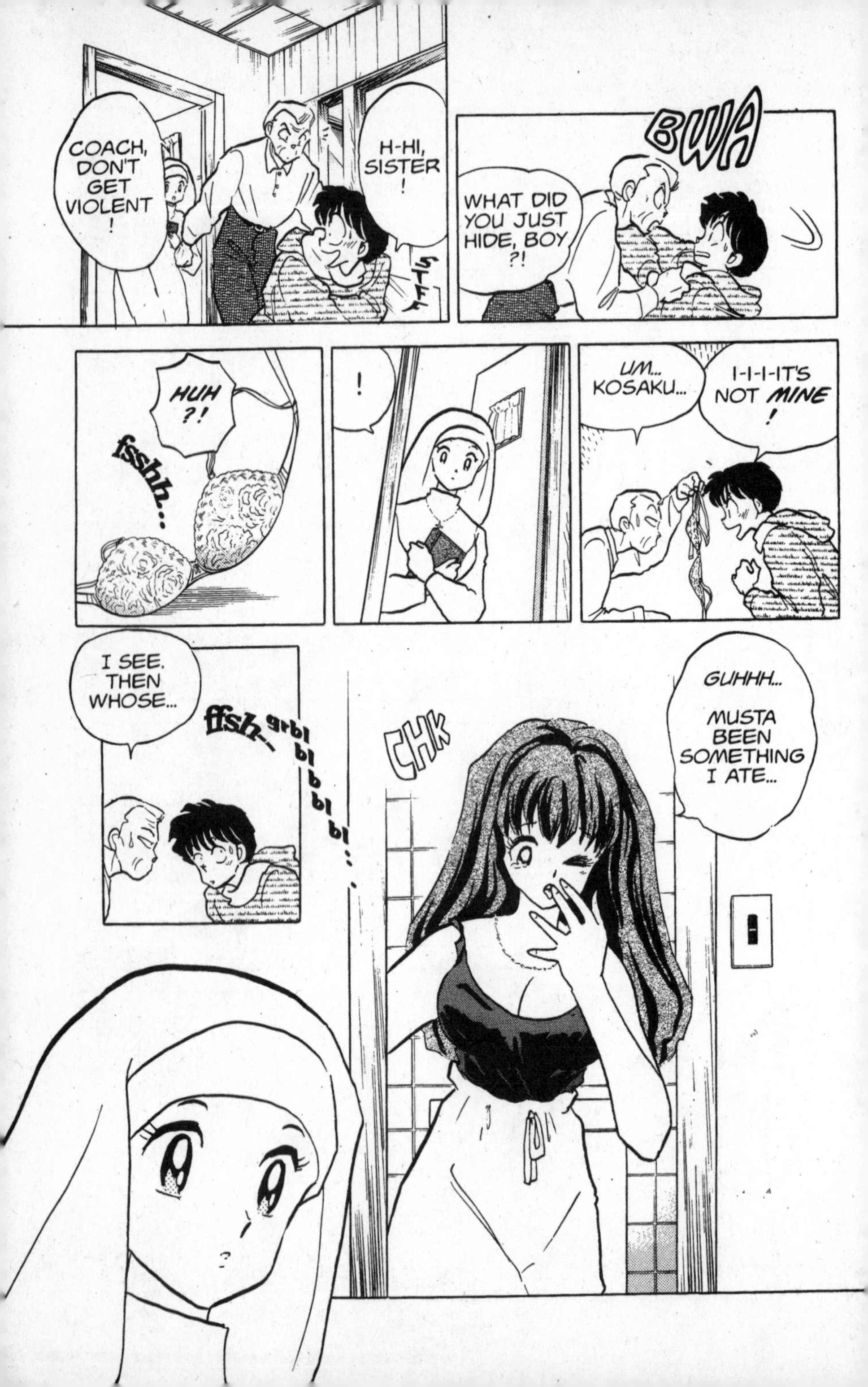
COACH, DON'T GET VIOLENT!
H-HI, SISTER!
STFF
BWA
WHAT DID YOU JUST HIDE, BOY?!
HUH?!
fsshh...
!
UM... KOSAKU...
I-I-I-IT'S NOT MINE!
I SEE. THEN WHOSE...
ffsh-
grbl bl b bl bl...
CHK
GUHHH...
MUSTA BEEN SOMETHING I ATE...

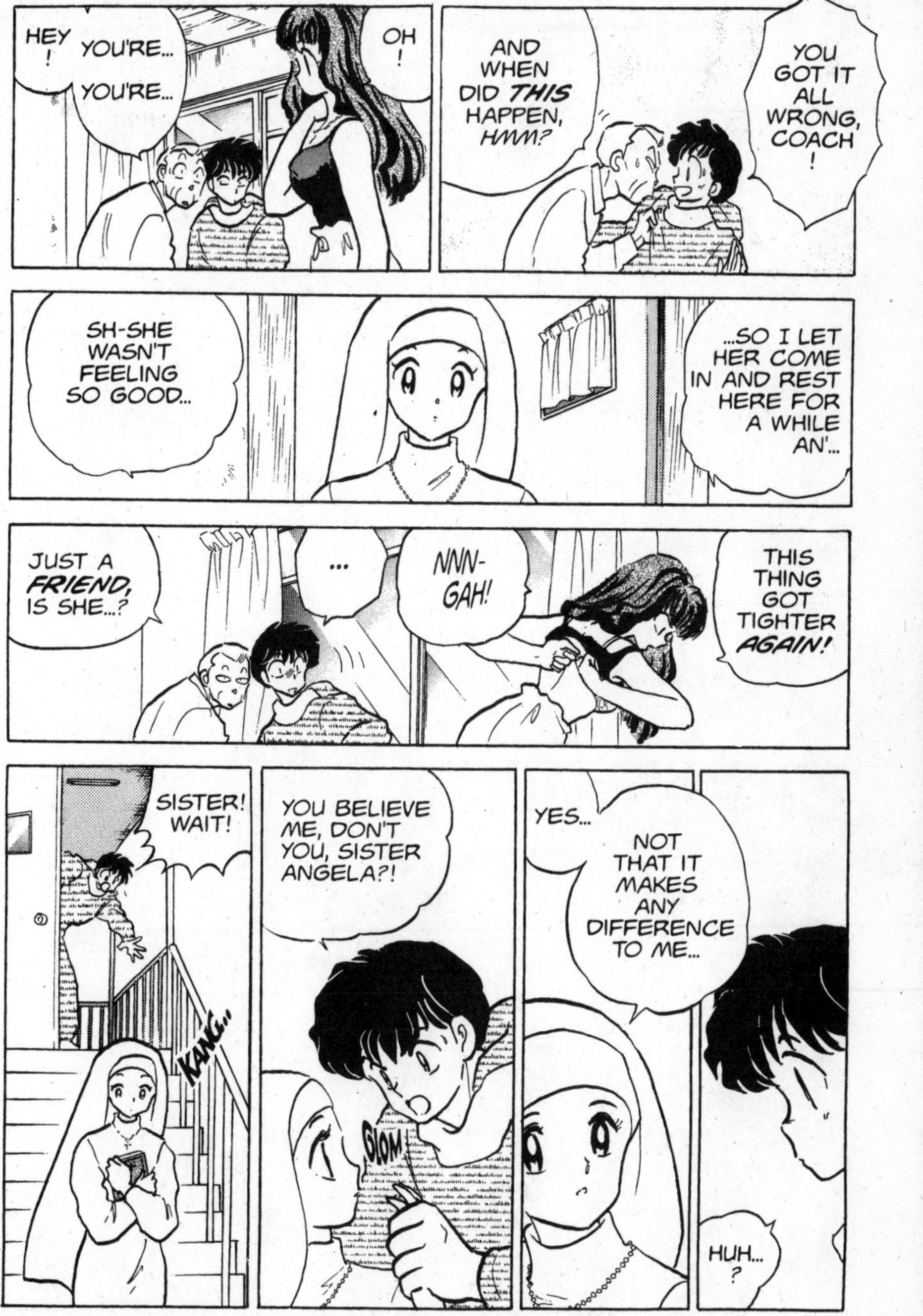
HEY!
YOU'RE... YOU'RE...
OH!
AND WHEN DID *THIS* HAPPEN, *HMM?*
YOU GOT IT ALL WRONG, COACH!
SH-SHE WASN'T FEELING SO GOOD...
...SO I LET HER COME IN AND REST HERE FOR A WHILE AN'...
JUST A *FRIEND,* IS SHE...?
...
NNN-GAH!
THIS THING GOT TIGHTER *AGAIN!*
SISTER! WAIT!
KANG..
YOU BELIEVE ME, DON'T YOU, SISTER ANGELA?!
GLOM
YES...
NOT THAT IT MAKES ANY DIFFERENCE TO ME...
HUH...?

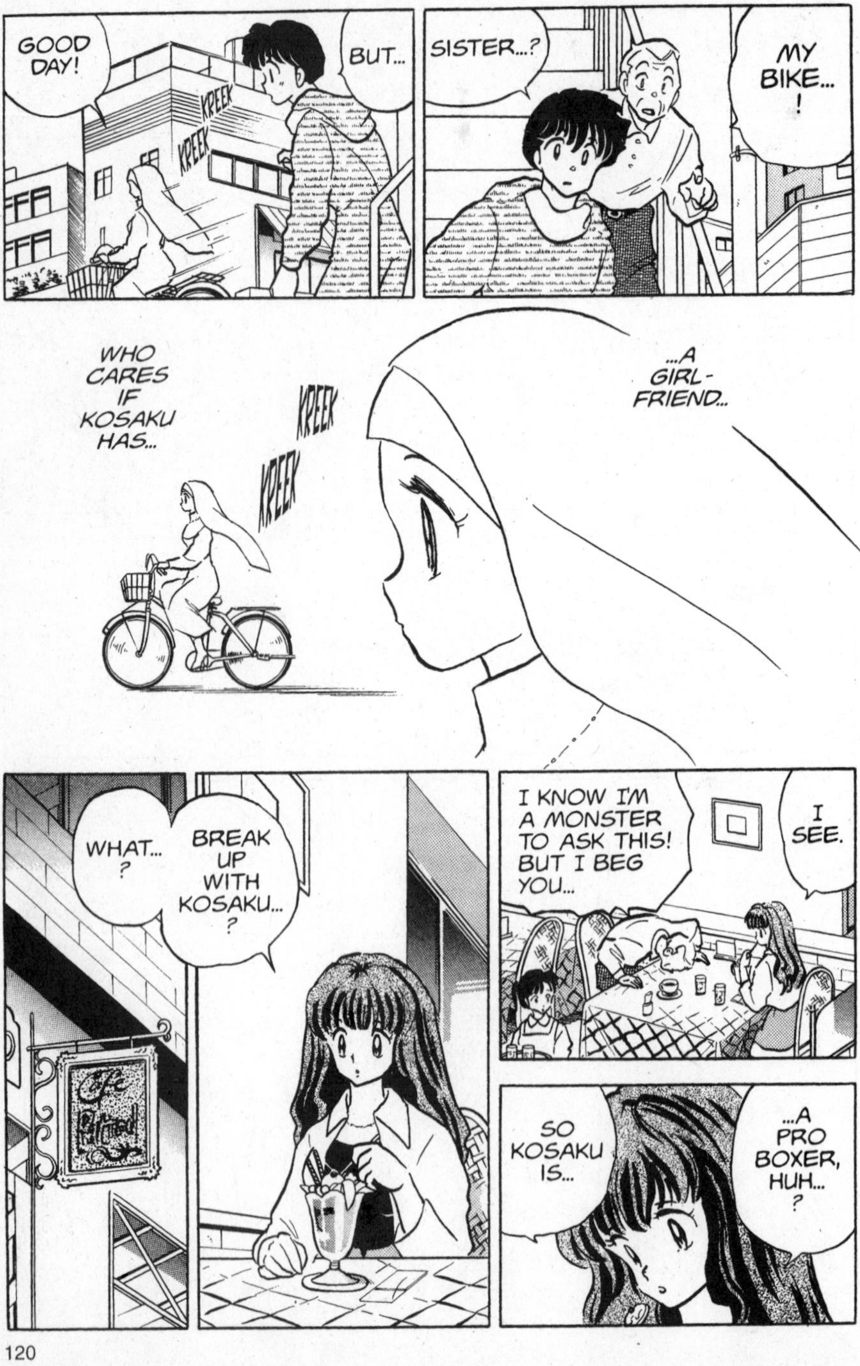
GOOD DAY!
KREEK
KREEK
BUT...
SISTER...?
MY BIKE...!
WHO CARES IF KOSAKU HAS...
KREEK
KREEK
...A GIRL-FRIEND...
WHAT...?
BREAK UP WITH KOSAKU...?
I KNOW I'M A MONSTER TO ASK THIS! BUT I BEG YOU...
I SEE.
SO KOSAKU IS...
...A PRO BOXER, HUH...?

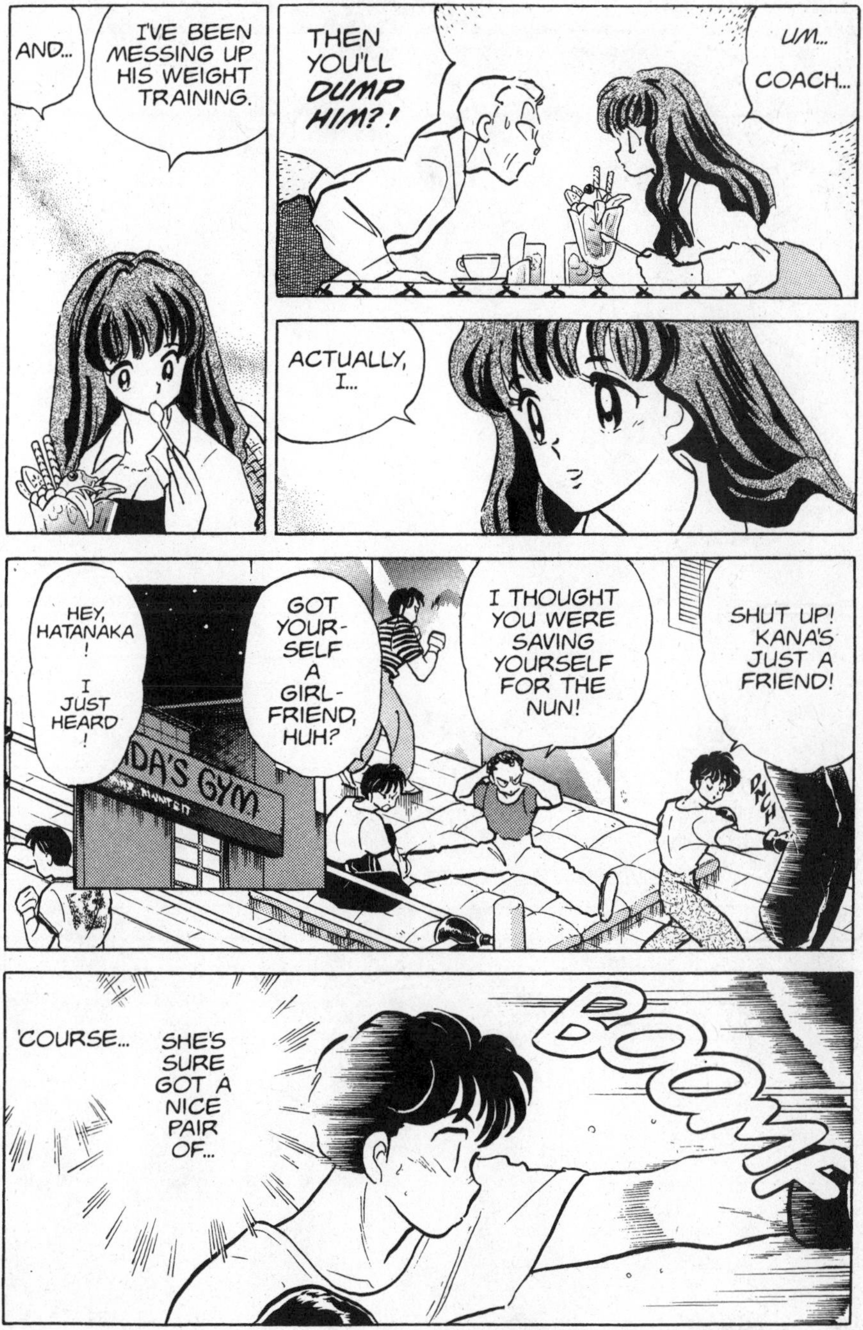
AND...
I'VE BEEN MESSING UP HIS WEIGHT TRAINING.
THEN YOU'LL *DUMP HIM?!*
UM... COACH...
ACTUALLY, I...
HEY, HATANAKA! I JUST HEARD!
GOT YOURSELF A GIRLFRIEND, HUH?
I THOUGHT YOU WERE SAVING YOURSELF FOR THE NUN!
SHUT UP! KANA'S JUST A FRIEND!
DNCH
'COURSE...
SHE'S SURE GOT A NICE PAIR OF...
BOOMF

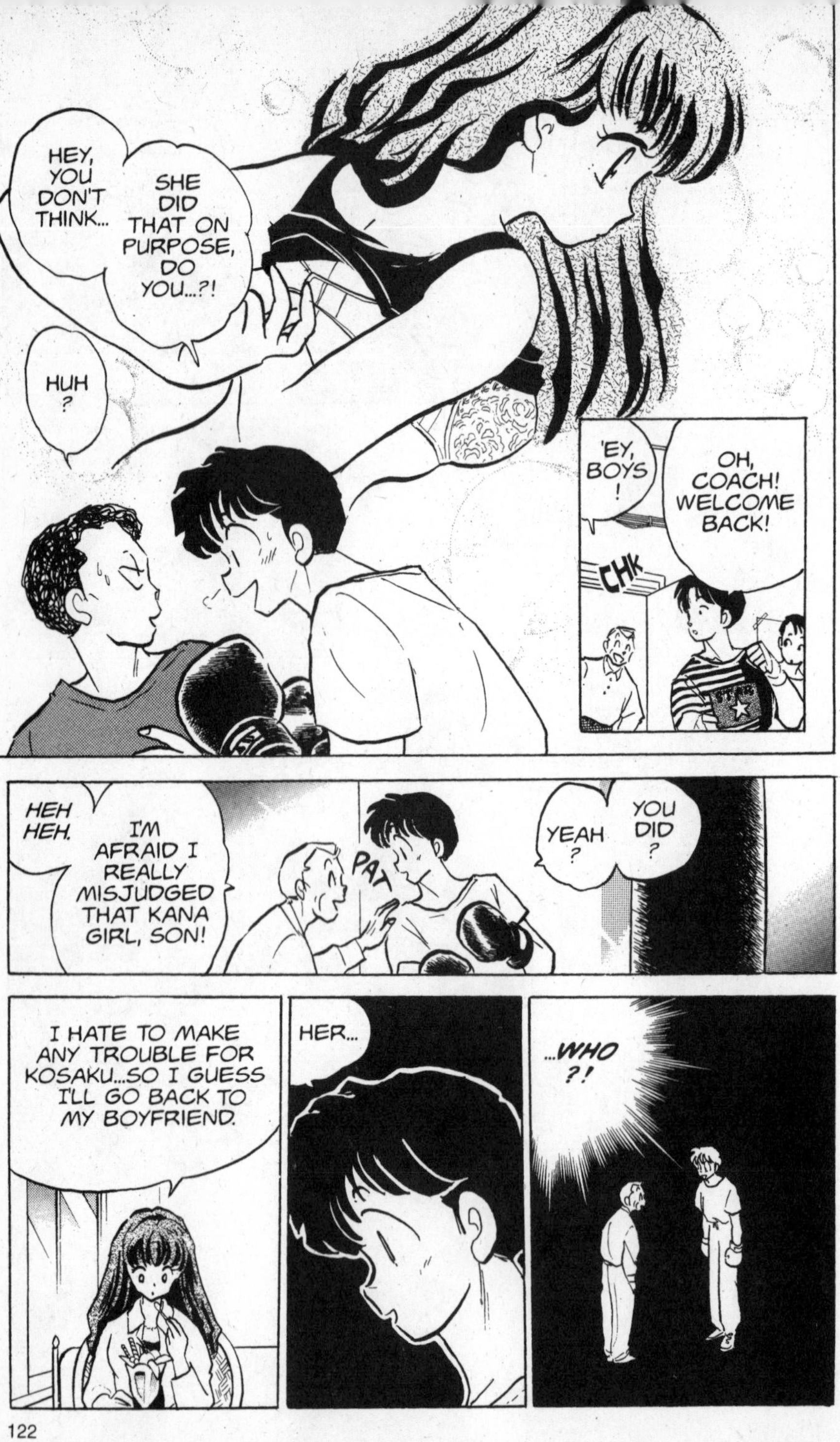
HEY, YOU DON'T THINK...
SHE DID THAT ON PURPOSE, DO YOU...?!
HUH?
'EY, BOYS!
OH, COACH! WELCOME BACK!
CHK
HEH HEH.
I'M AFRAID I REALLY MISJUDGED THAT KANA GIRL, SON!
PAT
YEAH?
YOU DID?
I HATE TO MAKE ANY TROUBLE FOR KOSAKU...SO I GUESS I'LL GO BACK TO MY BOYFRIEND.
HER...
...WHO?!

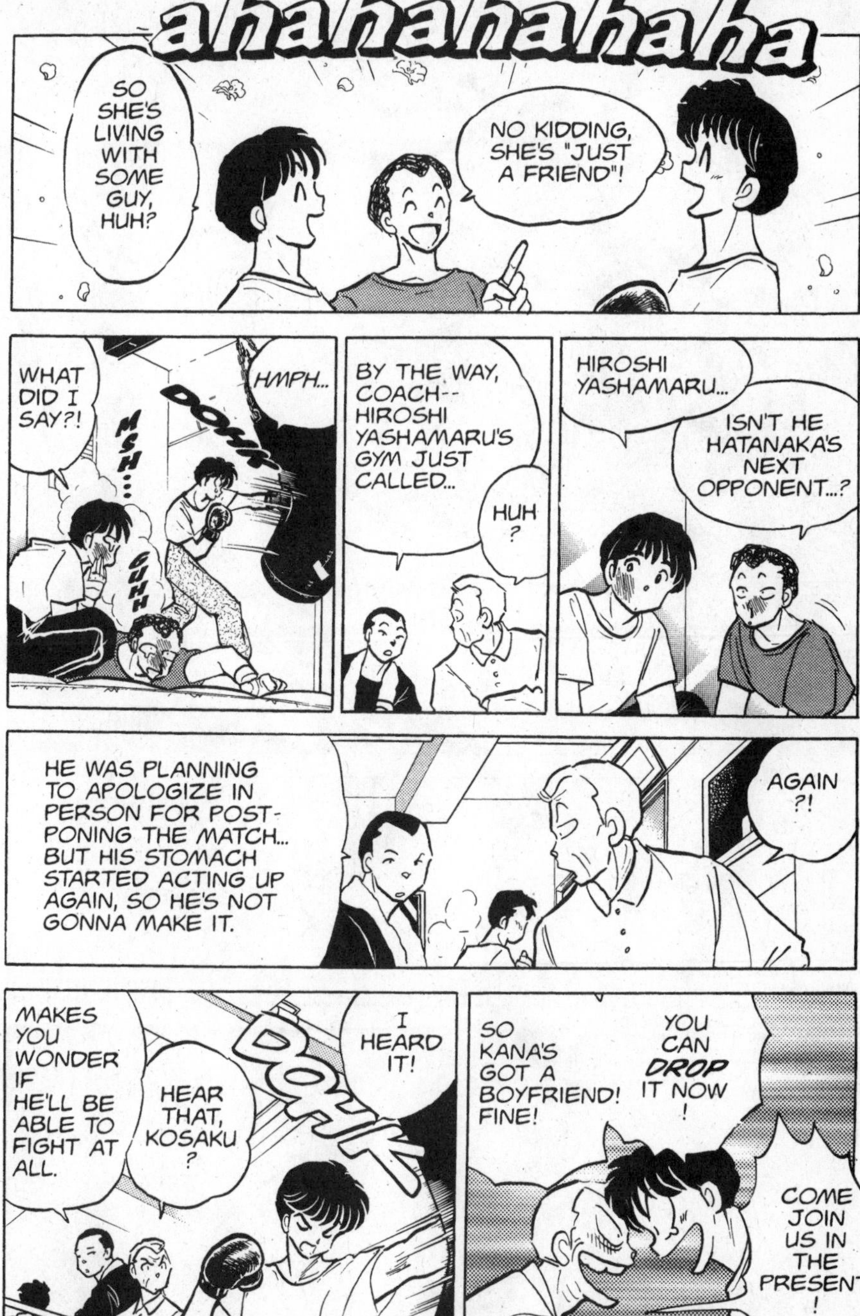
ahahahahaha
SO SHE'S LIVING WITH SOME GUY, HUH?
NO KIDDING, SHE'S "JUST A FRIEND"!
WHAT DID I SAY?!
HMPH...
DOHK
MSH...
GUHH
BY THE WAY, COACH-- HIROSHI YASHAMARU'S GYM JUST CALLED...
HUH?
HIROSHI YASHAMARU...
ISN'T HE HATANAKA'S NEXT OPPONENT...?
HE WAS PLANNING TO APOLOGIZE IN PERSON FOR POST-PONING THE MATCH... BUT HIS STOMACH STARTED ACTING UP AGAIN, SO HE'S NOT GONNA MAKE IT.
AGAIN?!
MAKES YOU WONDER IF HE'LL BE ABLE TO FIGHT AT ALL.
HEAR THAT, KOSAKU?
I HEARD IT!
DOHK
SO KANA'S GOT A BOYFRIEND! FINE!
YOU CAN DROP IT NOW!
COME JOIN US IN THE PRESENT!

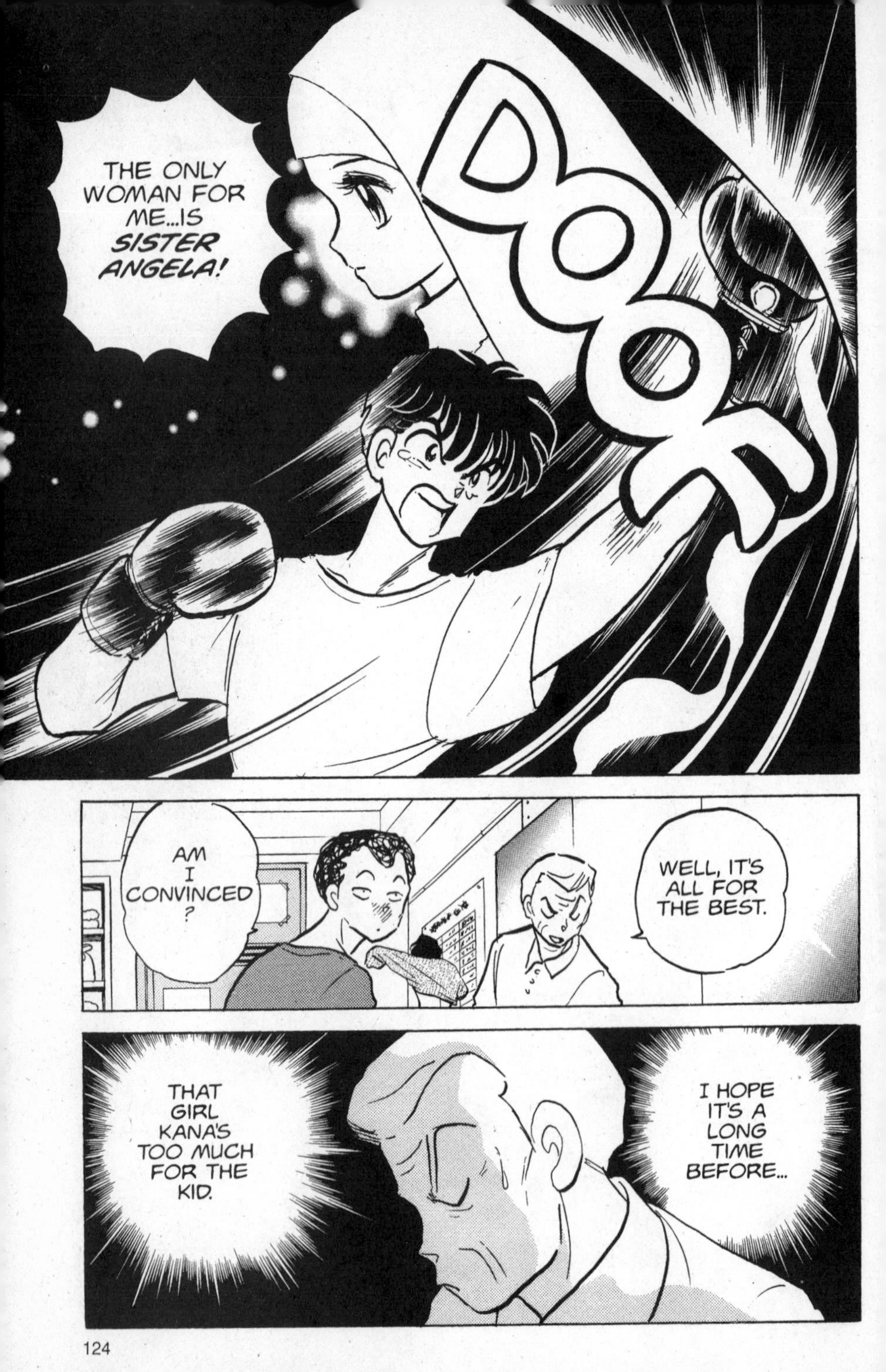
THE ONLY WOMAN FOR ME...IS SISTER ANGELA!
DOOF
AM I CONVINCED?
WELL, IT'S ALL FOR THE BEST.
THAT GIRL KANA'S TOO MUCH FOR THE KID.
I HOPE IT'S A LONG TIME BEFORE...

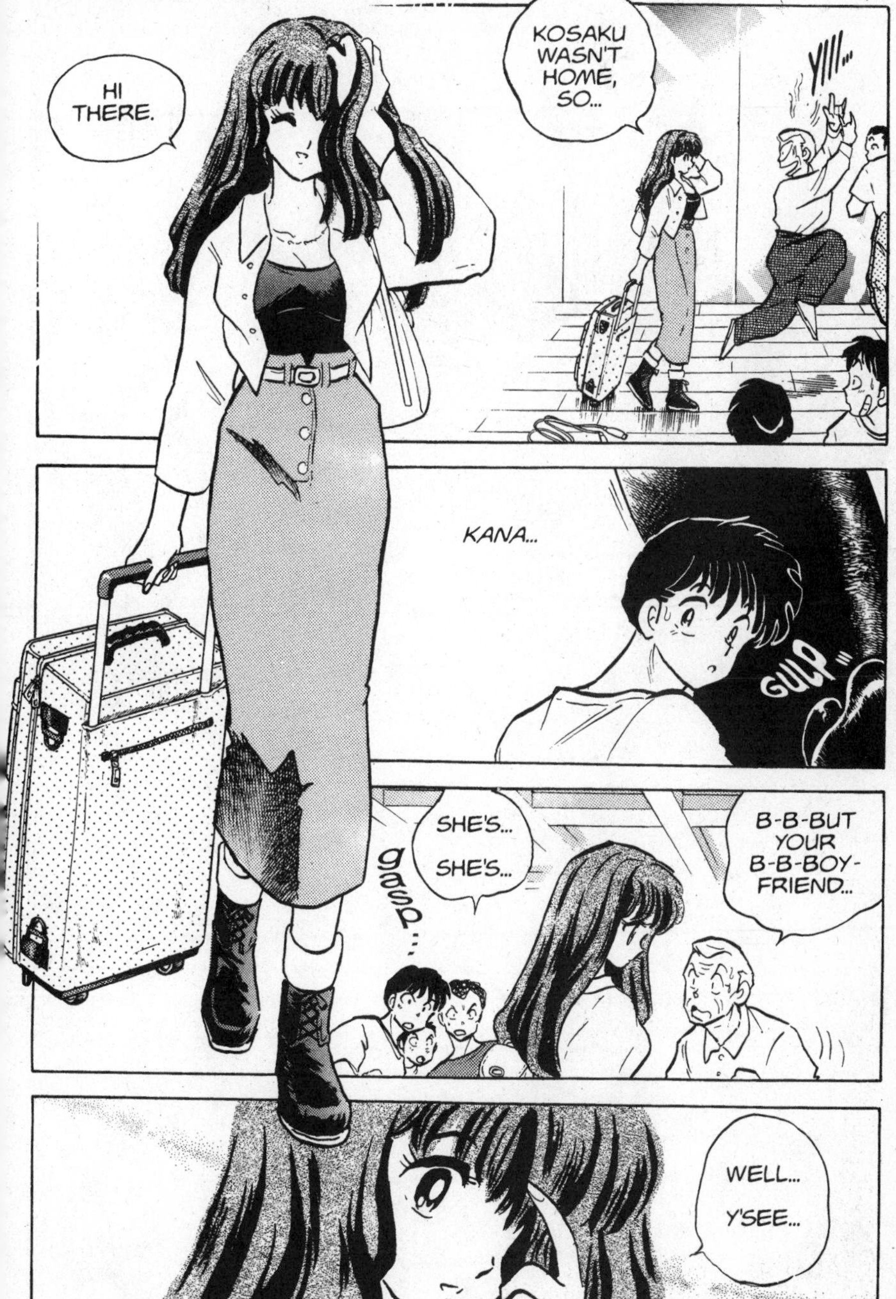
HI THERE.
KOSAKU WASN'T HOME, SO...
YIII...
KANA...
GULP
gasp...
SHE'S... SHE'S...
B-B-BUT YOUR B-B-BOY-FRIEND...
WELL... Y'SEE...

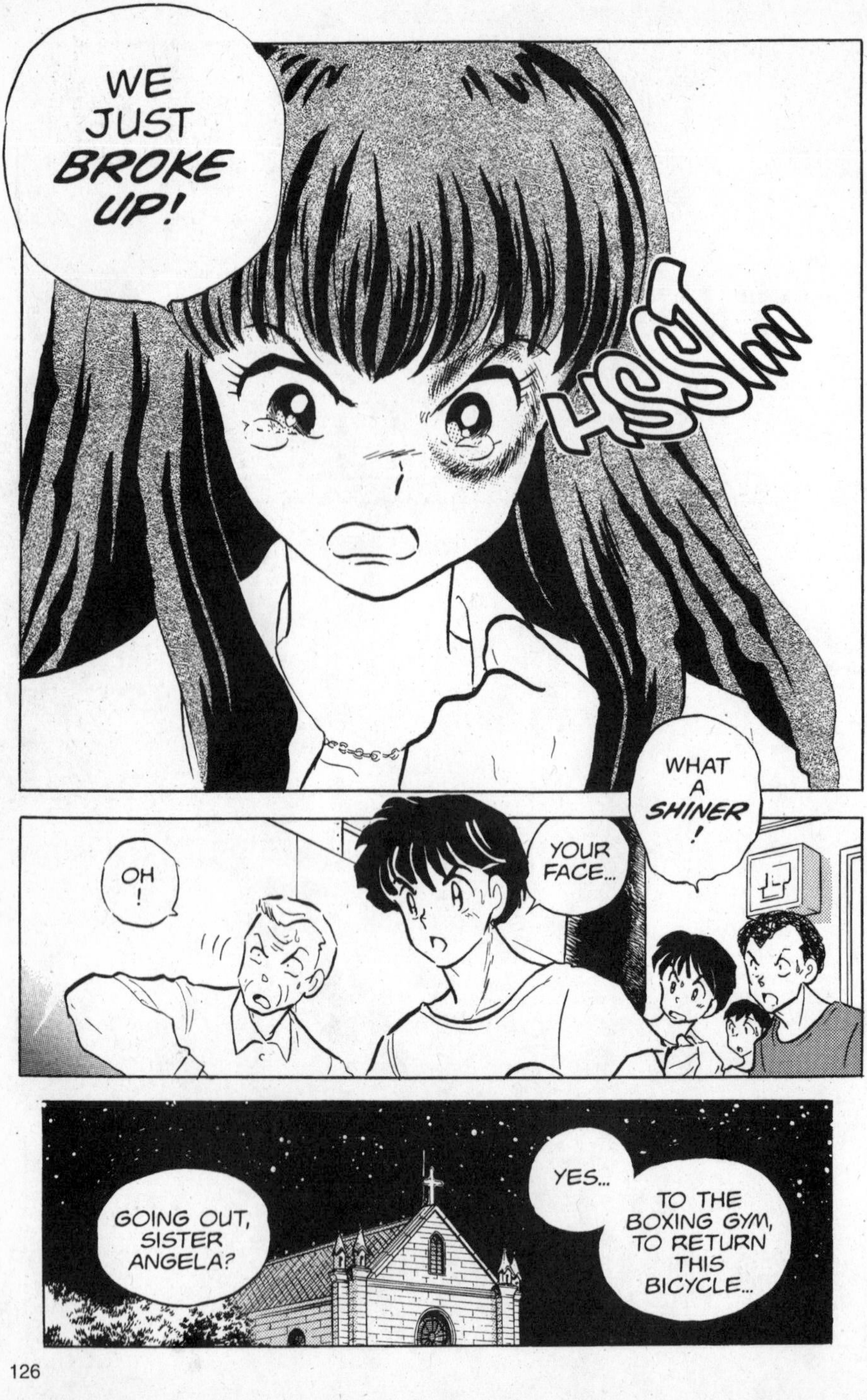
WE JUST BROKE UP!
HSSSS...
OH!
YOUR FACE...
WHAT A SHINER!
GOING OUT, SISTER ANGELA?
YES...
TO THE BOXING GYM, TO RETURN THIS BICYCLE...

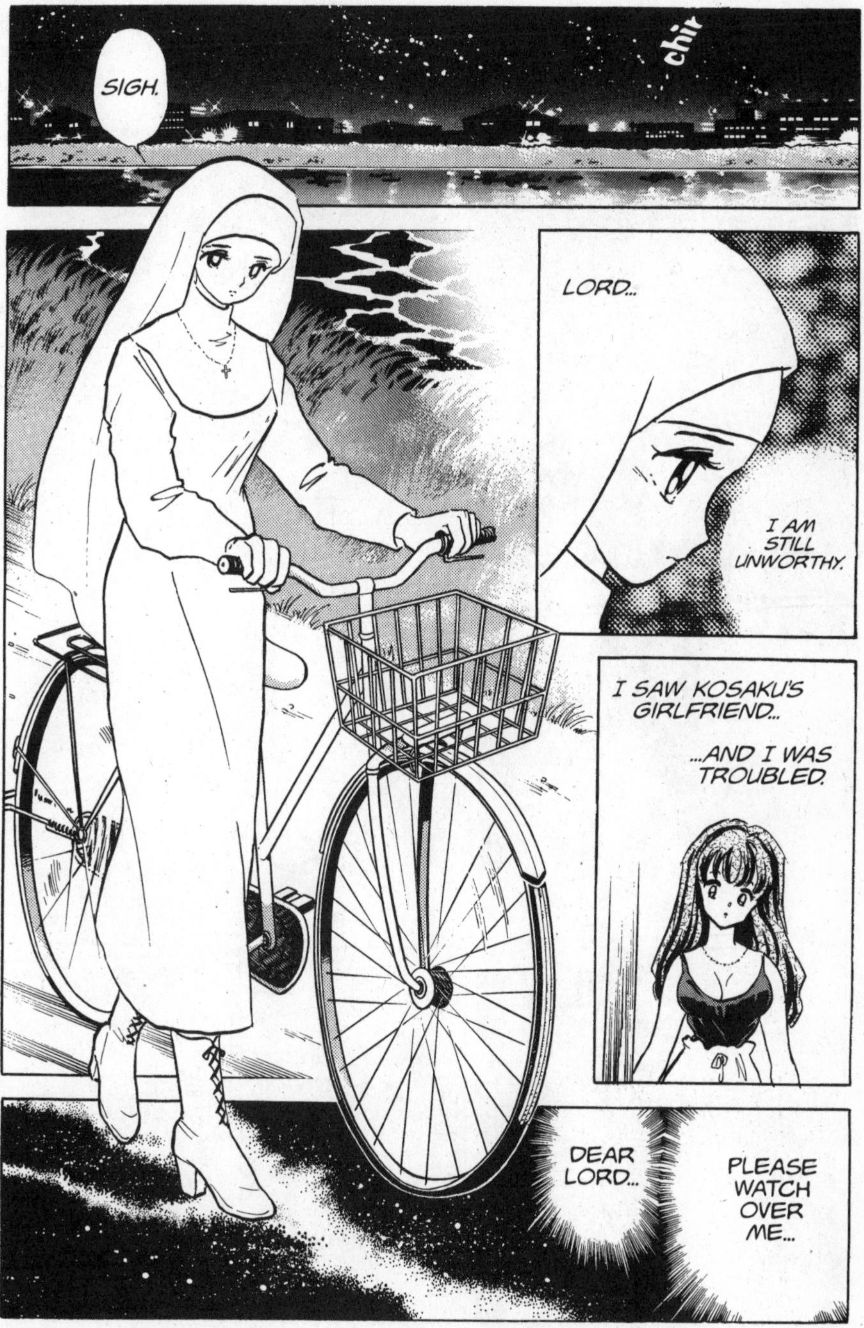
chir
SIGH.
LORD...
I AM STILL UNWORTHY.
I SAW KOSAKU'S GIRLFRIEND...
...AND I WAS TROUBLED.
DEAR LORD...
PLEASE WATCH OVER ME...

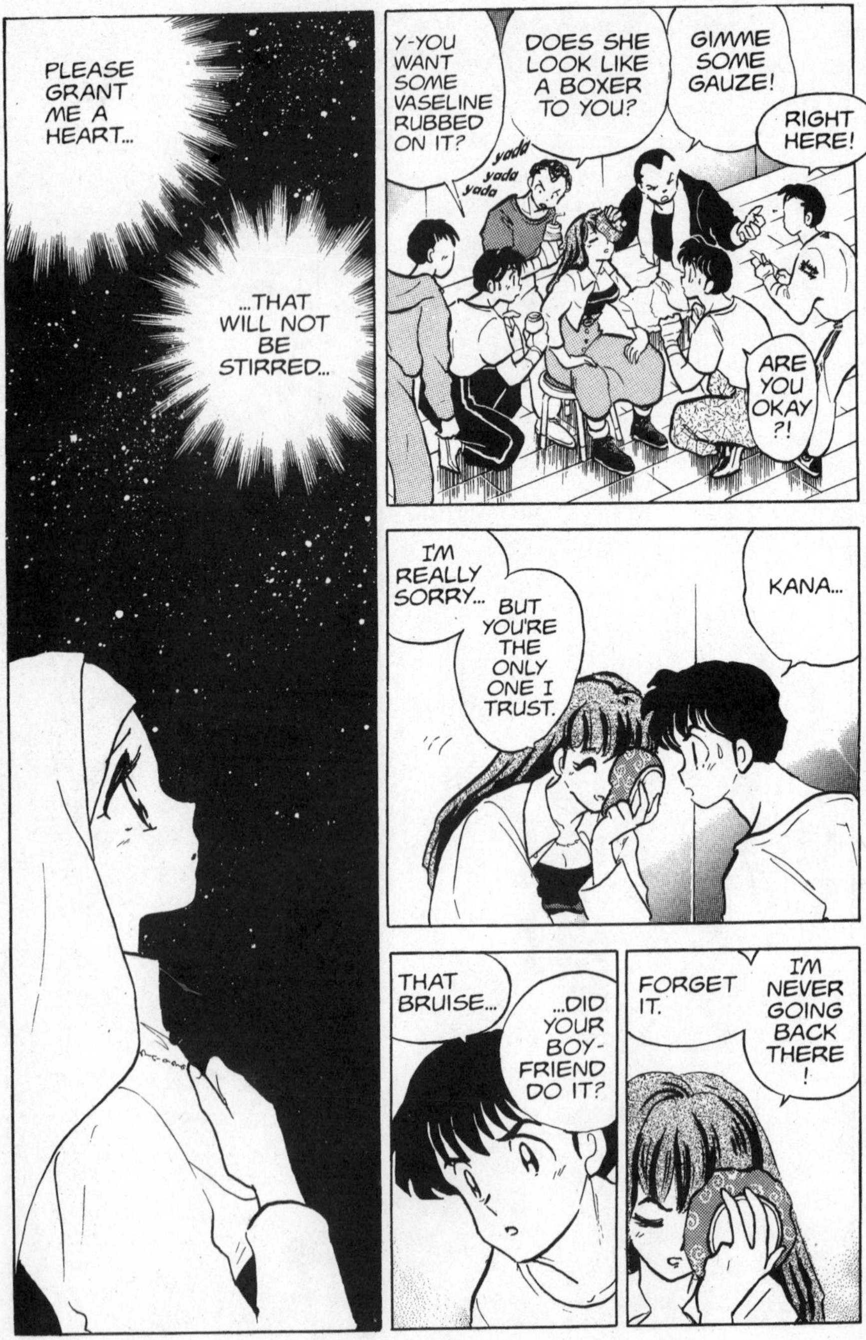
PLEASE GRANT ME A HEART...
...THAT WILL NOT BE STIRRED...
Y-YOU WANT SOME VASELINE RUBBED ON IT?
yada yada yada
DOES SHE LOOK LIKE A BOXER TO YOU?
GIMME SOME GAUZE!
RIGHT HERE!
ARE YOU OKAY?!
I'M REALLY SORRY... BUT YOU'RE THE ONLY ONE I TRUST.
KANA...
THAT BRUISE...
...DID YOUR BOY-FRIEND DO IT?
FORGET IT.
I'M NEVER GOING BACK THERE!

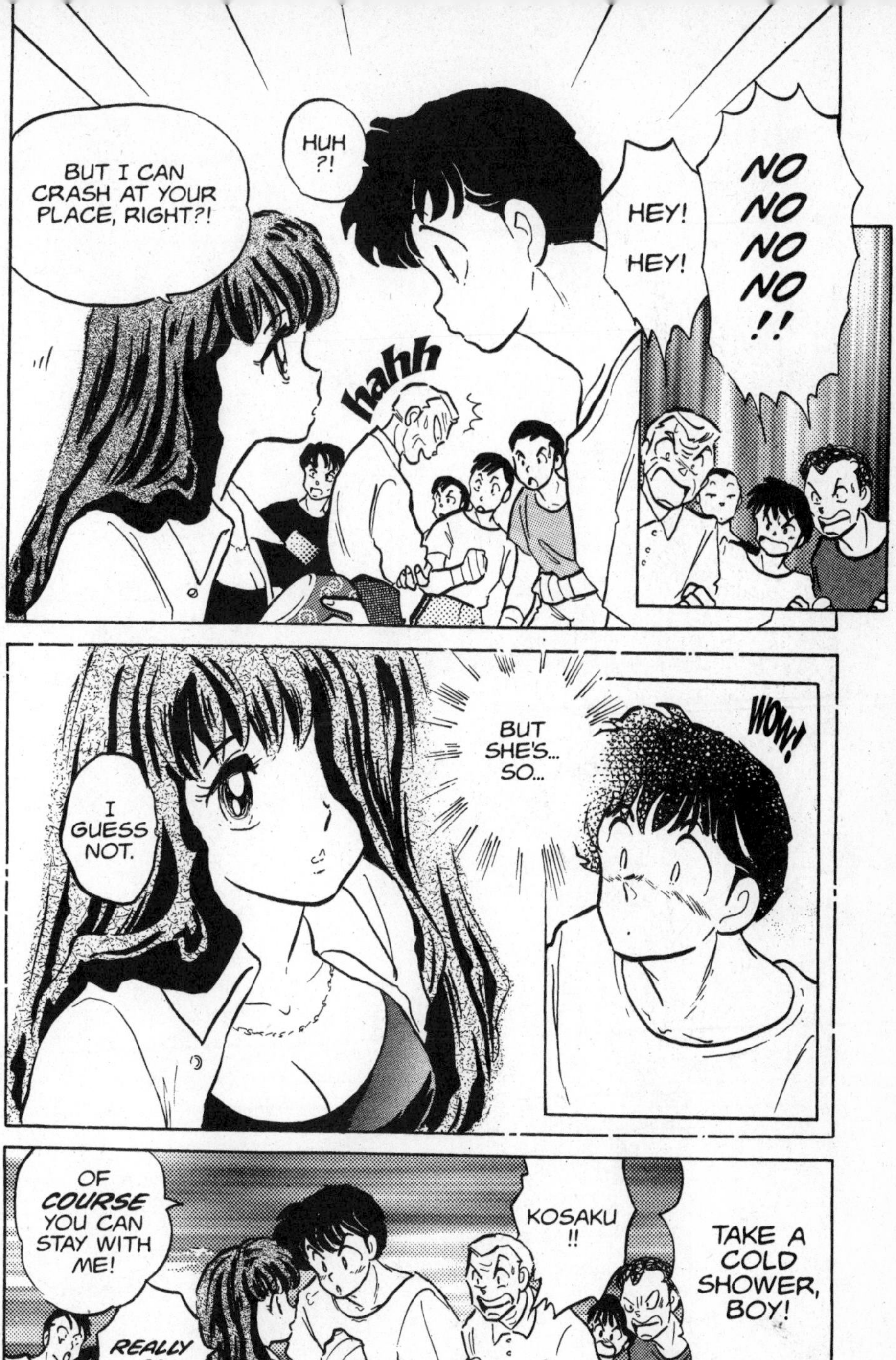
BUT I CAN CRASH AT YOUR PLACE, RIGHT?!
HUH ?!
hahh
HEY!
HEY!
NO NO NO NO !!
I GUESS NOT.
BUT SHE'S... SO...
WOW!
OF COURSE YOU CAN STAY WITH ME!
REALLY ?!
KOSAKU !!
TAKE A COLD SHOWER, BOY!

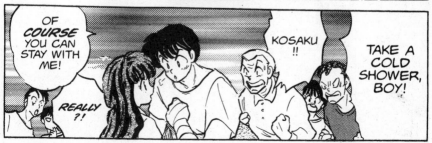

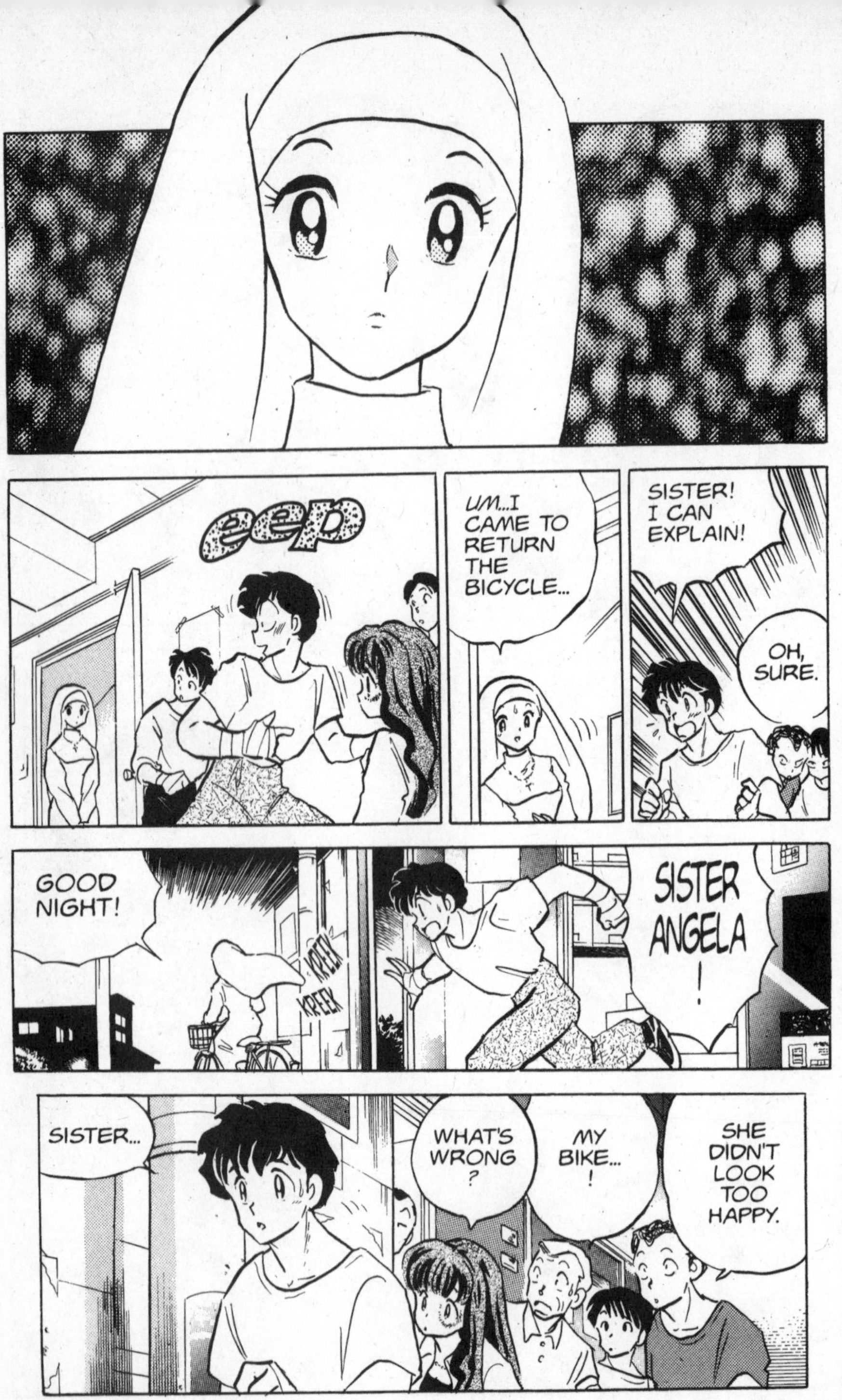
eep
UM...I CAME TO RETURN THE BICYCLE...
SISTER! I CAN EXPLAIN!
OH, SURE.
GOOD NIGHT!
KREEK KREEK
SISTER ANGELA!
SISTER...
WHAT'S WRONG?
MY BIKE...!
SHE DIDN'T LOOK TOO HAPPY.

CHAPTER THREE

THE FALLEN LAMB

PART TWO

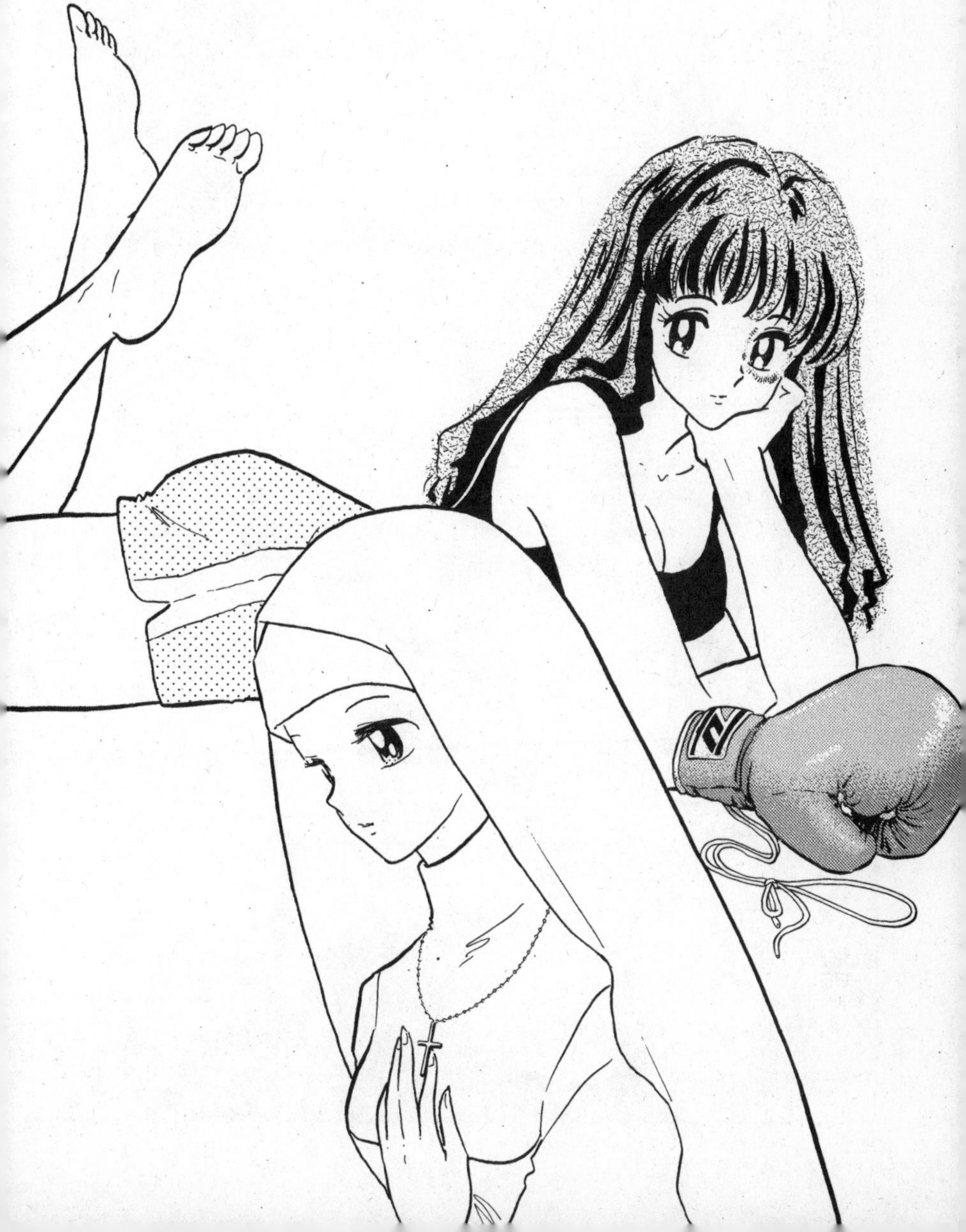

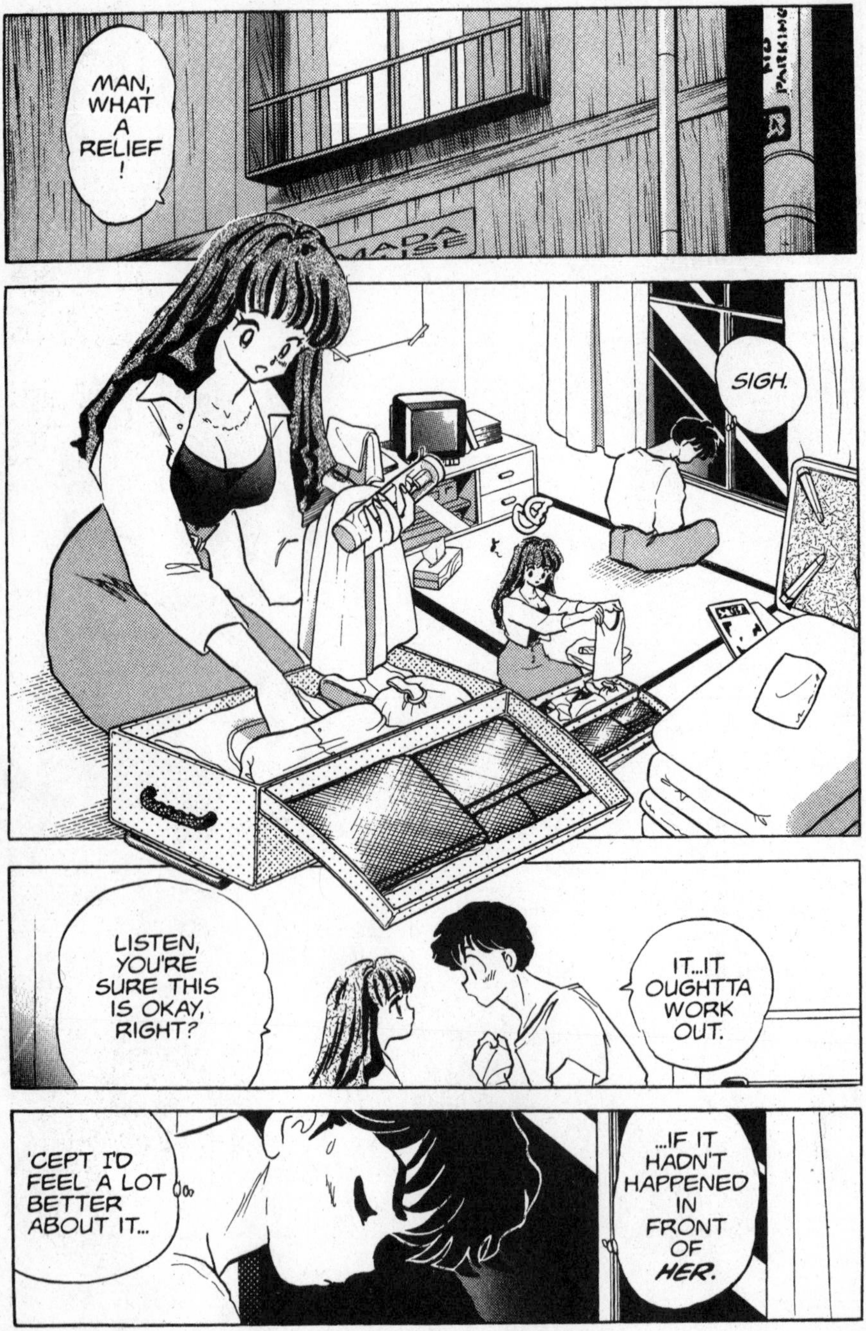
MAN, WHAT A RELIEF!
NO PARKING
SIGH.
LISTEN, YOU'RE SURE THIS IS OKAY, RIGHT?
IT...IT OUGHTTA WORK OUT.
'CEPT I'D FEEL A LOT BETTER ABOUT IT...
...IF IT HADN'T HAPPENED IN FRONT OF *HER*.

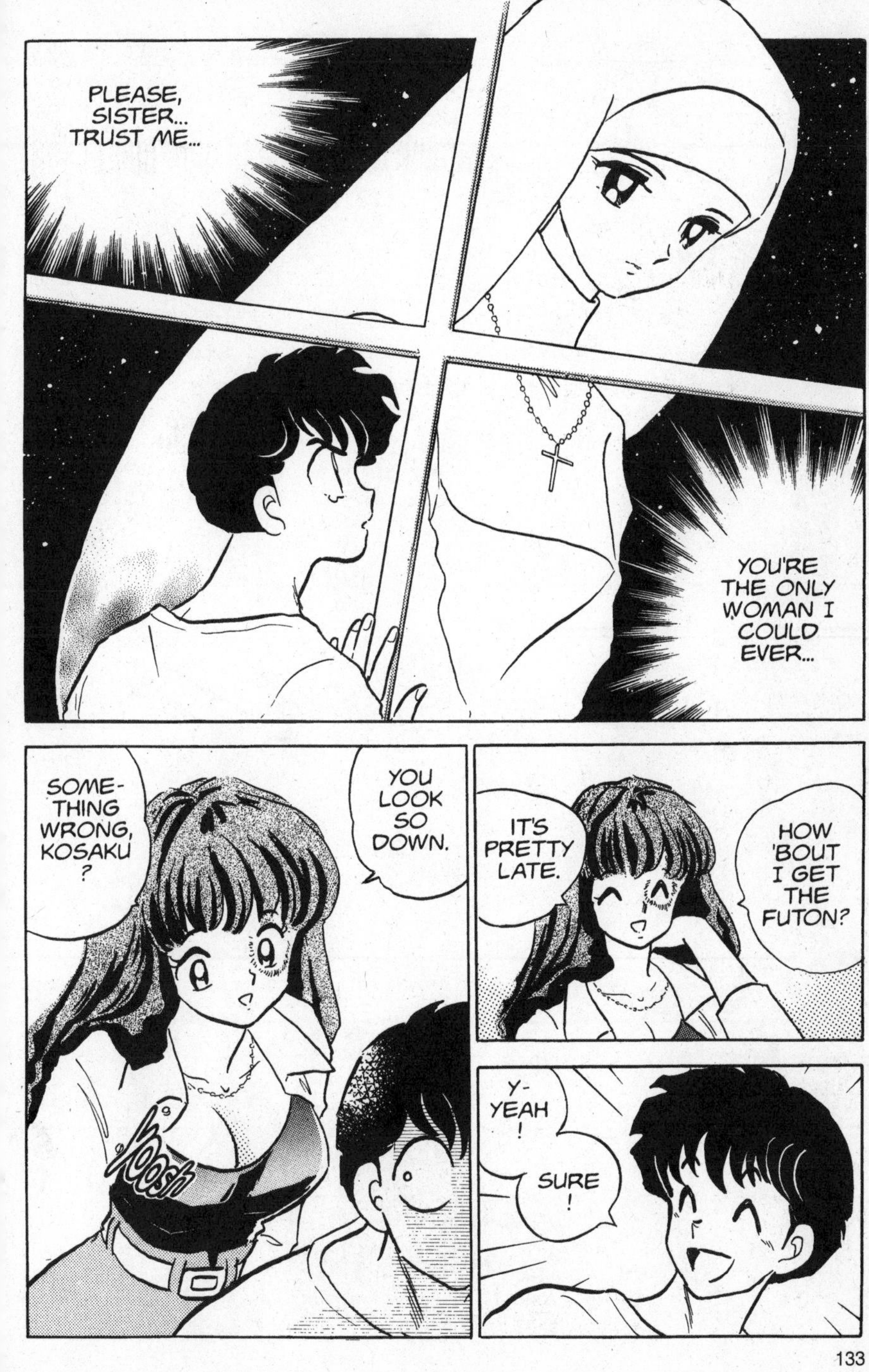
PLEASE, SISTER... TRUST ME...
YOU'RE THE ONLY WOMAN I COULD EVER...
SOME-THING WRONG, KOSAKU?
YOU LOOK SO DOWN.
YOOSH
IT'S PRETTY LATE.
HOW 'BOUT I GET THE FUTON?
Y-YEAH!
SURE!

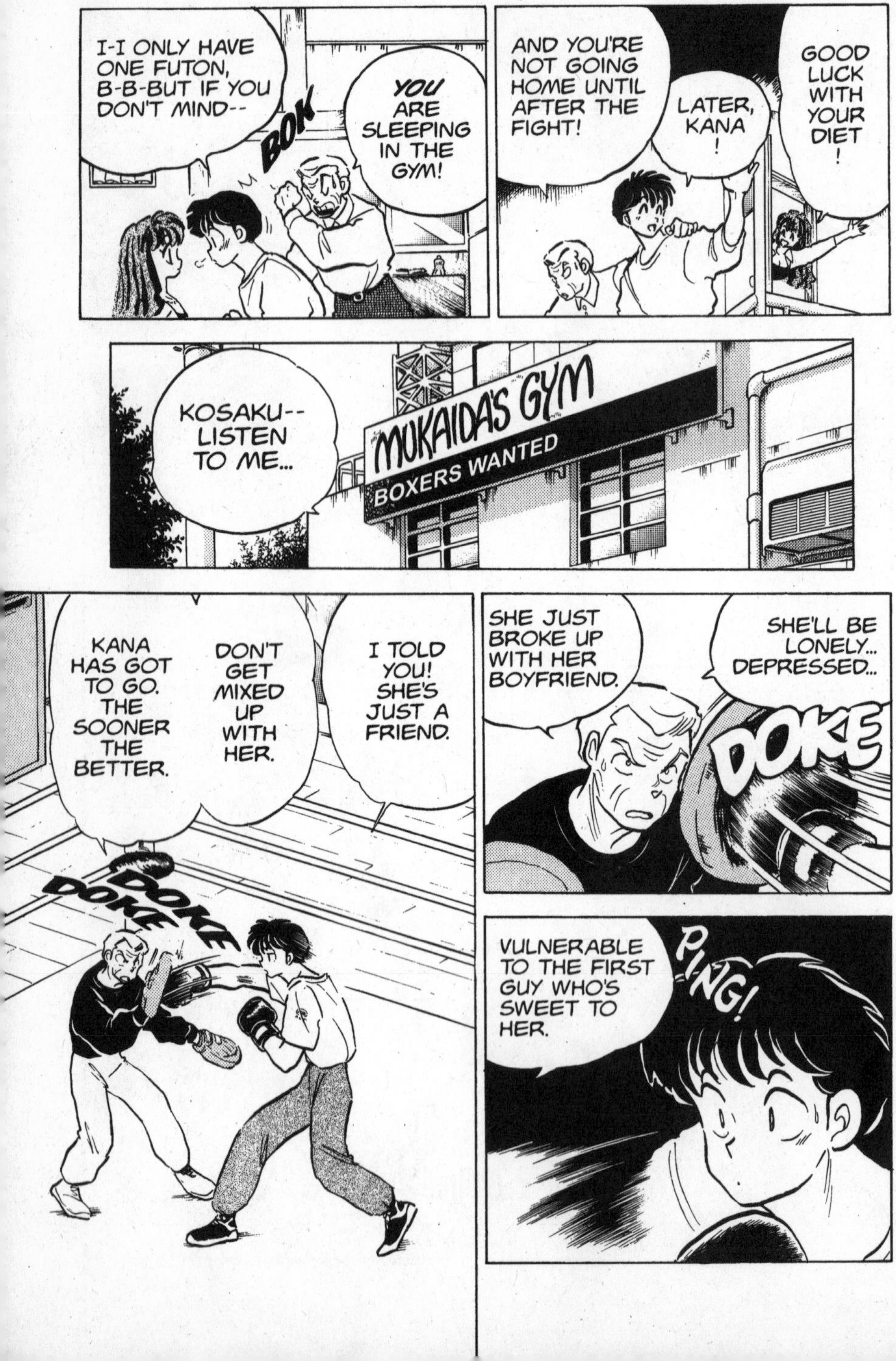
I-I ONLY HAVE ONE FUTON, B-B-BUT IF YOU DON'T MIND--
BOK
YOU ARE SLEEPING IN THE GYM!
AND YOU'RE NOT GOING HOME UNTIL AFTER THE FIGHT!
LATER, KANA!
GOOD LUCK WITH YOUR DIET!
KOSAKU-- LISTEN TO ME...
MUKAIDA'S GYM
BOXERS WANTED
KANA HAS GOT TO GO. THE SOONER THE BETTER.
DON'T GET MIXED UP WITH HER.
I TOLD YOU! SHE'S JUST A FRIEND.
DOKE
DOKE
SHE JUST BROKE UP WITH HER BOYFRIEND.
SHE'LL BE LONELY... DEPRESSED...
DOKE
VULNERABLE TO THE FIRST GUY WHO'S SWEET TO HER.
PING!

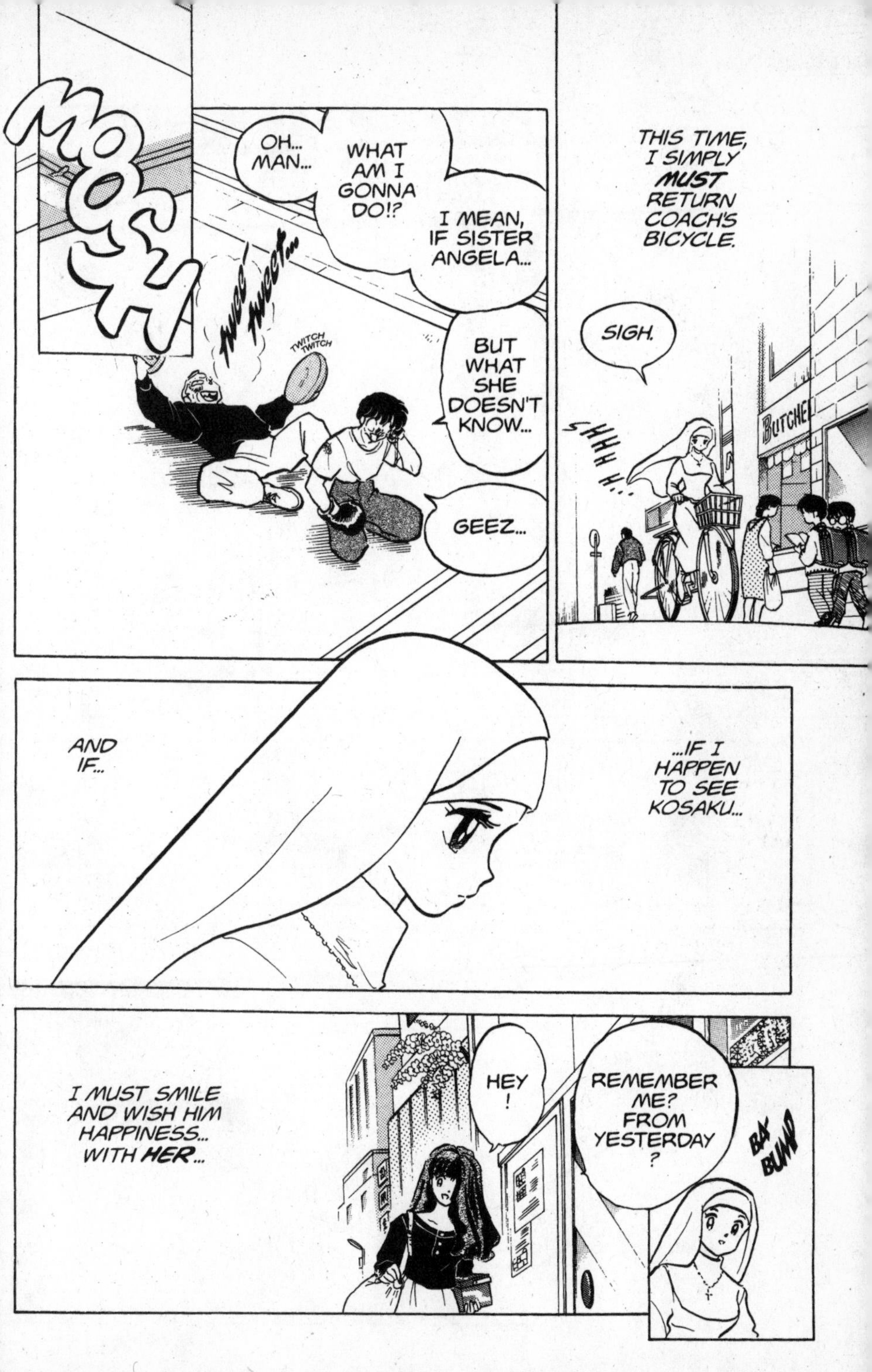
MOOSH
TWEET TWEET...
OH... MAN...
WHAT AM I GONNA DO!?
I MEAN, IF SISTER ANGELA...
TWITCH TWITCH
BUT WHAT SHE DOESN'T KNOW...
GEEZ...
THIS TIME, I SIMPLY **MUST** RETURN COACH'S BICYCLE.
SIGH.
SHHHH...
BUTCHE
AND IF...
...IF I HAPPEN TO SEE KOSAKU...
I MUST SMILE AND WISH HIM HAPPINESS... WITH **HER**...
HEY!
REMEMBER ME? FROM YESTERDAY?
BA-BUMP

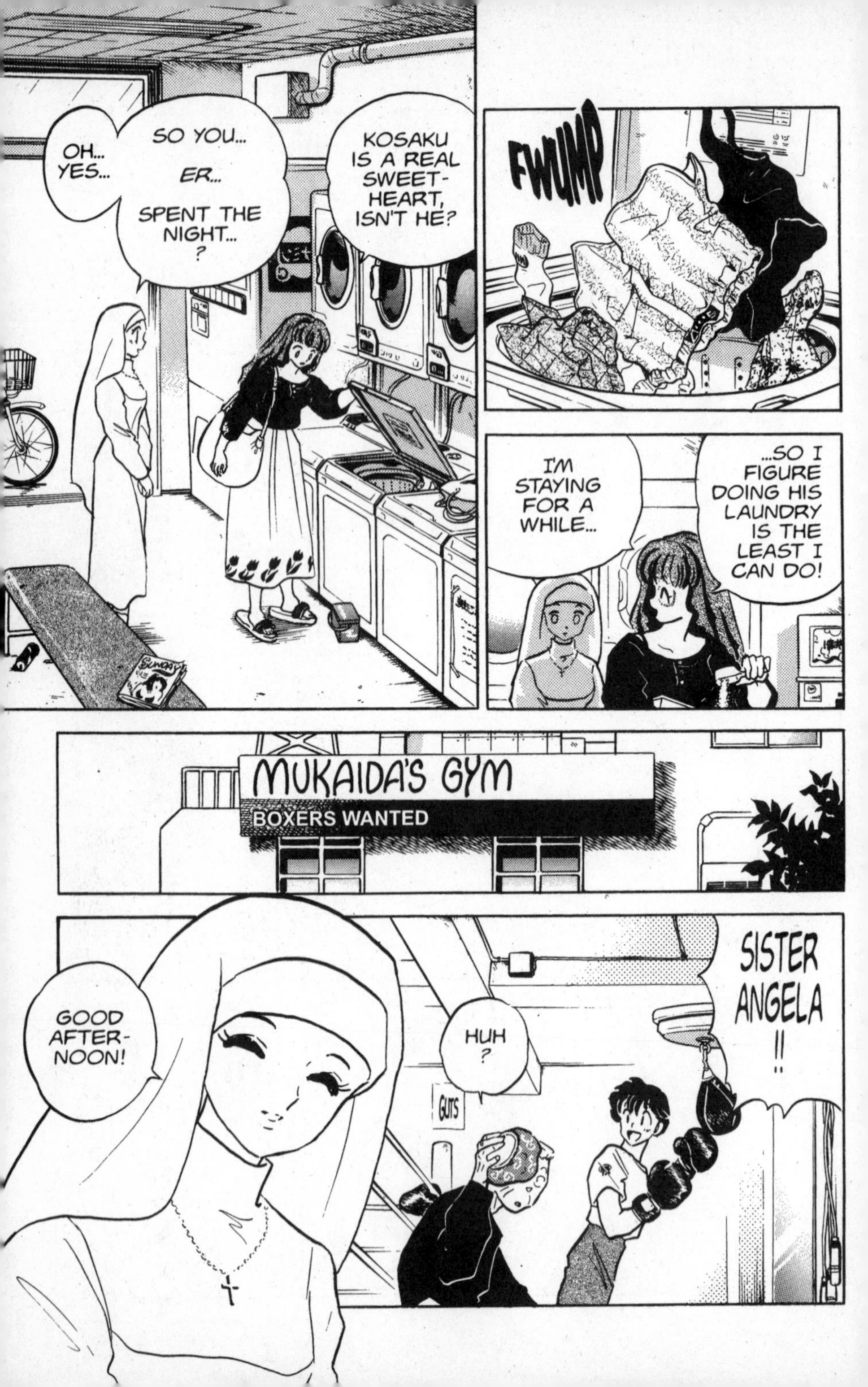
OH... YES...
SO YOU... ER... SPENT THE NIGHT... ?
KOSAKU IS A REAL SWEET-HEART, ISN'T HE?
FWUMP
I'M STAYING FOR A WHILE...
...SO I FIGURE DOING HIS LAUNDRY IS THE LEAST I CAN DO!
MUKAIDA'S GYM
BOXERS WANTED
GOOD AFTER-NOON!
HUH ?
GUTS
SISTER ANGELA !!

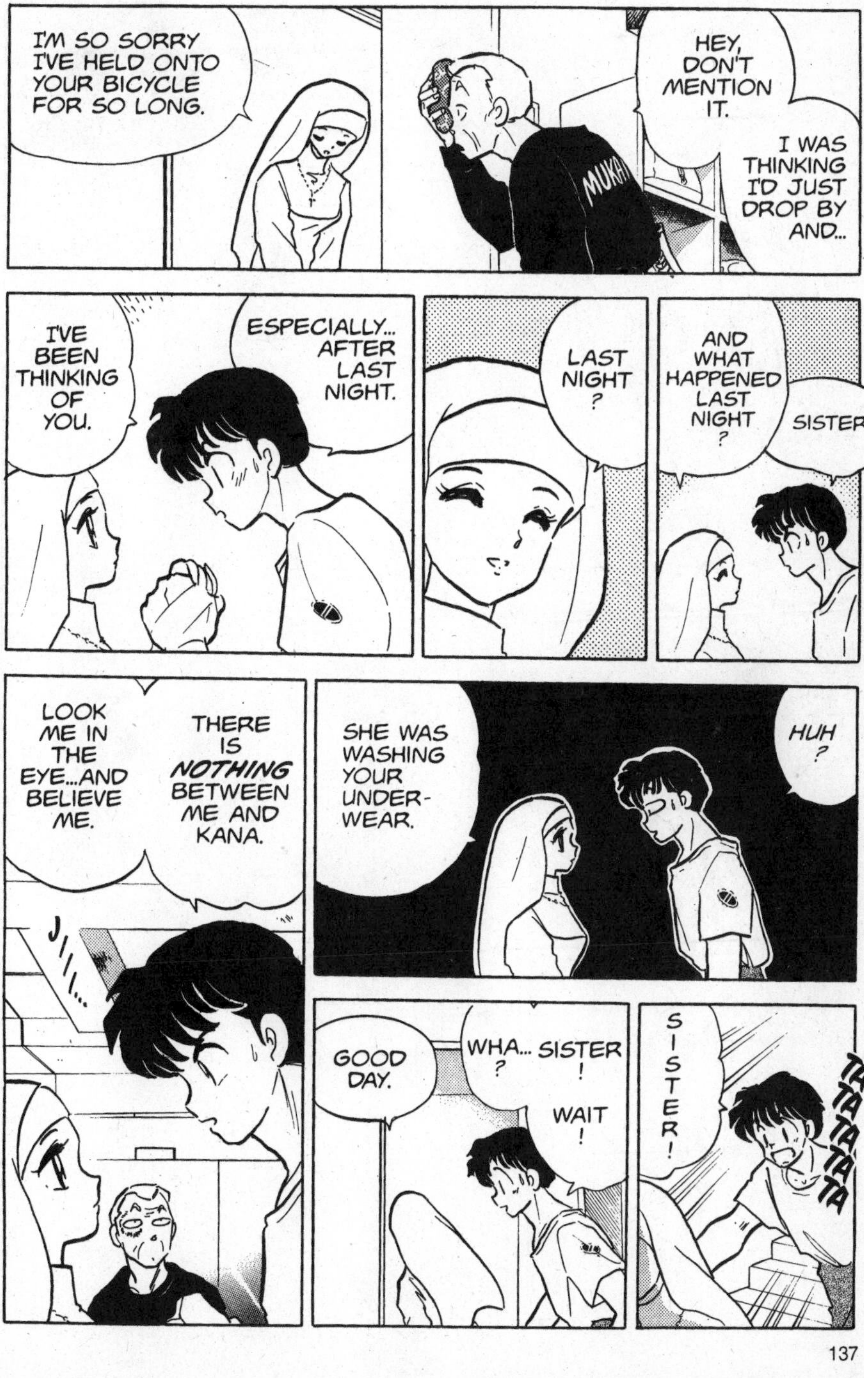
I'M SO SORRY I'VE HELD ONTO YOUR BICYCLE FOR SO LONG.
HEY, DON'T MENTION IT.
I WAS THINKING I'D JUST DROP BY AND...
MUKAI
I'VE BEEN THINKING OF YOU.
ESPECIALLY... AFTER LAST NIGHT.
LAST NIGHT?
AND WHAT HAPPENED LAST NIGHT?
SISTER...
LOOK ME IN THE EYE...AND BELIEVE ME.
THERE IS *NOTHING* BETWEEN ME AND KANA.
JIII...
SHE WAS WASHING YOUR UNDERWEAR.
HUH?
GOOD DAY.
WHA...? SISTER!
WAIT!
SISTER!
TA TA TA TA TA

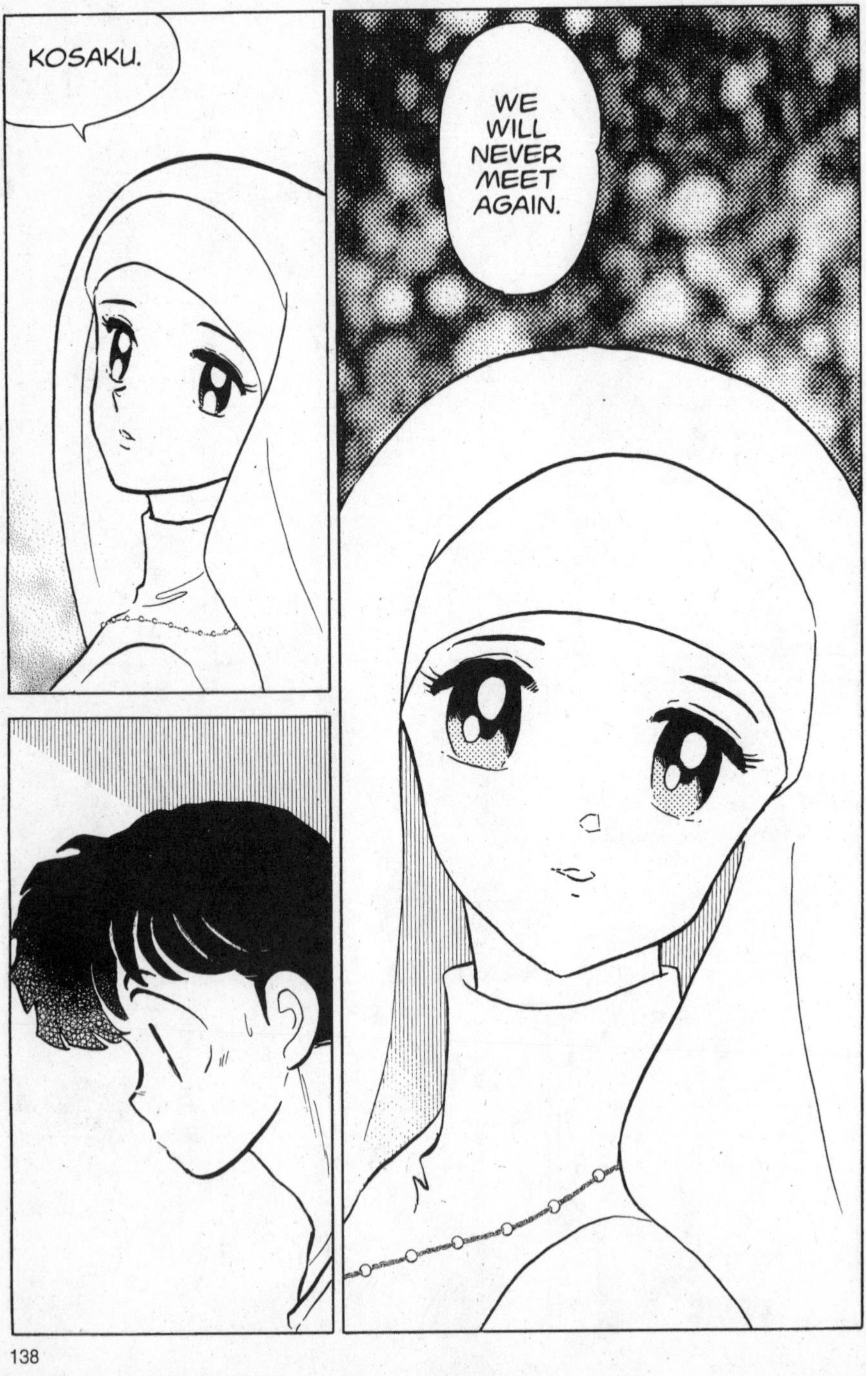
KOSAKU.
WE WILL NEVER MEET AGAIN.

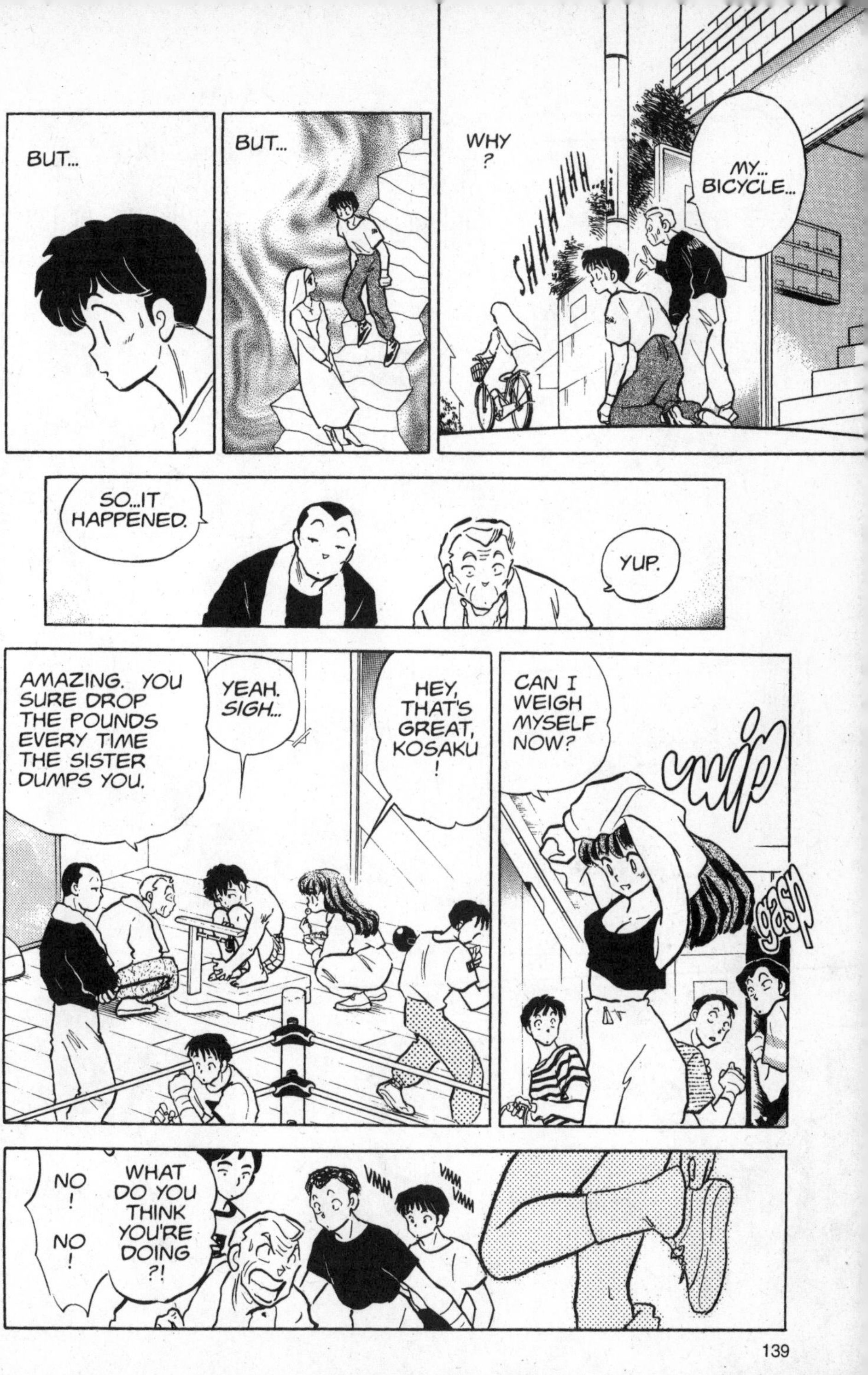
BUT...
BUT...
WHY ?
SHHHHHH...
MY... BICYCLE...
SO...IT HAPPENED.
YUP.
AMAZING. YOU SURE DROP THE POUNDS EVERY TIME THE SISTER DUMPS YOU.
YEAH. SIGH...
HEY, THAT'S GREAT, KOSAKU !
CAN I WEIGH MYSELF NOW?
WHIP
GASP
NO ! NO !
WHAT DO YOU THINK YOU'RE DOING ?!
VMM
VMM VMM

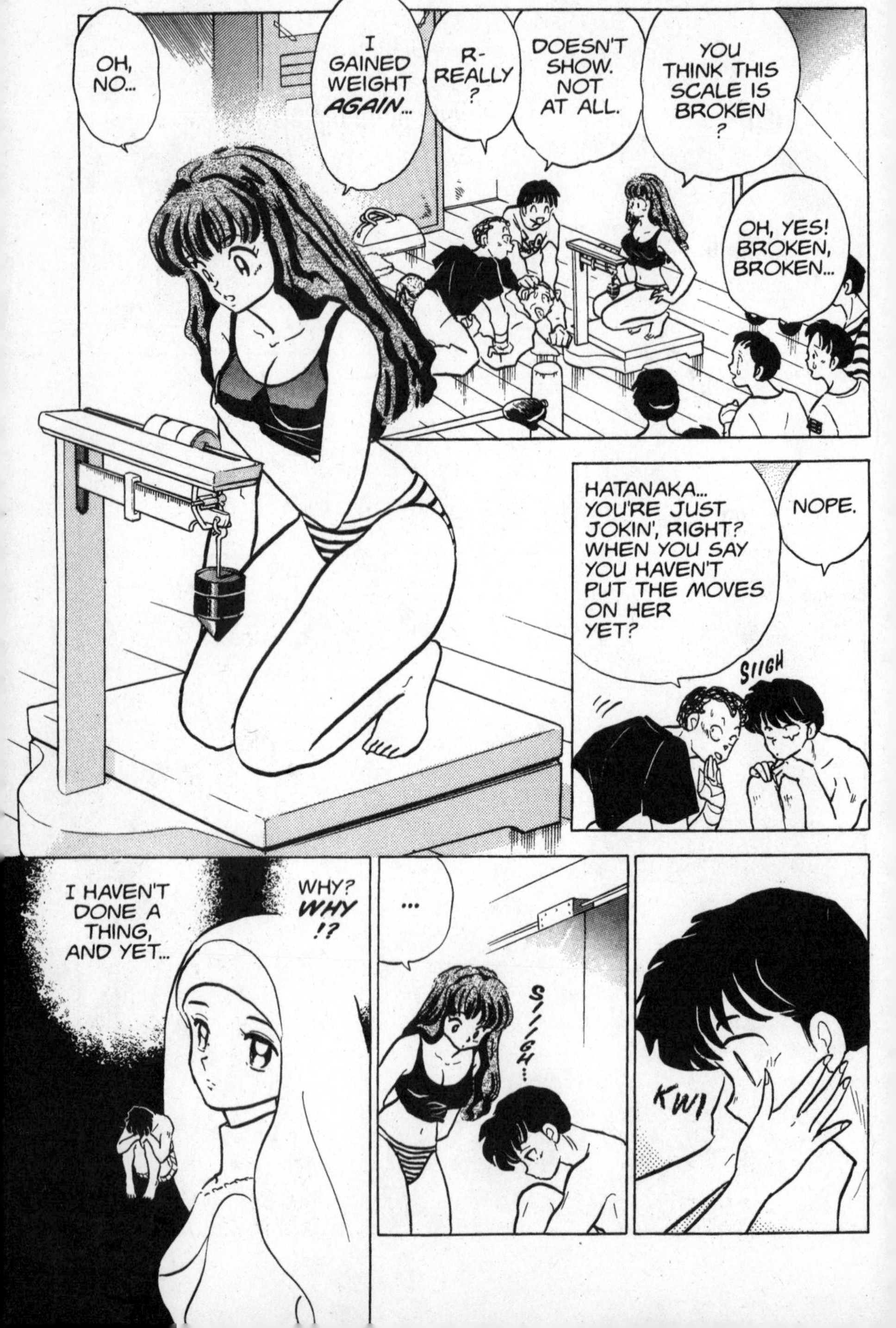
OH, NO...
I GAINED WEIGHT AGAIN...
R-REALLY?
DOESN'T SHOW. NOT AT ALL.
YOU THINK THIS SCALE IS BROKEN?
OH, YES! BROKEN, BROKEN...
HATANAKA... YOU'RE JUST JOKIN', RIGHT? WHEN YOU SAY YOU HAVEN'T PUT THE MOVES ON HER YET?
NOPE.
SIIGH
I HAVEN'T DONE A THING, AND YET...
WHY? WHY!?
...
SIIIGH...
KWI

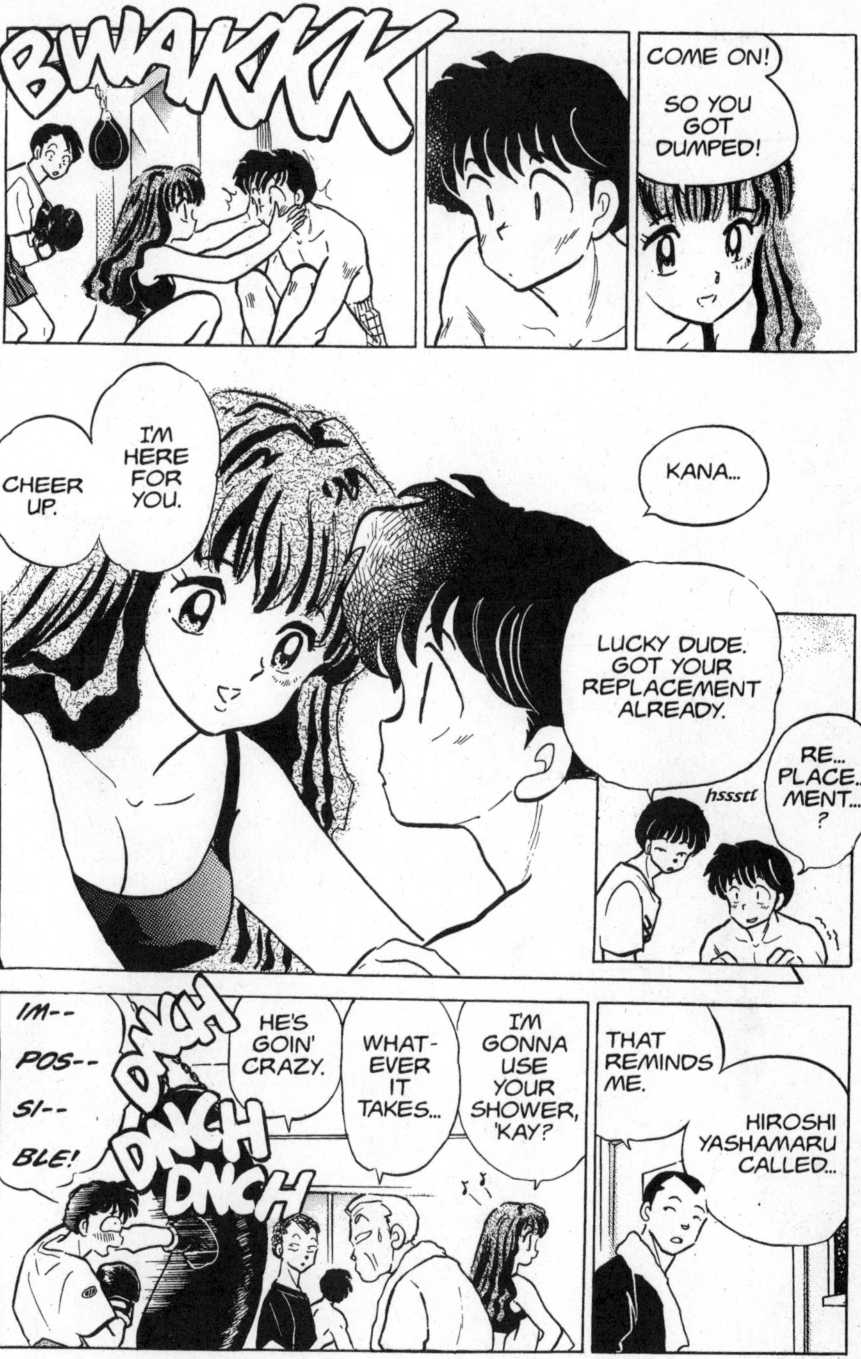
BWAKKK
COME ON!
SO YOU GOT DUMPED!
CHEER UP.
I'M HERE FOR YOU.
KANA...
LUCKY DUDE. GOT YOUR REPLACEMENT ALREADY.
hssstt
RE... PLACE... MENT... ?
IM-- POS-- SI-- BLE!
DNCH DNCH DNCH
HE'S GOIN' CRAZY.
WHAT-EVER IT TAKES...
I'M GONNA USE YOUR SHOWER, 'KAY?
THAT REMINDS ME.
HIROSHI YASHAMARU CALLED...

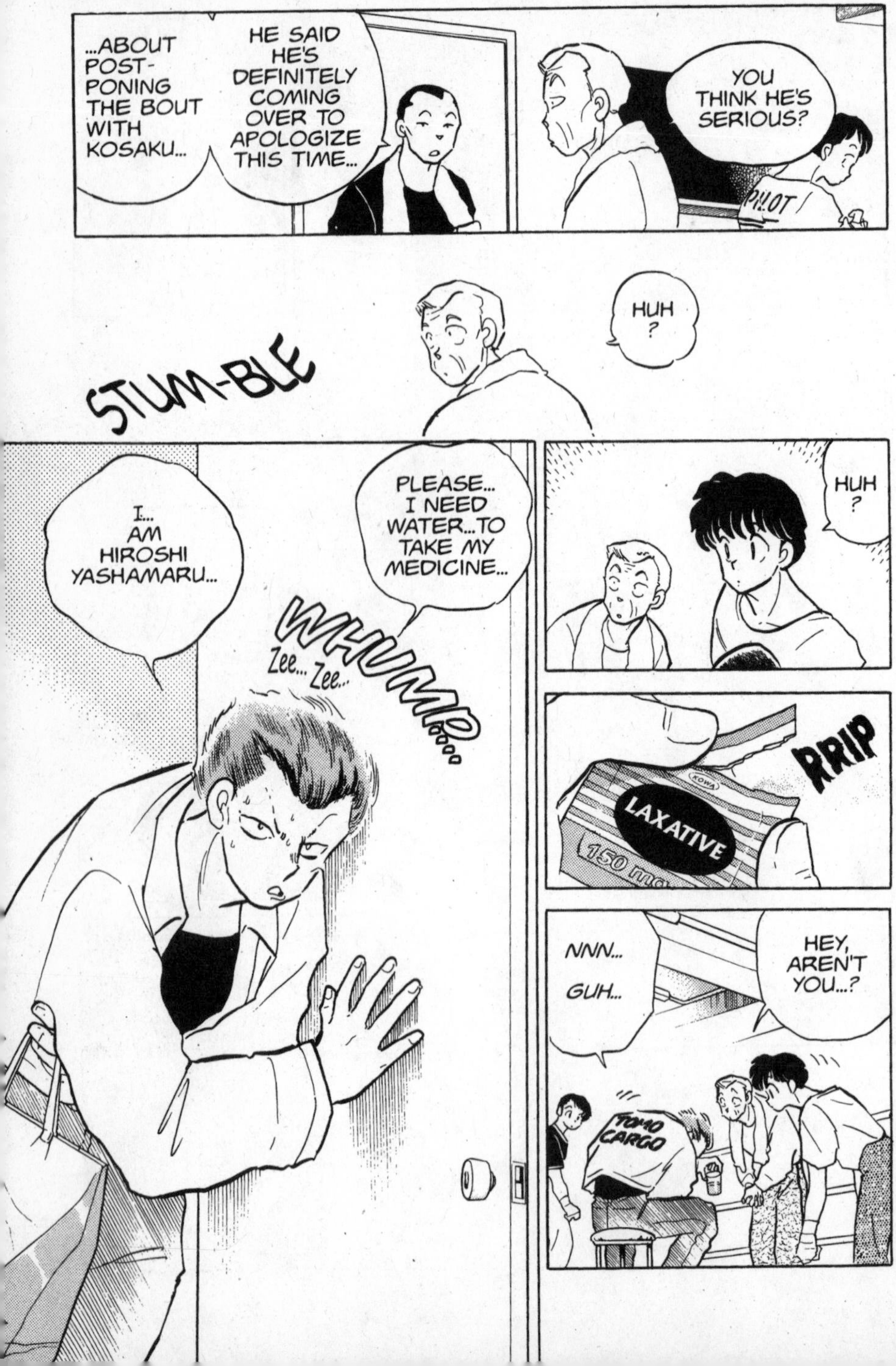
...ABOUT POST-PONING THE BOUT WITH KOSAKU...
HE SAID HE'S DEFINITELY COMING OVER TO APOLOGIZE THIS TIME...
YOU THINK HE'S SERIOUS?
PILOT
STUM-BLE
HUH?
I... AM HIROSHI YASHAMARU...
PLEASE... I NEED WATER...TO TAKE MY MEDICINE...
WHUMP...
Zee... Zee...
HUH?
RRIP
KOWA
LAXATIVE
150 mg
NNN... GUH...
HEY, AREN'T YOU...?
TOMO CARGO

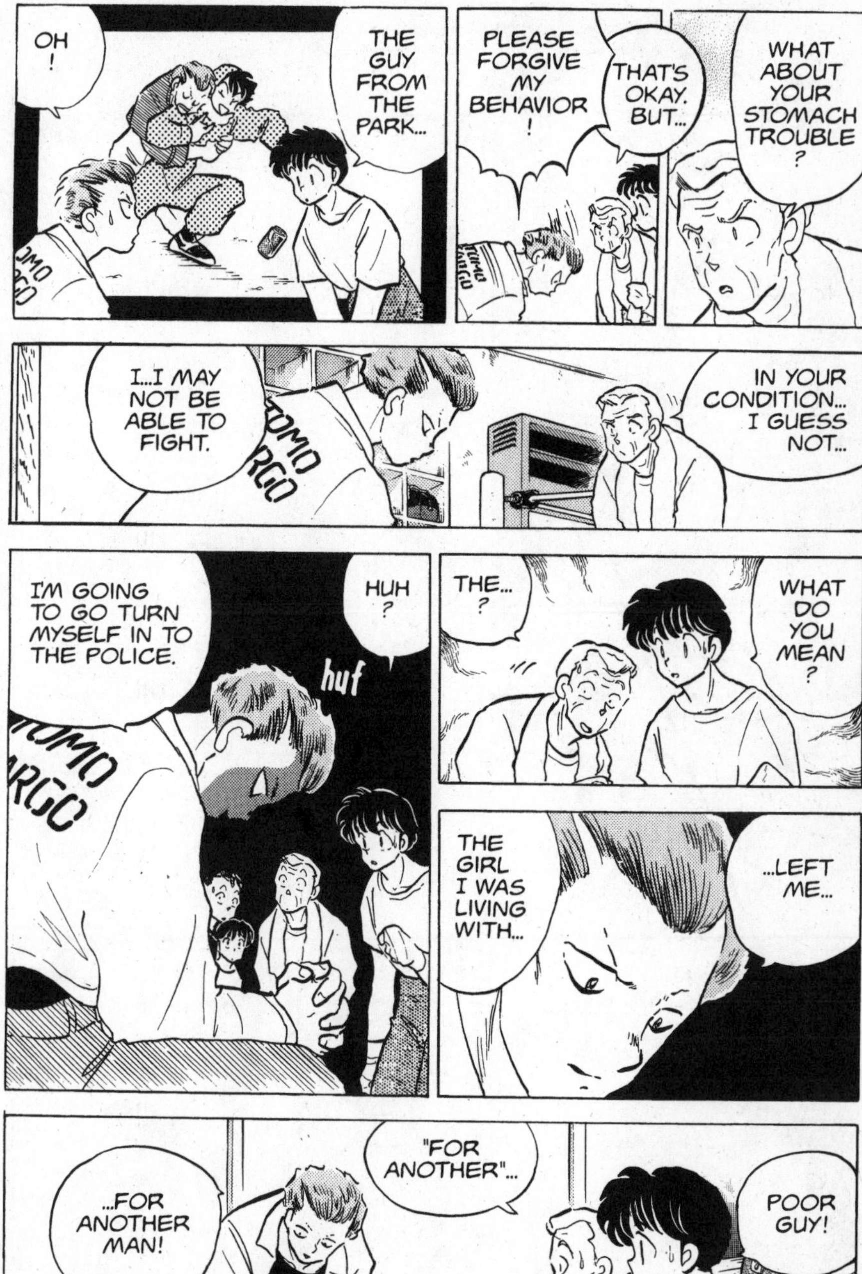
OH!
THE GUY FROM THE PARK...
PLEASE FORGIVE MY BEHAVIOR!
THAT'S OKAY. BUT...
WHAT ABOUT YOUR STOMACH TROUBLE?
I...I MAY NOT BE ABLE TO FIGHT.
IN YOUR CONDITION... I GUESS NOT...
I'M GOING TO GO TURN MYSELF IN TO THE POLICE.
HUH?
huf
THE...?
WHAT DO YOU MEAN?
THE GIRL I WAS LIVING WITH...
...LEFT ME...
...FOR ANOTHER MAN!
"FOR ANOTHER"...
POOR GUY!

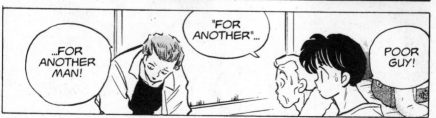

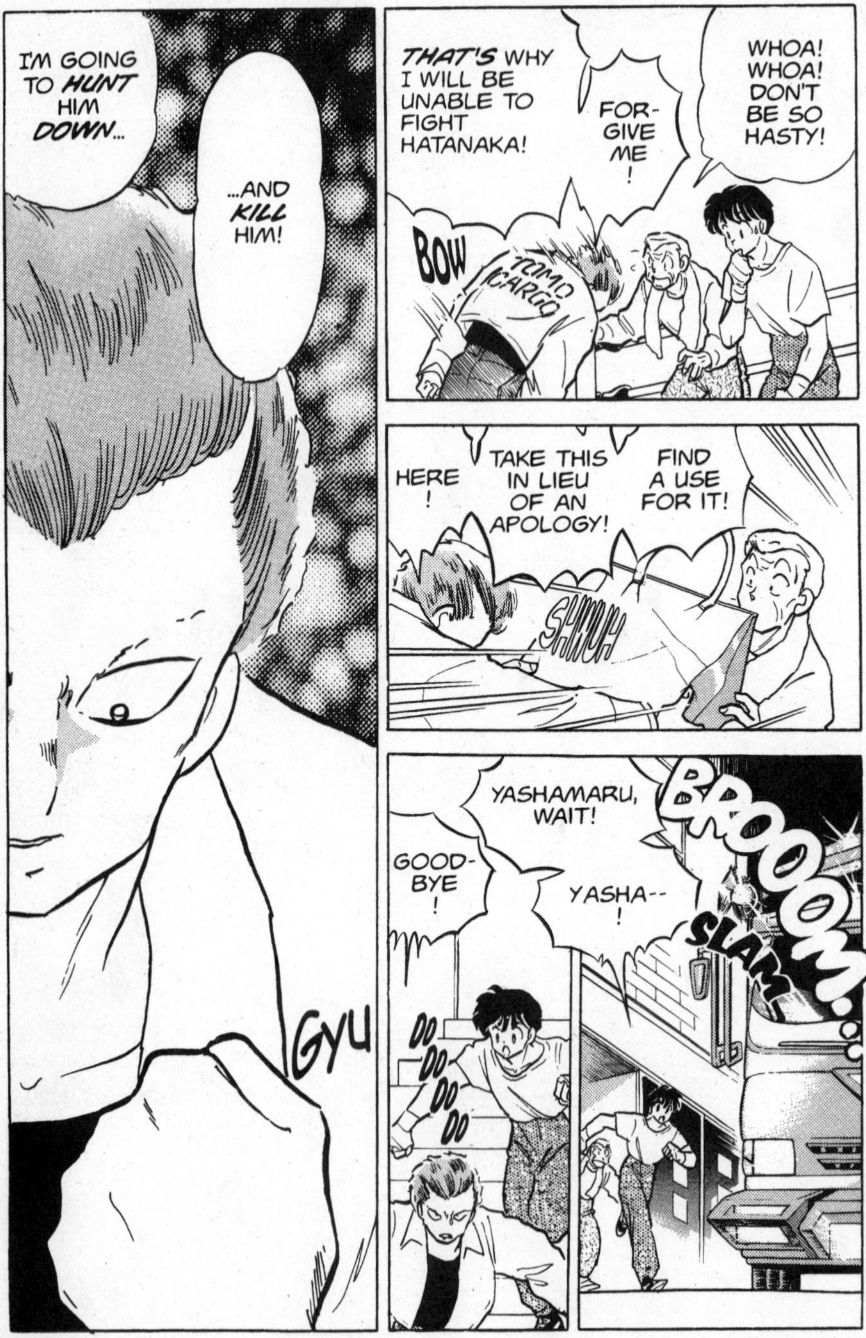
I'M GOING TO HUNT HIM DOWN...
...AND KILL HIM!
GYU
THAT'S WHY I WILL BE UNABLE TO FIGHT HATANAKA!
FOR-GIVE ME!
WHOA! WHOA! DON'T BE SO HASTY!
BOW
TOMO CARGO
HERE!
TAKE THIS IN LIEU OF AN APOLOGY!
FIND A USE FOR IT!
SHUUH
YASHAMARU, WAIT!
GOOD-BYE!
YASHA--!
BROOOOM...
SLAM
DO DO DO DO DO

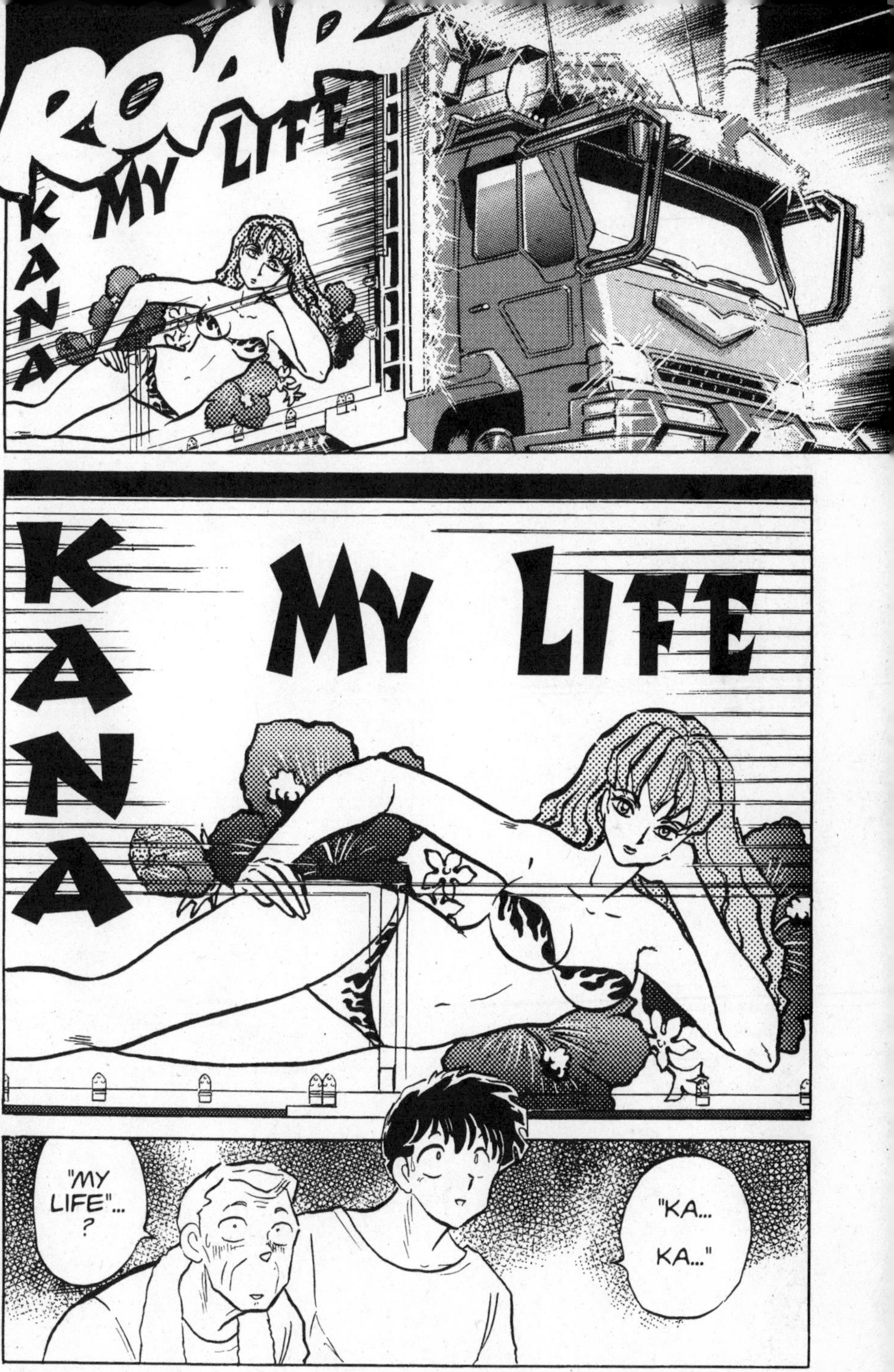
ROAR
KANA
MY LIFE
KANA
MY LIFE
"MY LIFE"... ?
"KA... KA..."

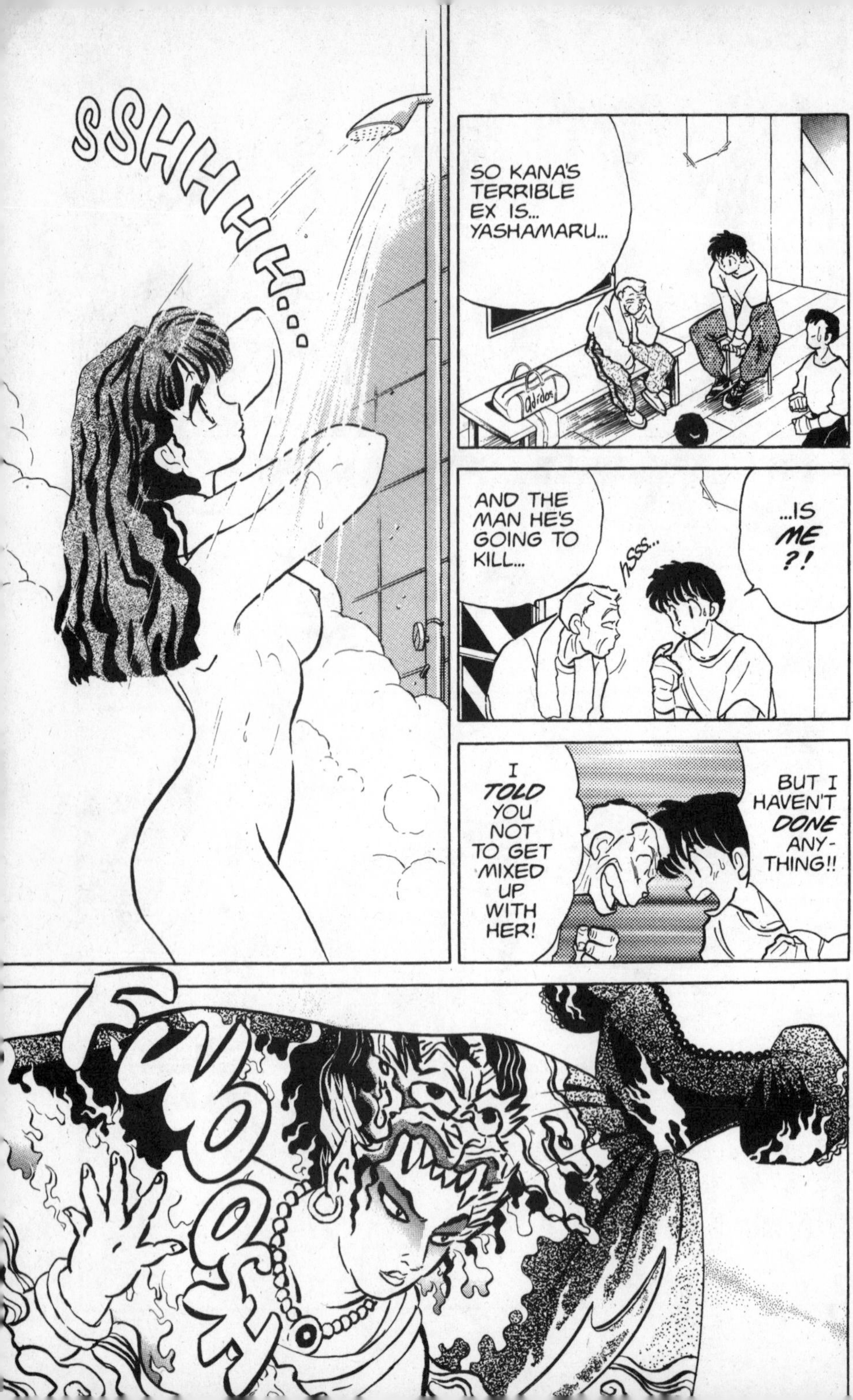
SSHHHHH...
SO KANA'S TERRIBLE EX IS... YASHAMARU...
AND THE MAN HE'S GOING TO KILL...
hsss...
...IS ME ?!
I TOLD YOU NOT TO GET MIXED UP WITH HER!
BUT I HAVEN'T DONE ANY-THING!!
FWOOOSH

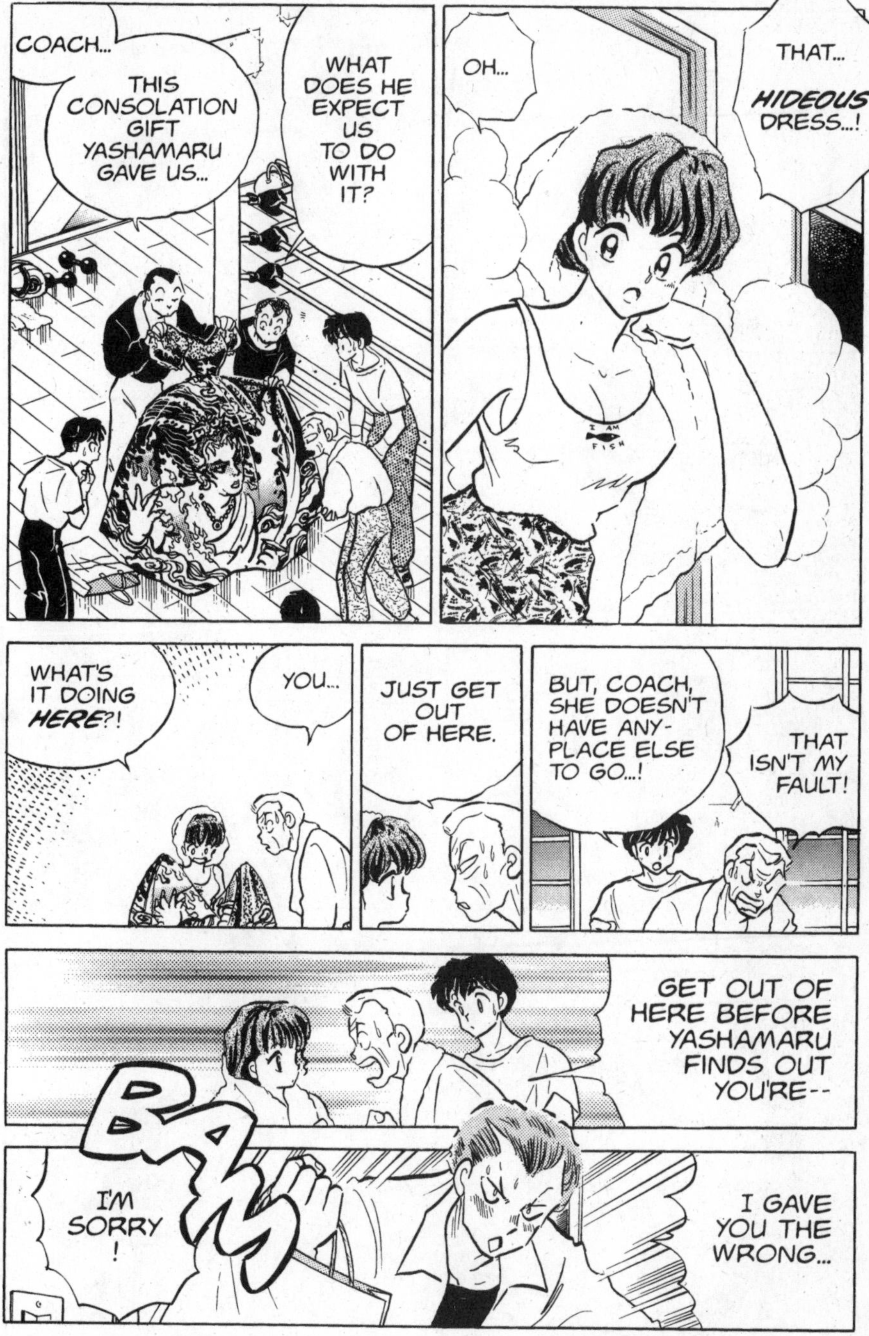
COACH...
THIS CONSOLATION GIFT YASHAMARU GAVE US...
WHAT DOES HE EXPECT US TO DO WITH IT?
OH...
THAT...
HIDEOUS DRESS...!
I AM FISH
WHAT'S IT DOING HERE?!
YOU...
JUST GET OUT OF HERE.
BUT, COACH, SHE DOESN'T HAVE ANY-PLACE ELSE TO GO...!
THAT ISN'T MY FAULT!
GET OUT OF HERE BEFORE YASHAMARU FINDS OUT YOU'RE--
BAM
I'M SORRY!
I GAVE YOU THE WRONG...

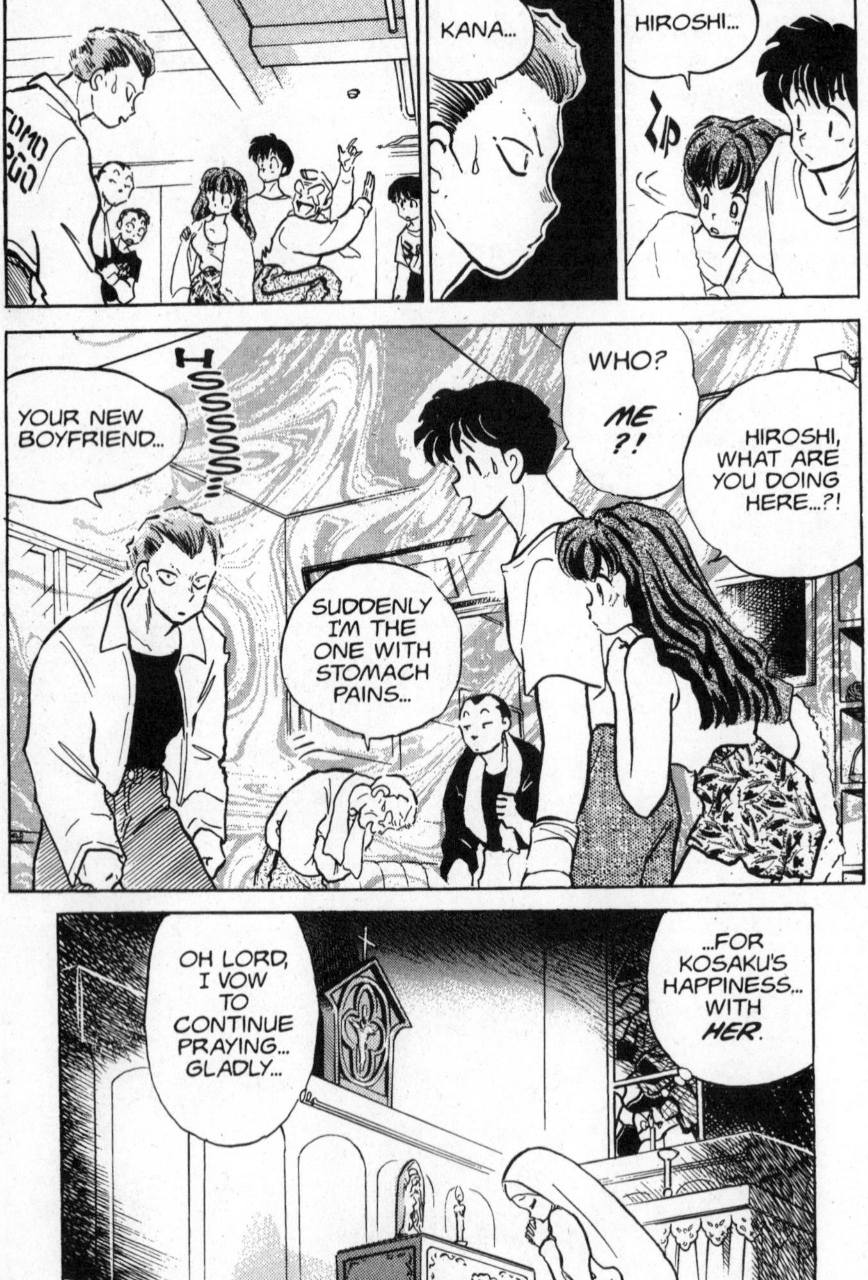
KANA...
HIROSHI...
ZIP
YOUR NEW BOYFRIEND...
HSSSSSS!!
WHO? *ME* ?!
HIROSHI, WHAT ARE YOU DOING HERE...?!
SUDDENLY I'M THE ONE WITH STOMACH PAINS...
OH LORD, I VOW TO CONTINUE PRAYING... GLADLY...
...FOR KOSAKU'S HAPPINESS... WITH *HER*.

CHAPTER THREE

THE FALLEN LAMB

PART THREE

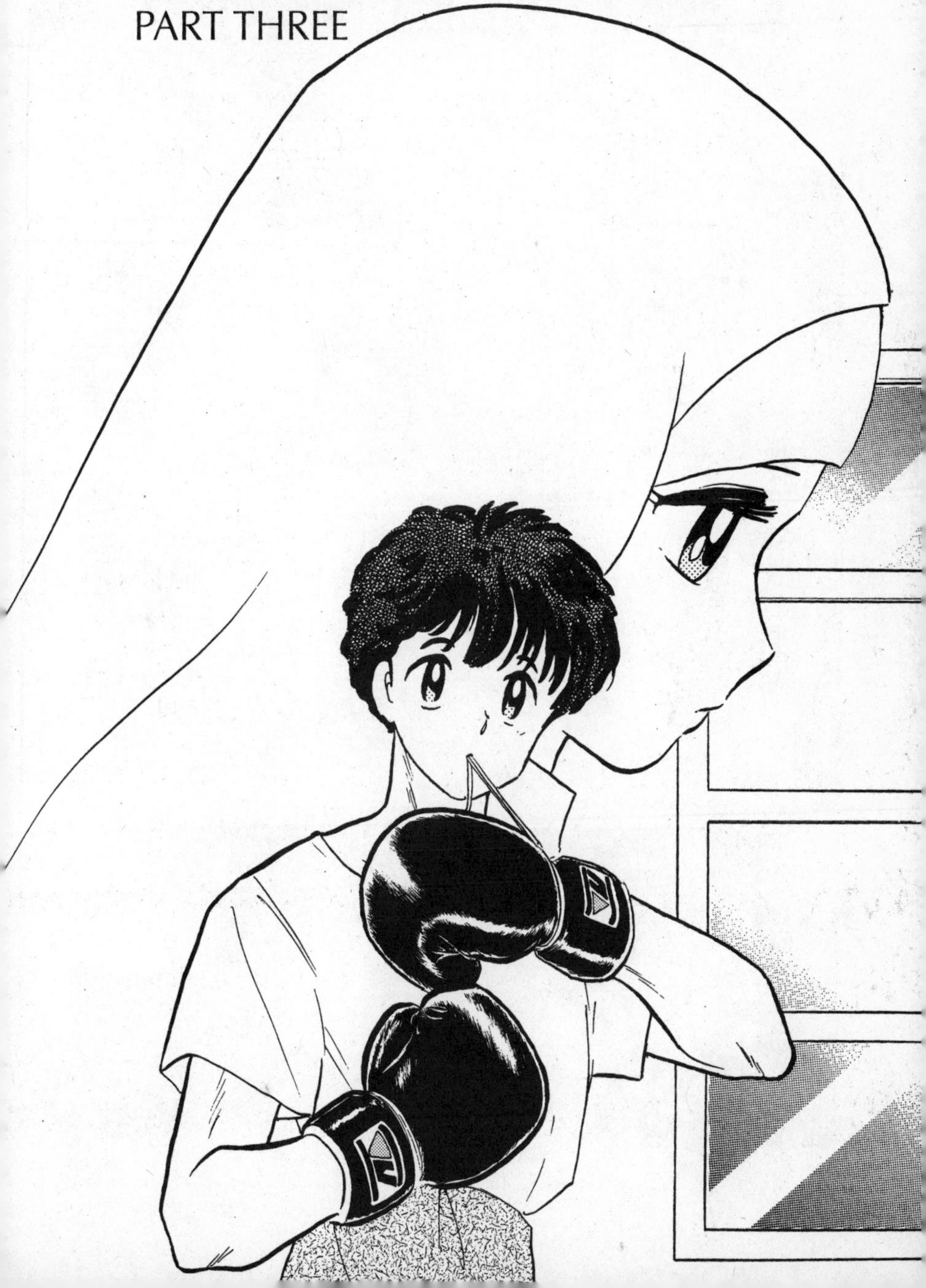

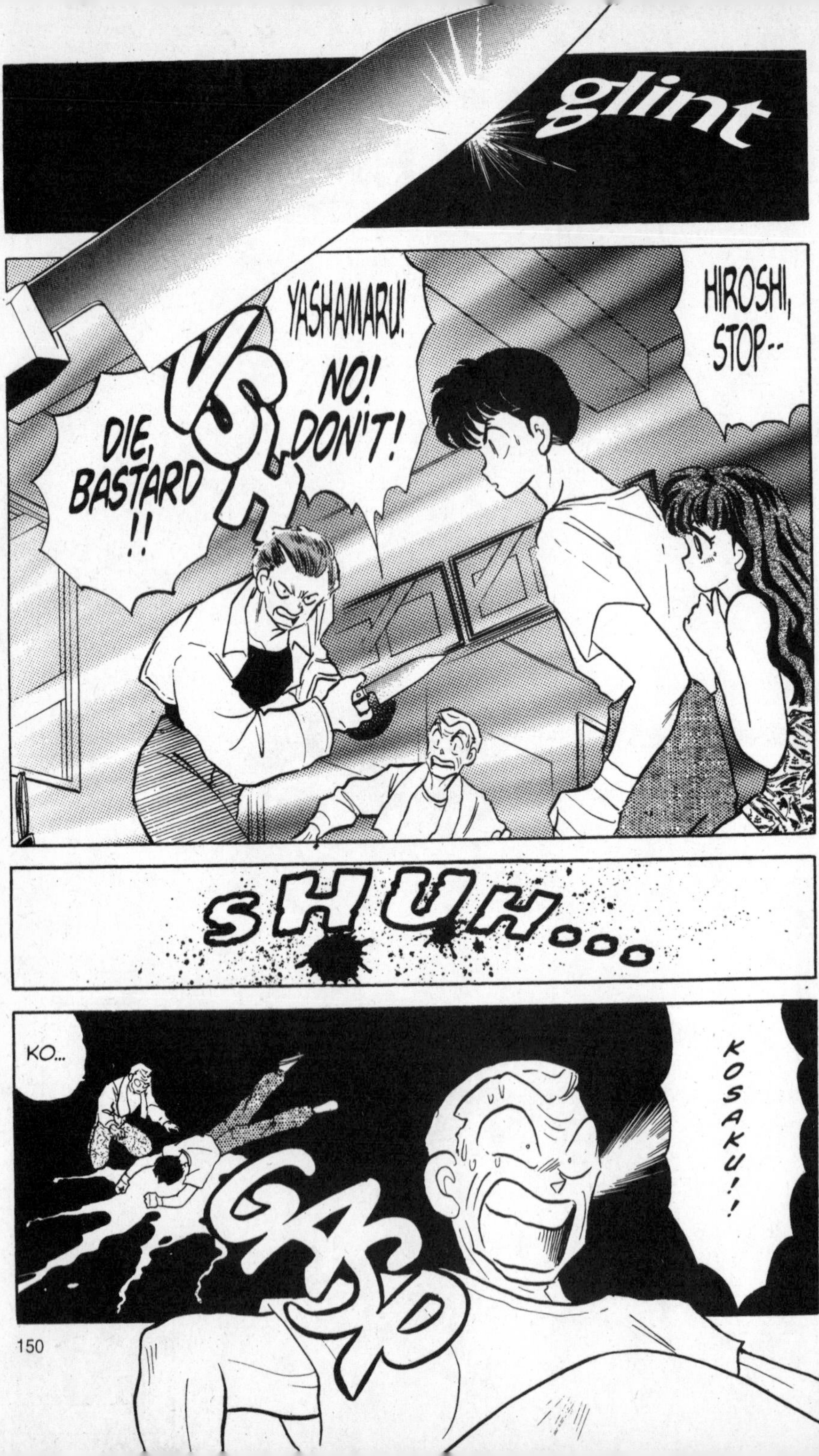
glint
DIE, BASTARD!!
VSH
YASHAMARU! NO! DON'T!
HIROSHI, STOP--
sHUH...
KO...
GASP
KOSAKU!!

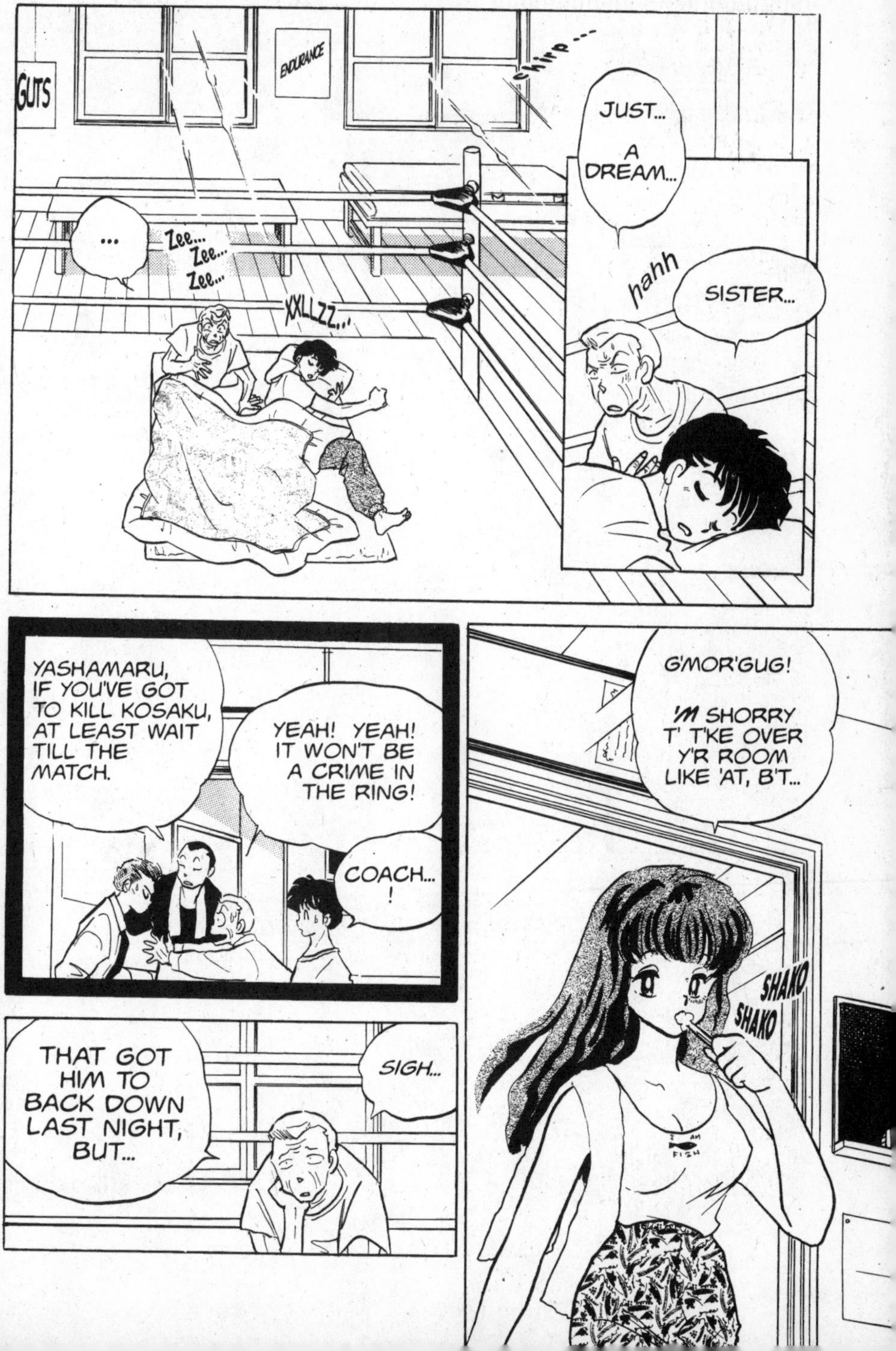
GUTS
ENDURANCE
chirp...
...
Zee... Zee... Zee...
XXLLZZ...
JUST... A DREAM...
hahh
SISTER...
YASHAMARU, IF YOU'VE GOT TO KILL KOSAKU, AT LEAST WAIT TILL THE MATCH.
YEAH! YEAH! IT WON'T BE A CRIME IN THE RING!
COACH... !
THAT GOT HIM TO BACK DOWN LAST NIGHT, BUT...
SIGH...
G'MOR'GUG!
'M SHORRY T' T'KE OVER Y'R ROOM LIKE 'AT, B'T...
SHAKO SHAKO
I AM FISH

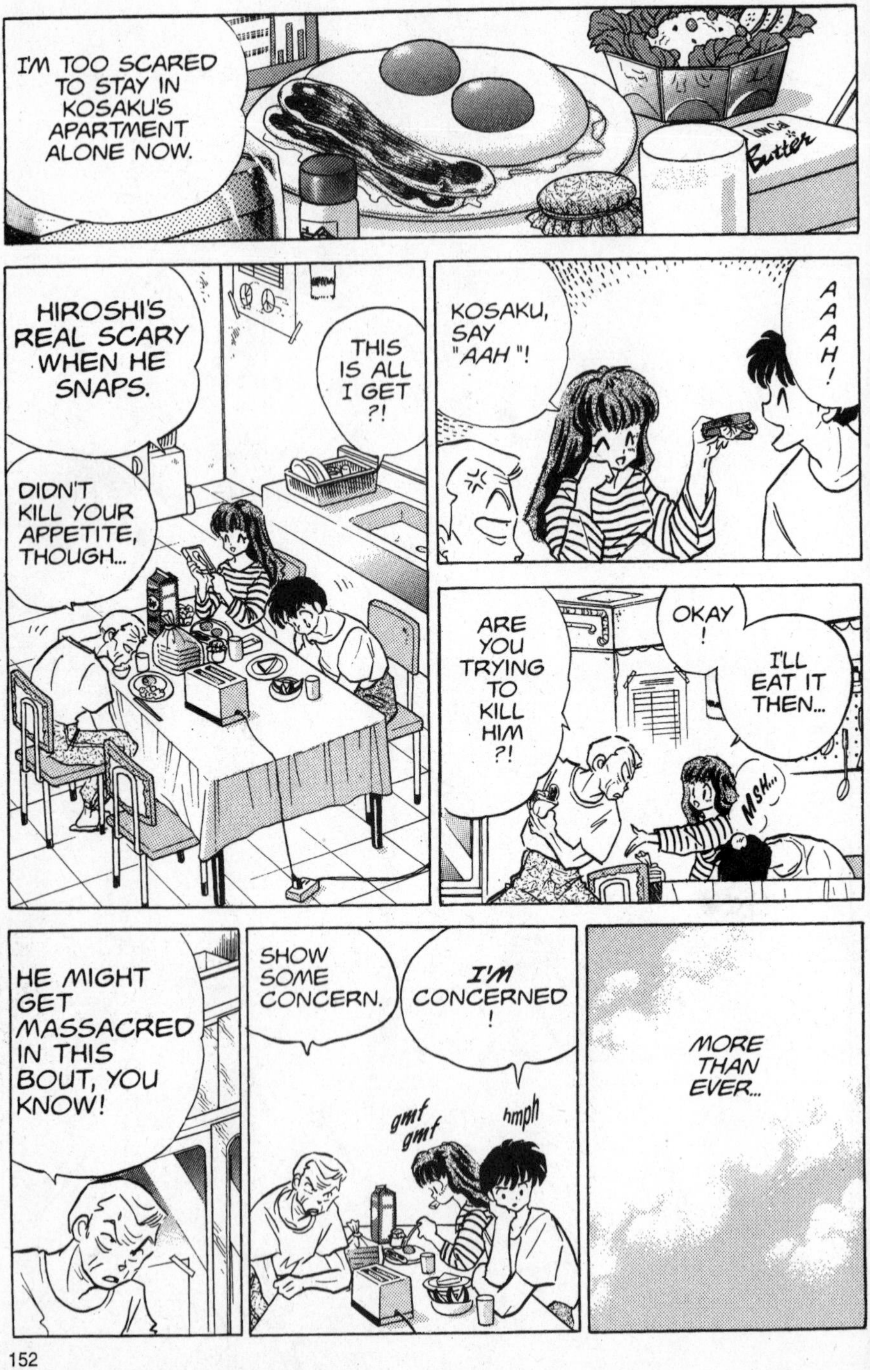

I'M TOO SCARED TO STAY IN KOSAKU'S APARTMENT ALONE NOW.
Low Cal Butter
HIROSHI'S REAL SCARY WHEN HE SNAPS.
THIS IS ALL I GET ?!
DIDN'T KILL YOUR APPETITE, THOUGH...
KOSAKU, SAY "AAH"!
AAAAH!
ARE YOU TRYING TO KILL HIM ?!
OKAY!
I'LL EAT IT THEN...
MSH...
HE MIGHT GET MASSACRED IN THIS BOUT, YOU KNOW!
SHOW SOME CONCERN.
I'M CONCERNED!
gmf gmf
hmph
MORE THAN EVER...

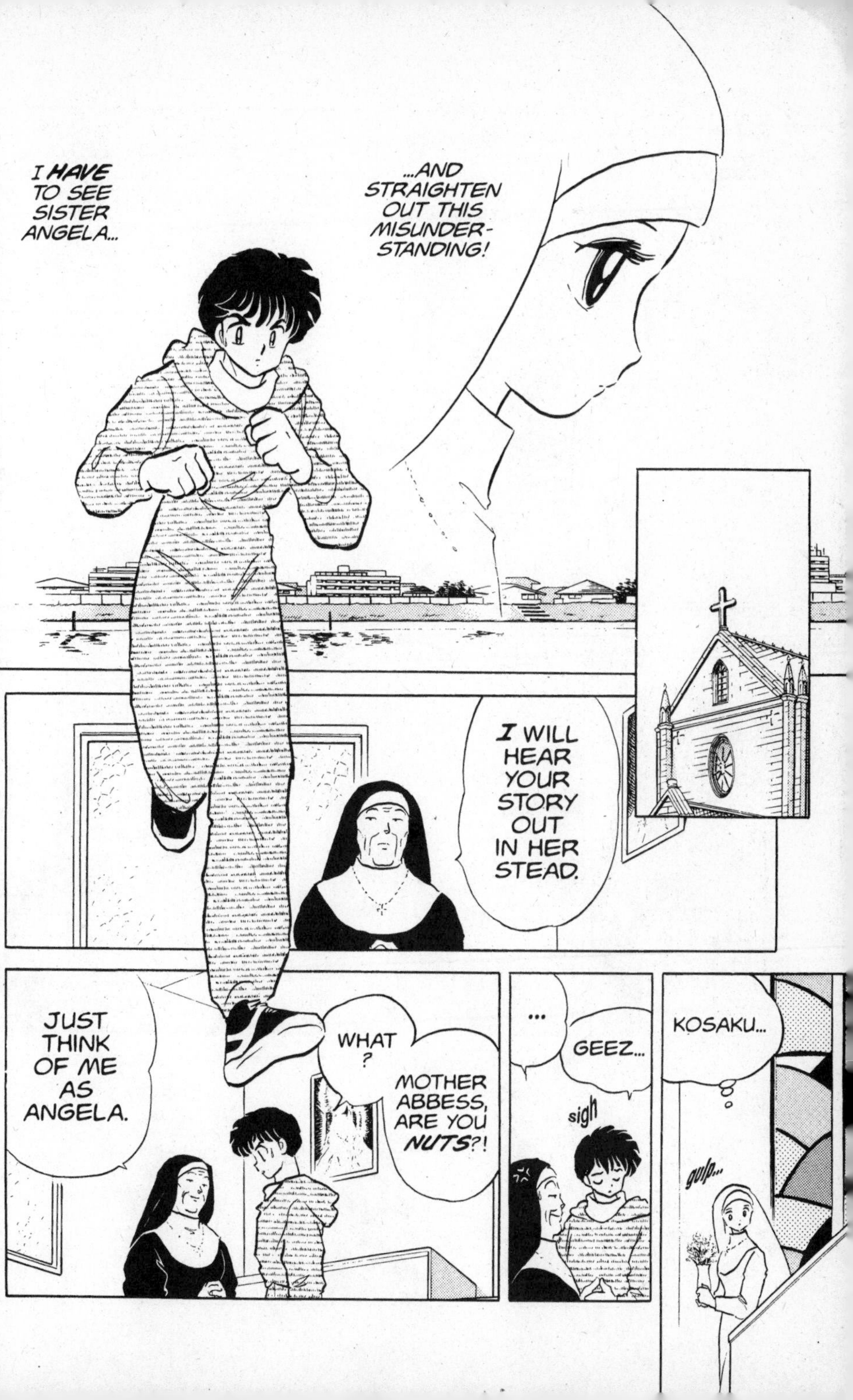
I HAVE TO SEE SISTER ANGELA...
...AND STRAIGHTEN OUT THIS MISUNDER-STANDING!
I WILL HEAR YOUR STORY OUT IN HER STEAD.
JUST THINK OF ME AS ANGELA.
WHAT?
MOTHER ABBESS, ARE YOU NUTS?!
...
GEEZ...
sigh
KOSAKU...
gulp...

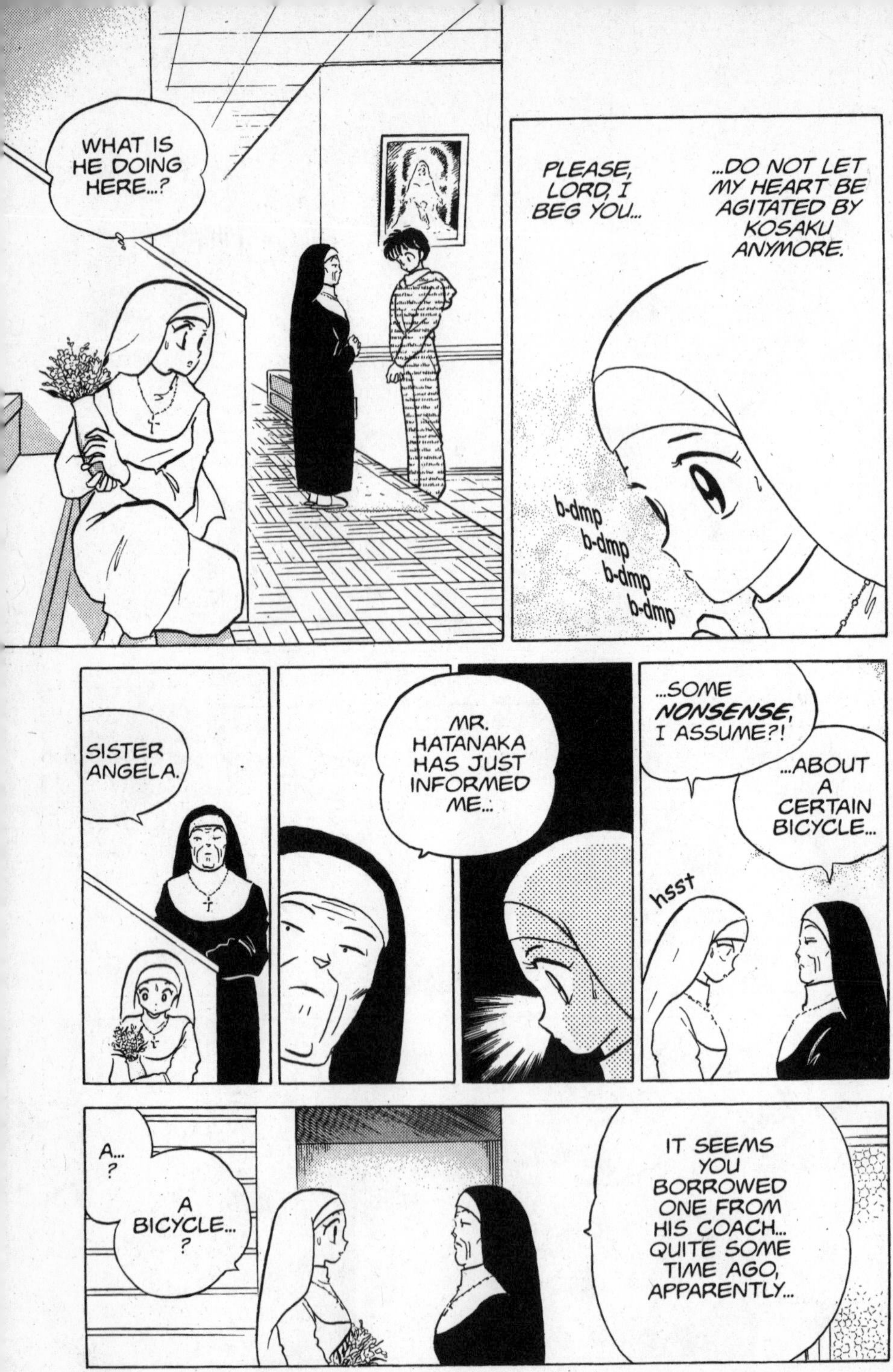
WHAT IS HE DOING HERE...?
PLEASE, LORD, I BEG YOU...
...DO NOT LET MY HEART BE AGITATED BY KOSAKU ANYMORE.
b-dmp b-dmp b-dmp b-dmp
SISTER ANGELA.
MR. HATANAKA HAS JUST INFORMED ME...
...SOME NONSENSE, I ASSUME?!
...ABOUT A CERTAIN BICYCLE...
hsst
A... ?
A BICYCLE... ?
IT SEEMS YOU BORROWED ONE FROM HIS COACH... QUITE SOME TIME AGO, APPARENTLY...

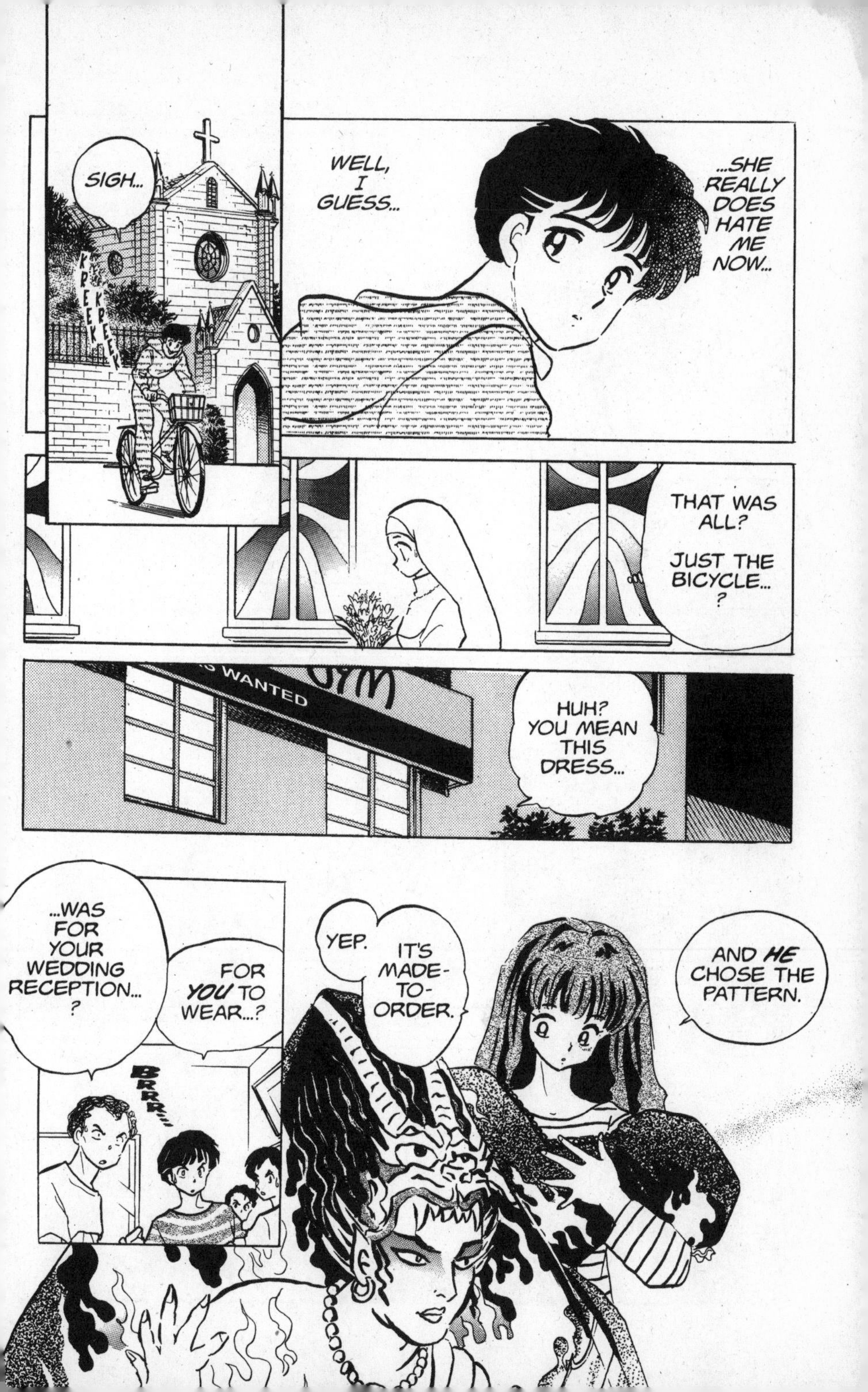
SIGH...
KREEK KREEK
WELL, I GUESS...
...SHE REALLY DOES HATE ME NOW...
THAT WAS ALL? JUST THE BICYCLE...?
WANTED
HUH? YOU MEAN THIS DRESS...
...WAS FOR YOUR WEDDING RECEPTION...?
FOR *YOU* TO WEAR...?
BRRRR...
YEP. IT'S MADE-TO-ORDER.
AND *HE* CHOSE THE PATTERN.

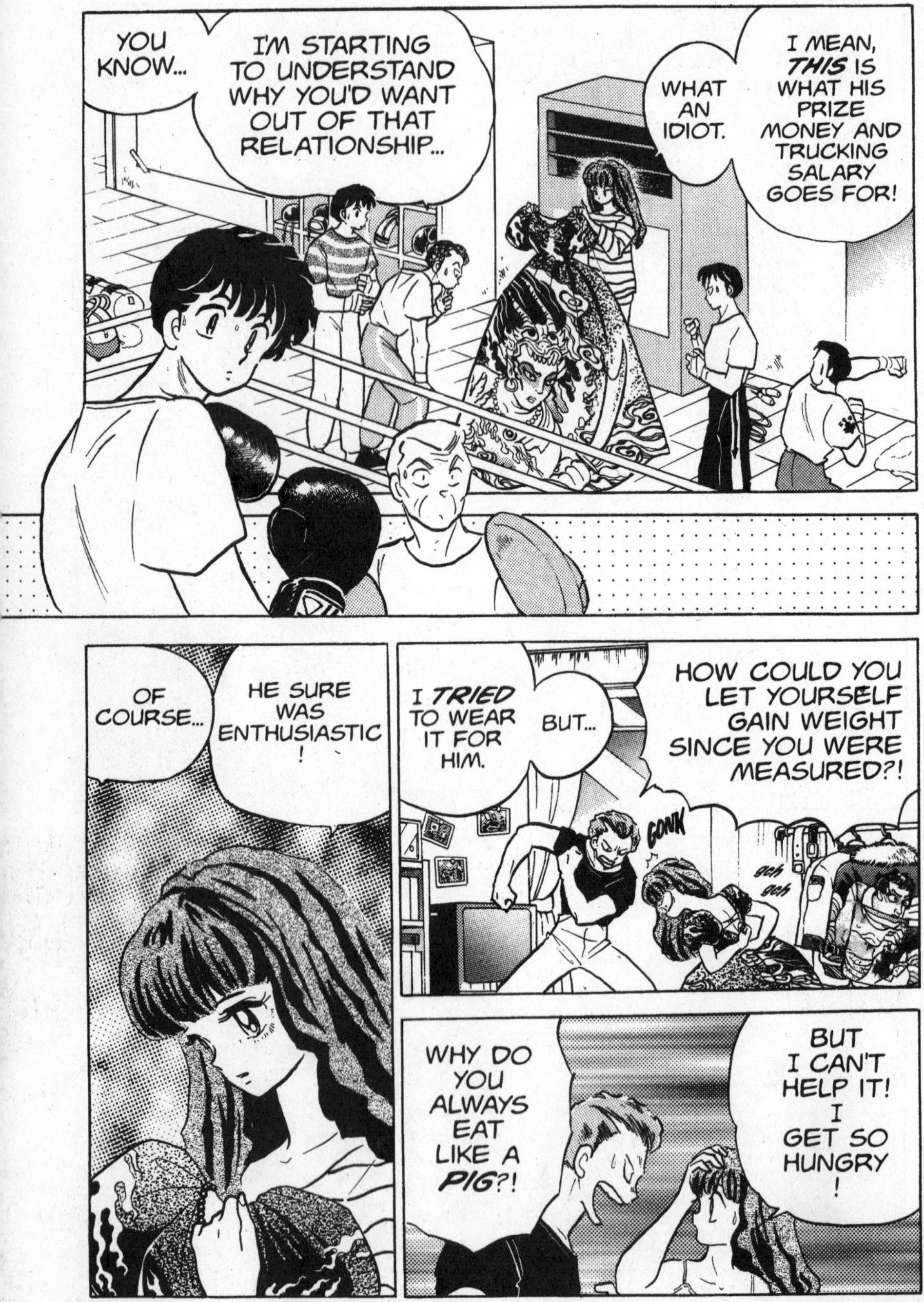
YOU KNOW...
I'M STARTING TO UNDERSTAND WHY YOU'D WANT OUT OF THAT RELATIONSHIP...
WHAT AN IDIOT.
I MEAN, *THIS* IS WHAT HIS PRIZE MONEY AND TRUCKING SALARY GOES FOR!
OF COURSE...
HE SURE WAS ENTHUSIASTIC!
I *TRIED* TO WEAR IT FOR HIM.
BUT...
HOW COULD YOU LET YOURSELF GAIN WEIGHT SINCE YOU WERE MEASURED?!
GONK
geh geh
WHY DO YOU ALWAYS EAT LIKE A *PIG*?!
BUT I CAN'T HELP IT! I GET SO HUNGRY!

BUT I WENT ON A DIET ANYWAY JUST TO SPITE HIM...

THAT'S WHY I LEFT HIM...

IT WOULD HAVE BEEN BETTER IF YOU NEVER MET...

AND THAT'S HOW YOU MET HATANAKA, RIGHT?

...

IT'S SICKENING!

YEAH! SLUGGING A *GIRL*...!

...REALLY WAS FROM HIM!

THAT MEANS THAT SHINER...

MEANWHILE...

YASHAMARU... YOU SURE YOU'RE UP TO THIS? YOUR STOMACH...

KANA!

DAY CA

WANTED

TRAINEE

COUGH-NO-MORE

K

DWOK

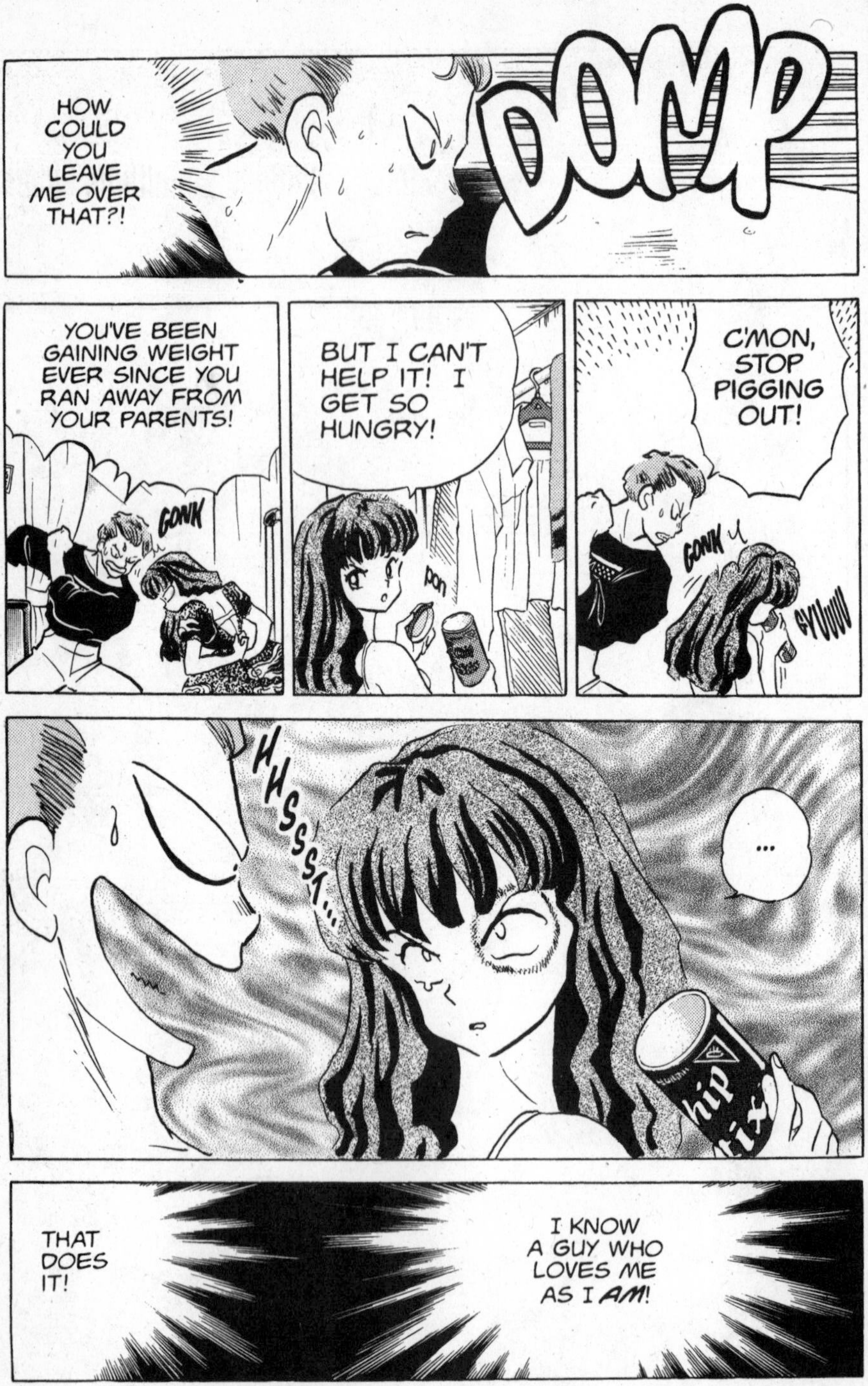
HOW COULD YOU LEAVE ME OVER THAT?!
DOMP
YOU'VE BEEN GAINING WEIGHT EVER SINCE YOU RAN AWAY FROM YOUR PARENTS!
GONK
BUT I CAN'T HELP IT! I GET SO HUNGRY!
pon
C'MON, STOP PIGGING OUT!
GONK
GYUUUU
HHSSS1...
...
hip
THAT DOES IT!
I KNOW A GUY WHO LOVES ME AS I *AM*!

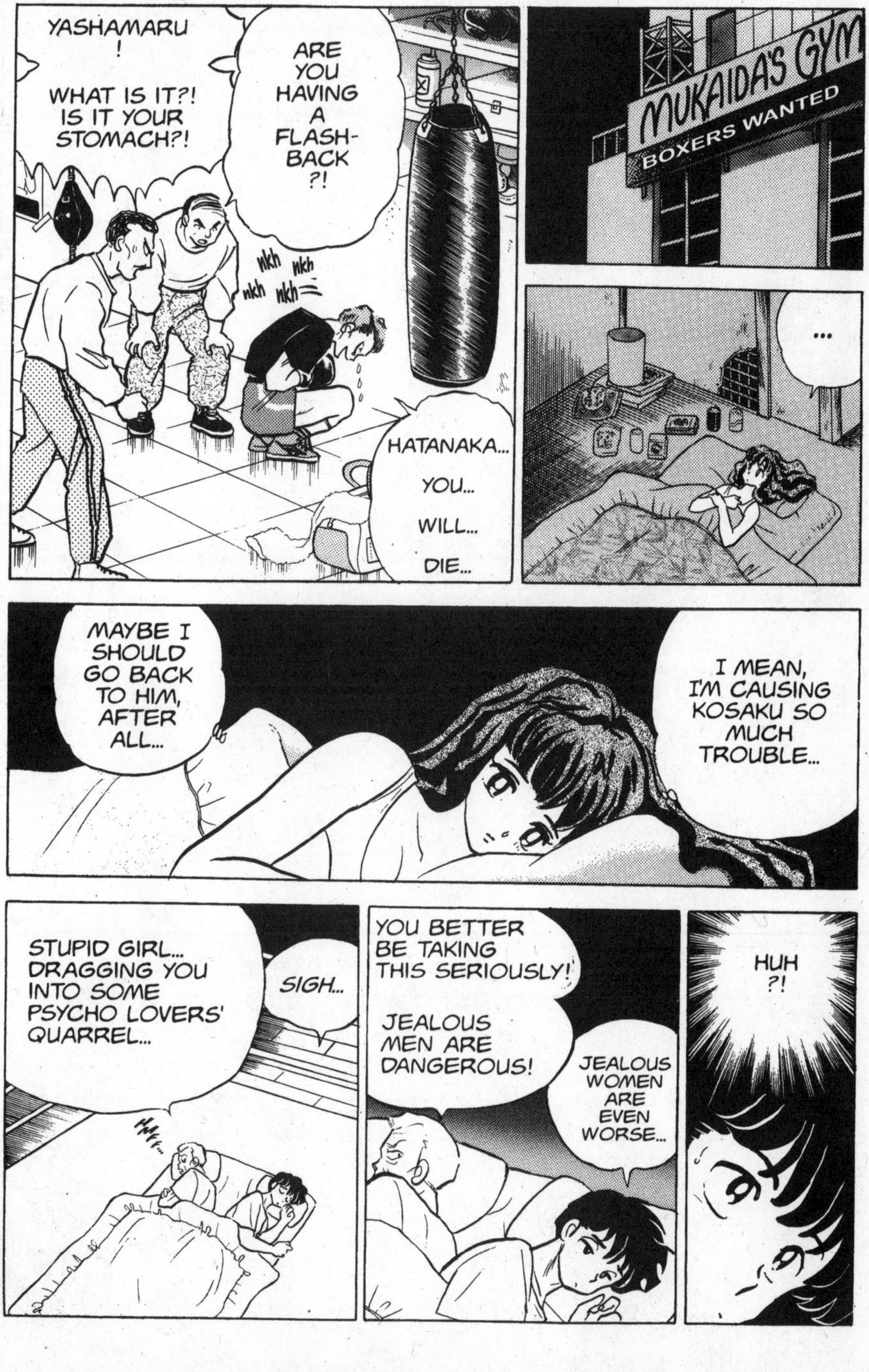
YASHAMARU!
WHAT IS IT?! IS IT YOUR STOMACH?!
ARE YOU HAVING A FLASH-BACK?!
nkh nkh nkh nkh
HATANAKA... YOU... WILL... DIE...
MUKAIDA'S GYM
BOXERS WANTED
...
MAYBE I SHOULD GO BACK TO HIM, AFTER ALL...
I MEAN, I'M CAUSING KOSAKU SO MUCH TROUBLE...
STUPID GIRL... DRAGGING YOU INTO SOME PSYCHO LOVERS' QUARREL...
SIGH...
YOU BETTER BE TAKING THIS SERIOUSLY!
JEALOUS MEN ARE DANGEROUS!
JEALOUS WOMEN ARE EVEN WORSE...
HUH?!

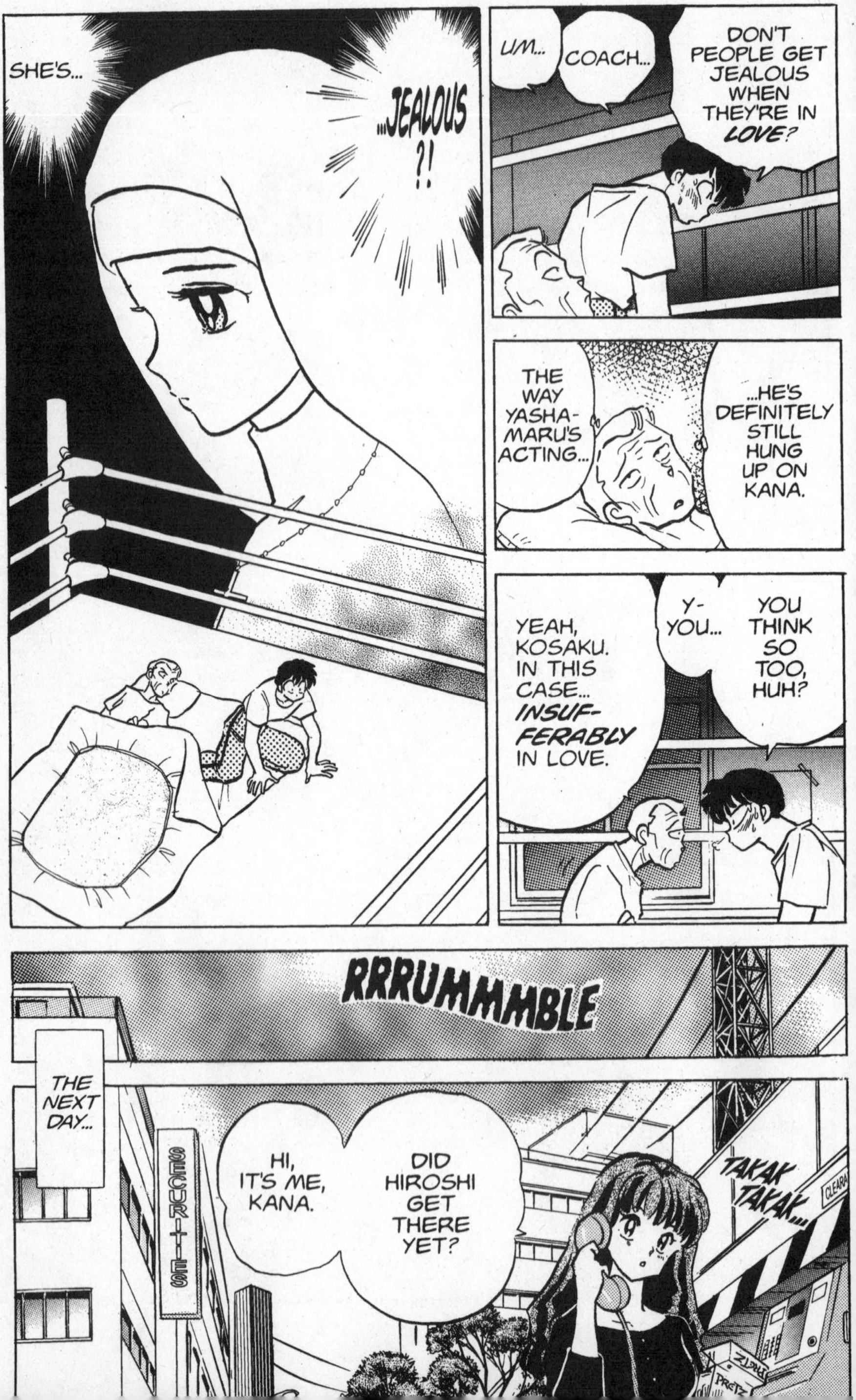
SHE'S...
...JEALOUS ?!
UM...
COACH...
DON'T PEOPLE GET JEALOUS WHEN THEY'RE IN LOVE?
THE WAY YASHA-MARU'S ACTING...
...HE'S DEFINITELY STILL HUNG UP ON KANA.
YEAH, KOSAKU. IN THIS CASE... INSUF-FERABLY IN LOVE.
Y-YOU...
YOU THINK SO TOO, HUH?
RRRUMMMBLE
THE NEXT DAY...
SECURITIES
HI, IT'S ME, KANA.
DID HIROSHI GET THERE YET?
TAKAK TAKAK...

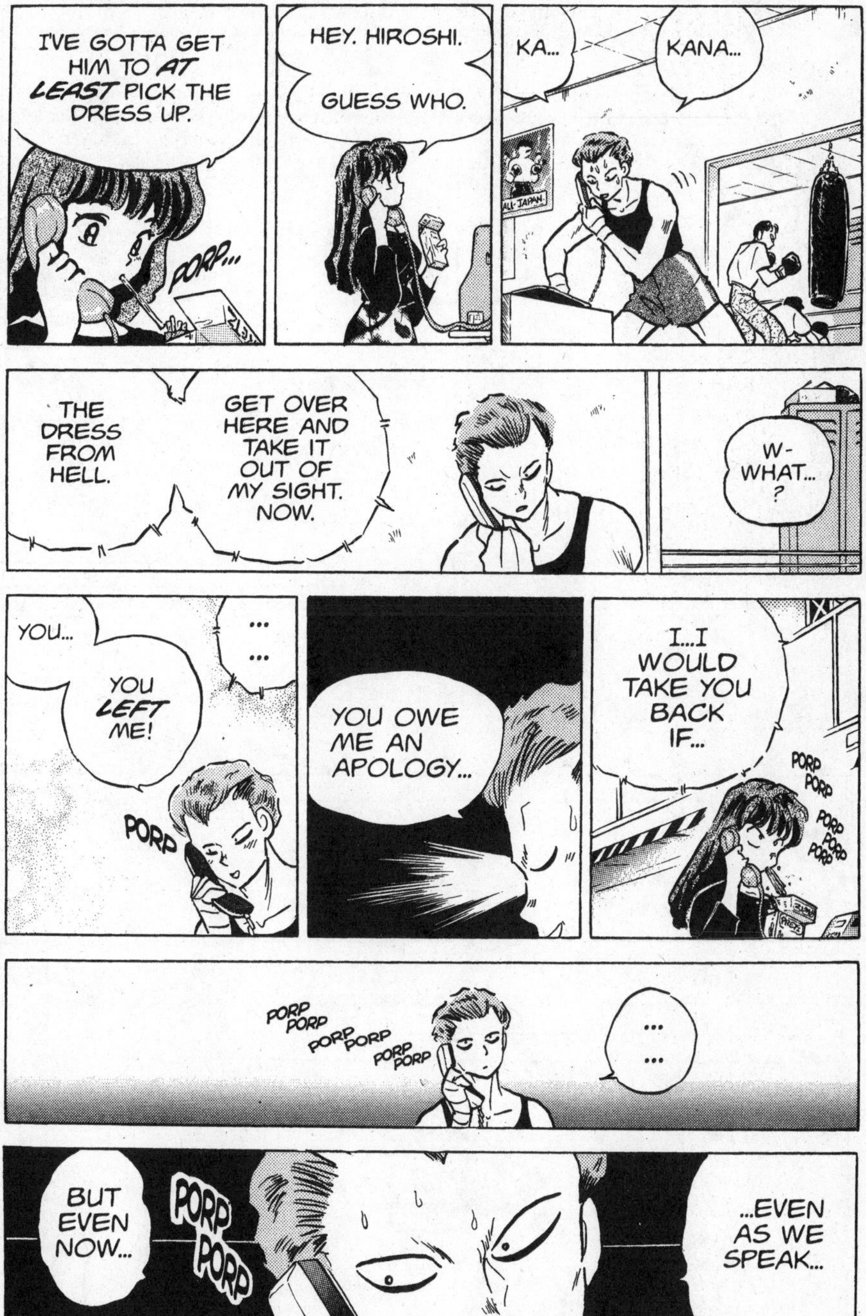
I'VE GOTTA GET HIM TO AT LEAST PICK THE DRESS UP.
PORP...
HEY. HIROSHI.
GUESS WHO.
KA...
KANA...
ALL-JAPAN.
THE DRESS FROM HELL.
GET OVER HERE AND TAKE IT OUT OF MY SIGHT. NOW.
W-WHAT...?
YOU...
YOU LEFT ME!
...
...
PORP
YOU OWE ME AN APOLOGY...
I...I WOULD TAKE YOU BACK IF...
PORP PORP PORP PORP PORP
PORP PORP PORP PORP PORP PORP
...
...
BUT EVEN NOW...
PORP PORP
...EVEN AS WE SPEAK...

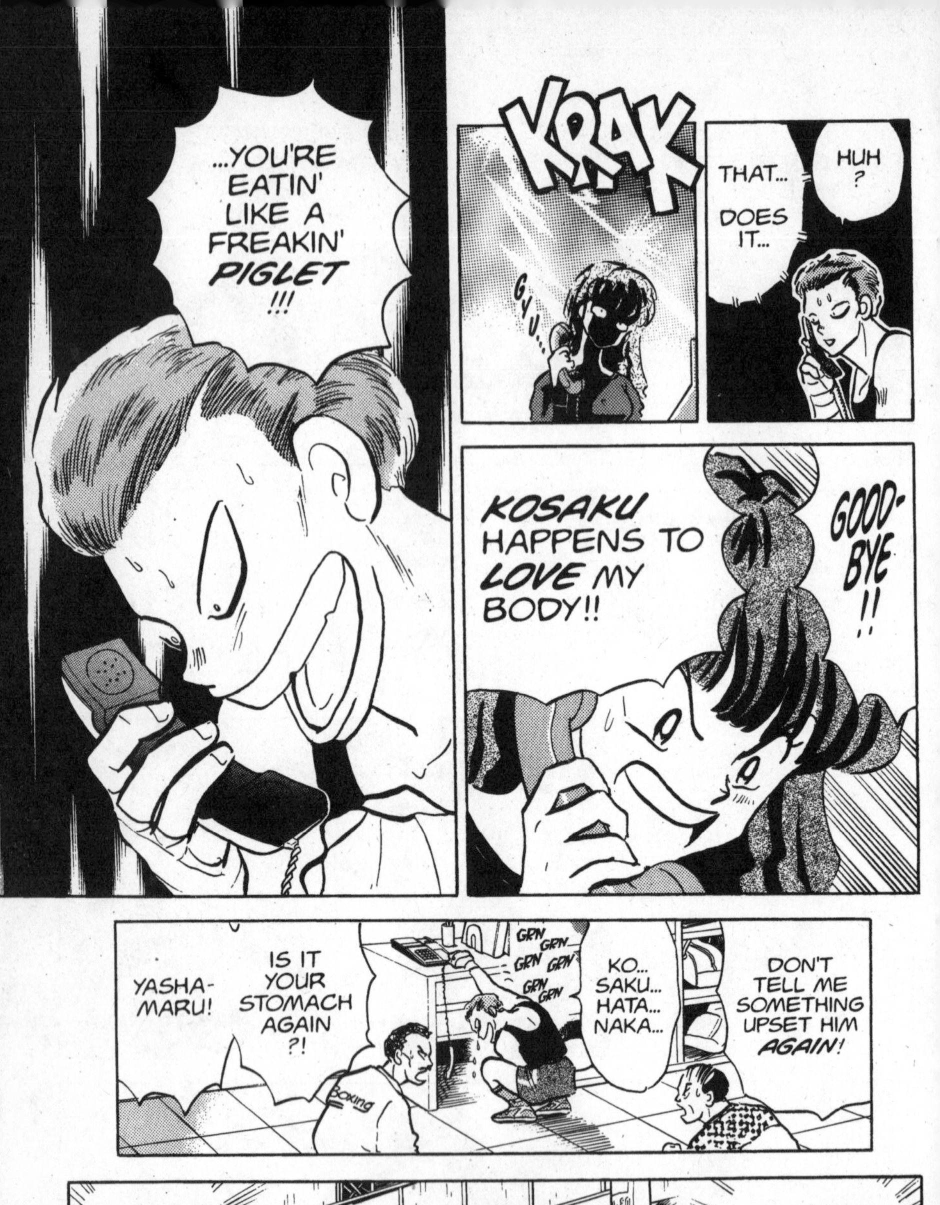
...YOU'RE EATIN' LIKE A FREAKIN' *PIGLET* !!!
KRAK
GYU...
THAT... DOES IT...
HUH ?
KOSAKU HAPPENS TO *LOVE* MY BODY!!
GOOD-BYE !!
YASHA-MARU!
IS IT YOUR STOMACH AGAIN ?!
GRN GRN GRN GRN GRN GRN
KO... SAKU... HATA... NAKA...
DON'T TELL ME SOMETHING UPSET HIM *AGAIN*!
Boxing
I'M GONNA CHEAT ON HIM!
I SWEAR I'M GONNA CHEAT ON HIM!

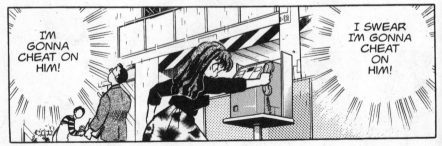

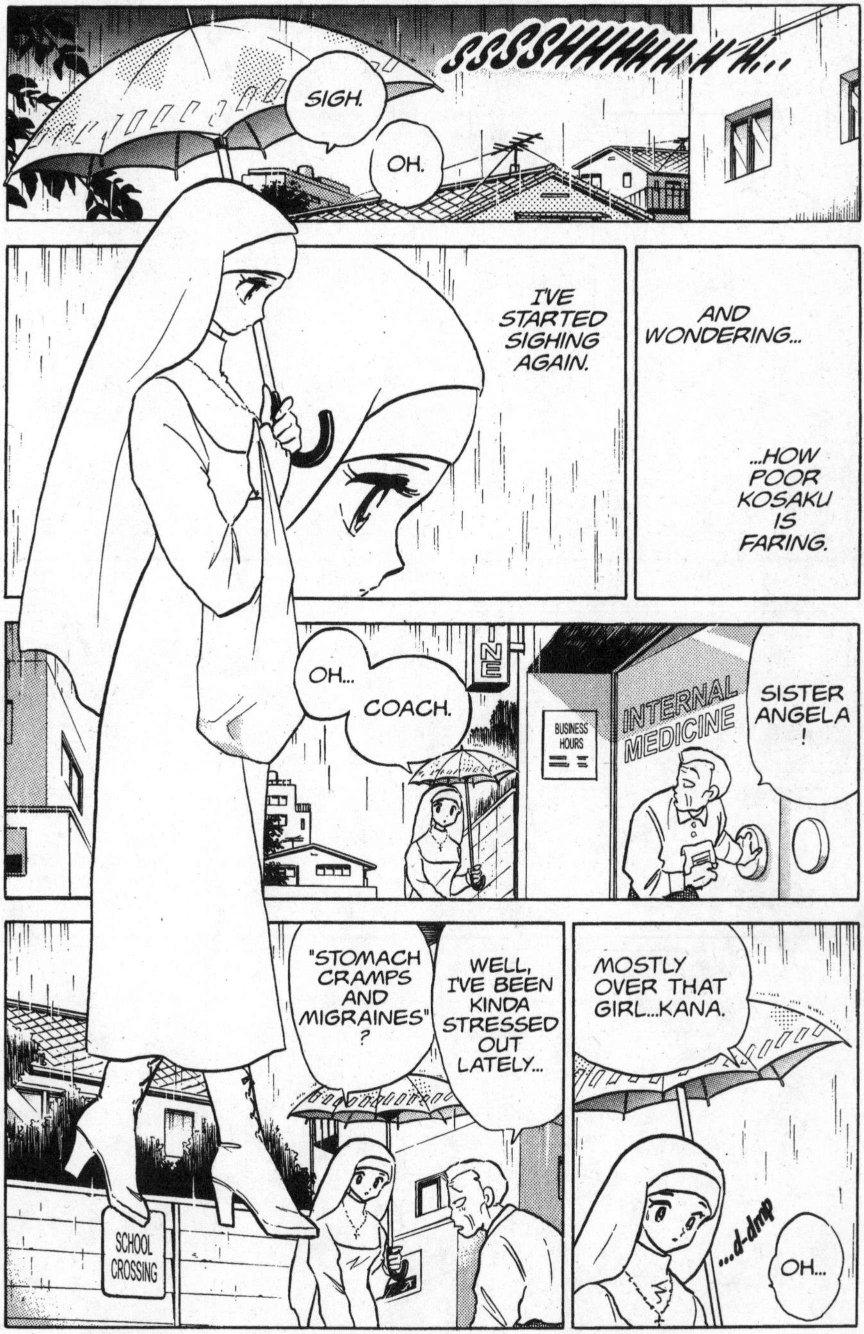
SSSSHHHHHH-H'H...
SIGH.
OH.
I'VE STARTED SIGHING AGAIN.
AND WONDERING...
...HOW POOR KOSAKU IS FARING.
INE
BUSINESS HOURS
OH... COACH.
INTERNAL MEDICINE
SISTER ANGELA!
"STOMACH CRAMPS AND MIGRAINES"?
WELL, I'VE BEEN KINDA STRESSED OUT LATELY...
SCHOOL CROSSING
MOSTLY OVER THAT GIRL...KANA.
...d-drrip
OH...

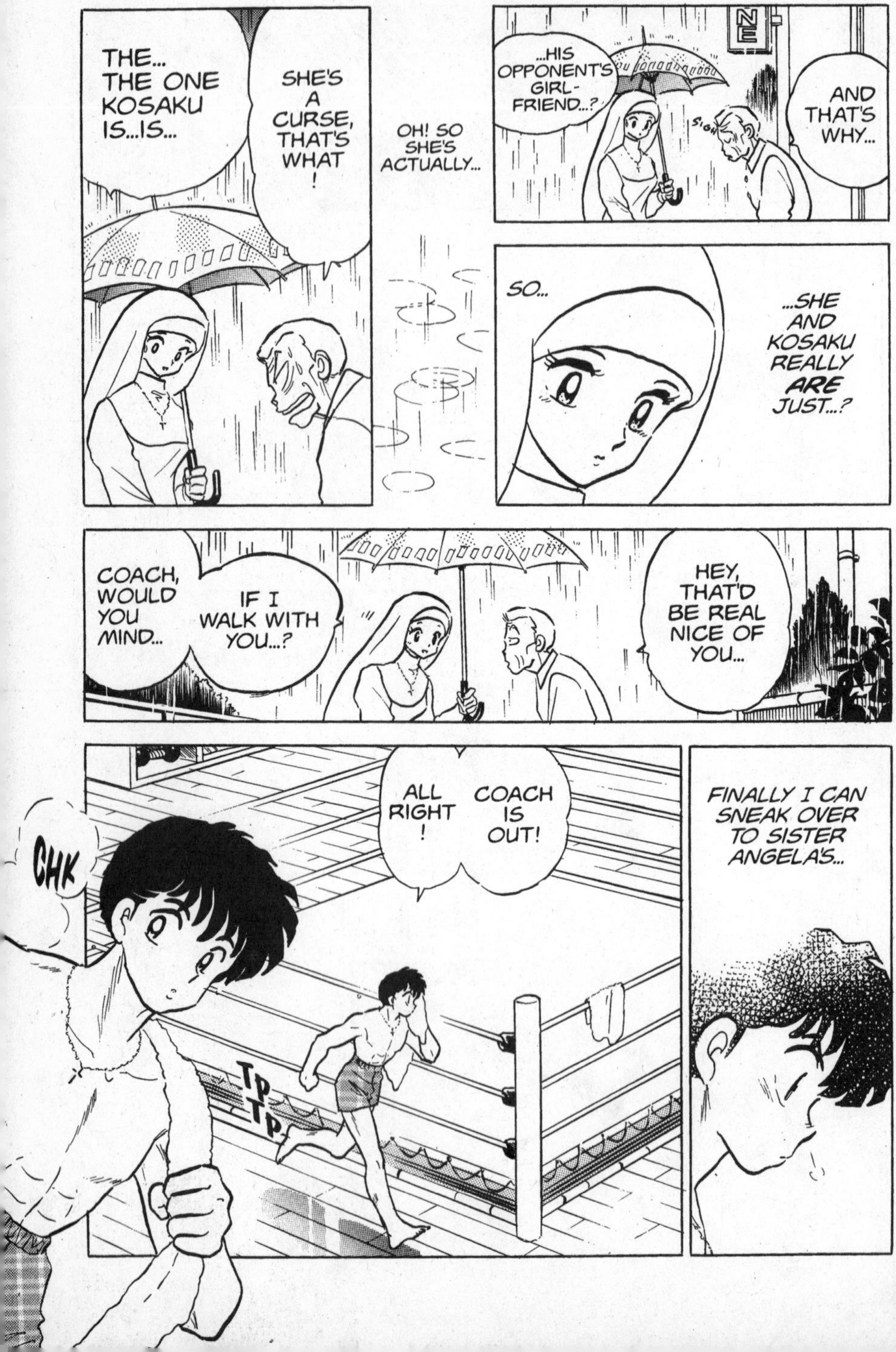
THE... THE ONE KOSAKU IS...IS...
SHE'S A CURSE, THAT'S WHAT!
OH! SO SHE'S ACTUALLY...
...HIS OPPONENT'S GIRL-FRIEND...?
SIGH
AND THAT'S WHY...
SO...
...SHE AND KOSAKU REALLY ARE JUST...?
COACH, WOULD YOU MIND...
IF I WALK WITH YOU...?
HEY, THAT'D BE REAL NICE OF YOU...
CHK
ALL RIGHT!
COACH IS OUT!
TP TP
FINALLY I CAN SNEAK OVER TO SISTER ANGELA'S...

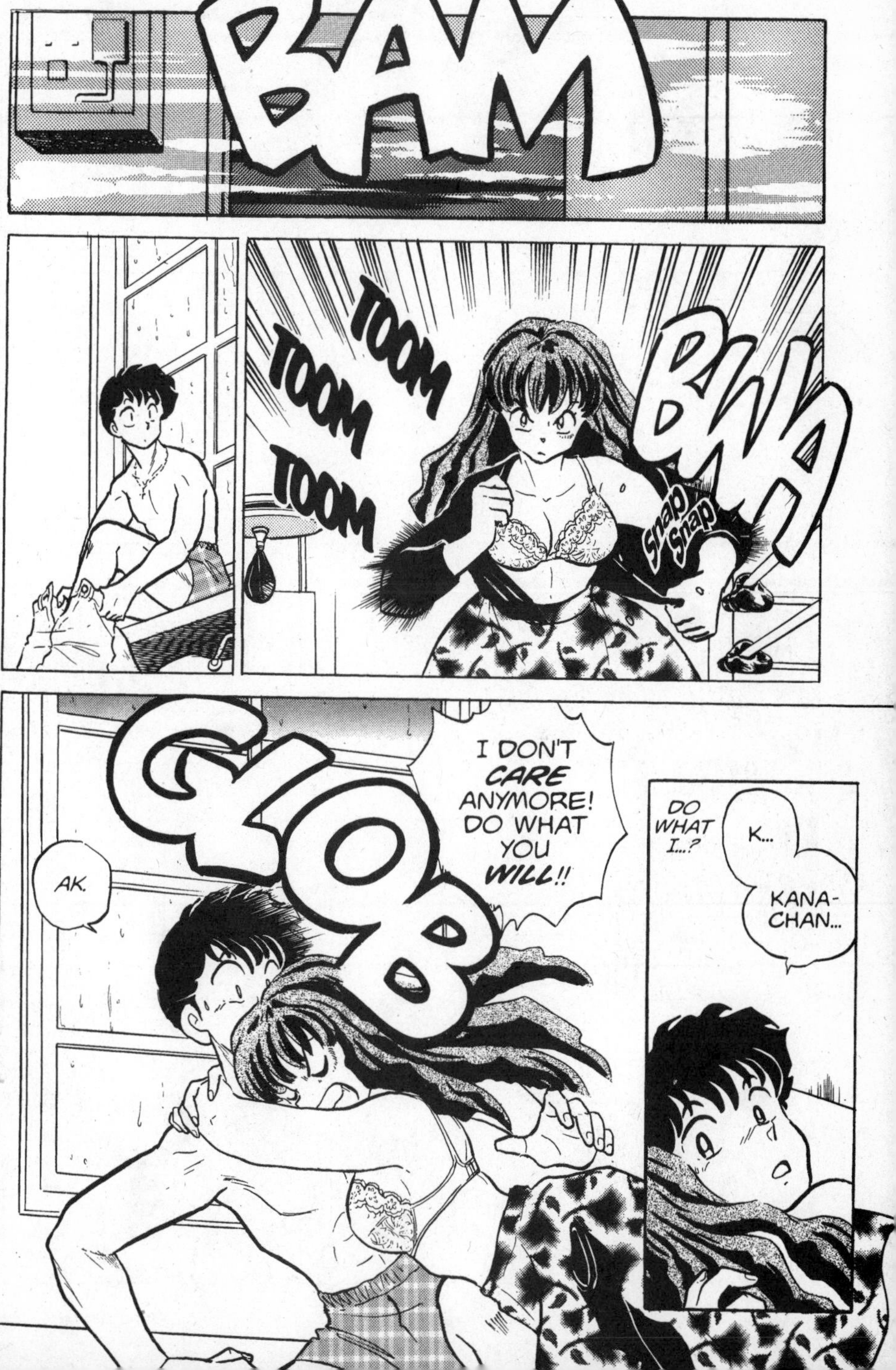
BAM
TOOM
TOOM
TOOM
TOOM
BWA
Snap
Snap
CLOB
I DON'T CARE ANYMORE! DO WHAT YOU WILL!!
AK.
DO WHAT I...?
K...
KANA-CHAN...

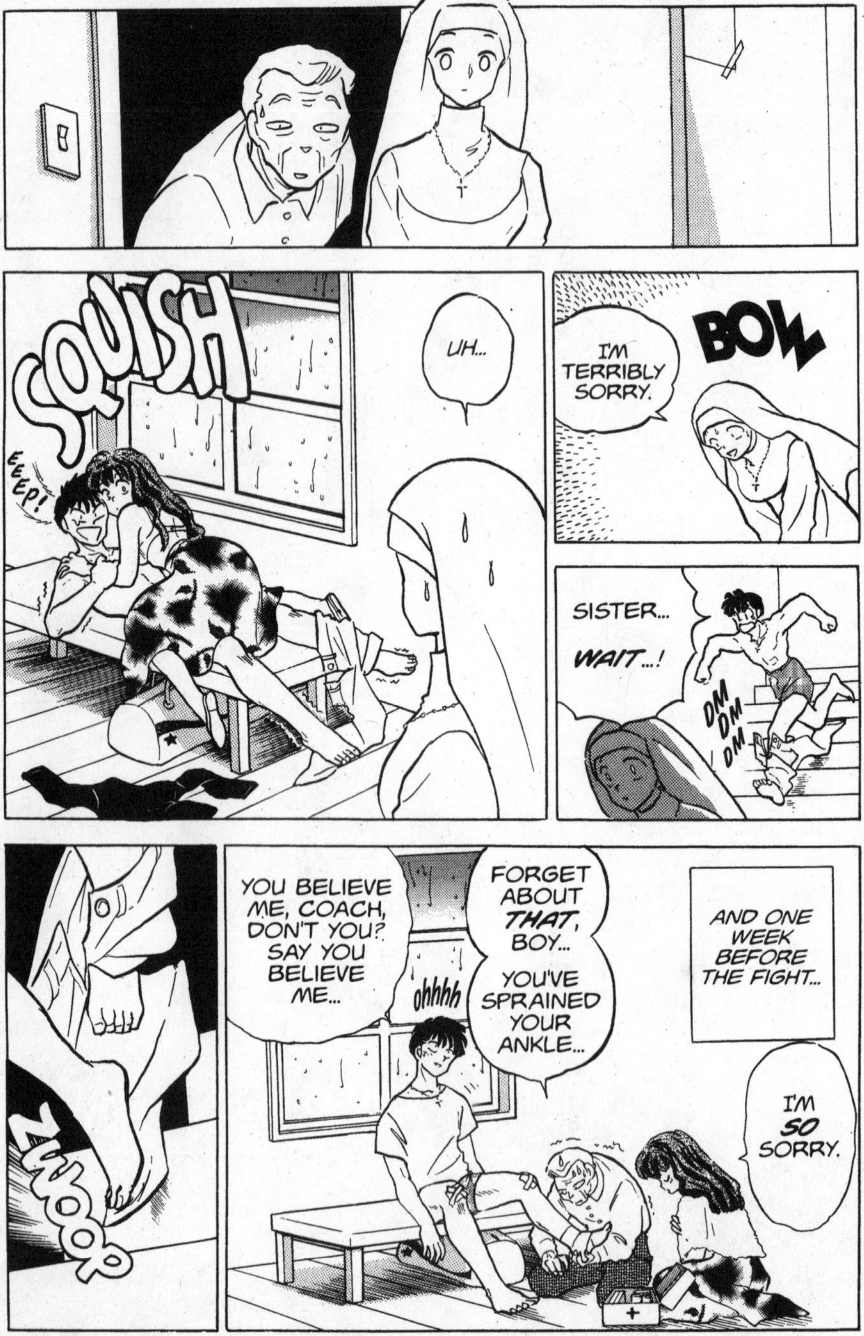
SQUISH
EEEP!
UH...
I'M TERRIBLY SORRY.
BOW
SISTER... WAIT...!
DM DM DM
ZWOOP
YOU BELIEVE ME, COACH, DON'T YOU? SAY YOU BELIEVE ME...
ohhhh
FORGET ABOUT THAT, BOY...
YOU'VE SPRAINED YOUR ANKLE...
AND ONE WEEK BEFORE THE FIGHT...
I'M SO SORRY.

CHAPTER THREE
THE FALLEN LAMB
PART FOUR

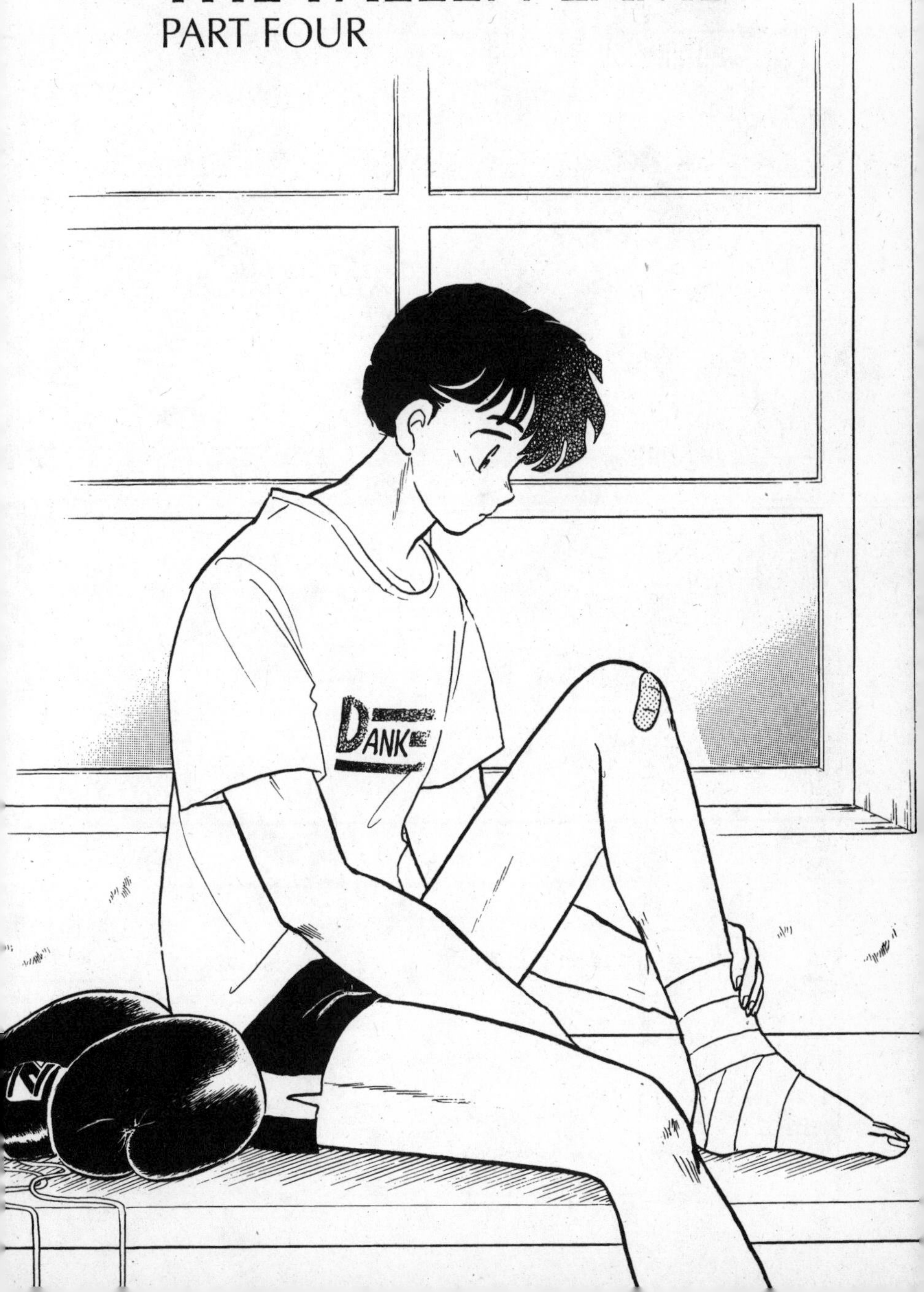
DANK

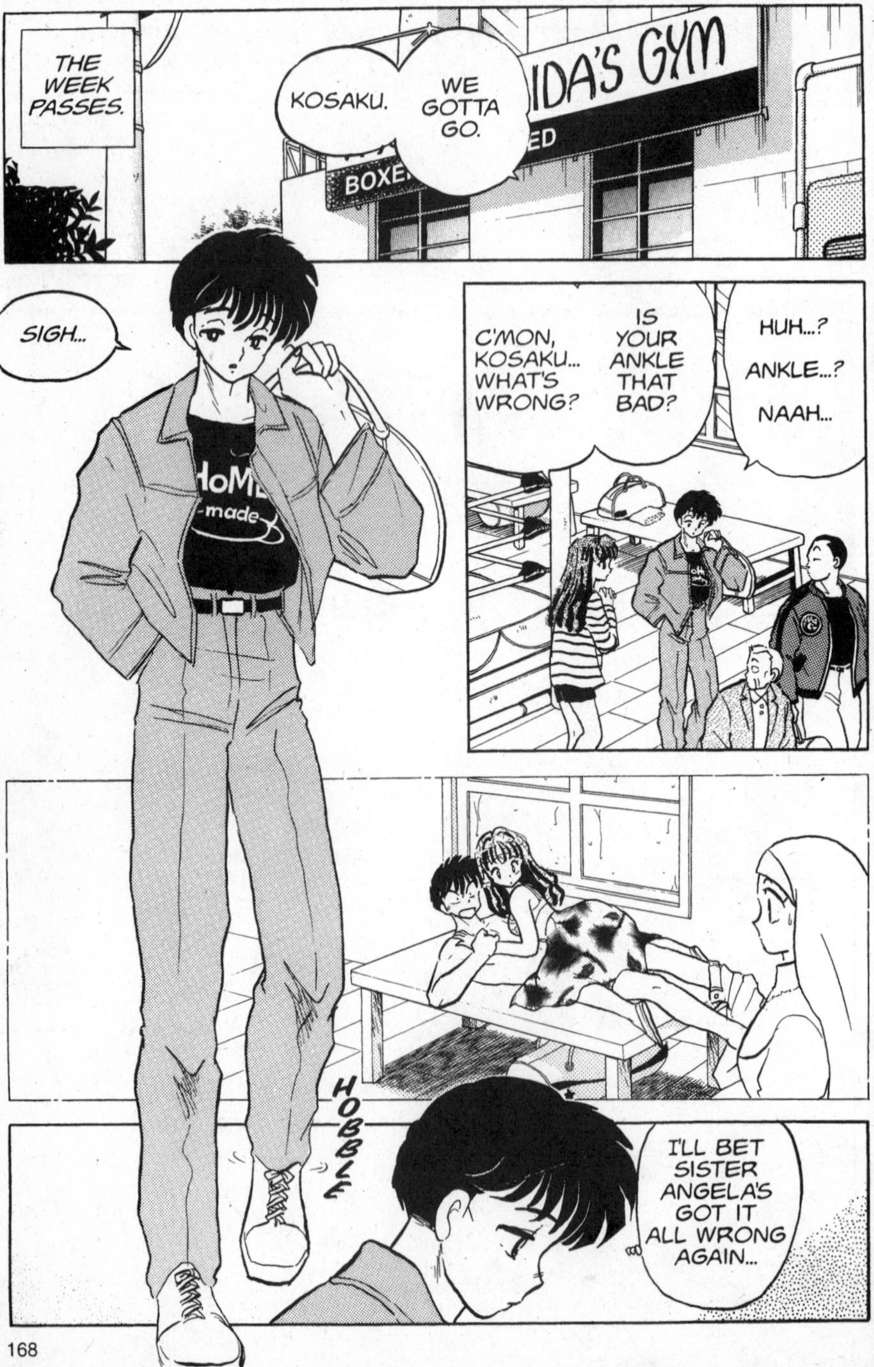
THE WEEK PASSES.
KOSAKU.
WE GOTTA GO.
SIGH...
HOBBLE
C'MON, KOSAKU... WHAT'S WRONG?
IS YOUR ANKLE THAT BAD?
HUH...? ANKLE...? NAAH...
I'LL BET SISTER ANGELA'S GOT IT ALL WRONG AGAIN...

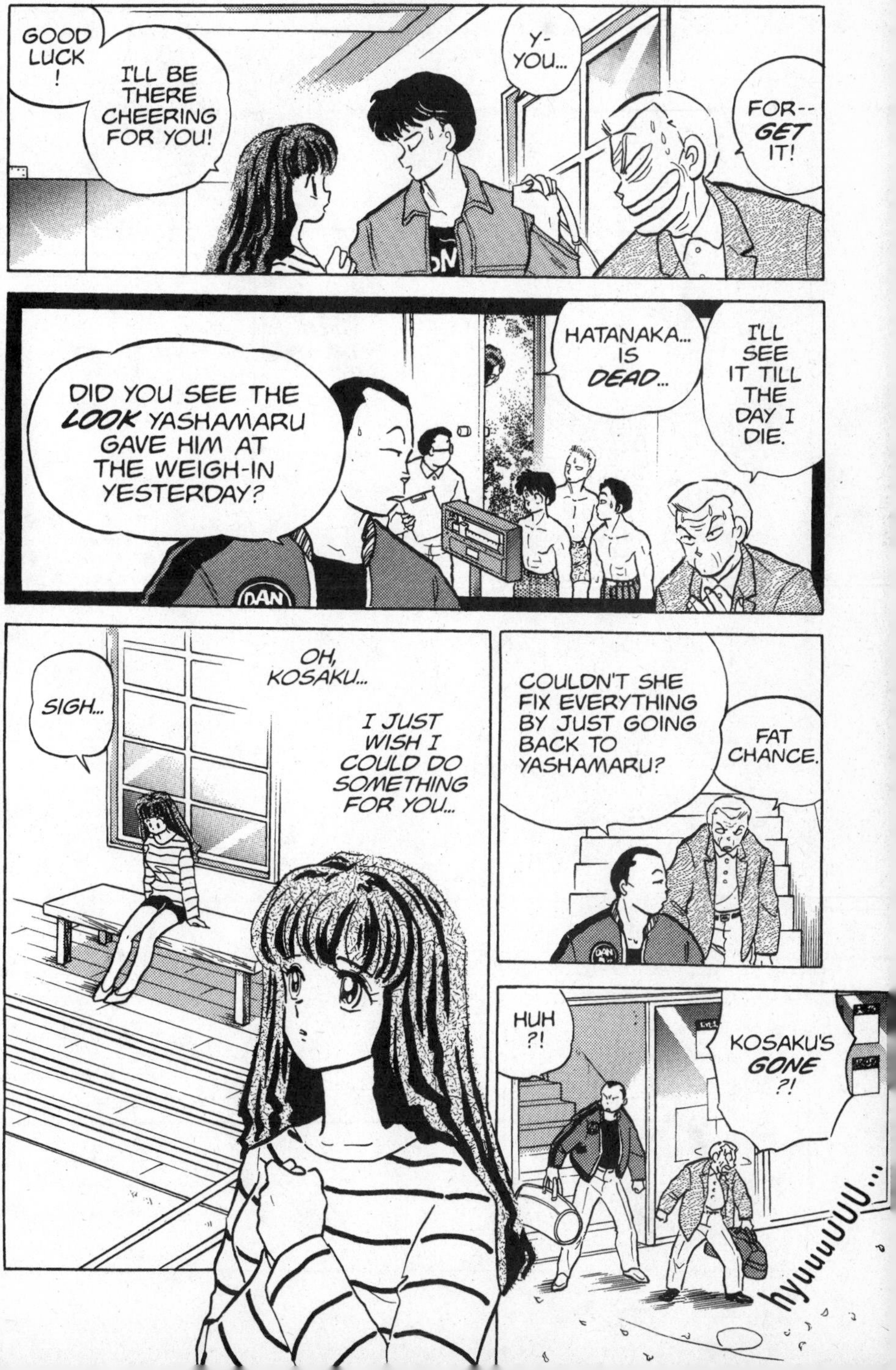
GOOD LUCK!
I'LL BE THERE CHEERING FOR YOU!
Y-YOU...
FOR--GET IT!
DID YOU SEE THE LOOK YASHAMARU GAVE HIM AT THE WEIGH-IN YESTERDAY?
HATANAKA... IS DEAD...
I'LL SEE IT TILL THE DAY I DIE.
SIGH...
OH, KOSAKU...
I JUST WISH I COULD DO SOMETHING FOR YOU...
COULDN'T SHE FIX EVERYTHING BY JUST GOING BACK TO YASHAMARU?
FAT CHANCE.
HUH?!
KOSAKU'S GONE?!
hyuuuuuu...

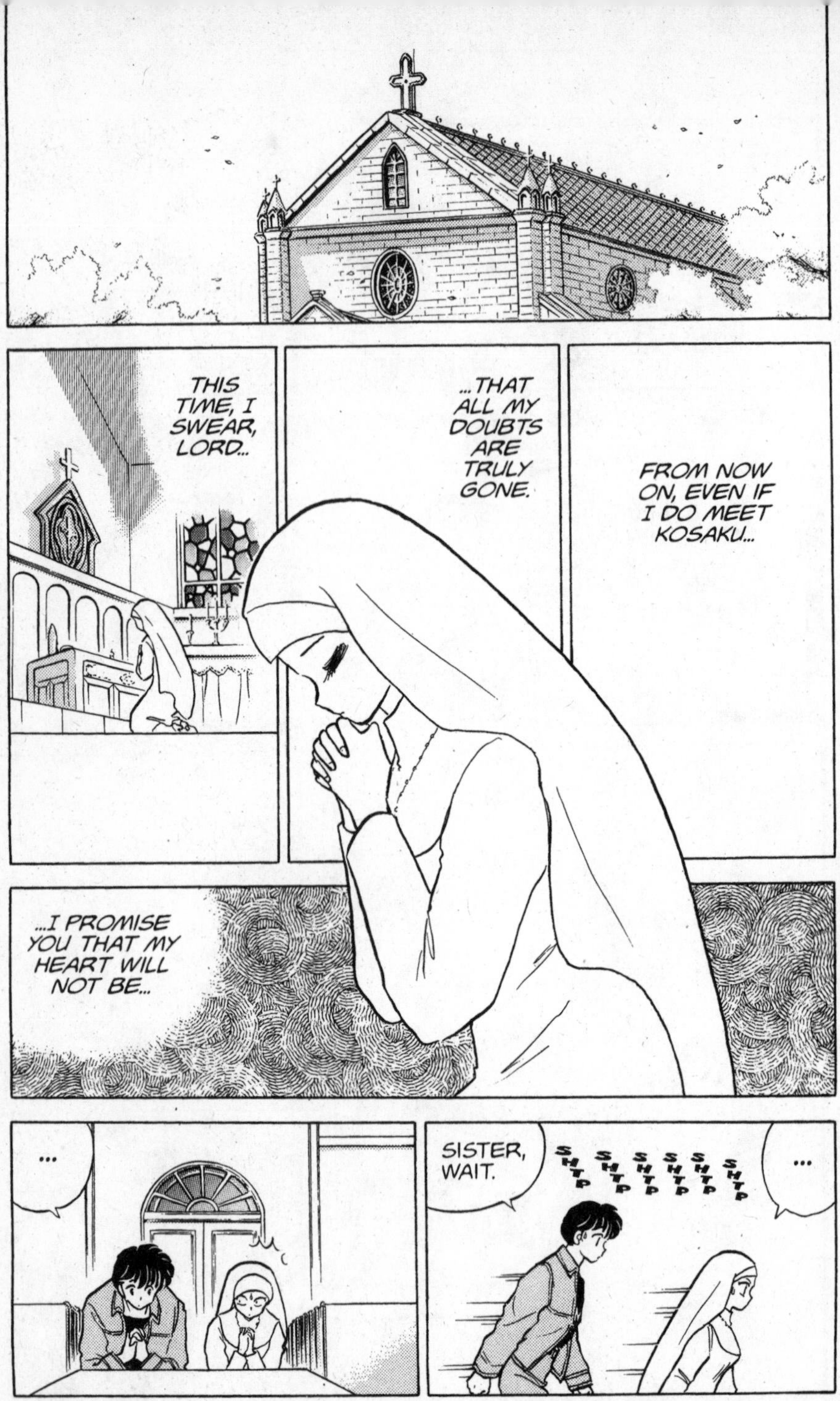
THIS TIME, I SWEAR, LORD...
...THAT ALL MY DOUBTS ARE TRULY GONE.
FROM NOW ON, EVEN IF I DO MEET KOSAKU...
...I PROMISE YOU THAT MY HEART WILL NOT BE...
...
SISTER, WAIT.
SHTP SHTP SHTP SHTP SHTP SHTP
...

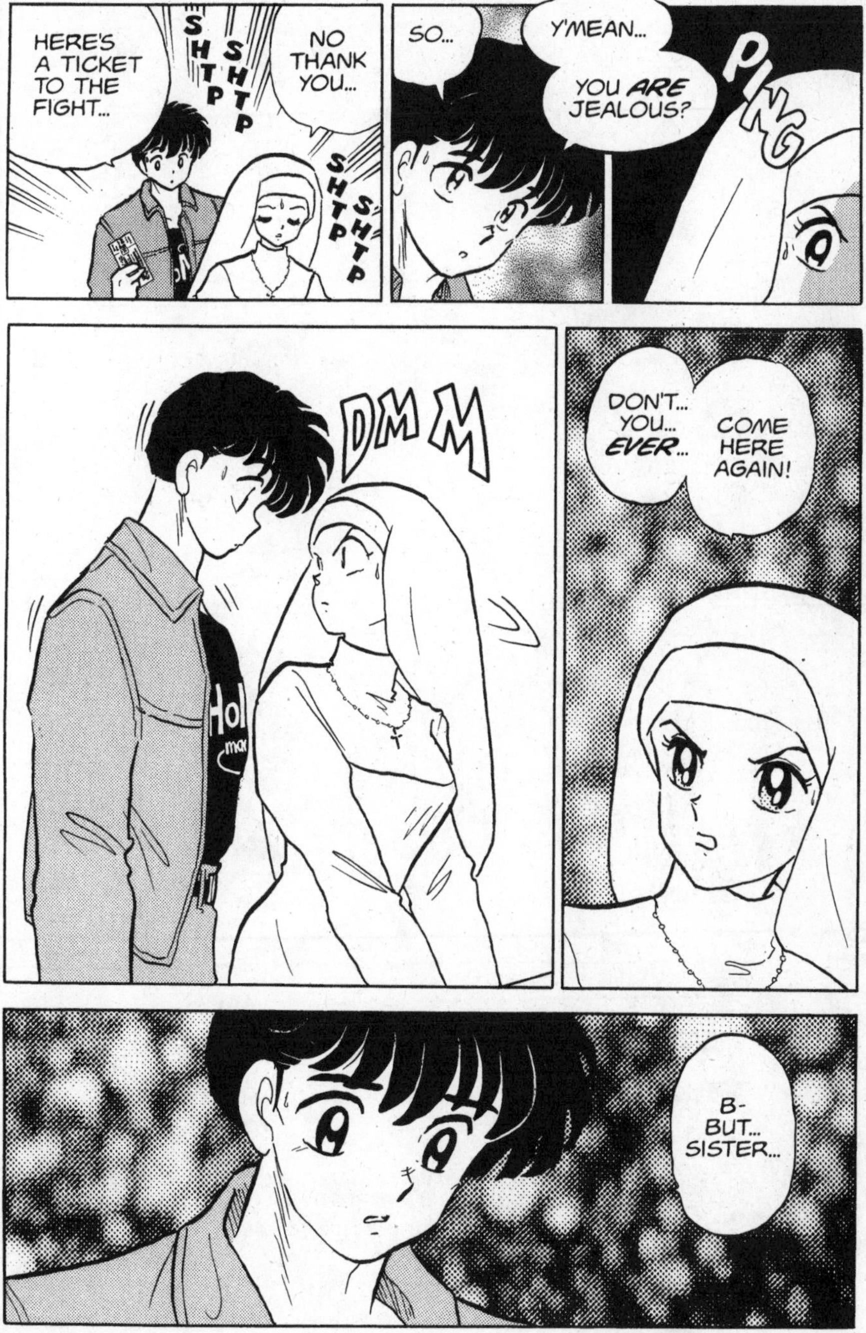
HERE'S A TICKET TO THE FIGHT...
SHTP SHTP
NO THANK YOU...
SHTP SHTP
SO...
Y'MEAN...
YOU **ARE** JEALOUS?
PING
DMM
DON'T... YOU... **EVER**...
COME HERE AGAIN!
B-BUT... SISTER...

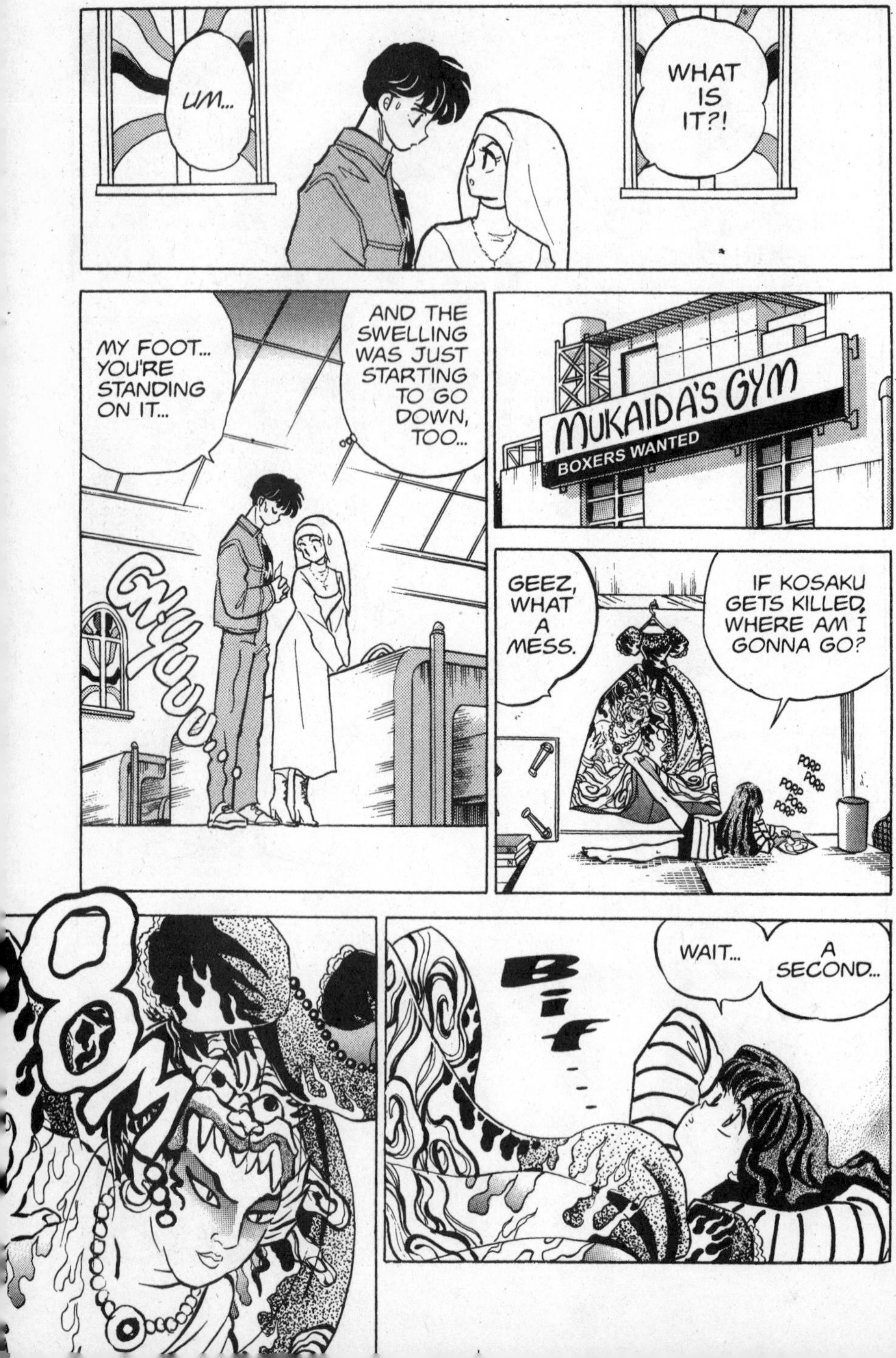
UM...
WHAT IS IT?!
MY FOOT... YOU'RE STANDING ON IT...
AND THE SWELLING WAS JUST STARTING TO GO DOWN, TOO...
GNYUUUU...
MUKAIDA'S GYM
BOXERS WANTED
GEEZ, WHAT A MESS.
IF KOSAKU GETS KILLED, WHERE AM I GONNA GO?
PORP PORP PORP PORP PORP PORP
BOM
BIFF
WAIT...
A SECOND...

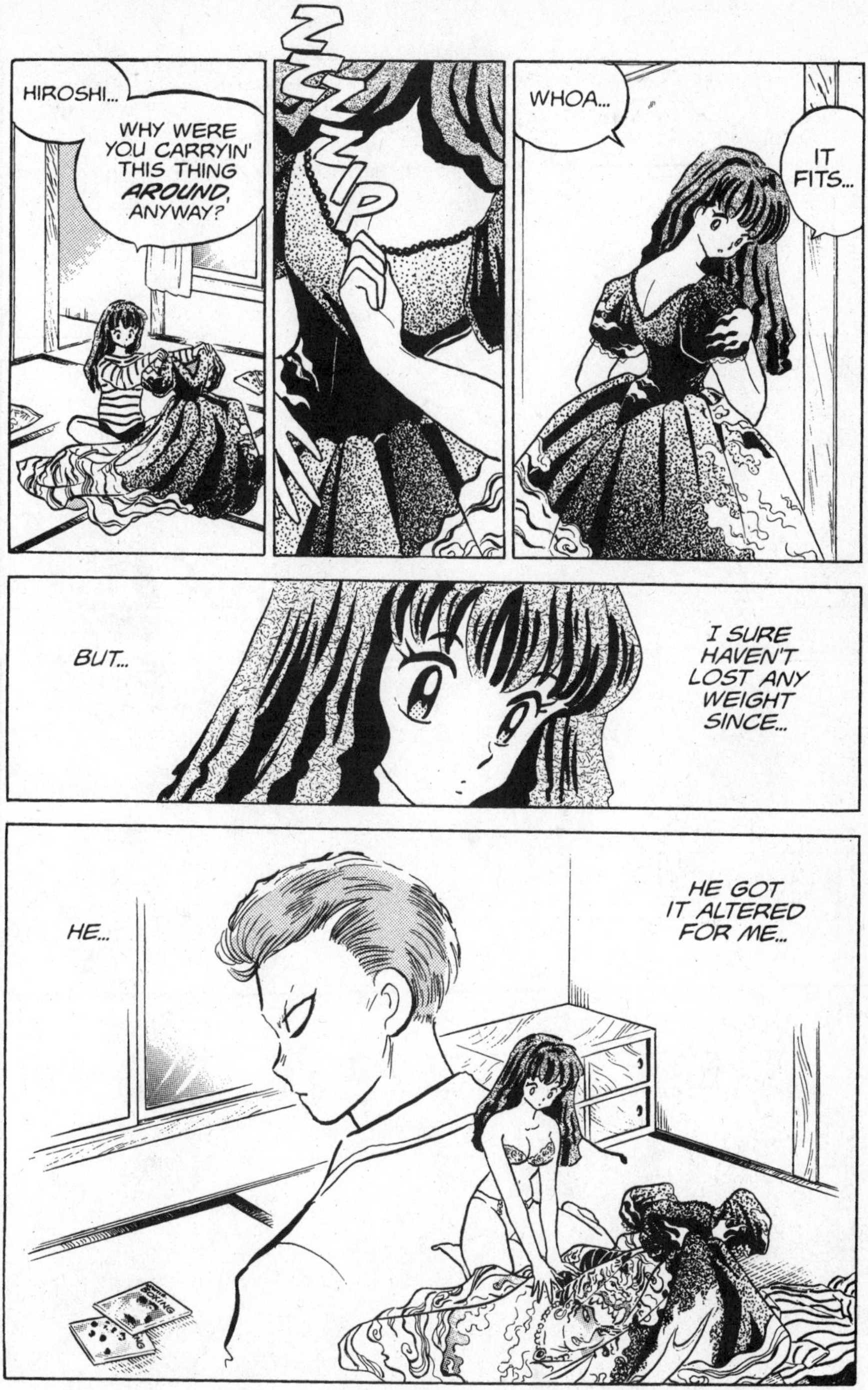
HIROSHI...
WHY WERE YOU CARRYIN' THIS THING *AROUND*, ANYWAY?
ZZZZZIP
WHOA...
IT FITS...
BUT...
I SURE HAVEN'T LOST ANY WEIGHT SINCE...
HE...
HE GOT IT ALTERED FOR ME...

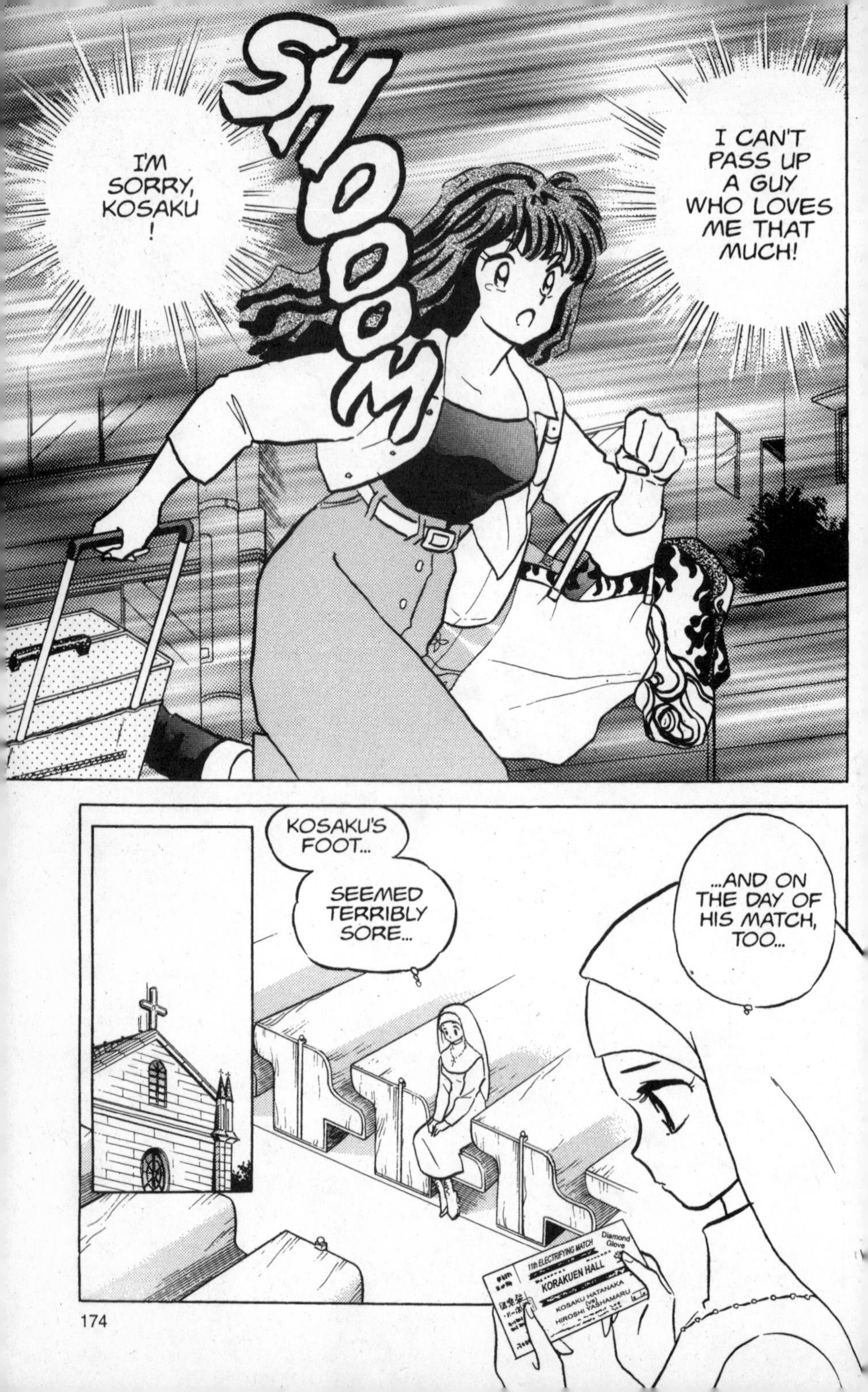

I'M SORRY, KOSAKU!
SHOOOM
I CAN'T PASS UP A GUY WHO LOVES ME THAT MUCH!
KOSAKU'S FOOT...
SEEMED TERRIBLY SORE...
...AND ON THE DAY OF HIS MATCH, TOO...
Diamond Glove
11th ELECTRIFYING MATCH
KORAKUEN HALL
KOSAKU HATANAKA (vs) HIROSHI YASHAMARU

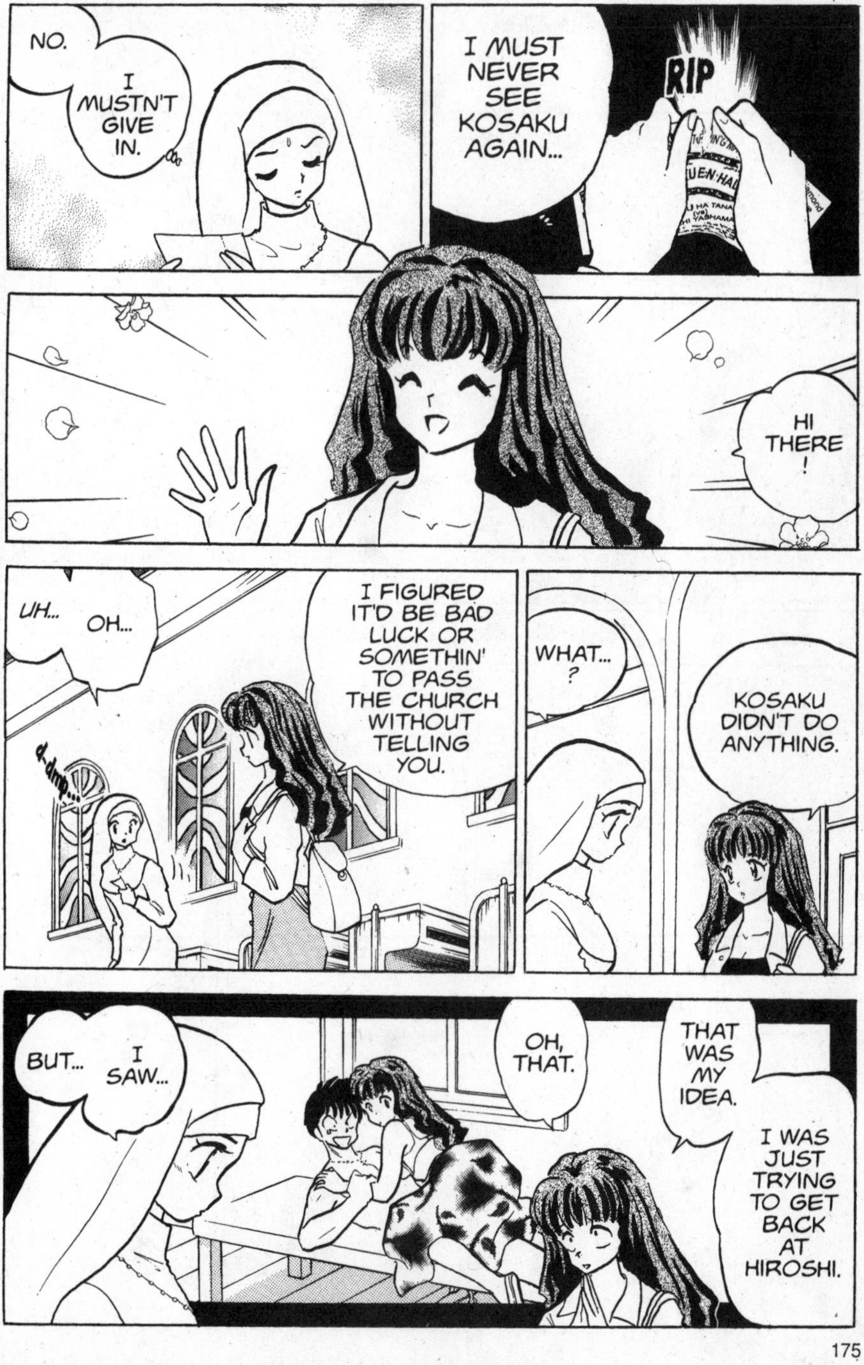
NO.
I MUSTN'T GIVE IN.
I MUST NEVER SEE KOSAKU AGAIN...
RIP
HI THERE!
UH...
OH...
I FIGURED IT'D BE BAD LUCK OR SOMETHIN' TO PASS THE CHURCH WITHOUT TELLING YOU.
d-drop...
WHAT...?
KOSAKU DIDN'T DO ANYTHING.
BUT...
I SAW...
OH, THAT.
THAT WAS MY IDEA.
I WAS JUST TRYING TO GET BACK AT HIROSHI.

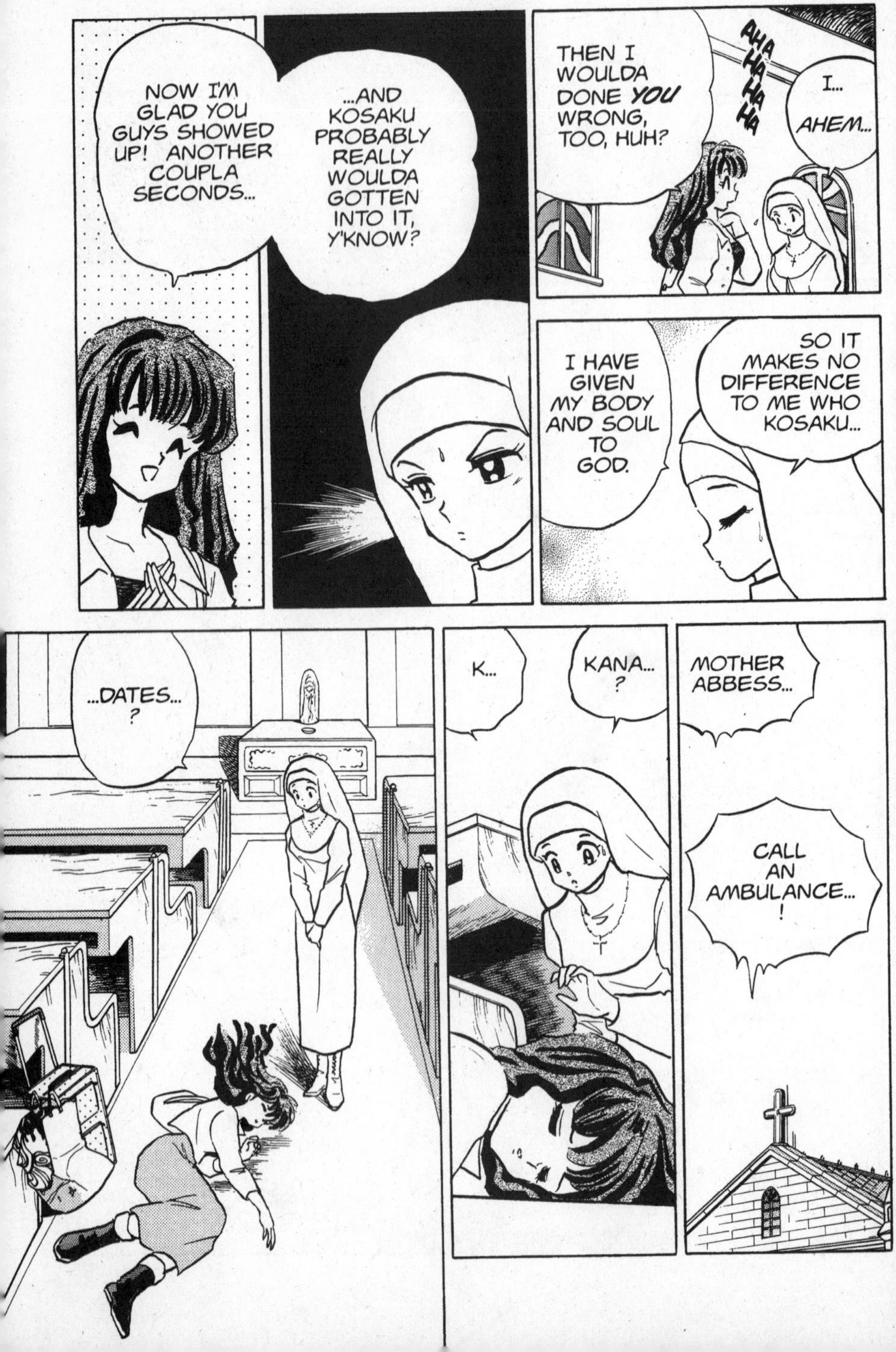
NOW I'M GLAD YOU GUYS SHOWED UP! ANOTHER COUPLA SECONDS...
...AND KOSAKU PROBABLY REALLY WOULDA GOTTEN INTO IT, Y'KNOW?
THEN I WOULDA DONE *YOU* WRONG, TOO, HUH?
AHAHAHAHA
I...
AHEM...
I HAVE GIVEN MY BODY AND SOUL TO GOD.
SO IT MAKES NO DIFFERENCE TO ME WHO KOSAKU...
...DATES...?
K...
KANA...?
MOTHER ABBESS...
CALL AN AMBULANCE...!

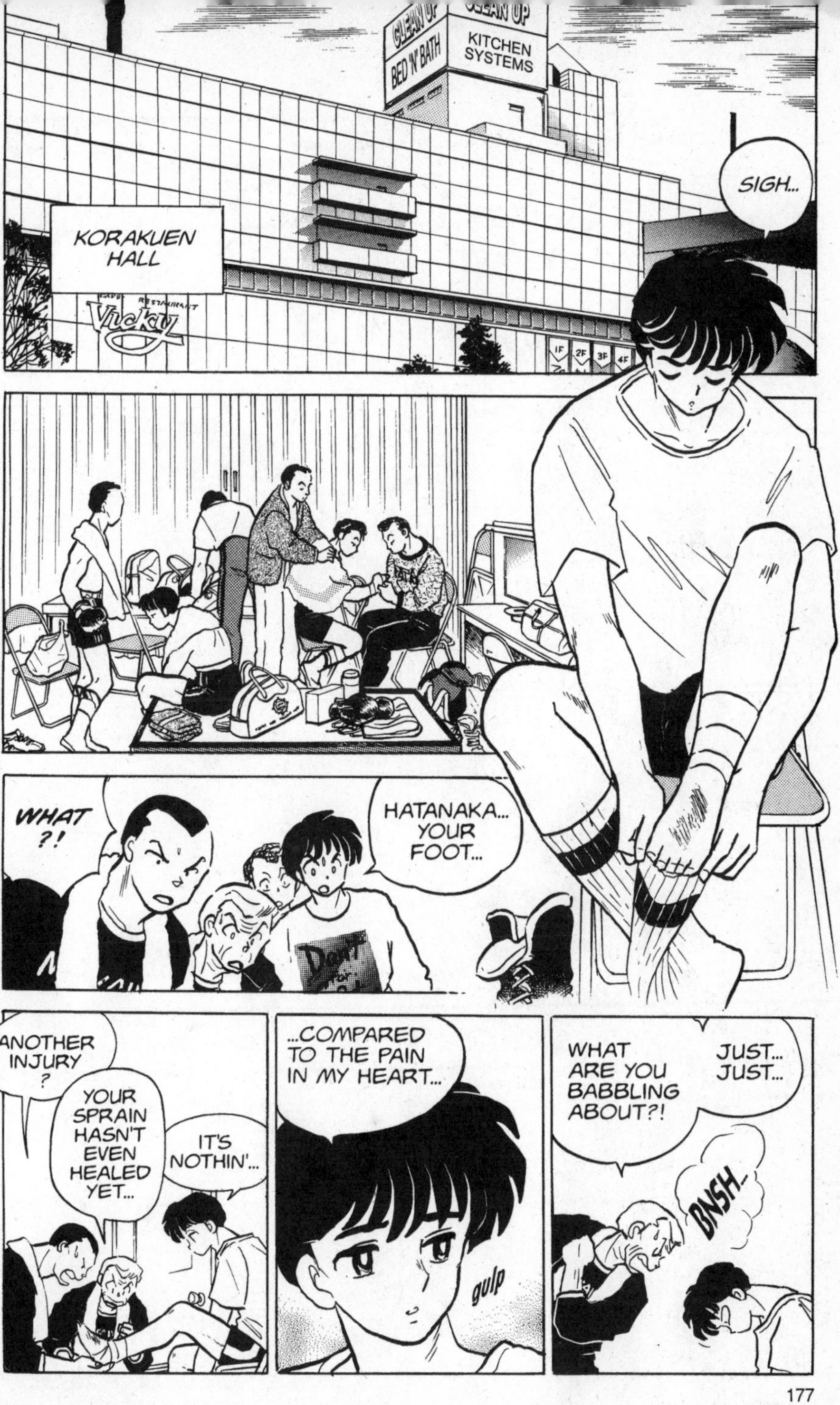
CLEAN UP
BED 'N' BATH
CLEAN UP
KITCHEN SYSTEMS
KORAKUEN HALL
SIGH...
WHAT ?!
HATANAKA... YOUR FOOT...
ANOTHER INJURY ?
YOUR SPRAIN HASN'T EVEN HEALED YET...
IT'S NOTHIN'...
...COMPARED TO THE PAIN IN MY HEART...
gulp
WHAT ARE YOU BABBLING ABOUT?!
JUST... JUST...
BNSH..

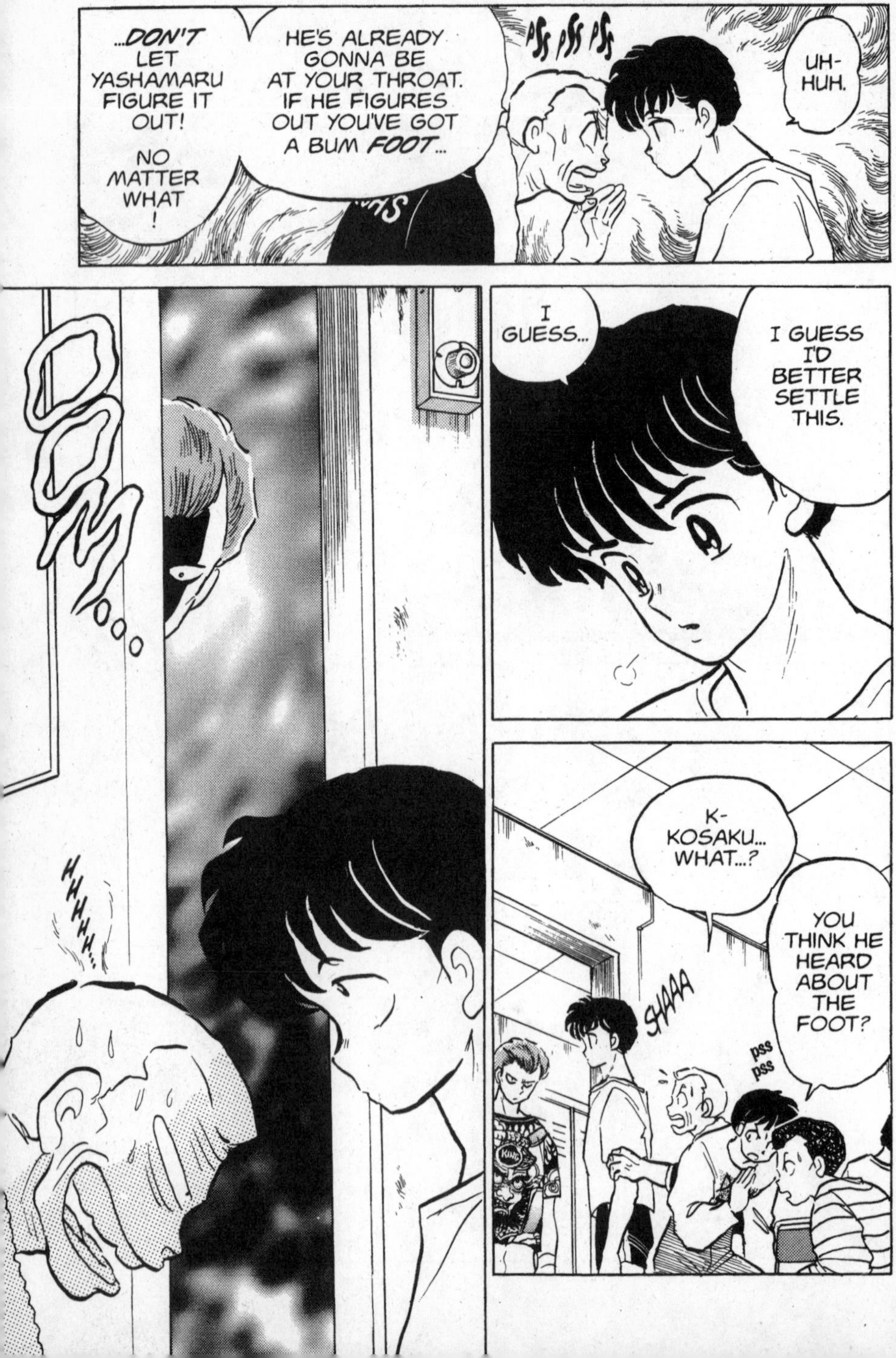
...DON'T LET YASHAMARU FIGURE IT OUT! NO MATTER WHAT!
HE'S ALREADY GONNA BE AT YOUR THROAT. IF HE FIGURES OUT YOU'VE GOT A BUM FOOT...
PSS PSS PSS
UH-HUH.
DOOM
OOO
HHHHH...
I GUESS...
I GUESS I'D BETTER SETTLE THIS.
K-KOSAKU... WHAT...?
YOU THINK HE HEARD ABOUT THE FOOT?
SHAAA
pss pss

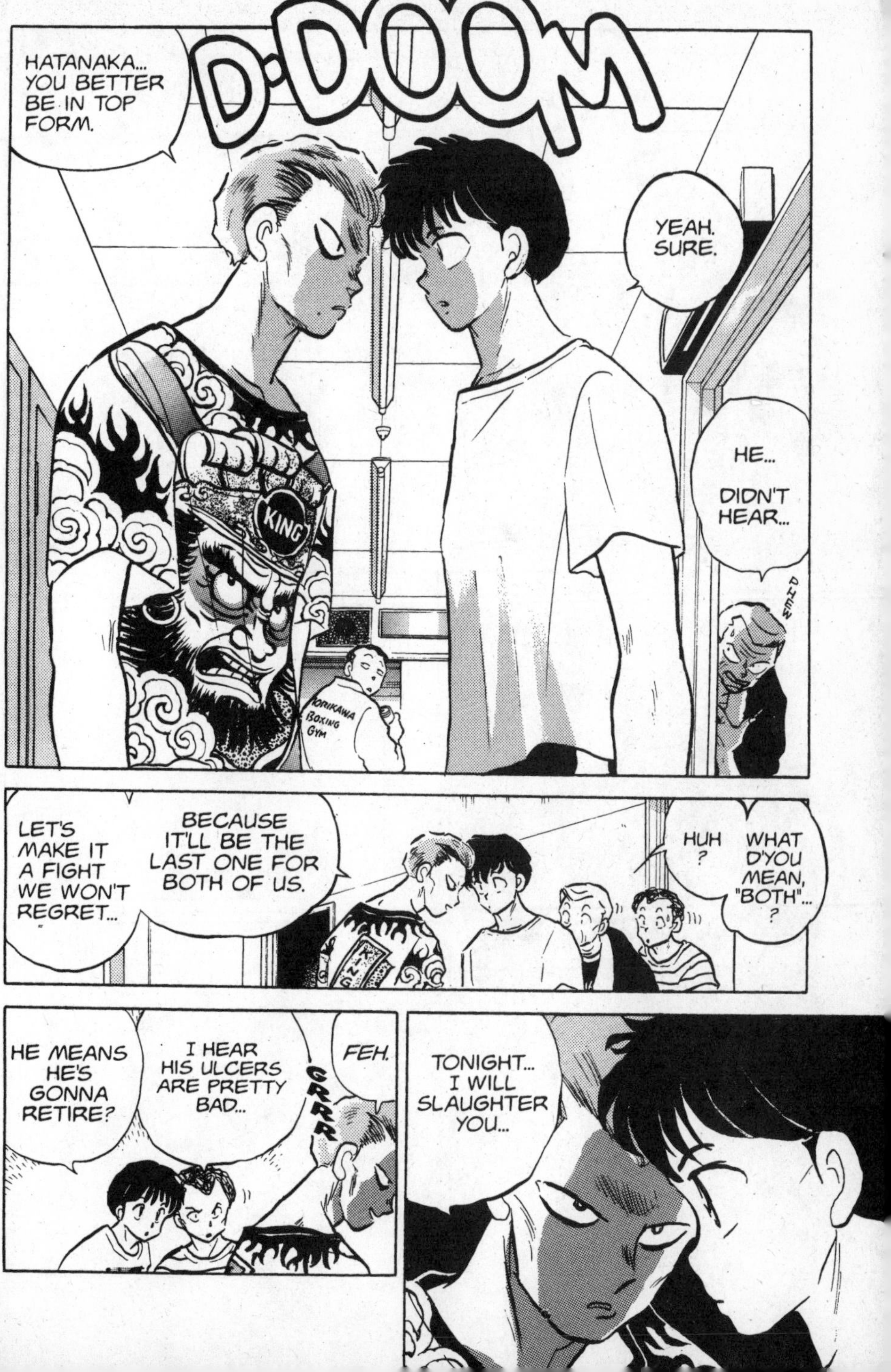
HATANAKA... YOU BETTER BE IN TOP FORM.
D-DOOM
YEAH. SURE.
HE... DIDN'T HEAR...
KING
BOXING GYM
LET'S MAKE IT A FIGHT WE WON'T REGRET...
BECAUSE IT'LL BE THE LAST ONE FOR BOTH OF US.
HUH?
WHAT D'YOU MEAN, "BOTH"...?
HE MEANS HE'S GONNA RETIRE?
I HEAR HIS ULCERS ARE PRETTY BAD...
GRRR
FEH.
TONIGHT... I WILL SLAUGHTER YOU...

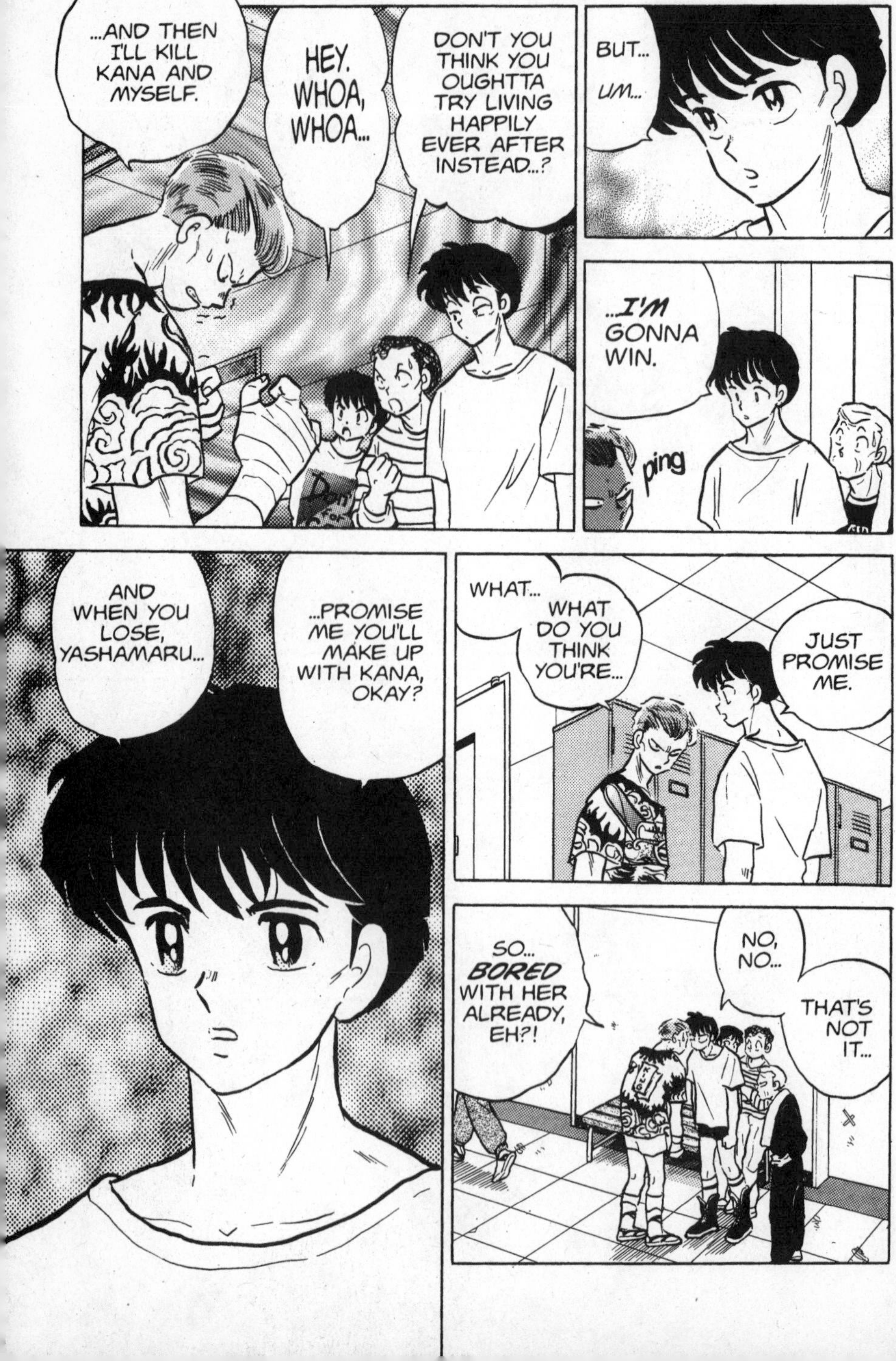
...AND THEN I'LL KILL KANA AND MYSELF.
HEY. WHOA, WHOA...
DON'T YOU THINK YOU OUGHTTA TRY LIVING HAPPILY EVER AFTER INSTEAD...?
BUT...
UM...
...*I'M* GONNA WIN.
ping
AND WHEN YOU LOSE, YASHAMARU...
...PROMISE ME YOU'LL MAKE UP WITH KANA, OKAY?
WHAT...
WHAT DO YOU THINK YOU'RE...
JUST PROMISE ME.
SO... ***BORED*** WITH HER ALREADY, EH?!
NO, NO...
THAT'S NOT IT...

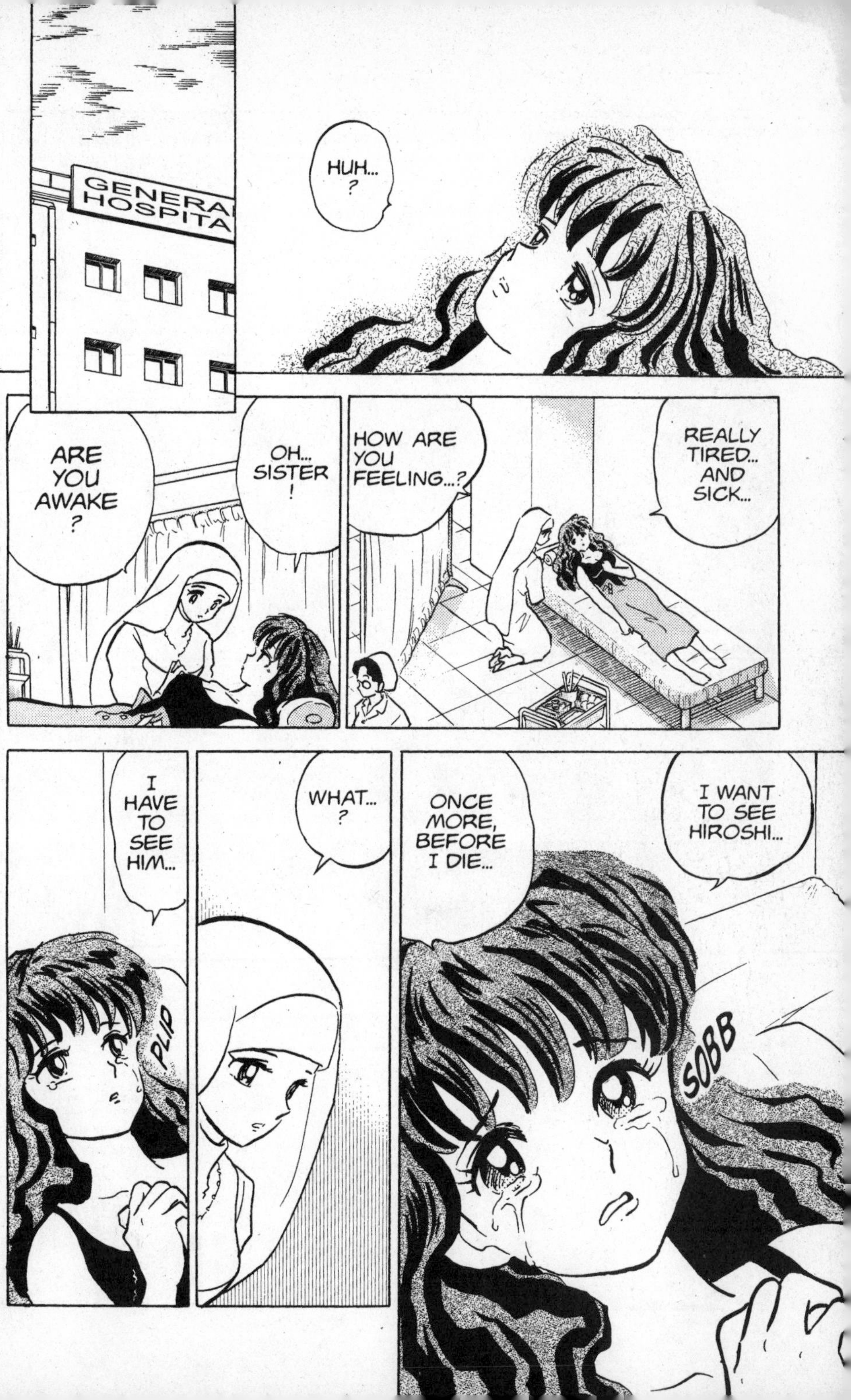
GENERAL HOSPITAL
HUH... ?
ARE YOU AWAKE ?
OH... SISTER !
HOW ARE YOU FEELING...?
REALLY TIRED... AND SICK...
I HAVE TO SEE HIM...
PLIP
WHAT... ?
ONCE MORE, BEFORE I DIE...
I WANT TO SEE HIROSHI...
SOBB

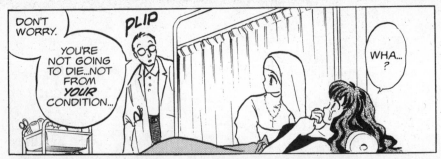

DON'T WORRY.
YOU'RE NOT GOING TO DIE...NOT FROM YOUR CONDITION...
PLIP
WHA...?
CLEAN UP
KITCHEN SYSTEMS
FIRST... FEATHER-WEIGHT EIGHT-ROUNDERS!
YASHA-MARU, YOU SURE YOU'RE OKAY?
WITH YOUR ULCERS AND EVERY-THING...
...
YADDA YADDA
THAT SCUM, HATANAKA... "MAKE UP WITH KANA," HE SAYS?!
FEH.
LOOK AT HIM. HE'S COMING RIGHT AT YOU! NO FINESSE...NO FEINTS...

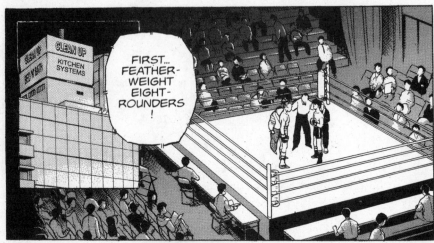

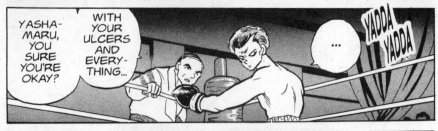

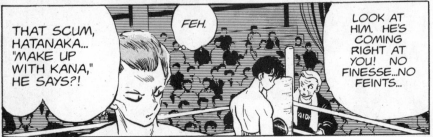

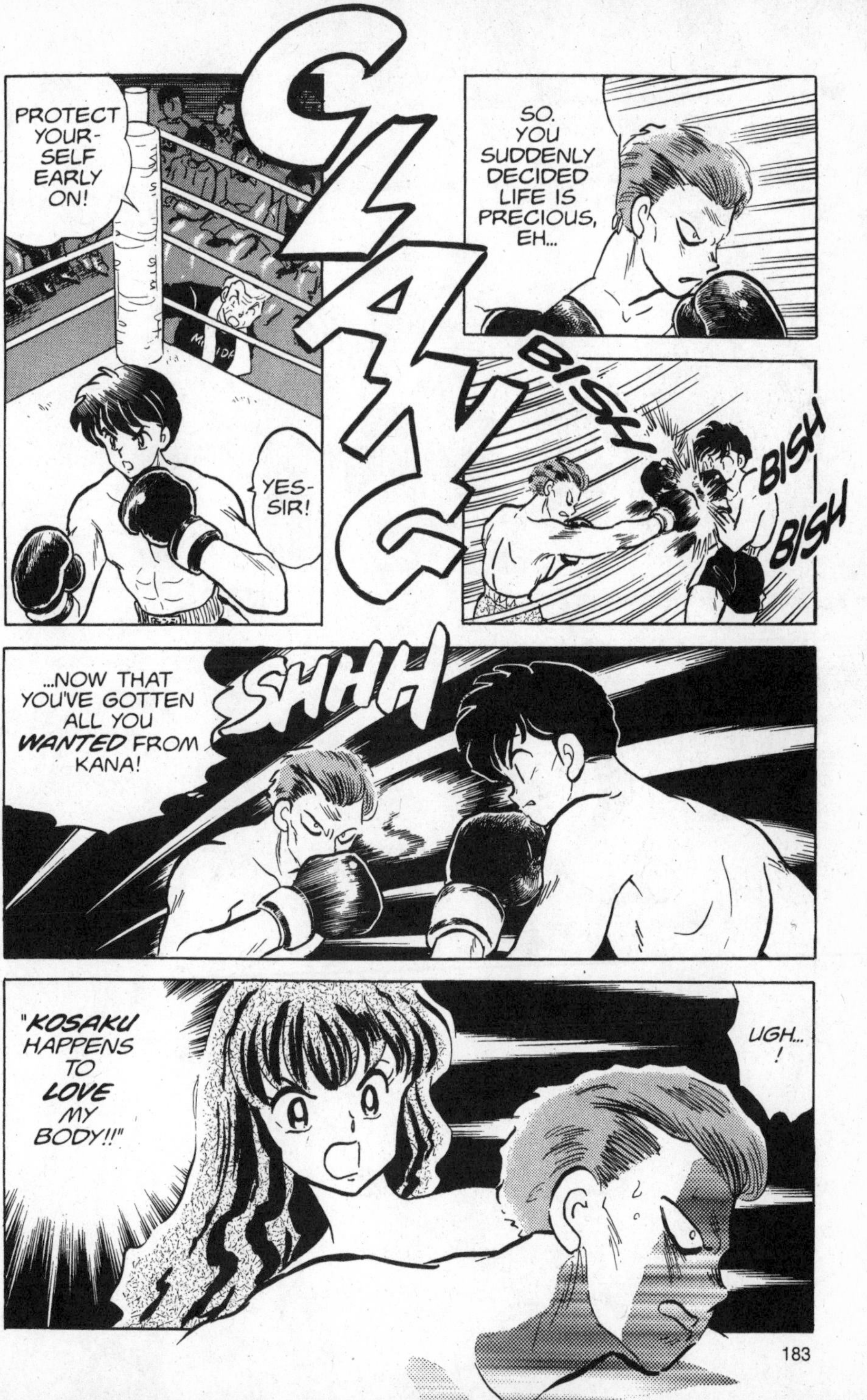
CLANG
PROTECT YOUR-SELF EARLY ON!
YES-SIR!
SO. YOU SUDDENLY DECIDED LIFE IS PRECIOUS, EH...
BISH
BISH
BISH
SHHH
...NOW THAT YOU'VE GOTTEN ALL YOU WANTED FROM KANA!
"KOSAKU HAPPENS TO LOVE MY BODY!!"
UGH... !

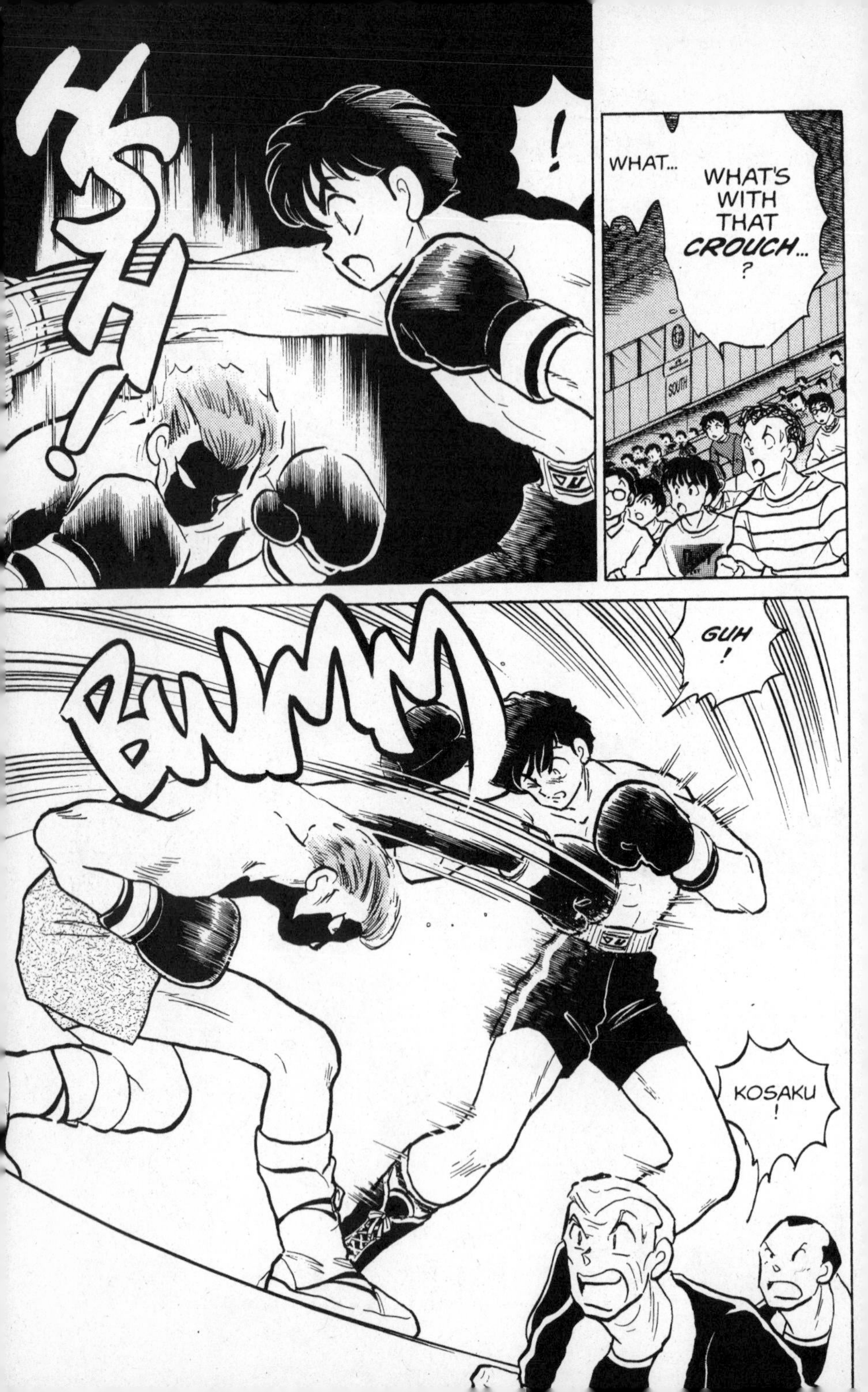
!
WHAT...
WHAT'S WITH THAT CROUCH... ?
SOUTH
GUH !
KOSAKU !

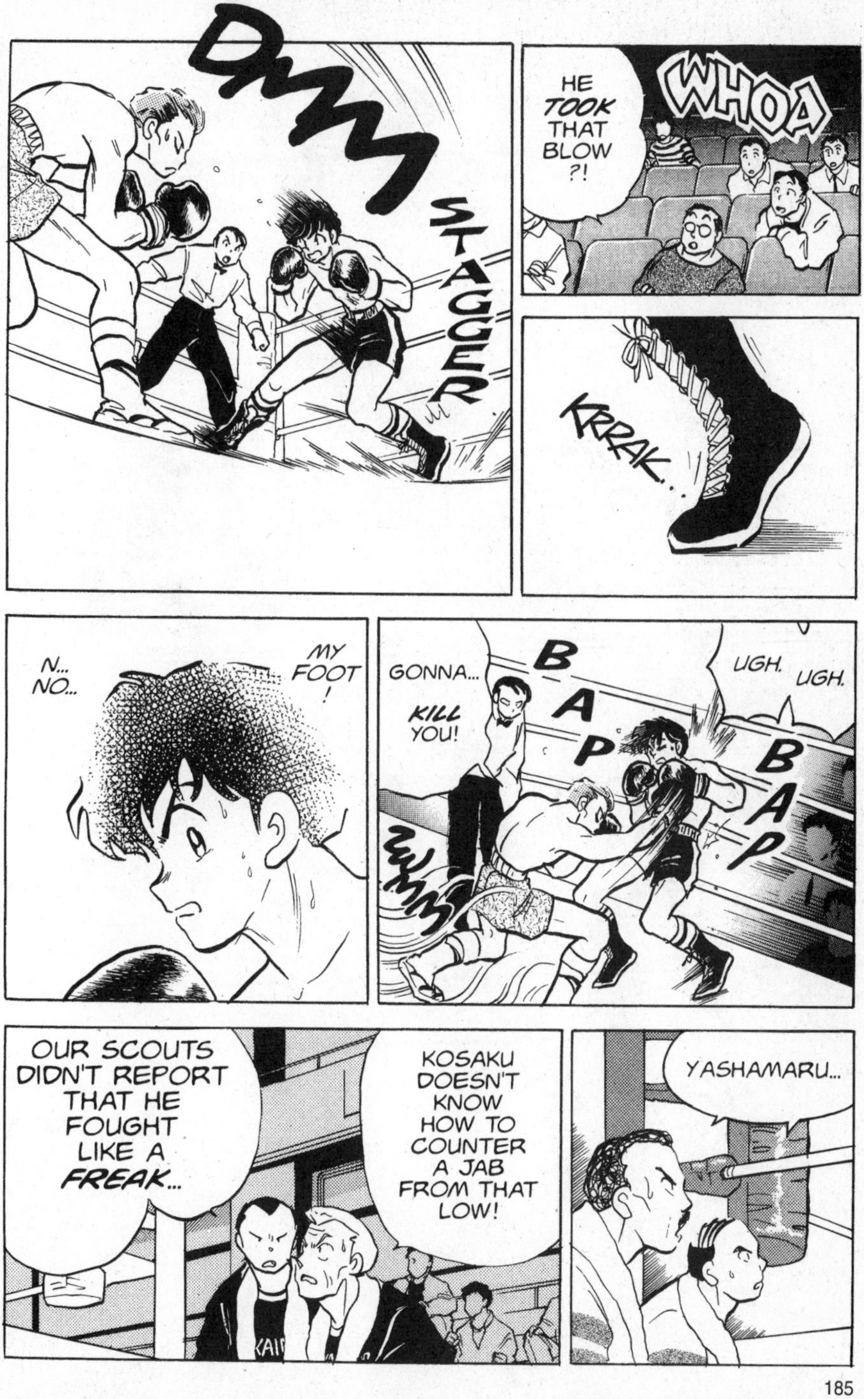
DMMM
STAGGER
HE TOOK THAT BLOW ?!
WHOA
KRRAK...
N... NO...
MY FOOT !
GONNA...
KILL YOU!
BAP
UGH. UGH.
BAP
OUR SCOUTS DIDN'T REPORT THAT HE FOUGHT LIKE A FREAK...
KOSAKU DOESN'T KNOW HOW TO COUNTER A JAB FROM THAT LOW!
YASHAMARU...

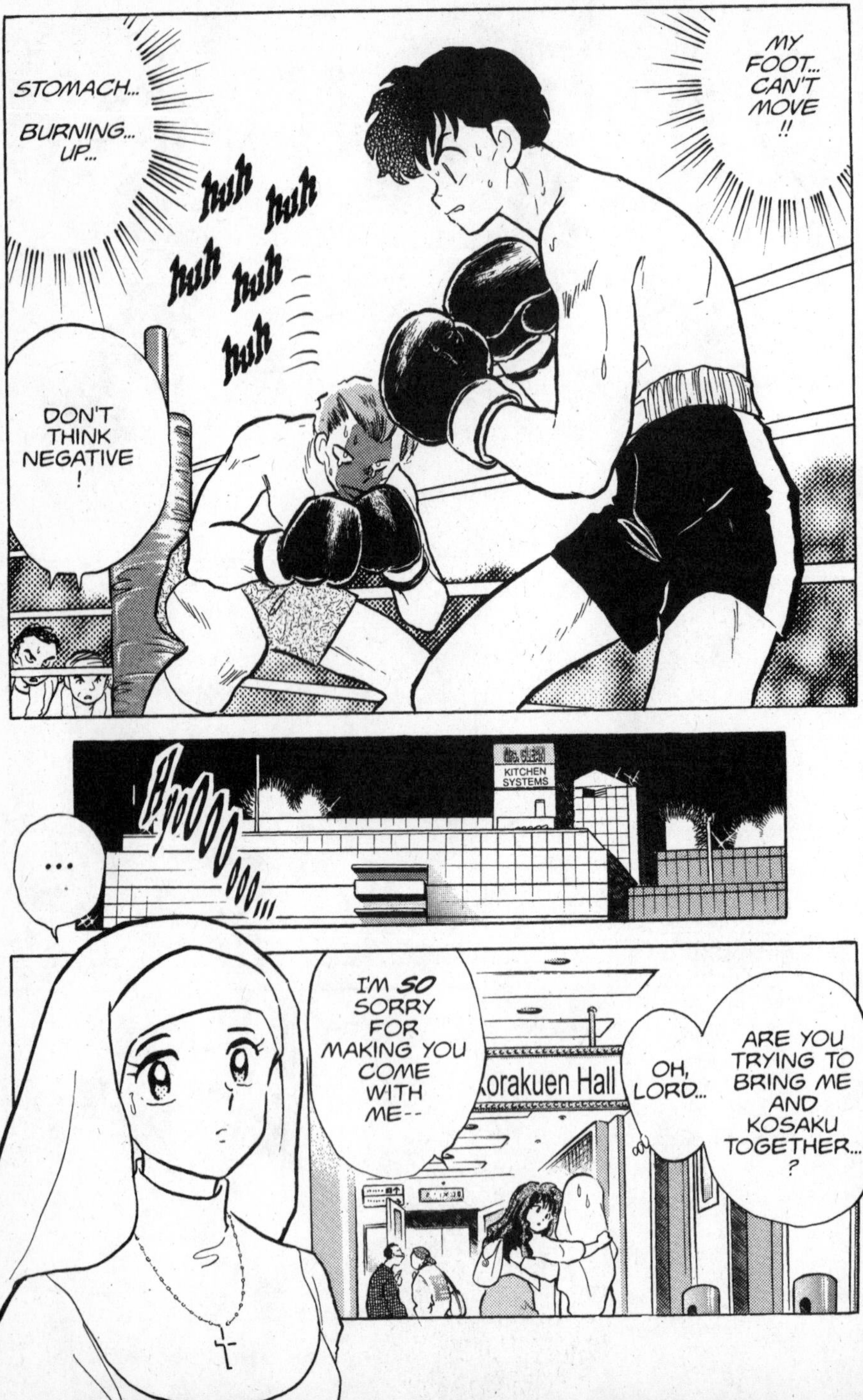
STOMACH... BURNING... UP...
huh huh huh huh huh
MY FOOT... CAN'T MOVE !!
DON'T THINK NEGATIVE !
...
KITCHEN SYSTEMS
I'M SO SORRY FOR MAKING YOU COME WITH ME--
Korakuen Hall
OH, LORD...
ARE YOU TRYING TO BRING ME AND KOSAKU TOGETHER... ?

CHAPTER THREE

THE FALLEN LAMB

PART FIVE

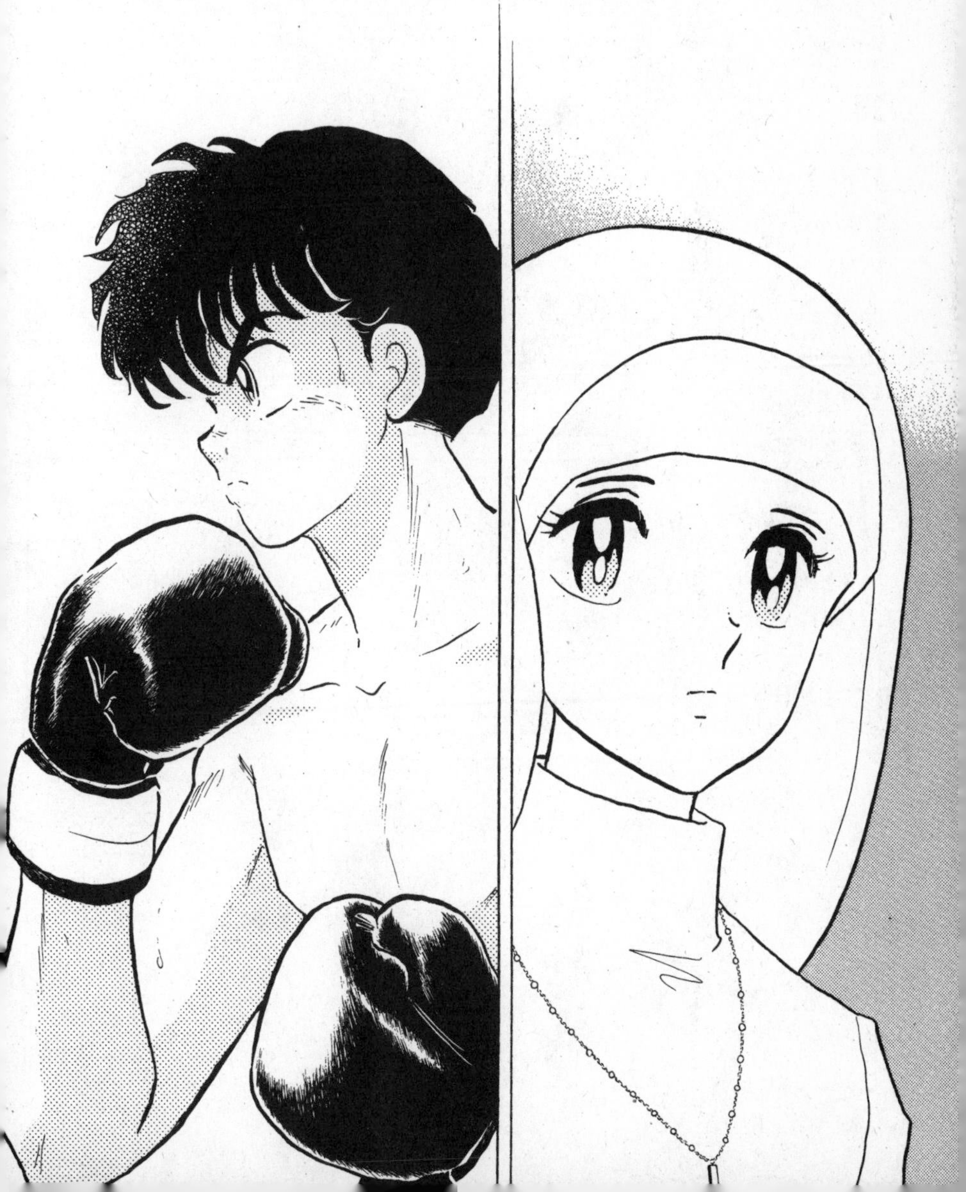

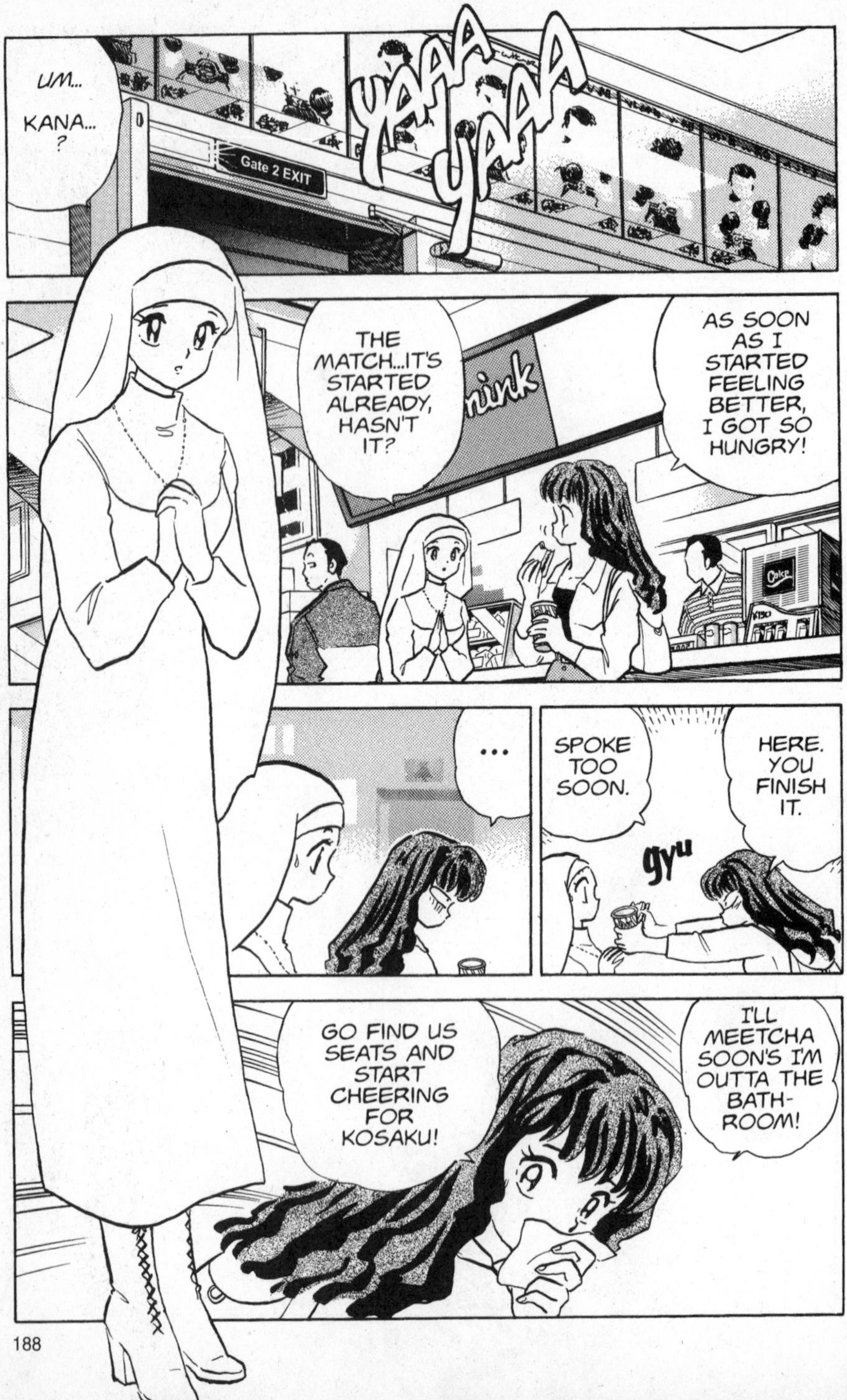
UM...
KANA...?
YAAA YAAA YAAA
Gate 2 EXIT
THE MATCH...IT'S STARTED ALREADY, HASN'T IT?
AS SOON AS I STARTED FEELING BETTER, I GOT SO HUNGRY!
...
SPOKE TOO SOON.
HERE. YOU FINISH IT.
GYU
GO FIND US SEATS AND START CHEERING FOR KOSAKU!
I'LL MEETCHA SOON'S I'M OUTTA THE BATH-ROOM!

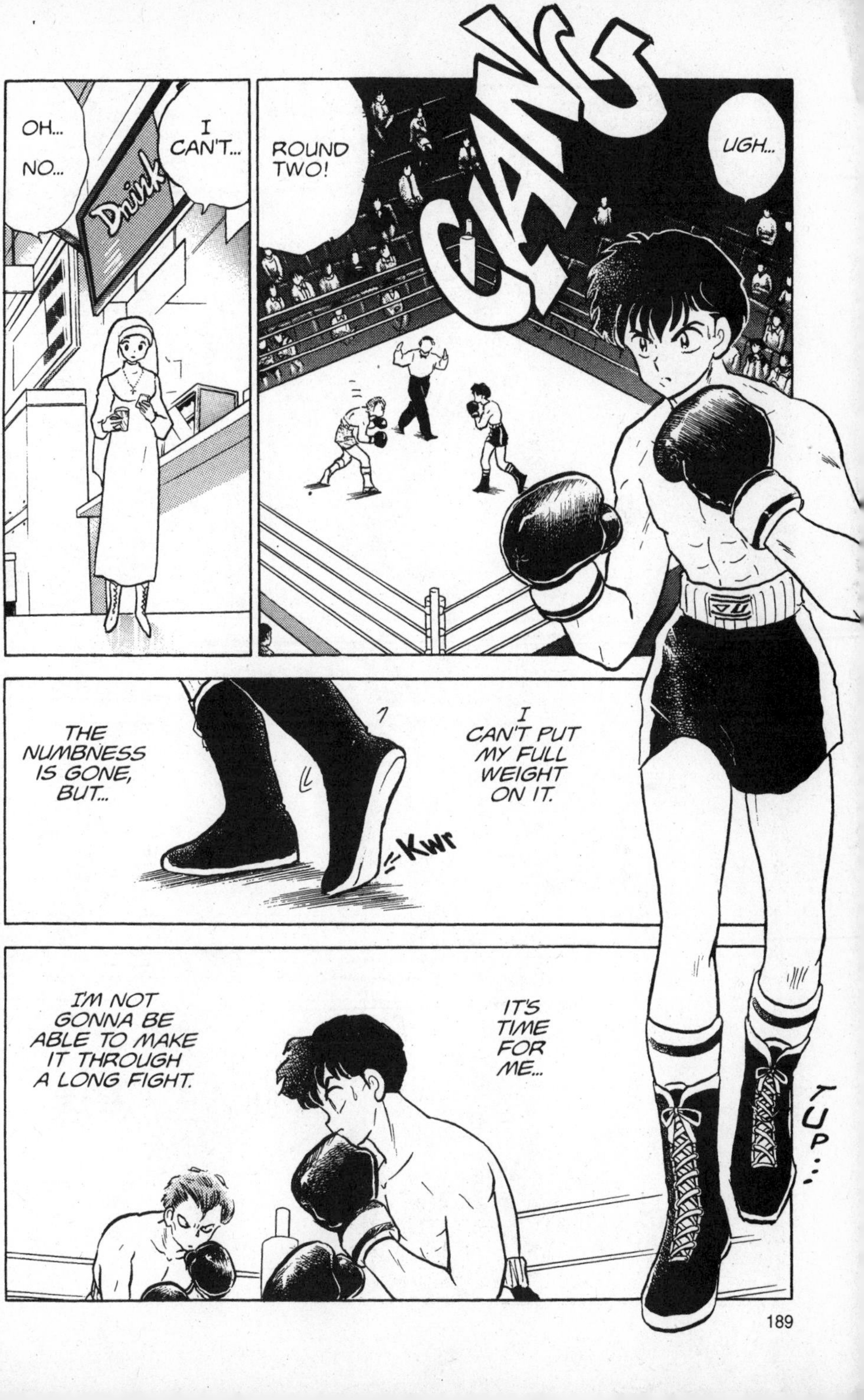
OH... NO...
I CAN'T...
Drink
ROUND TWO!
GANG
UGH...
THE NUMBNESS IS GONE, BUT...
I CAN'T PUT MY FULL WEIGHT ON IT.
KWR
I'M NOT GONNA BE ABLE TO MAKE IT THROUGH A LONG FIGHT.
IT'S TIME FOR ME...
TUP...

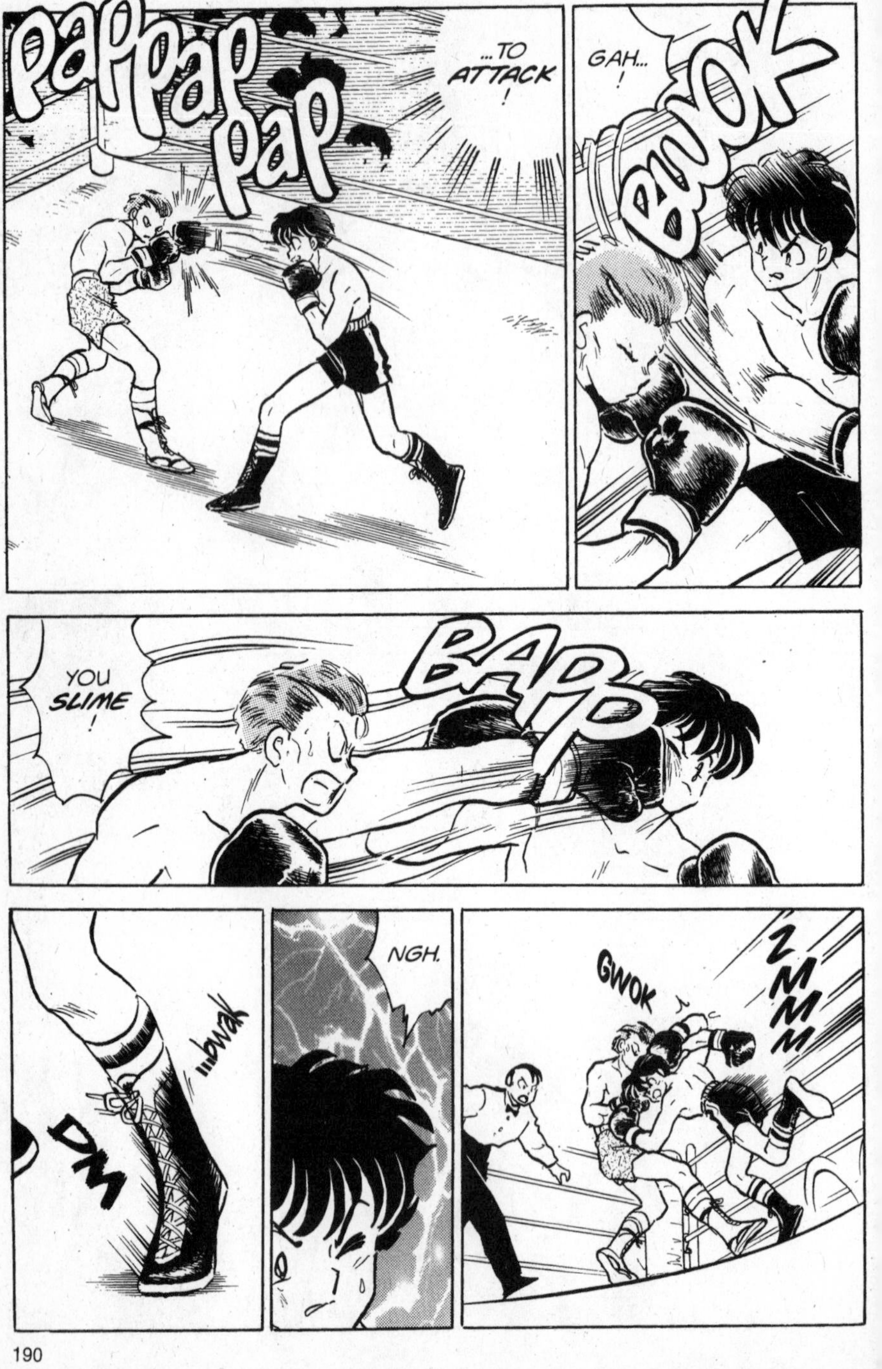
PAPPAP PAP
...TO ATTACK!
GAH...!
BWOK
YOU SLIME!
BAP
...bwak
DM
NGH.
GWOK
ZMMM

Y'CALL THIS A FIGHT?!

YADDA YADDA YADDA YADDA

C'MON, SHOW US WHATCHA GOT!

HEY, SISTER!

gasp

SHH!

HUH? ME?

H-HOW IS KOSAKU DOING...?

OMG

LOOKIN' PRETTY LAME, IF YOU WANT THE TRUTH.

HIS FOOT'S MESSED UP. HE CAN'T PLANT HIMSELF FOR A SOLID PUNCH.

G'ULP

IT'S LOOKIN' PRETTY BAD FOR HIM!

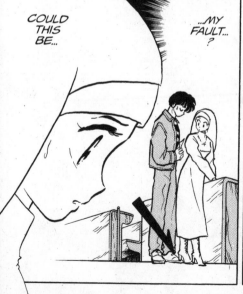

COULD THIS BE...

...MY FAULT...?

OH, KOSAKU...

UGH...

DMF DMF

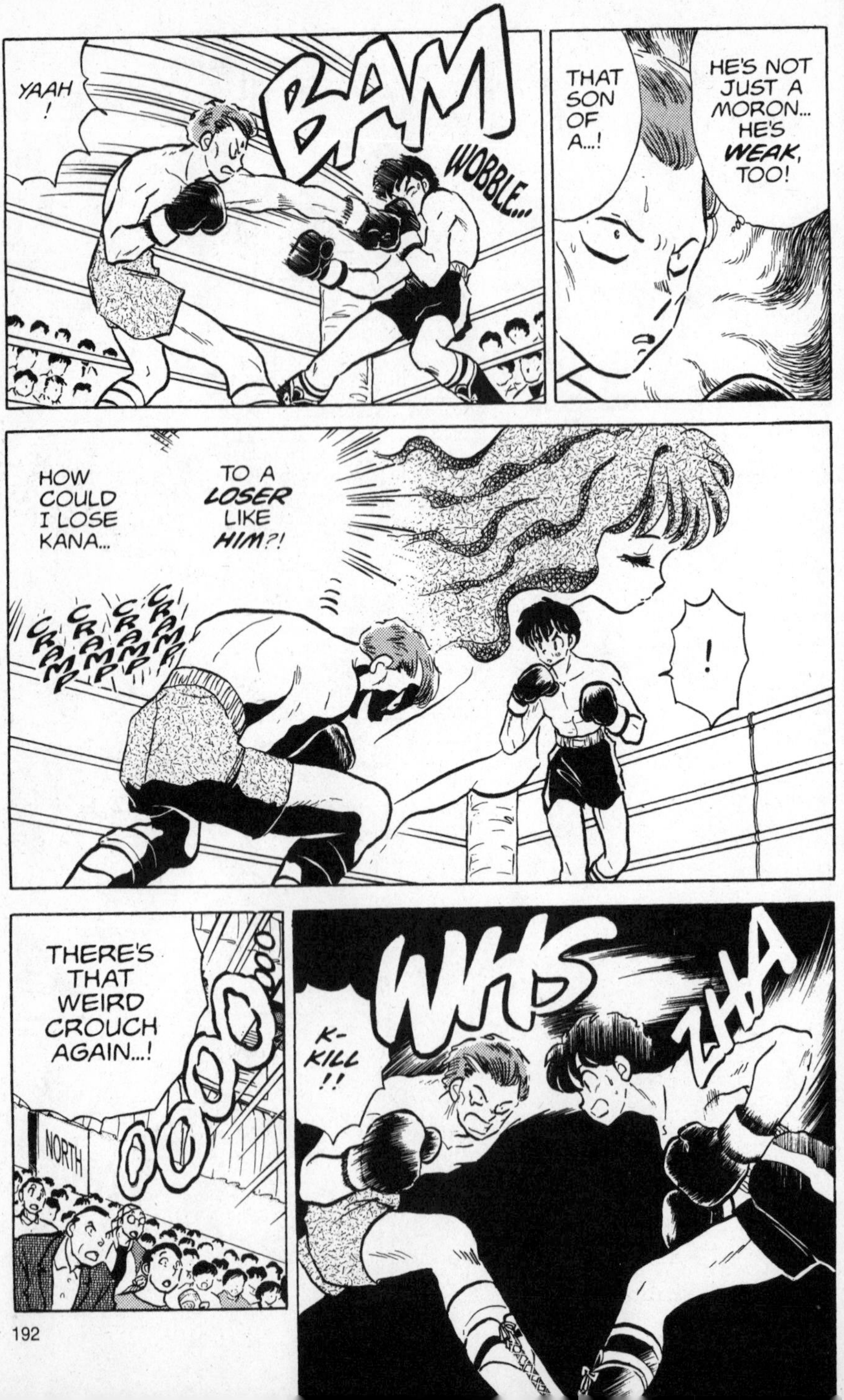
YAAH!
BAM
WOBBLE...
THAT SON OF A...!
HE'S NOT JUST A MORON... HE'S WEAK, TOO!
HOW COULD I LOSE KANA...
TO A LOSER LIKE HIM?!
CRAMP CRAMP CRAMP CRAMP
!
THERE'S THAT WEIRD CROUCH AGAIN...!
NORTH
WHS
K-KILL!!
ZHA

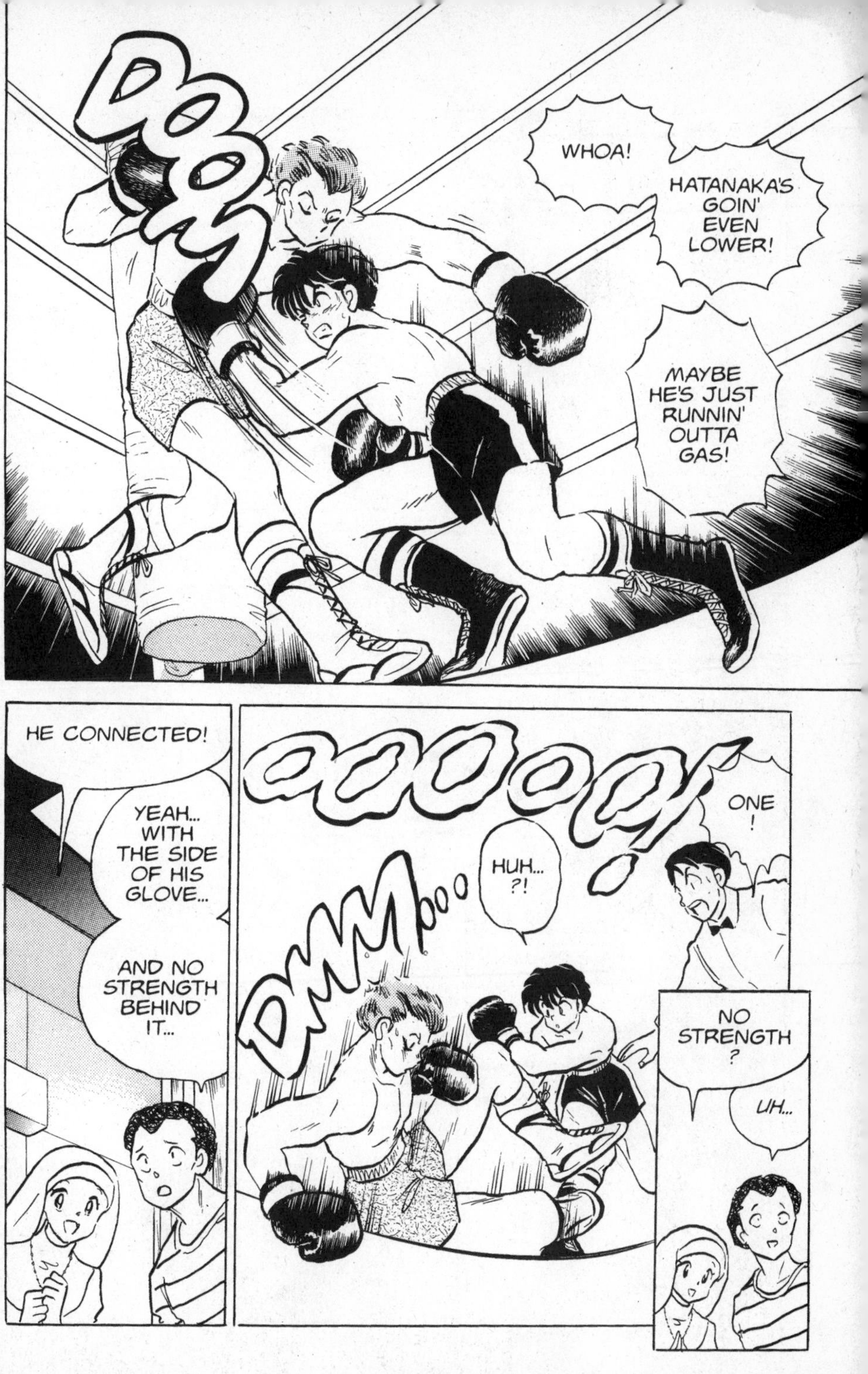
DOOM
WHOA!
HATANAKA'S GOIN' EVEN LOWER!
MAYBE HE'S JUST RUNNIN' OUTTA GAS!
HE CONNECTED!
YEAH... WITH THE SIDE OF HIS GLOVE...
AND NO STRENGTH BEHIND IT...
OOOOOO!
HUH...?!
DMMPOO
ONE!
NO STRENGTH?
UH...

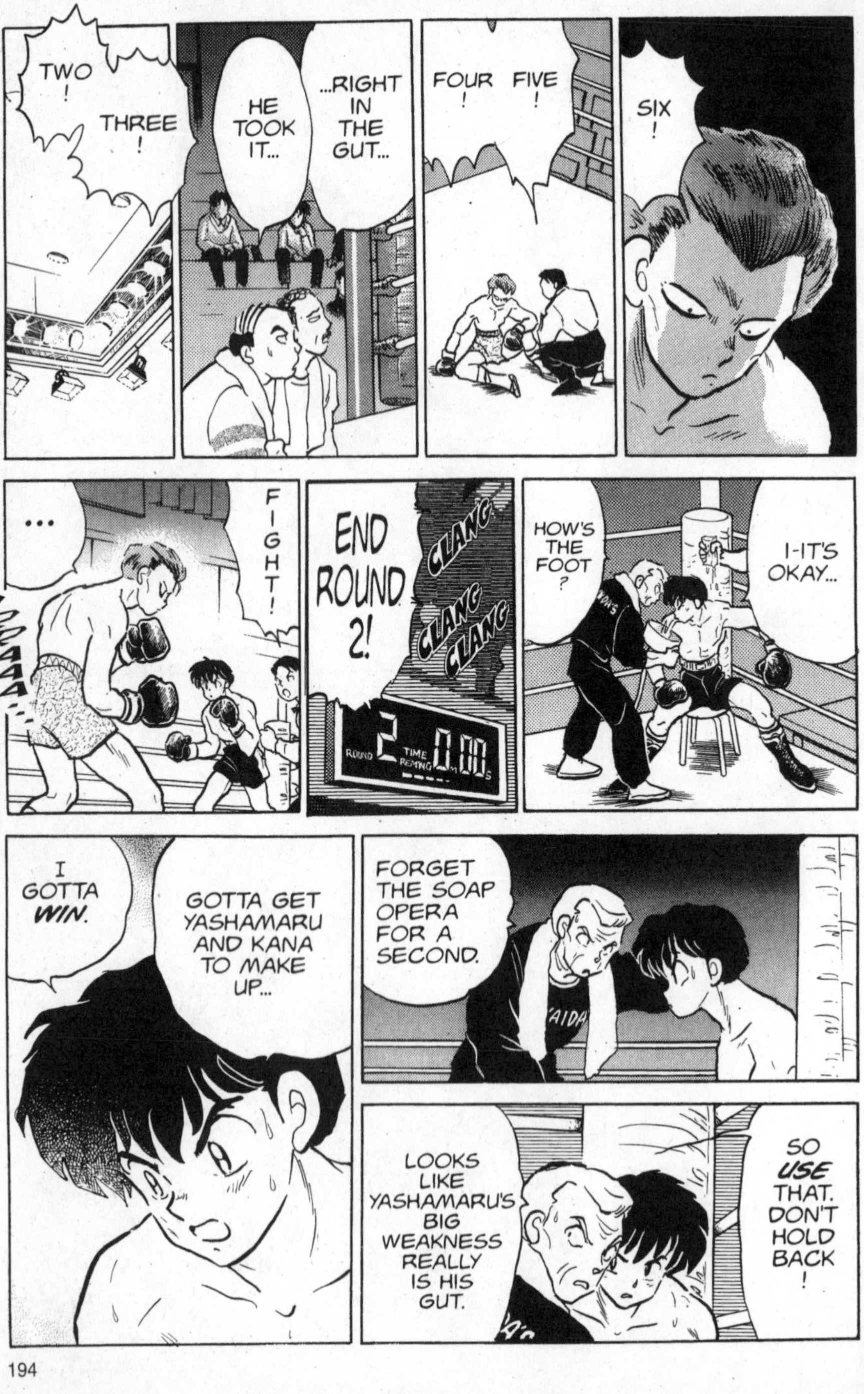
TWO!
THREE!
HE TOOK IT...
...RIGHT IN THE GUT...
FOUR! FIVE!
SIX!
...
RRRAAA...
FIGHT!
END ROUND 2!
CLANG
CLANG
CLANG
HOW'S THE FOOT?
I-IT'S OKAY...
I GOTTA *WIN*.
GOTTA GET YASHAMARU AND KANA TO MAKE UP...
FORGET THE SOAP OPERA FOR A SECOND.
LOOKS LIKE YASHAMARU'S BIG WEAKNESS REALLY IS HIS GUT.
SO *USE* THAT. DON'T HOLD BACK!

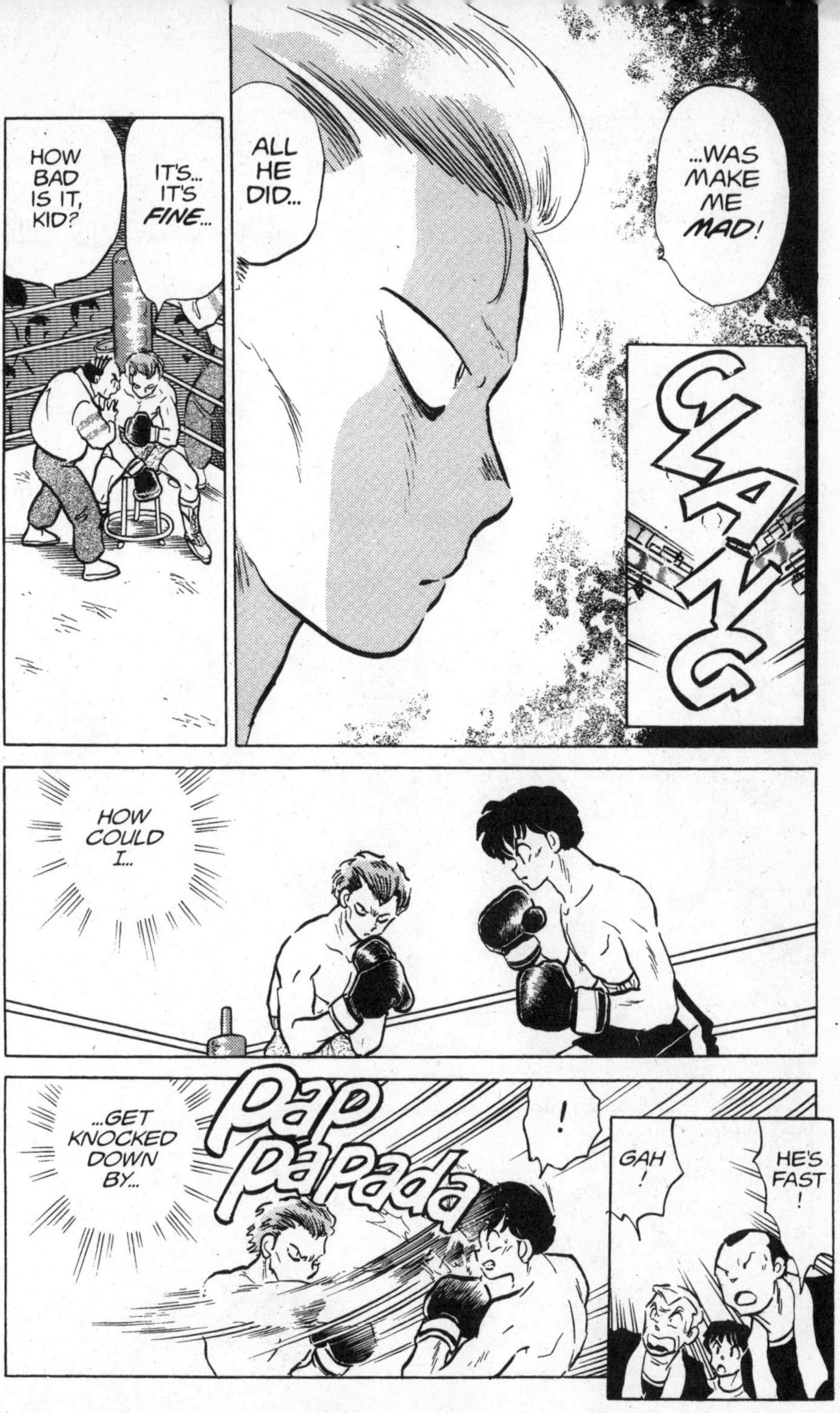
HOW BAD IS IT, KID?
IT'S... IT'S *FINE*...
ALL HE DID...
...WAS MAKE ME *MAD*!
CLANG
HOW COULD I...
...GET KNOCKED DOWN BY...
pap papada
!
GAH!
HE'S FAST!

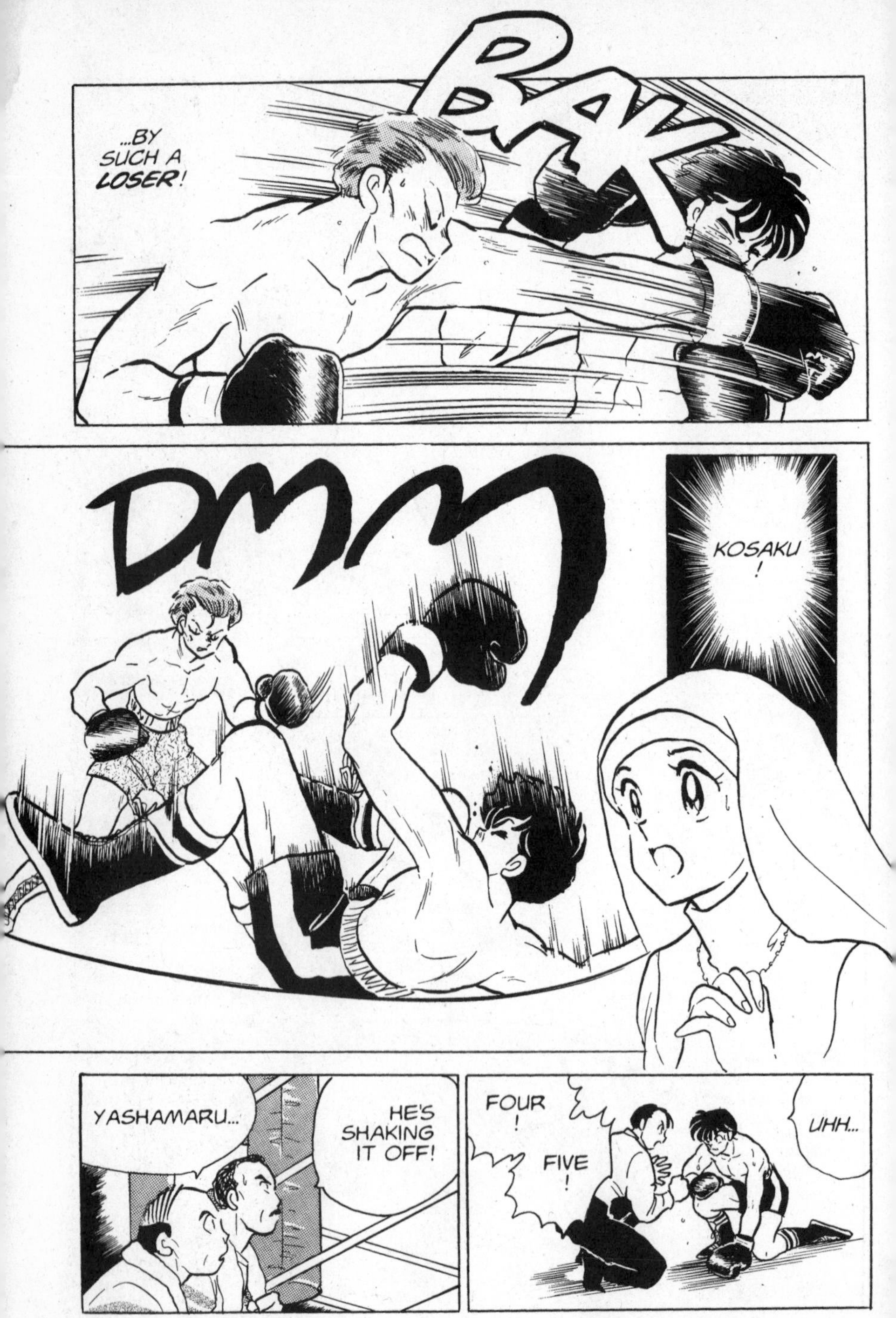
BAK
...BY SUCH A LOSER!
DMM
KOSAKU!
YASHAMARU...
HE'S SHAKING IT OFF!
FOUR!
FIVE!
UHH...

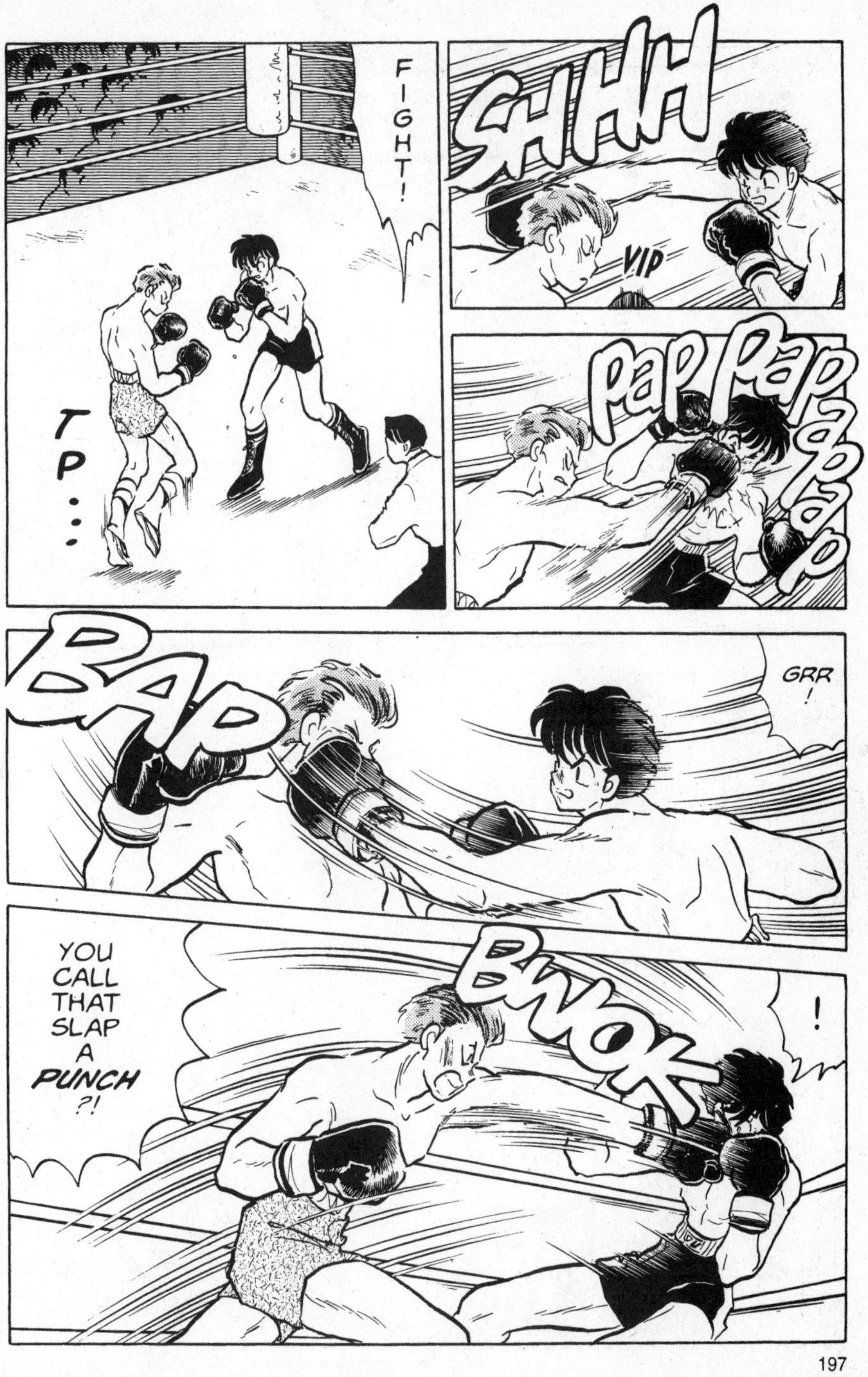

FIGHT!
TP...
SHHH
VIP
PAP PAP PAPAPAP
BAP
GRR!
YOU CALL THAT SLAP A PUNCH?!
BWOK
!

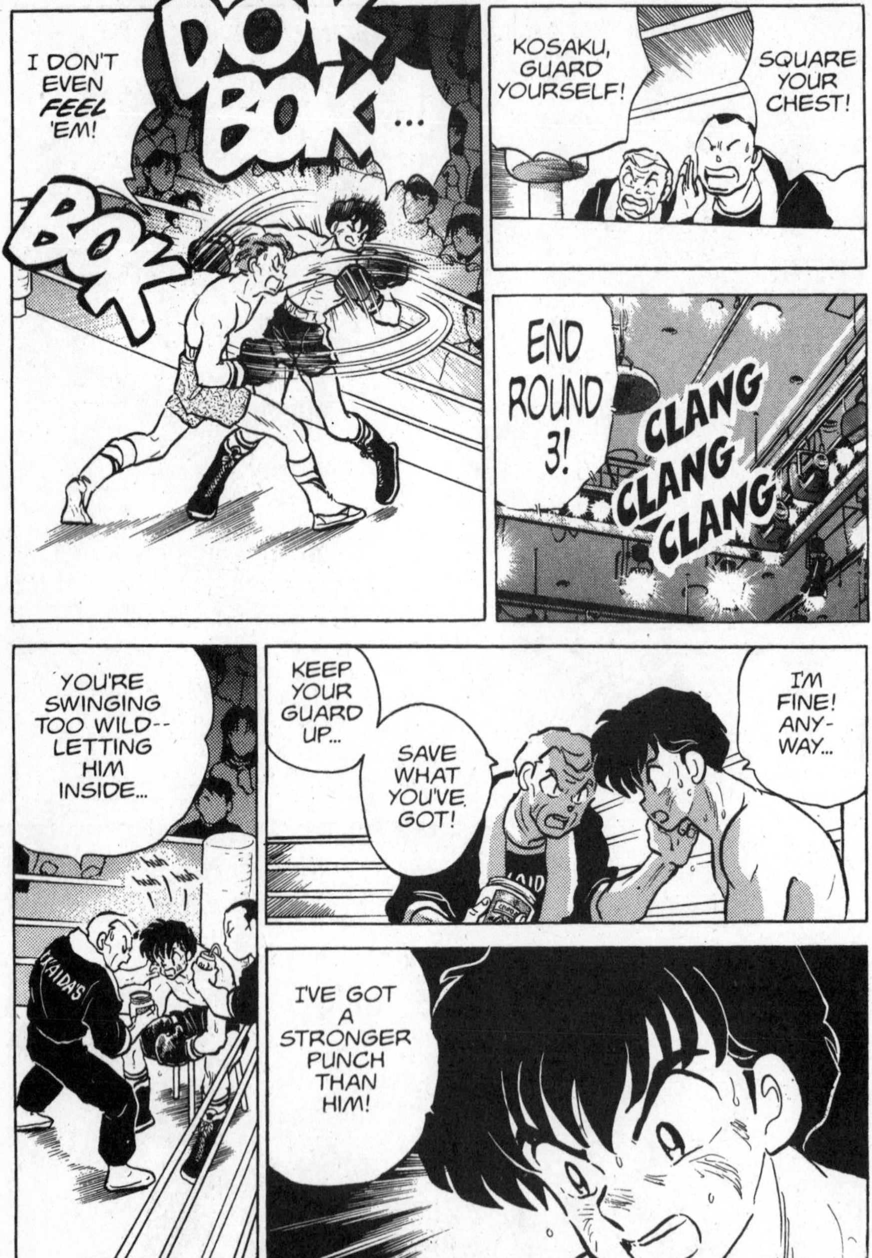

I DON'T EVEN FEEL 'EM!
DOK BOK...
BOK
KOSAKU, GUARD YOURSELF!
SQUARE YOUR CHEST!
END ROUND 3!
CLANG CLANG CLANG
YOU'RE SWINGING TOO WILD-- LETTING HIM INSIDE...
KEEP YOUR GUARD UP...
SAVE WHAT YOU'VE GOT!
I'M FINE! ANY-WAY...
I'VE GOT A STRONGER PUNCH THAN HIM!

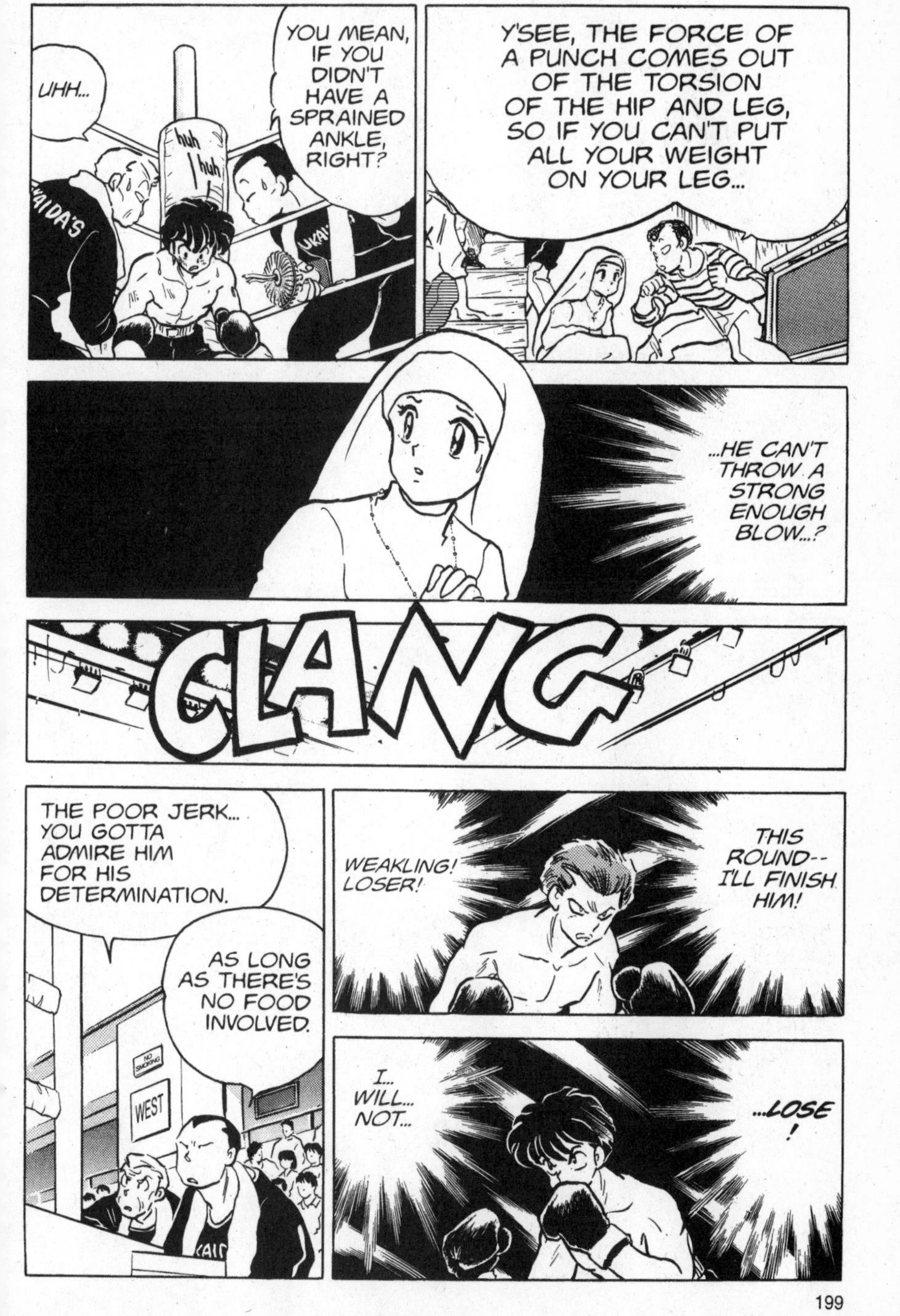
UHH...
YOU MEAN, IF YOU DIDN'T HAVE A SPRAINED ANKLE, RIGHT?
huh huh
Y'SEE, THE FORCE OF A PUNCH COMES OUT OF THE TORSION OF THE HIP AND LEG, SO IF YOU CAN'T PUT ALL YOUR WEIGHT ON YOUR LEG...
...HE CAN'T THROW A STRONG ENOUGH BLOW...?
CLANG
THE POOR JERK... YOU GOTTA ADMIRE HIM FOR HIS DETERMINATION.
AS LONG AS THERE'S NO FOOD INVOLVED.
NO SMOKING
WEST
WEAKLING! LOSER!
THIS ROUND-- I'LL FINISH HIM!
I... WILL... NOT...
...LOSE!

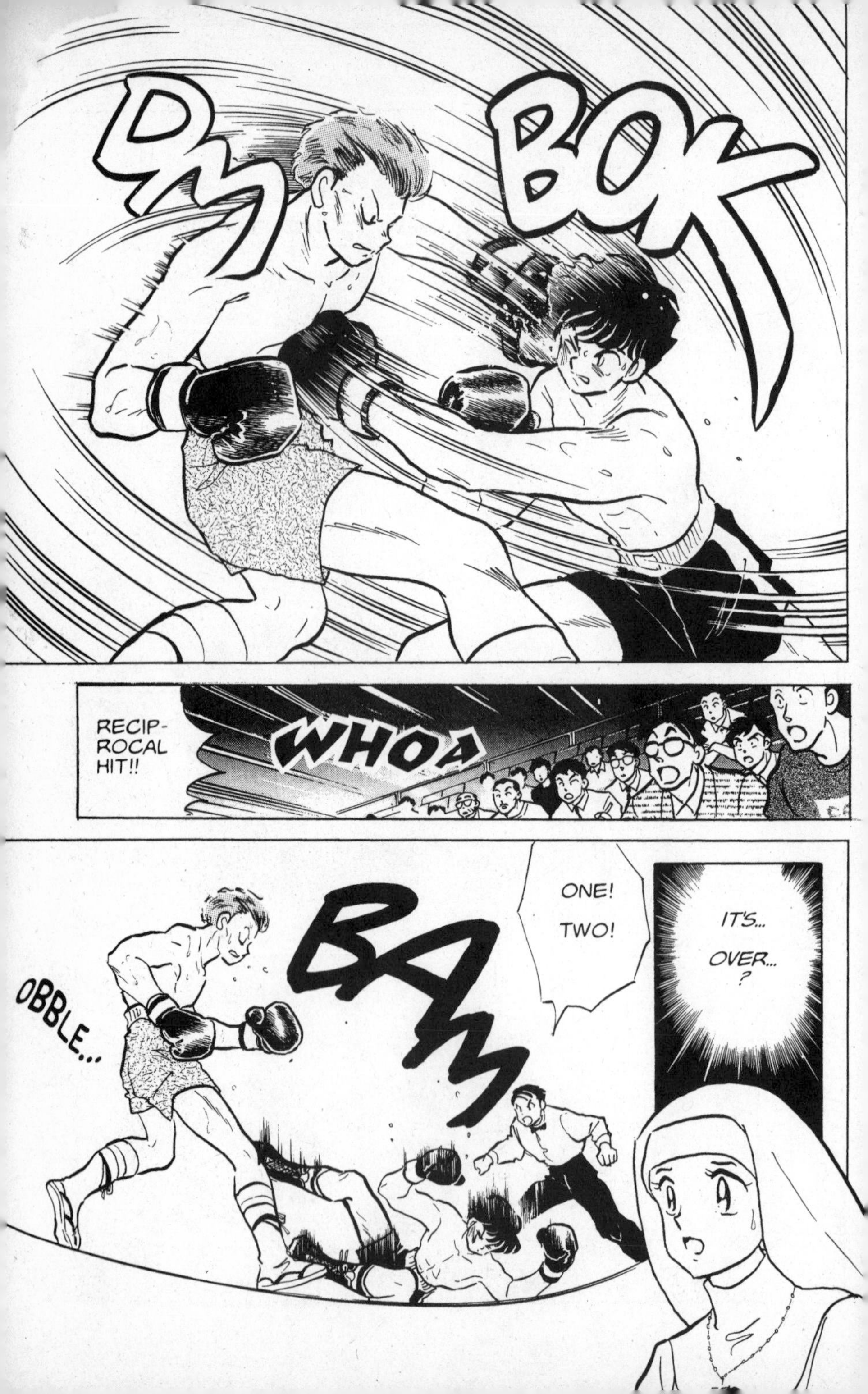
DM
BOK
RECIP-ROCAL HIT!!
WHOA
OBBLE...
BAM
ONE! TWO!
IT'S... OVER...?

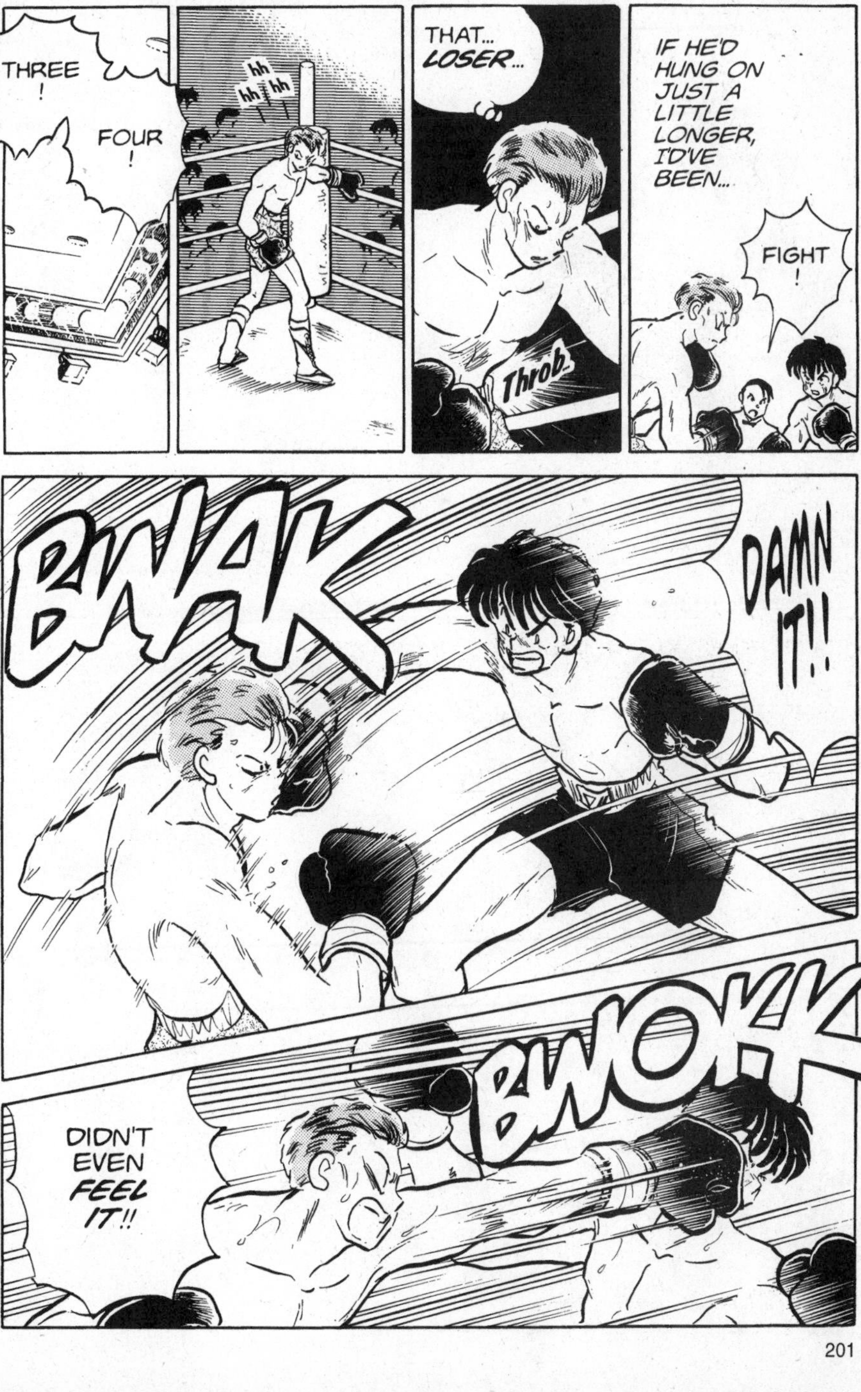
THREE!
FOUR!
hh hh hh
THAT... LOSER...
Throb
IF HE'D HUNG ON JUST A LITTLE LONGER, I'D'VE BEEN...
FIGHT!
BWAK
DAMN IT!!
BWOKK
DIDN'T EVEN FEEL IT!!

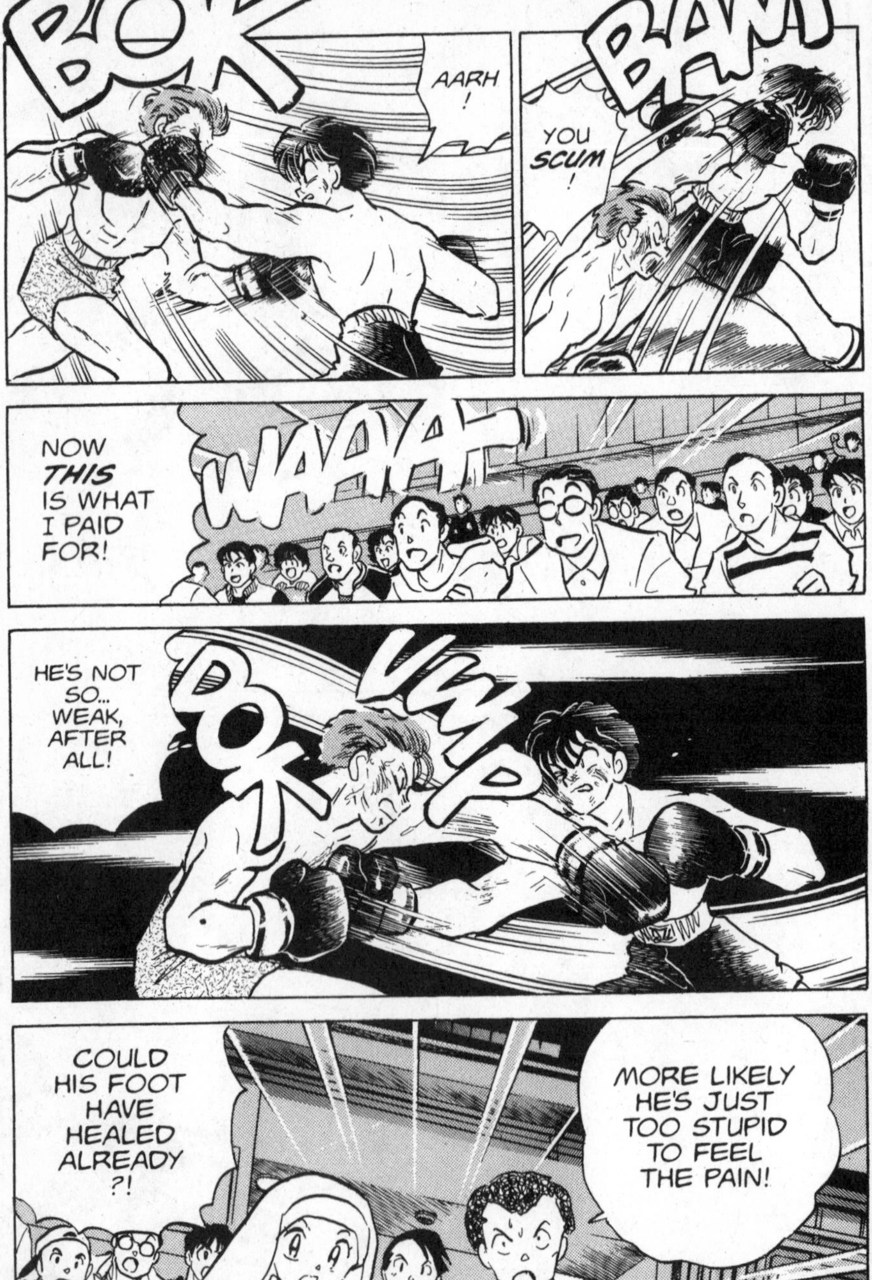
BOK
AARH!
BAM
YOU SCUM!
NOW THIS IS WHAT I PAID FOR!
WAAA
HE'S NOT SO... WEAK, AFTER ALL!
DOK
VUMP
COULD HIS FOOT HAVE HEALED ALREADY?!
MORE LIKELY HE'S JUST TOO STUPID TO FEEL THE PAIN!
CANNES

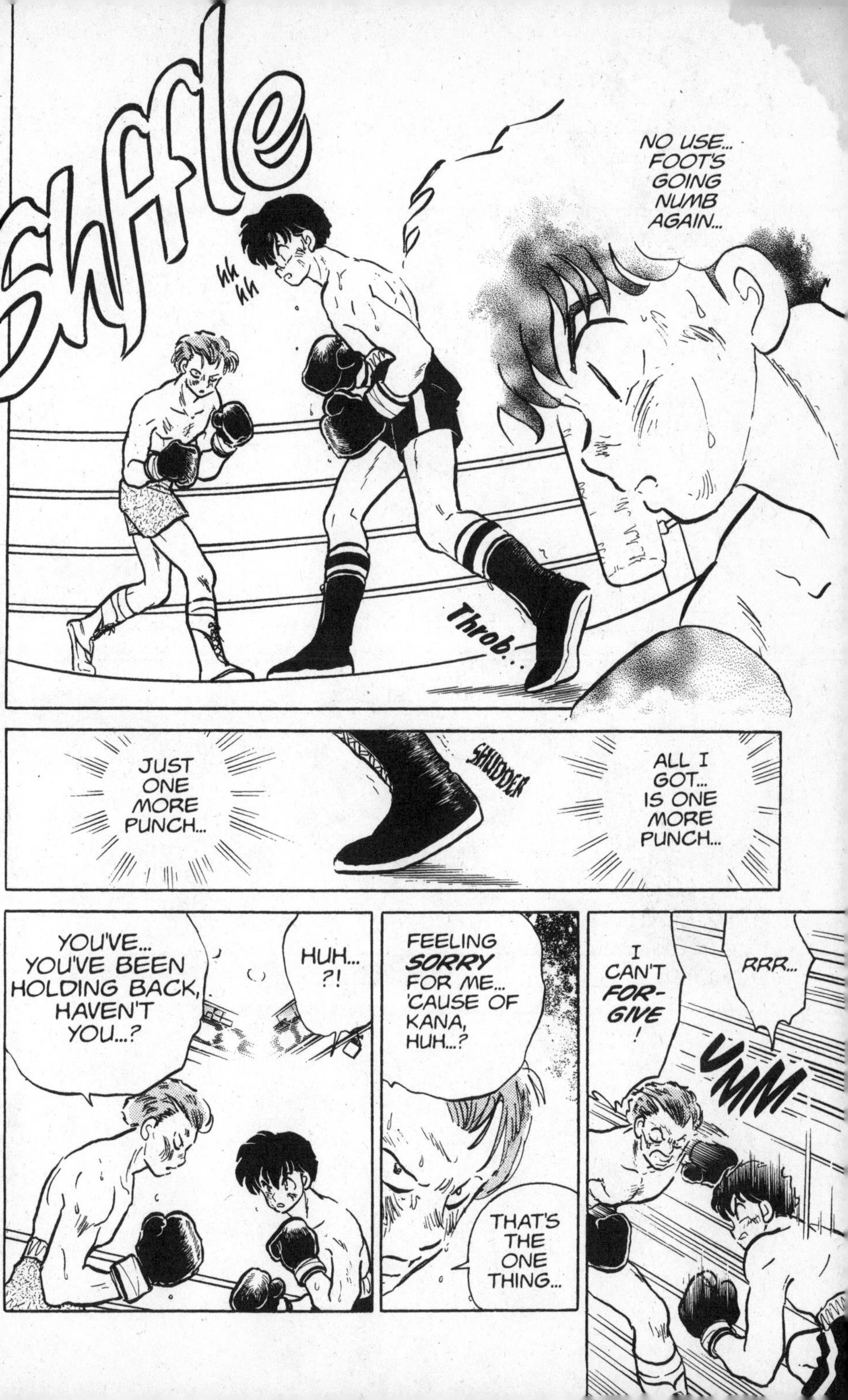

Shuffle
NO USE... FOOT'S GOING NUMB AGAIN...
hh hh
Throb...
JUST ONE MORE PUNCH...
SHUDDER
ALL I GOT... IS ONE MORE PUNCH...
YOU'VE... YOU'VE BEEN HOLDING BACK, HAVEN'T YOU...?
HUH... ?!
FEELING SORRY FOR ME... 'CAUSE OF KANA, HUH...?
THAT'S THE ONE THING...
I CAN'T FORGIVE!
RRR...
VMM

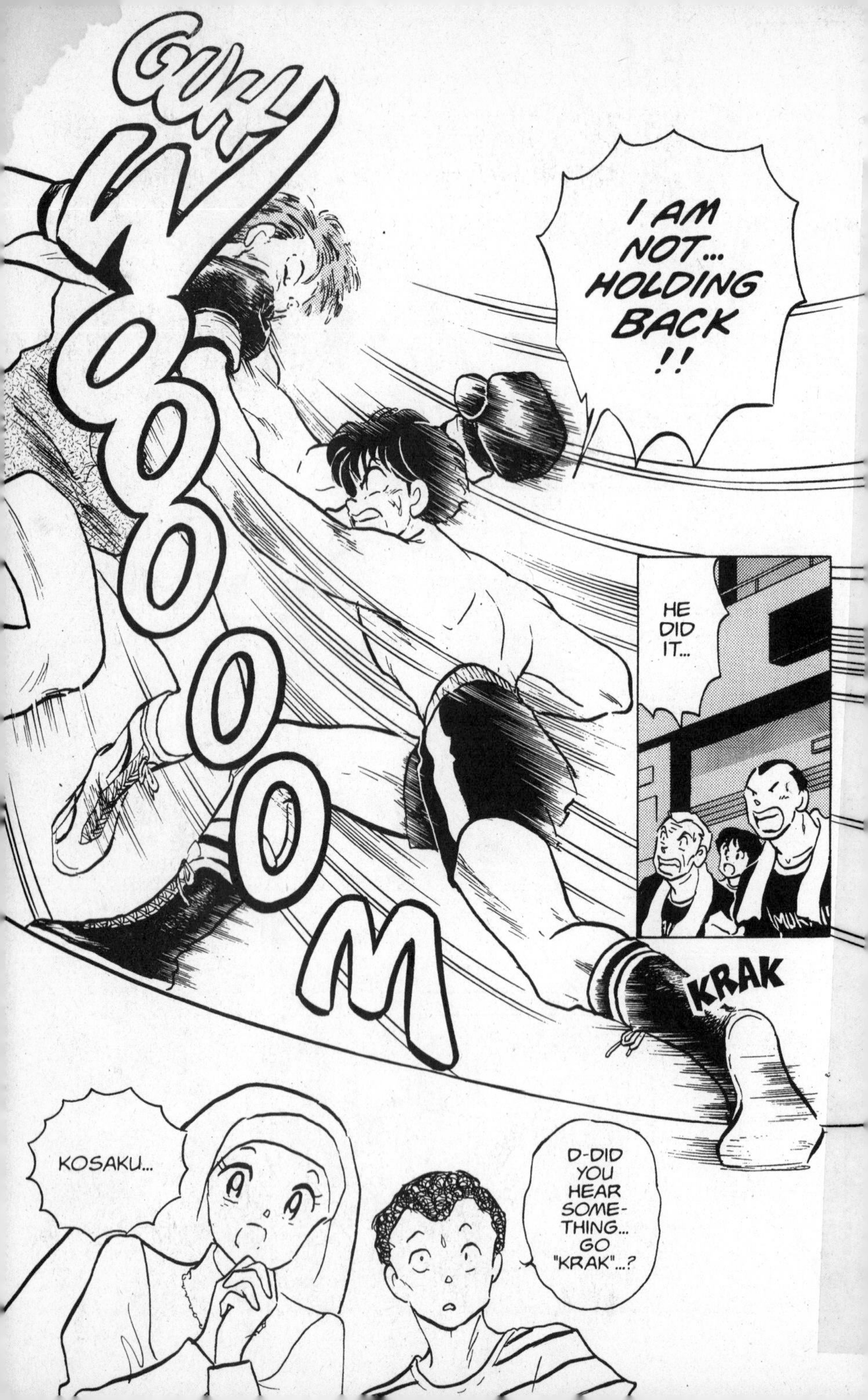
I AM NOT... HOLDING BACK !!
HE DID IT...
KRAK
KOSAKU...
D-DID YOU HEAR SOME-THING... GO "KRAK"...?

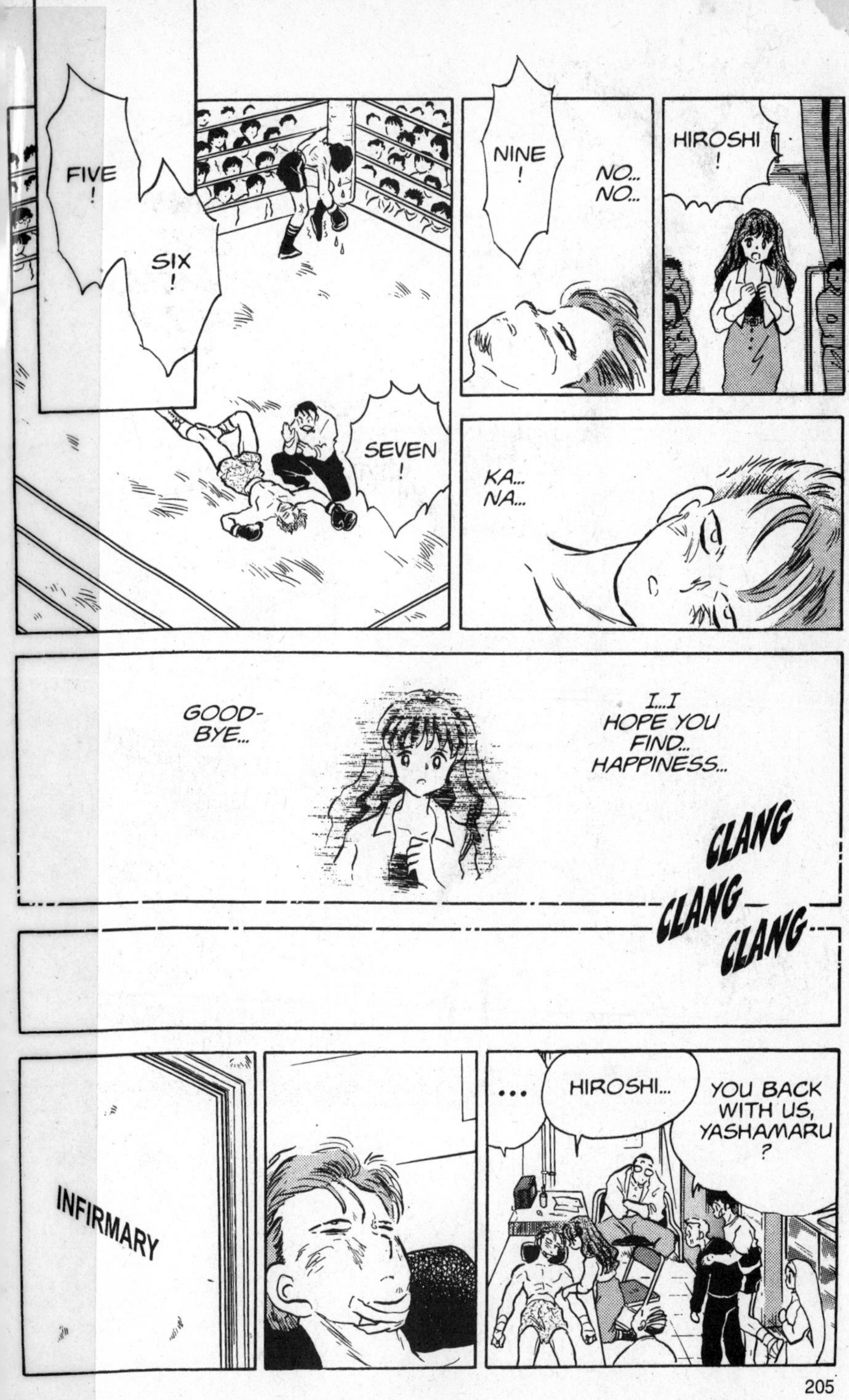
FIVE!
SIX!
SEVEN!
NINE!
NO... NO...
HIROSHI!
KA... NA...
GOOD-BYE...
I...I HOPE YOU FIND... HAPPINESS...
CLANG
CLANG
CLANG
INFIRMARY
...
HIROSHI...
YOU BACK WITH US, YASHAMARU?

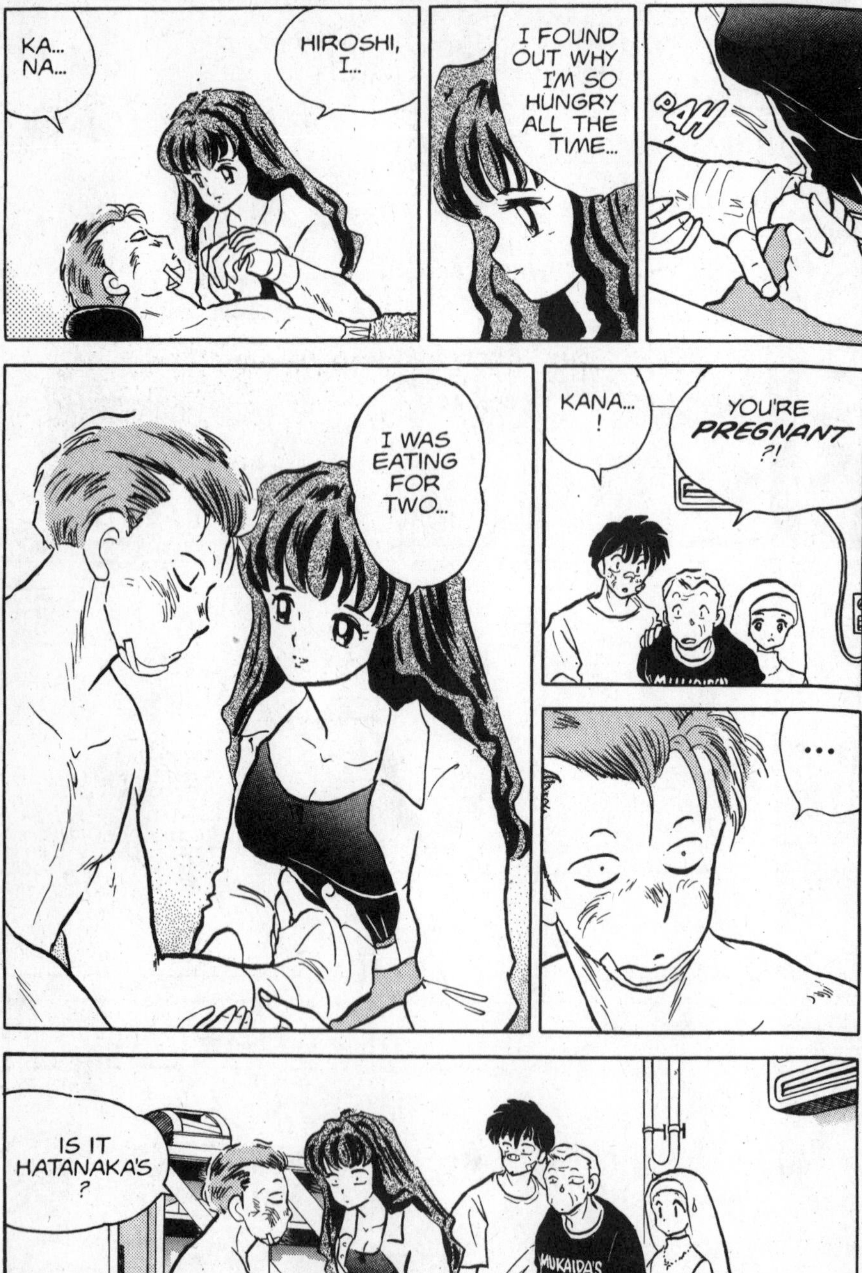
KA... NA...
HIROSHI, I...
I FOUND OUT WHY I'M SO HUNGRY ALL THE TIME...
PAH
I WAS EATING FOR TWO...
KANA... !
YOU'RE PREGNANT ?!
MUKAIDA'S
...
IS IT HATANAKA'S ?
MUKAIDA'S

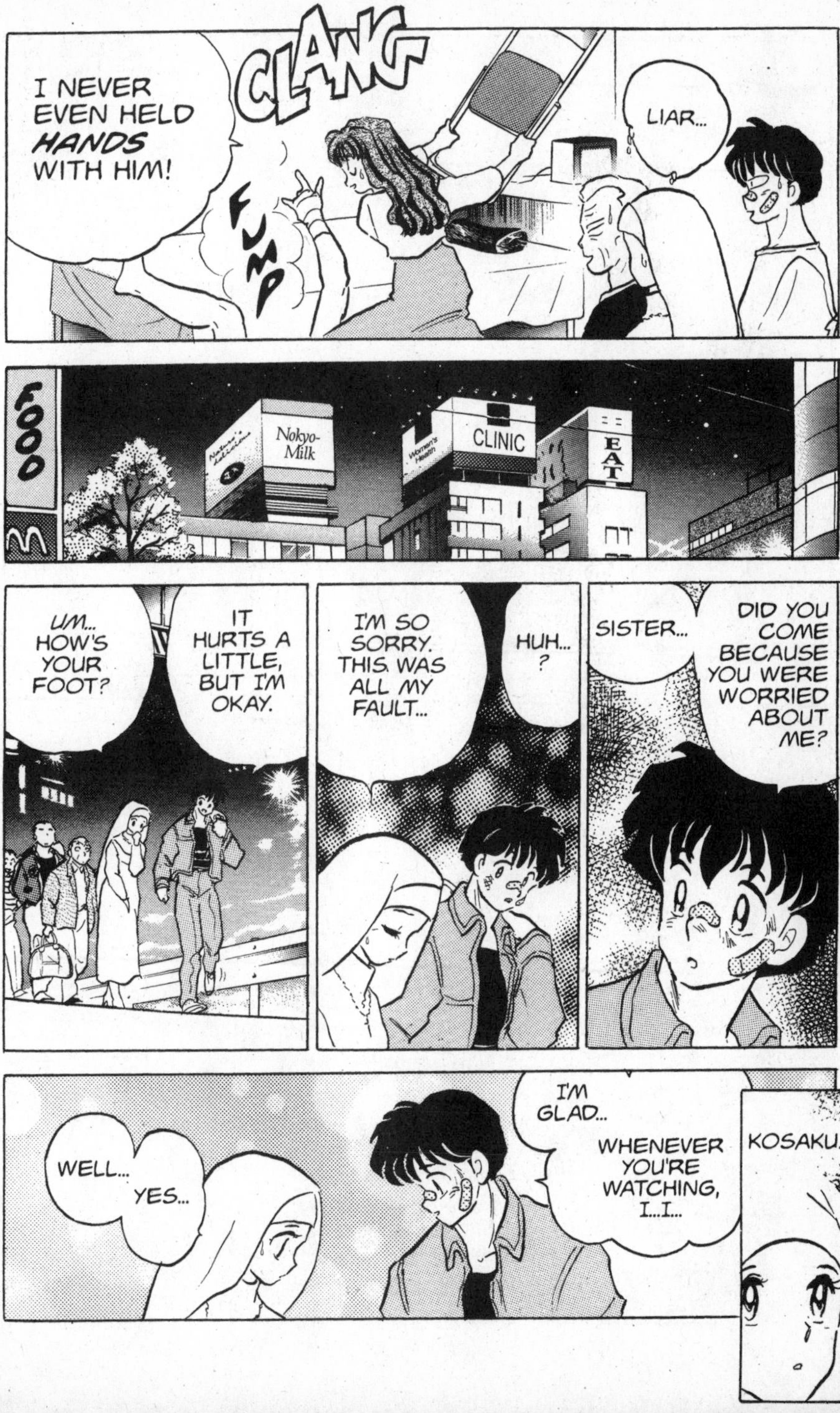

I NEVER EVEN HELD HANDS WITH HIM!
CLANG
FUMP
LIAR...
FOOD
M
Nature's delicious
Nokyo-Milk
Women's Health
CLINIC
EAT
UM... HOW'S YOUR FOOT?
IT HURTS A LITTLE, BUT I'M OKAY.
I'M SO SORRY. THIS WAS ALL MY FAULT...
HUH... ?
SISTER...
DID YOU COME BECAUSE YOU WERE WORRIED ABOUT ME?
WELL... YES...
I'M GLAD...
WHENEVER YOU'RE WATCHING, I...I...
KOSAKU...

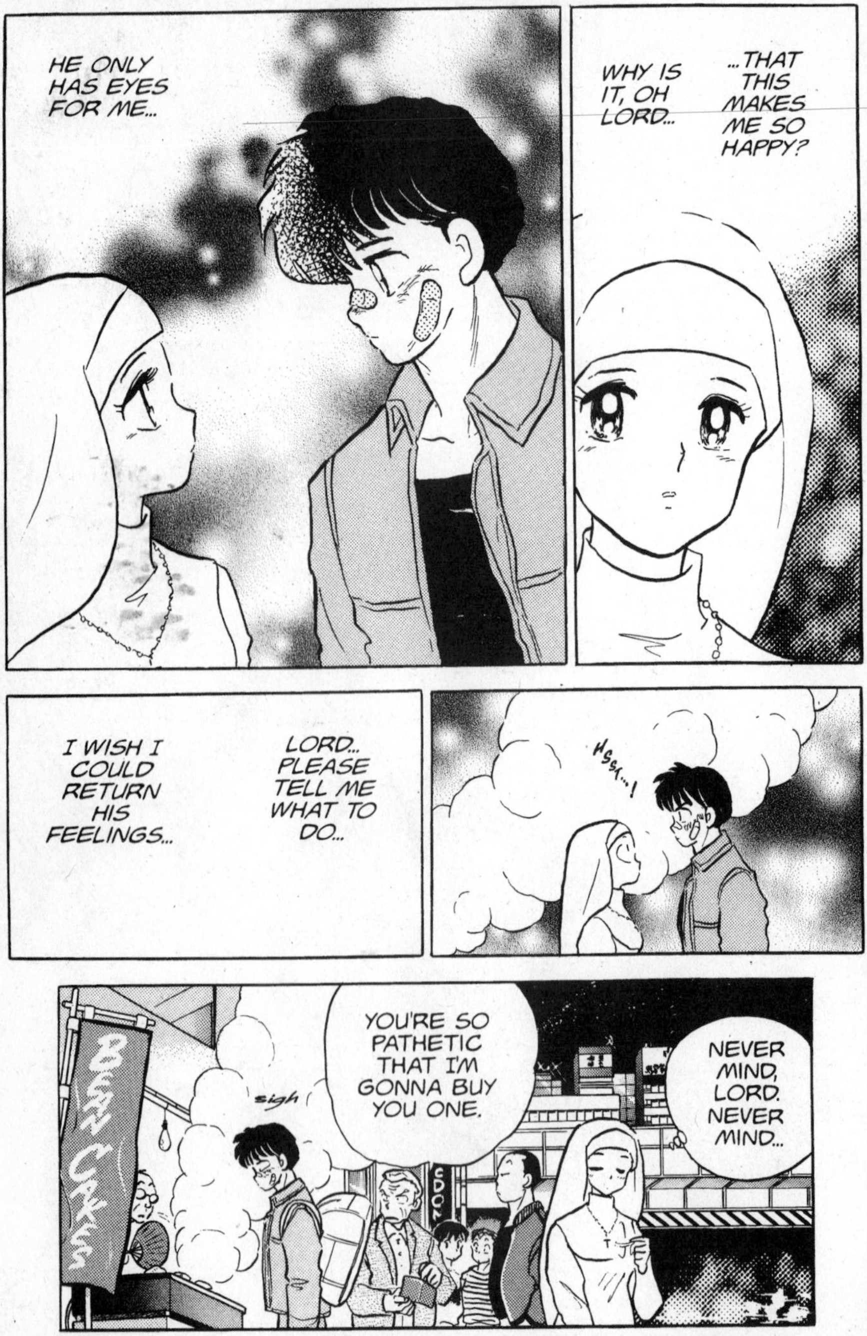
HE ONLY HAS EYES FOR ME...
WHY IS IT, OH LORD...
...THAT THIS MAKES ME SO HAPPY?
I WISH I COULD RETURN HIS FEELINGS...
LORD... PLEASE TELL ME WHAT TO DO...
BEAN CAKES
sigh
YOU'RE SO PATHETIC THAT I'M GONNA BUY YOU ONE.
NEVER MIND, LORD. NEVER MIND...

END OF ONE-POUND GOSPEL: KNUCKLE SANDWICH!